The Immigrant
Paradox
in Children
and Adolescents

The Immigrant
Paradox

in Children
and Adolescents

IS BECOMING AMERICAN
A DEVELOPMENTAL RISK?

EDITED BY

Cynthia García Coll
Amy Kerivan Marks

AMERICAN PSYCHOLOGICAL ASSOCIATION

WASHINGTON, DC

Published by
American Psychological Association
750 First Street, NE
Washington, DC 20002
www.apa.org

To order
APA Order Department
P.O. Box 92984
Washington, DC 20090-2984
Tel: (800) 374-2721; Direct: (202) 336-5510
Fax: (202) 336-5502; TDD/TTY: (202) 336-6123
Online: www.apa.org/pubs/books
E-mail: order@apa.org

In the U.K., Europe, Africa, and the Middle East, copies may be ordered from
American Psychological Association
3 Henrietta Street
Covent Garden, London
WC2E 8LU England

Typeset in Goudy by Circle Graphics, Inc., Columbia, MD

Printer: United Book Press, Baltimore, MD
Cover Designer: Berg Design, Albany, NY

The opinions and statements published are the responsibility of the authors, and such opinions and statements do not necessarily represent the policies of the American Psychological Association.

Library of Congress Cataloging-in-Publication Data

The immigrant paradox in children and adolescents : is becoming American a developmental risk? / edited by Cynthia Garcia Coll and Amy Kerivan Marks. — 1st ed.
    p. cm.
 Includes bibliographical references and index.
 ISBN-13: 978-1-4338-1053-4
 ISBN-10: 1-4338-1053-0
 1. Children of immigrants—United States. 2. Children of immigrants—United States—Social conditions. 3. Children of immigrants—Education—United States. 4. Child development—Cross-cultural studies. I. García Coll, Cynthia T. II. Marks, Amy Kerivan.

 HQ792.U5I47 2012
 305.23086'912—dc23

                                   2011016589

British Library Cataloguing-in-Publication Data

A CIP record is available from the British Library.

Printed in the United States of America
First Edition

DOI: 10.1037/13094-000

CONTENTS

CONTRIBUTORS

Meghan Salas Atwell, PhD, George Washington University, Washington, DC

Victoria L. Blanchard, MS, University at Albany, State University of New York

Hoan N. Bui, PhD, University of Tennessee at Knoxville

Raymond Buriel, PhD, Pomona College, Claremont, CA

Cynthia García Coll, PhD, Brown University, Providence, RI

Dylan Conger, PhD, George Washington University, Washington, DC

Robert Crosnoe, PhD, University of Texas at Austin

Nancy A. Denton, PhD, University at Albany, State University of New York

Andrew J. Fuligni, PhD, University of California, Los Angeles

Roberto G. Gonzales, PhD, University of Chicago, Chicago, IL

Tristan Guarini, Doctoral Student, Suffolk University, Boston, MA

Wen-Jui Han, PhD, New York University, New York, NY

Lingxin Hao, PhD, Johns Hopkins University, Baltimore, MD

Donald J. Hernandez, PhD, Hunter College and the Graduate Center, City University of New York, New York, NY

Hyeyoung Kang, PhD, University of Binghamton, State University of New York

Grace Kao, PhD, University of Pennsylvania, Philadelphia

Yingyi Ma, PhD, Syracuse University, Syracuse, NY

Suzanne Macartney, MA, Poverty and Health Statistics Branch, U.S. Census Bureau, Suitland, MD

Amy Kerivan Marks, PhD, Suffolk University, Boston, MA

Natalia Palacios, PhD, University of Virginia, Charlottesville

Suet-ling Pong, PhD, The Pennsylvania State University, State College

Marcela Raffaelli, PhD, University of Illinois at Urbana–Champaign

Kristin Turney, PhD, University of California, Irvine

Kristina L. Zeiser, PhD, The Pennsylvania State University, State College

PREFACE

Aside from those of us who can claim Native American roots in the United States, our family histories reflect individual and collective stories of migration. The majority of the U.S. population is originally from somewhere else. This is not a uniquely American phenomenon: Migration is very much part of being human, not only recently, but throughout the history of the civilized world. Since the beginning of permanent settlement, people have picked up whatever they could and roamed to new lands in search of better lives, better locations, and better communities for their families. For some migrants, famine, natural disaster, war, and persecution may have been the main initiator of the voyage. By foot, by boat, and more recently by plane, we have left our roots and our familiar surroundings in the process of immigration. What propels individual and mass migrations has filled countless pages within the academic discourse.

But no matter the cause of migration, the children of immigration are born to new lands or brought from old shores at various ages and with a wide range of familiarity with the new culture. For these children, growing up in America is filled not only with the normative developmental tasks of childhood but also with the necessary adaptations to new cultural frameworks and demands. Families are disrupted and reorganized, responding to both the supports and obstacles placed by both their original and receiving communities. They are forced to respond to the stimuli of two cultures: to combine them, to forget them, retain them, reject them, and constantly negotiate them. If contact is possible, family members left behind become the umbilical cord to the native land, but the migrants' current life is situated in a brand new culture and environment.

Today, the complexity of acculturation grows deeper for the increasing number of immigrants in the United States: Transnational communities have developed as constant communication and transferring of assets becomes accessible all over the world. Communication by cell phone, e-mail, Skype, and electronic social media, as well as networking and money transfers, can become part of daily routines. Funerals, baptisms, and weddings create opportunities for the home and new cultures to reconnect and to reflect the strength of kinship. Such opportunities also allow children to participate in both cultures and to adopt skills from both, to create meaningful relations with uncles and cousins and longtime family friends. Many of today's children of immigration are living as part of these transnational communities. At the same time, they are creating cultures of their own that are related to but distinct from both their family's culture of origin and their new host society. The myriad permutations and combinations that emerge from these individual adaptations challenge not only the parent's culture but the host culture as well. The experiences within social environments of children of migrants, then, are uniquely individualized: They are an amalgam of their home culture; their new culture; their own unique adaptations; and the strength of the connection, if any, that these migrants maintain with their relatives "back home."

As a result, many immigrant families and their children have the enormous task of becoming bicultural: proficient and successful at responding to new ecological demands with no clear road maps while retaining the values, skills, and modes of being that connect them with their country of origin. For developing new competencies required to succeed, they have to rely on institutions (ethnic and mainstream) and individuals that take their adaptation to heart. In contrast, native mainstream families have access to extended family, institutional, community, and other cultural mediums that provide important and sometimes critical information on how to navigate the necessary systems (e.g., schools, communities, employment) to ensure their children's access to promoting environments. Devoid of family and institutional connections, most immigrant parents can only hope that the sacrifices they made for a better life for their children are actualized, believing sometimes blindly that their move into a new culture will automatically result in better opportunities. Hard work, obedience, and respect will make you succeed, they say to their children. But can their children navigate schools and obtain jobs that justify the initial impulse to migrate? When and how does this happen? Why do some children succeed while others do not?

Using empirical research, this book documents the educational, health, and behavioral outcomes among immigrant children and adolescents across a variety of nationality groups, ages, and immigrant generations. Our goal is to understand both success and failure as a function of immigrant generation and acculturation. In so doing, we pose the following questions: Is there really an immigrant paradox in educational outcomes and risky behaviors? For children of immigrants, is becoming American, in this time and place, a developmental risk? Why? What are the nuances of the paradox (e.g., in which developmental domains and at what ages do we observe these patterns of findings)? What individual, family, school, or community mechanisms may be responsible for these patterns?

Trying to elucidate some of the mechanisms behind the immigrant paradox as well as its generality, we convened scholars at Brown University in Providence, Rhode Island, in the spring of 2009. All invited scholars were known for their research contributions to our understanding of immigrant adaptations to the United States. Most of us were sociologists and psychologists, but many had never directly addressed the paradox in their research. Most had heard of the phenomenon, primarily the early results reported in the 1980s, but had not yet focused their attention on the more recent work in this area. Some were skeptical of the notion of the paradox, and many were even apprehensive that if we disseminated the conference findings, money and programs targeting immigrants might be cut. Nevertheless, the organizers of the conference (and editors of this book) felt not only intrigued by the paradox and the discourse at the conference but also excited at the prospect of understanding resilience among U.S. immigrant child populations. The notion of learning from the strengths of individuals and groups and using this knowledge to inform our discussion of immigrant adaptation and necessary policies in the United States might constitute a shift in the way that developmental outcomes could be conceived in these populations.

Near the end of our journey in editing this volume, two of our students and conveners and participants in the conference, Tam Ngoc Tran, and Cinthya Nathalie Felix Perez, passed away. They died on Saturday, May 18, 2010, in an automobile accident. Despite many hardships, Cinthya and Tam, who were both first-generation college students from undocumented families, had lifelong commitments to the field of education and immigrant rights; their ethic and dedication were true inspirations to the editors of this volume.

Professor Matt García, one of Tam's advisors, wrote eloquently at the time of her death,

> Tam embodied everything that this country expects of its citizens: virtue, love of country, civic engagement, community activism, and support for each other. She was a daughter and a sister. She was born in Germany to Vietnamese refugee parents who fought Communism in their country.

When Tam was 6 years old, the family moved to the United States. They requested asylum here, but their application remains in limbo. Tam and her family are stateless: Germany will not accept them back because they are not of German origin, and return to Vietnam is impossible given the family's anti-Communist history. A budding scholar, Tam was pursuing her PhD in the Department of American Civilization at Brown University at the time of her death. Her dissertation planned to merge historical inquiry with participant observation, documenting the trajectory and power of student politics over the last half century.

Tam Tran was a dedicated and fearless leader for immigrant rights. She advocated on behalf of undocumented immigrant youth in search of education. As an undergraduate at the University of California, Los Angeles, she worked with fellow undocumented and documented students to extend public funding to undocumented students. On May 18, 2007, Tam took the courageous step of testifying in Congress in support of the Development, Relief and Education for Alien Minors Act (The "DREAM Act"), a bill that would provide pathways to citizenship by granting a 6-year conditional permanent legal residency to undocumented students who met certain criteria. Although the bill failed, Tam continued to work for its passage and was a tireless activist until the day of her untimely death.

Cinthya Felix, like Tam, was fearlessly committed to seeing the DREAM Act become a reality. She was a founding member of the undocumented youth group at UCLA (IDEAS) and the first undocumented student admitted to Columbia University's School of Public Health in 2007. Cinthya was fearless in overcoming the obstacles in her way: Being undocumented, she was unable to secure public funding for her education. She saw this as an injustice and was determined to see her education through, no matter the sacrifice. She saw her education as a way of extending her ability to serve her community: Her story and struggle inspire us in the deepest and most sincere way.

Though young, Cynthia and Tam were responsible and important members of our intellectual community. We are inspired by their struggle and hope this book serves as an inspiration to those in the field.

The Immigrant
Paradox
in Children
and Adolescents

INTRODUCTION

CYNTHIA GARCÍA COLL AND AMY KERIVAN MARKS

In this edited volume, we seek to provide a better understanding of child and adolescent development in the contexts of parent immigration to the United States during the end of the 20th century and the beginning of the 21st. The families studied in this book represent those who have experienced immigration processes in a particular time and place, or perhaps better said—times and places. They represent part of a major demographic shift in the United States (See Chapter 1, this volume). They differ from previous waves of U.S. migrants by place of origin, language, race, and ethnicity. The earlier waves were mostly from Europe; the more recent have been from Latin America and Asia. More recent immigrants also immigrate into very different neighborhoods, schools, and employment situations than earlier immigrants. For many immigrants, for example, there are higher requirements and greater barriers (e.g., a greater need for formal education) to be successful in this time and place. U.S. school systems are failing not only in promoting the successful integration of recent immigrants but in the quality of education for all. Neighborhoods with concentrated poverty and segregation have also grown exponentially and are in many cases the only affordable first destinations for many immigrants.

This book is the first to devote itself to the documentation and explanation of the immigrant paradox in childhood, adolescence, and young adulthood. The book is intended for advanced undergraduates, graduate students, and colleagues in the area of immigration or ethnic studies, sociology, psychology, and education. Policymakers' and practitioners' work might be informed by the research contained in this book. It is an interdisciplinary compendium and as such uses a variety of methods from psychology, sociology, demography, and anthropology. Each, with its strengths and limitations, adds some answers to the puzzle that the immigrant paradox represents. Both authors and editors hope that our readers will increase their knowledge of immigration in general as well as of the specific and sometimes extraordinary demands this process entails and the assets and liabilities that these families have to cope with these demands. In addition, readers will learn where the immigrant paradox exists in education and behavior as well as some health outcomes among youth in immigrant families. Also elucidated here is how both settings and personal attributes contribute to the paradox and the differential outcomes observed not only by generation but by ethnic group and age. Most important, the implications for policy and practice, we hope, will come not only from our own writing but from our readers' informed interpretation and understanding of the phenomena.

SKETCHING OUT THE IMMIGRANT PARADOX

The fundamental question posed by this book, "Is there support for the immigrant paradox?" comes from a series of findings that perplexes our field. They originated in the astonishing finding that babies of immigrant women and immigrant adults had better health outcomes in a variety of indexes such as birth weight, infant mortality, adult obesity, cardiovascular functioning, longevity, and mortality when compared with native born or later generation immigrants (Argeseanu Cunningham, Ruben, & Venkat Narayan, 2008). These reports were followed more recently by findings in education in which more highly acculturated immigrant youth displayed less academic excellence and/or more risky behaviors than their less acculturated peers. Of course the literature is nuanced, and the patterns of these findings vary widely across ethnic–racial subgroups and by the developmental age range studied. But overall, a myriad of examples document a pattern of worsening developmental outcomes as acculturation into American culture proceeds—what we are calling the "immigrant paradox." In other words, as some children of immigrants become "more American" (e.g., speak more English and less of their parent's native language; see Chapters 7 and 8, this volume), the worse their chances are for positive developmental outcomes compared with their less acculturated peers. Echoing these patterns of research findings, we have also directly observed immigrant parents of elementary school children of various ethnic backgrounds expressing their fears that their children will "become American." Numerous reports have shown what the parents fear: "American children" lose respect for their elderly; question parents' authority; and get involved in gangs, premature pregnancies, and drugs (Garcia Coll & Marks, 2009).

One of the clear messages of the research in this book is that the questions surrounding the immigrant paradox are not only timely but complex. The evidence reported in this book examines why becoming American, being more acculturated, represents a developmental risk for some ethnic groups, ages, developmental outcomes, and circumstances, and in others, it does not. For instance, in Chapters 9 and 12, the authors found a stronger immigrant paradox for Asians than for Latinos in educational outcomes. The erosion of good attitudes toward school in part explains the downward trend in academic outcomes observed over time. It appears that academic attitudes, conceived as attachment to school and positive feelings toward school and peers, might be a good area for a preventive intervention.

This view—that becoming American is risky—is incongruent with traditional academic and public policy views regarding the incorporation of immigrants into the U.S. population. Historically, academic perspectives of incorporation emphasized assimilation; becoming American as quickly as you could was taken as the best course of action for newly arrived immigrants (see, e.g., Infeld, 1940). This view is still reflected in English-only policies or English immersion programs today (see Auerbach, 1993). Similarly, most of the immigration policies in this country have been based on the belief that full assimilation—leaving your culture behind—is the exemplary adaptation for immigrants and that only as "Americans" in a strict, normative sense will immigrants succeed to the best of their abilities (see Chapter 2, this volume). Schools have been seen as major machineries of immersion and a key mechanism for the assimilation of first-generation immigrant children. This is in spite of the fact that contemporary research has shown the complexities of acculturation with a myriad of outcomes representing both successful and unsuccessful adaptations (Berry, 2008; Porter & Washington, 1993). Assimilation or total acculturation does not automatically result in positive developmental outcomes.

This book was also inspired by the notion that widespread negative views of immigrants and their children should be informed and challenged by the mounting data available in the social sciences literature and not simply by ideological impulses. We know from history that ideological movements can strengthen when economic and social resources are scarce, and this is just such a time in the United States. The view that immigrants are bad students, prone to risky behavior, and uninterested in doing well is wildly inaccurate. Nevertheless, these views remain powerful motivators for many of the immigration reform policies spreading through the United States. A review of the policies toward bilingual education over 150 years reflects these patterns clearly (Peréa & Garcia Coll, 2008), whereby more favorable bilingual education policies come and go as a function of perceived economic constraints. Unfortunately, scholarly research on the advantages and disadvantages of bilingual education has had limited effects on these changes.

Today, we are seeing a similar pattern of disconnect between research and policy toward children of immigrants. Some of the ideologically based views of immigrants have inspired enthusiastic voices pleading for changing the 14th amendment to the U.S. Constitution. That is, these ideologically negative views have inspired some Americans to call for a change in some of the defining features of our country, such that children of immigrants would not be granted citizenship even if they were born here. Systematic research with this population has documented a variety of positive and promising developmental outcomes, a far cry from what some of these ideologies suggest. Even if we can find evidence that some children of immigrants can and do succumb to poverty and low-performing schools or do not successfully integrate into American society, many children of immigrants become exemplar citizens, and some even excel beyond their social and economic risk factors (see Chapter 11, this volume). In fact, research studies, including some in this book, have shown that first-generation immigrant youth can, and often do, outperform their native-born peers across a variety of developmental outcomes. So a portion of these children, even if they are challenged by growing up in poverty, in households with little formal education and English language fluency, manage to make it. Why? Why are some individuals and groups able to beat the odds better than others? Does nationality matter? How does the context of reception, including historical period, matter? In what circumstances do some immigrant children start to excel while others fall behind? What are the roles of family, peers, school, and neighborhood in these immigrant youth success stories? How might self-selection play a role in the initial immigrant advantage (see Chapters 2 and 12, this volume)?

In Chapter 3, Crosnoe raises several important areas to advance our understanding and theory regarding the paradox, in part by examining the inconsistencies in and diversity of the paradox. Developmental stage, type of outcome studied, and socioeconomic status (SES) are explored as meaningful lenses through which to understand the paradox and consider policy implications. For example, Crosnoe highlights the particularly salient role that parent education might have in eliminating the developmental disparities between earlier and later generations of immigrant children. He also points out that the topic of the paradox is an extremely important one, that "what we do not know or understand about the immigrant paradox still outweighs what we do know," and calls for new research in the area.

ACCULTURATION AND GENERATION

An important aspect of unpacking the paradox is attending to the nuances in definitions and measurement of the constructs used to study it. The term *acculturation* typically denotes a process by which an individual (or group of individuals) encounters a new cultural context and begins a series of complex social, interpersonal, and context-sensitive psychological processes of assuming new cultural attitudes, abilities, and traditions while maintaining (or not maintaining) those from the individual's culture of origin (see Berry, 1997). To operationalize such a complex idea in research is challenging and requires multifaceted approaches, including psychological measures tapping cultural attitudes, beliefs, and practices with both the culture of origin and the new culture.

Alongside the notion of acculturation, researchers often use the concept of immigrant generation as a marker of immigration context. *Immigrant generation*, captured by distinctions between the "first generation," "second generation," and so forth, refers in developmental research to the child's nativity with respect to immigration. A *first-generation* child is one who is born abroad, typically with parents who are born abroad as well. A *second-generation* child is one who is born in the United States, with one or both parents born abroad. A *third-generation* child is one who is born in the United States, with both parents U.S.-born as well. Although seemingly straightforward, here too we find variability in approaches to measurement. For example, many researchers use the third generation as a reference group in analyses and incorporate into their third-generation group those who may be effectively fourth+ generation as well. Furthermore, when studying adolescents and young adults, some researchers have made sound cases for distinguishing among the first and second generations by utilizing designations such as the *1.5 generation*. Here, we see researchers find that the age at which a child immigrates to the United States has important implications for development. Therefore, denoting a youth as being 1.5 generation would indicate that the child, although born abroad, moved to the United States before the age of 5 (Rumbaut & Portes, 2006) . These young ages at migration yield distinct social, language, and psychological acculturation processes for the individual compared with an adolescent who moves to the United States when he or she is 13 years old. Note, however, that using the 1.5 generation distinction is most relevant when studying developmental processes and outcomes in adolescence and early adulthood.

This book is consequently bound to some of the methodological approaches that have historically dominated the topic and inquiry of the immigrant paradox. Most researchers in this volume operationalize immigrant context by using the generational distinctions and do not speak directly to psychological acculturation as defined earlier. Other authors incorporate language use as a proxy of acculturation as well. Generation markers can show interesting and robust developmental patterns but also leave many questions unanswered as to the psychological acculturation processes underscoring group differences (or explaining inter- or intraindividual variability over time). Although less than ideal, the use of generations, which permeates much of the recent research on the paradox, stems from our reliance on large-scale, nationally representative studies in which valid and nuanced measures of acculturation are simply not available. Although the use of generations alone is not ideal (and we urge future researchers to incorporate multifaceted, dimensional measures of acculturation into the national developmental studies they design), there is still much we can learn from generational associations and interactions. By examining them with contexts and language markers to explain outcomes, the authors in this volume add important and nuanced findings to the literature on the paradox in numerous ways and advance our understanding of the potential mechanisms underlying the generational patterns observed.

THEORETICAL FRAMEWORKS

Guided by contemporary theoretical frameworks, many of the chapters in this book examine the contexts of children of immigrants such as families, peers, school, and neighborhoods to look for explanations of the immigrant paradox. The early 20th century's psychological notion of an individual acting and reacting to development on his or her own is replaced by a more nuanced vision in which interactive, sometimes bidirectional, associations are to be expected between the child and his or her environment (Bronfenbrenner, 1979). Characteristics of families, schools, peers, and neighborhoods are examined to help explain changes over time in an individual's life and across generations. For example, in keeping with past research, Raffaeli and colleagues present data in Chapter 5 in this volume documenting evidence of the paradox in sex risk behaviors and sexual involvement among immigrant adolescents from the Add Health study. They then propose an adapted theoretical model emphasizing the role of contexts in explaining the paradoxical patterns of findings observed. Among many of the chapters in this book (see, e.g., Chapters 4 and 6), the fact that multiple environments interact over time leads to the use of complex statistical analyses to help isolate causal explanations. In such research, developmental outcomes are multiply determined by interacting contexts, and any statements of causal associations must take into account other theoretically linked explanations (such as parent education and poverty). Palacios's work (see Chapter 8, this volume) also supports the notion that a longitudinal lens is necessary for this work. She reports that the immigrant advantage is not present at school entry, but it is presented in growth over time and in actual outcomes 5 years later.

LENSES USED TO FIND EVIDENCE
FOR AN IMMIGRANT PARADOX

We have stated that this book constitutes an interdisciplinary effort to elucidate data that inform the phenomenon of the immigrant paradox in behavioral, health, and educational outcomes of youth in immigrant families. We feel that given our theoretical orientation toward explaining developmental outcomes as the product of growing up in particular contexts, no single discipline could be used to ascertain all the complexities we expected to arise. From psychology we have examples like the study of unfolding individual lives through longitudinal designs and individual differences in propensity to migrate. From sociology, the study of institutions such as families, schools, and communities represents our attempt to take context seriously and not as a background, categorical variable. In the study of new populations such as undocumented students, qualitative sociology and anthropological methods like participant observation and in-depth interviews were deemed more appropriate. Other longitudinal and cross-sectional designs are used to fit the particular question under study. Large, nationally representative, publically available data sets like the Early Childhood Longitudinal Study—Kindergarten cohort and Add Health were used to address our questions with the hope that we could generalize the findings to the national scene. In contrast, geographically narrower studies were also deemed appropriate to inform the debate by providing in-depth understanding of a particular locality. Finally, many ethnic–racial groups were used, emphasizing that generalities can only be derived if they are found across various groups.

BEHAVIORAL EVIDENCE

In general, this collection of studies found consistent evidence of an immigrant paradox in risky behaviors in adolescence. In other words, more highly acculturated or later generation youth reported being engaged in substance use and abuse, unprotected sex, and delinquency more often than their less acculturated or first-generation peers. In Chapter 6 in this volume, Bui presents strong evidence of the paradox for delinquency in adolescence. Examining patterns by ethnic–racial subgroup, we see that the paradox holds for most groups except Asians. How do we explain this? One possibility for future research may be to examine the differential patterns by ethnicity and generation according to characteristics of the family context. It is important to note that Bui reports that characteristics of the school context yield full mediation of the delinquency paradox for White and Black adolescents but only partial mediation for Hispanic youth. For White and Black adolescents, then, school programs emphasizing academics and school engagement might be indicated to prevent juvenile delinquency. On the basis of the results reported in Chapter 6, our theories also need to begin addressing why some ethnic groups show the paradox (for some outcomes) and not others. The broadly applied theories most currently used in the study of immigrant youth are limited because they do not articulate fully important acculturation-related variables under study (such as a complete articulation of acculturation processes, the roles of ethnic identities and development, and why some children espouse strong family obligations whereas others do not), further hindering our ability to extend our findings into policy and intervention work (see Chapter 2).

The behavioral paradox effects appear to be most pronounced in adolescence, when these behaviors tend to be most salient for a significant number of youth. For instance, Turney and Kao, in Chapter 4, lead us to consider that the early elementary years may be too early to conclusively see the first-versus second-generation differences in behavioral problems that are later observed in the risky behavioral paradoxes documented in adolescence. However, even in these early ages, there are still some important nuances in these findings. It is noteworthy that Turney and Kao do not find evidence of the paradox using parents' reports of their children's behavior but do see some evidence of the paradox when examining teacher-reported behavior. Further, when using within-ethnic-group analyses, there *is* evidence of the paradox at this early age range. Taken together, these results highlight the importance of studying early childhood behavioral problems and the role of teachers because interventions might be most efficacious in these years prior to the establishment of the paradox in adolescence. In addition, because teasing apart potential 1.5 generation effects is difficult in young children, this remains an important and interesting age group to study because it may be key to providing clues for how the paradox unfolds. Something appears to be happening in development later in childhood and into adolescence that establishes the behavioral and delinquency paradox patterns we so widely observe in adolescence. Future research should therefore target understanding behavioral problem patterns in middle childhood and early adolescence.

From the work on risky behaviors that is presented in this book, a fundamental question remains: What are the long-term consequences of these risky behaviors? We understand that some youth will emerge successfully from a risky behavioral profile in adolescence whereas others may be set for a life in the juvenile justice and adult prison systems. Do these early behavioral patterns persist into adulthood, and for which outcomes—drugs, unprotected sex, and/or delinquency? Do the patterns persist for all cultural groups and genders? Rumbaut (1994) extended these notions to adulthood in terms of involvement with the law. He found that among adults, members of the first generation are arrested and convicted less frequently than those of later generations. Do these findings differ by ethnic group? Future studies in this area should examine the immigrant paradox in risk behaviors from childhood as it may extend into the adult years.

EDUCATIONAL OUTCOMES

A different picture of the paradox is presented by the findings in educational outcomes compared with the findings for behavioral outcomes. Trying to obtain a more nuanced picture of development, a variety of educational outcomes was studied in this book, including scholastic attitudes, grade point average, and standardized test scores. From the earliest grades and up through college, we have found indices that reflect age-appropriate attitudes and behaviors toward school as well as more concrete measures of academic achievement. These include general attitudes toward school and learning, testing scores, grades, high school graduation rates, and attendance at postsecondary institutions. Overall, the studies in this book show that Latinos and Asians have very positive attitudes about school, across all ages (see Chapter 9). Nevertheless, more recent immigrants still show an advantage over second and third generations, having the most positive attitudes of all groups studied. What is perplexing is that these positive attitudes do not appear to translate into positive academic outcomes for Latinos, whereas they *are* associated with high achievement for Asian groups (see Chapters 9 and 12, respectively). In other words, Asian students who are more recent immigrants have not only more positive academic attitudes but also higher grades, test scores, graduation rates, and postsecondary attendance than their later generation peers. What might explain these ethnic differences? Differences in ethnic enclaves and parents' knowledge of how to make use of educational programs, resources, and institutions seem to play a role in explaining the differences observed between these populations (Zhou, 2009). Indeed, several authors in this volume suggest that access to critical, institutionally regulated resources is more important for academic outcomes than for socioemotional ones (see Chapters 3 and 13), perhaps explaining the universality of the behavioral paradox and the appearance of the educational paradox in some groups and not others.

With an emphasis on community context, Conger and Atwell also study the educational paradox in adolescence (see Chapter 10, this volume), directly examining how the type of immigrant community (traditional, emerging, and reemerging gateways) may be related to the paradox. In this work, community type did not have a consistent relationship with the presence or absence of the paradox in scholastic test scores. As we observed in Bui (Chapter 6) and Turney and Kao (Chapter 4), we are again reminded of how important it is to examine the paradox specifically by ethnic–racial subgroups. Evidence of the paradox in academic outcomes was found, for example, among Asian and Black students living in Miami but not for Hispanic students. Another important theme in this chapter is the role of language use at home as it relates to the paradox. For two of the communities studied by Conger and Atwell, a second-generation advantage in math scores was observed for native-born students living in non-English-speaking homes. These findings highlight the potential benefits of bilingualism in promoting positive math academic achievement among second-generation adolescents.

Many of the families whose children show the immigrant education advantage do so when the SES of the family is controlled for; in other words, studies compare across generations and acculturation statuses among children that live in families of similar SES. This is the first volume of studies that has tried to explain this phenomenon from a series of mostly contextual factors, after controlling for family SES. It seems that as generations go by and as acculturation proceeds, developmental risks do increase for some of these children. For example, family values might be a major mechanism protecting less acculturated youth from having poor academic achievement. Such values include the importance of education, valuing hard work, and a sense of family obligation. In schools, these children and youth maintain positive outlooks even if the institutions they attend are deprived of the many resources that are typically needed for a high-quality education. Self-selection (the most motivated and skillful individuals migrate while others stay behind) has also been invoked to explain the first-generation advantage, although the present research on the immigrant paradox has not been able to provide any definitive data on this possible explanation (see Chapters 2, 12, and 13, this volume).

In sum, by exploring these important social questions through research, we hope to promote research-informed policies and practices that follow logically from the studies presented here. For example, when we state that one of our aims is to understand how some immigrant children succeed in spite of all odds, this is not to say that immigrant families and their children do not need supports to be successful in this country. It only says that perhaps by understanding the mechanisms by which some immigrant youth (even if they represent a minority of the overall population) overcome social and economic obstacles to become successful, we might learn how to create better contexts and policies to support success by a larger proportion of immigrant children. Similarly, by understanding characteristics of the contexts related to immigrant children's negative outcomes and the seeming deterioration of well-being over time and with acculturation, we might be in a better position to prevent declines in educational and risky behavioral outcomes for future populations of immigrant youth.

REFERENCES

Argeseanu Cunningham, S., Ruben, J. D., & Venkat Narayan, K. M. (2008). Health of foreign-born people in the United States: A review, *Health & Place, 14*, 623–635. doi:10.1016/j.healthplace.2007.12.002

Auerbach, E. R. (1993). Reexamining English only in the ESL classroom. *TESOL Quarterly, 27*(1), 9–32. doi:10.2307/3586949

Berry, J. W. (1997). Immigration, acculturation, and adaptation. *Applied Psychology, 46*, 5–34. doi:10.1111/j.1464-0597.1997.tb01087.x

Berry, J. W. (2008). Globalisation and acculturation. *International Journal of Intercultural Relations, 32*, 328–336.

Bronfenbrenner, U. (1979). *The ecology of human development: Experiments by nature and design*. Cambridge, MA: Harvard University Press.

Garcia Coll, C., & Marks, A. K. (2009). *Immigrant stories: Ethnicity and academics in middle childhood*. New York, NY: Oxford University Press.

Infeld, H. (1940). The aged in the process of ethnic assimilation. *Sociometry, 3*(4), 353–365. doi:10.2307/2785087

Peréa, F., & Garcia Coll, C. (2008). The social and cultural contexts of bilingualism. In J. Altarriba & R. R. Heredia (Eds.), *An introduction to bilingualism: Principles and processes* (pp. 199–241). Mahwah, NJ: Erlbaum.

Porter, J. R., & Washington, R. E. (1993). minority identity and self-esteem. *Annual Review of Sociology, 19*, 139–161.

Rumbaut, R. G. (1994). The crucible within: Ethnic identity, self-esteem, and segmented assimilation among children of immigrants. *The International Migration Review, 28*(4), 748–794. doi:10.2307/2547157

Rumbaut, R., & Portes, A. (2006). *Immigrant America: A portrait* (3rd ed.). Berkeley: University of California Press.

Zhou, M. (2009, March). *Segmented assimilation and the Asian paradox: The multifaceted educational experiences of Chinese and Vietnamese children*. Paper presented at the conference "The Immigrant Paradox in Education and Behavior," Brown University, Providence, RI.

I

IS THERE AN "IMMIGRANT PARADOX"?

1

CHILDREN IN IMMIGRANT FAMILIES: DEMOGRAPHY, POLICY, AND EVIDENCE FOR THE IMMIGRANT PARADOX

DONALD J. HERNANDEZ, NANCY A. DENTON,
SUZANNE MACARTNEY, AND VICTORIA L. BLANCHARD

According to Hernandez, Denton, Macartney, and Blanchard

Children of immigrants often are viewed as posing challenges to the American health and education systems because of various circumstances that disadvantage them, such as lack of fluency in English. But first- and second-generation children in many immigrant groups are, in fact, doing about as well as or better than their peers in native-born families along many dimensions, a phenomenon which has been referred to as the *immigrant paradox* because it is contrary to the broadly held view just described. In this context, the purpose of this chapter is threefold.

In this chapter, we first present new results for children in immigrant families from the Census Bureau's American Community Survey (ACS) for 2005–2007 to describe important family and socioeconomic circumstances separately for children whose parents differ in their English fluency. These circumstances reflect resources, constraints, and opportunities available in families and communities that shape the developmental progress of children and that are influenced by public policies. (See http://www.albany.edu/csda/children for more detailed results from the ACS.) Insofar as the aim is to portray important features of the demographic circumstances of children in immigrant families as a backdrop for this and subsequent chapters in this volume, comparative results for key indicators also are presented for major groups children in native-born families.

Second, the chapter summarizes results from two national studies that were among the first to provide basic findings concerning the nature and magnitude of the immigrant paradox regarding health-related and education outcomes for a variety of immigrant groups. The aim is broad description, leaving more theoretical discussions to subsequent chapters.

Third, the chapter discusses public policies that could enhance successful development among children of immigrants. These policies focus on language, education, health, income, and immigrant enforcement.

At the outset, it is important to highlight why all Americans should be concerned about the children of immigrants (Hernandez, Denton, & Macartney, 2008). They account for nearly one fourth (24%) of all children in the United States, they live in substantial numbers in every state, and they are leading the racial–ethnic transformation of America. As a result, as the predominantly White baby boomers retire, they will depend increasingly for support on the economic productivity and civic participation, including voting, of working-age adults who belong to a wide range of racial–ethnic minorities, many of whom grew up in immigrant families.

THE LANGUAGE ENVIRONMENTS OF CHILDREN OF IMMIGRANTS

English fluency is essential to achieving educational and occupational success in the United States, and the language environment of children, both at home and at school, is important in shaping their language development. Children who lack fluency in the English language often are referred to as *English language learners* (ELLs), but this term also is applicable to many parents. The linguistic environments of immigrant families vary in this continuum. Six percent of children in immigrant families live with parents who speak no English at home, more than twice as many (14%) have parents who speak only English, and the vast majority (81%) have parents who speak both English and another language. Thus, most immigrant parents have learned at least some English, and most will, no doubt, learn more English the longer they live in the United States. This pattern holds true for immigrants from most countries of origin.

The diversity of languages spoken in the United States is enormous. For example, Census 2000 sample data identified 93 distinct languages in immigrant children's homes. Insofar as children living with parents who speak two languages have the opportunity to maintain or develop bilingual speaking and literacy skills, they are also well positioned to act as language ambassadors, connecting the United States to nations throughout the world. This includes regions where the United States has major economic or geopolitical interests, such as Latin America, China, and the Arabic- and Persian-speaking nations of West Asia. Thus, education policies fostering bilingualism among children in immigrant families can provide a valuable competitive edge as the United States seeks success in the increasingly competitive global economy.

Parents differ greatly not only in languages spoken but also in English fluency. Because children learn language first from their parents, children whose parents have limited English proficiency are most likely themselves to have limited English skills and to be classified by schools as ELLs, whereas children with English-fluent parents are least likely to be classified as ELLs. Parental English fluency has additional important implications. Parents learning English are less likely than fluent speakers to find well-paid, full-time, year-round jobs, and they may be less able to help their children study for subjects taught in English. Many education, health, and social service institutions do not provide outreach in the heritage language of parents, so parents and their children may be cut off from access to important public and private services and benefits.

For these reasons, this chapter presents results for three sets of children in immigrant families who are distinguished not by what language their parents speak but instead by the level of English proficiency of their parents. First are children with English-fluent parents only, that is, parents who speak only English or who speak English very well. Second are those with one English-fluent parent and one ELL parent, that is, a parent who speaks English well, not well, or not at all. Third are those with only ELL parents. Forty percent of children of immigrants live with English-fluent parents only, 16% live with mixed English proficiency parents, and 40% live with ELL parents only.

CITIZENSHIP OF PARENTS AND CHILDREN

One reason some immigrant groups have low proportions of parents who are ELL and comparatively high proportions with parents who all are English fluent is that English is commonly spoken in the country of origin. A second reason is that many children of immigrants have not only a foreign-born parent, but also a U.S.-born parent who has, therefore, been an American citizen since birth. The proportions with a U.S.-born parent are 42% for children with English-fluent parents only and 33% for those with mixed-fluency parents. However, among children with ELL parents only, a small 4% have a U.S.-born parent. The importance of having a U.S.-born or U.S. citizen parent, as discussed in greater detail later in this chapter, results from the lack of access that children may have to critical resources for which they are eligible as U.S. citizens, even when their parents are not themselves eligible because the parents are not U.S. citizens. All children of immigrants have at least one foreign-born parent who, therefore, was not a U.S. citizen at birth, but many have parents who have become naturalized citizens. In fact, large majorities live with at least one U.S. citizen parent among children with English fluent only parents (80%) and among those with mixed-proficiency parents (73%). Even among children with ELL parents only, more than one third (34%) live with an American citizen parent. Large proportions of parents who are naturalized citizens reflect a high level of commitment among these parents to their adopted homeland. Recent research also indicates that naturalizations are increasing (Passel, 2007). Between 1990 and 2005, the percentage of legal, permanent, foreign-born residents who were naturalized climbed from 38% to 52%. American citizenship is high among parents regardless of their country or region of origin. For only 12 of the 115 origins analyzed here does the proportion with a least one U.S. citizen parent fall below 50%, and for 11 of these 12 groups, at least 42% have U.S. citizen parents. Even among children in immigrant families with ELL parents only who are least likely to have a citizen parent, with few exceptions at least 30% have a parent who is a U.S. citizen. These results reflect a strong commitment to U.S. residency and citizenship.

Higher still are the proportions of children in immigrant families who are themselves life-long U.S. citizens because they were born in the United States. Among children in immigrant families with English-fluent parents only or mixed-proficiency parents, 87% to 88% were born in the United States, and even among those with ELL parents only, 79% were U.S. born. Thus, the vast majority of children of immigrants, regardless of parental language skills, share with children in native-born families the same rights as U.S. citizens, including eligibility for publicly funded health care and services. In fact, although 11% of children in immigrant families are undocumented, even among children with undocumented parents, nearly two thirds (63%) are themselves U.S. citizens because they were born in the United States (Passel, 2006). These figures are critically missing in the current discourse about undocumented residents of the United States and the policies to handle their rights and responsibilities

The 1996 federal welfare reform drew, for the first time, a sharp distinction between noncitizen immigrants and citizens, with noncitizens becoming ineligible for important public benefits and services. As a consequence, many noncitizen parents who are ineligible for specific public programs may not be aware that their citizen children are eligible, or they may hesitate to contact government authorities to obtain benefits or services for their children because they fear jeopardizing their own prospects for becoming citizens. This chilling effect of welfare reform may have serious negative consequences for U.S. citizen children who do not obtain needed resources (Capps, Kenney, & Fix, 2003; Fix & Passel, 1999; Fix & Zimmerman, 1995; Hernandez & Charney,

1998; Zimmermann & Tumlin, 1999). Among children of immigrants, more than half (55%) live in mixed-citizenship-status families with at least one U.S. citizen and one noncitizen, ranging from 42% for those with English-fluent parents only to 64% for those with at least one ELL parent. Insofar as children in mixed-citizenship-status families may experience barriers to access to services for which they are eligible, service-providing organizations should make special efforts to reach these children and their families.

RESOURCES IN IMMIGRANT FAMILIES

Children benefit from supportive parents with a good work ethic and ties to the community in which they live. Most children of immigrants benefit from the advantages and strengths associated with having two parents in the home; 82% live with two parents compared with 71% of children in native-born families. The proportion is very high among children in immigrant families for all three English language fluency groups, at 77% or more. Insofar as children living with two parents tend, on average, to be somewhat advantaged in their educational success (Cherlin, 1999; McLanahan & Sandefur, 1994), many children in immigrant families benefit from this family strength.

In addition to strong and supportive families, most children in immigrant families live in families with a strong work ethic. Among the three English fluency groups, 95% to 96% have fathers who work to support their families, a level similar to most native-born groups. For children of immigrants with ELL parents only, 85% or more have working fathers, and that is true for most country-of-origin groups. The exceptions include Cambodia, Laos, and Thailand (81%–84%) and the Hmong (73%). Many of these fathers arrived as refugees from the Vietnam War after suffering extremely traumatic events, experiences that may have limited their capacity to find work in the U.S. economy. The two other exceptions are children with origins in Armenia (82%) and Iraq (70%).

Most children in immigrant and native-born families also have working mothers. Although the proportion is somewhat lower for children with at least one ELL parent, a substantial majority (58%–65%) of these children have a working mother. Adding to the economic contribution of parents, 12% to 16% of children have another adult worker in the home among most native-born groups and in the two immigrant groups with at least one English-fluent parent. This jumps to 24% for children in immigrant families with ELL parents only.

Homeownership represents both an asset and resource for children and a family commitment to the community. In the United States, many children live in homes owned by their parents or other relatives. Homeownership rates are an extraordinary 73% to 79% for Whites and Asians in native-born families, whereas the range is 38% to 59% for most other native-born groups. Although all children of immigrants have at least one foreign-born parent, homeownership rates are 71% for those with English-fluent parents only, 63% for the mixed-fluency group, and 46% for those with ELL parents only. Even among the children with ELL parents only, homeownership rates are 35% or more for most specific countries of origin. Immigrants are strongly committed to putting down roots and joining in their local communities. This commitment by parents is an important feature that may help to foster the integration of their children into U.S. society, in part because it is associated with reduced residential mobility and hence with increased continuity for children in schools and with peers. These results are especially striking in view of the poverty rates for these groups (see the next section in this chapter) and the recency of their arrival in the United States. It is clear that many children in immigrant families live with parents who are contributing to the U.S. economy through their work and by investing in their adopted cities, towns, and neighborhoods. These practices can have positive effects on the integration of children into U.S. society, insofar as parents provide strong models of hard work and commitment to local communities.

CONSTRAINTS IN IMMIGRANT FAMILIES

Despite the resources we have discussed thus far in this chapter, many children in immigrant families experience major challenges associated with limited parental educational attainments and employment opportunities that contribute to poverty level incomes for families. Overall, a large 32% of children in immigrant families have fathers who are not high school graduates. Among the English fluency groups, children with English-fluent parents only are least likely to have fathers who have not graduated from high school at 10%, which is similar to Whites and Asians in native-born families. But this rises to 32% for the mixed-fluency immigrant group and to 54% for children in immigrant families with ELL parents only. The proportions with a father not graduating from high school are especially high among children with ELL parents only at 29% to 42% for the Dominican Republic, Haiti, Ecuador, Hong Kong, Indochina, and Iraq. This rises to the extraordinary level of 63% to 69% for Mexico, Central America, and Portugal/Azores.

No more than 3% of children in most native-born groups have fathers with 8 years of school or less. The proportion is equally low at 3% for children of immigrants with English-fluent parents only, but this increases fivefold to 16% for children with mixed-proficiency parents, and 11-fold to 35% for children with ELL parents only. Very large proportions of some immigrant groups have fathers with no more than 8 years of school. Among those with ELL parents only, the proportions are 21% to 23% for the Dominican Republic, Ecuador, Indochina, and Iraq and 42% to 46% for Mexico, Central America, and Portugal/Azores. Not only are these parents not familiar with the U.S. education system, they have no formal schooling in any country beyond the elementary level. This is a real challenge given the importance of parental education in the child's school readiness, early literacy, and eventual success in educational outcomes.

Another challenge for many parents is to find full-time, year-round work. Limited parental education not only limits the ability of parents to help their children in school, it also leads to somewhat higher levels of part-time work, low wages, and high poverty levels. The proportions with fathers not working full-time year-round among children with ELL parents only are highest at 33% to 46% for children with origins in Indochina, the Middle East, Romania, and the Commonwealth of Independent States (excluding Russia) and for Blacks and Whites from Africa.

Children in low-income families may experience serious deprivation in such basic areas as education, nutrition, clothing, housing, and health care. Many racial–ethnic minority children in native-born groups experience official poverty rates that are 2 to 4 times greater than for White or Asian children in native-born families, at 15% to 33% versus 8% to 9%. Official poverty for children in immigrant families with English-fluent parents is about the same as for Whites and Asians in native-born families at 8% to 9%, but this jumps to 15% for children with mixed-fluency parents and 31% for those with ELL parents only. Official poverty among specific country of origin groups ranges from only 3% to as much as 27% for those with English-fluent parents only or with mixed-proficiency parents. For children with ELL parents, this jumps to between 31% and 57% for a dozen origins: Mexico, Guatemala, Honduras, Dominican Republic, English-speaking Caribbean, the Hmong, Bangladesh, Pakistan, Afghanistan, Iraq, Israel/Palestine, and Blacks and Whites from Africa.

Many scholars, and others, feel that official poverty underestimates the level of real poverty in the United States, and public policy discussions often use a measure focusing on children with family incomes below 200% of the official poverty threshold (Annie E. Casey Foundation, 2006; Citro & Michael, 1995; Hernandez, Denton & Macartney, 2007). By this measure, the proportion of poor families rises from 26% for children with English-fluent parents only to 44% for mixed-fluency parents to 68% for children with ELL parents only. The highest rates of families living below the 200% poverty rate are again for children with origins in Mexico, Central America, Dominican Republic,

Haiti, English-Speaking Caribbean, the Hmong, Bangladesh, Pakistan, Middle East, and Blacks and Whites from Africa.

These results suggest the need for policy initiatives directed toward parents that would enhance the lives and foster the success and integration of their children by reducing constraints and fostering capacities of parents to achieve the goals they had in coming to the United States. In light of the commitment of immigrant parents to U.S. citizenship, to investing in their communities, and to working hard to support themselves and their families, public investments directed toward helping parents achieve their goal of learning English, as well as additional education and training opportunities for parents, are likely to pay off for the parents, their children, and the broader society.

THE IMMIGRANT PARADOX: HEALTH, RISK BEHAVIORS, AND EDUCATION

Despite the substantial constraints experienced by many children in immigrant families, it is paradoxical that they often fare about as well or better in the first generation than in the second generation, and that in many cases both generations often fare about as well as or better than third and later generations of children. Although this pattern has not been found universally true, early research with national data commissioned by the National Academies/ Institute of Medicine found strong support for these conclusions (Hernandez, 1999). Two sets of illustrative results are presented here. The first set pertains mainly to health and risky behaviors among adolescents with nine specific origins: Mexico, Cuba, Central/South America, Puerto Rico, China, Philippines, other Asia, Africa/Afro-Caribbean, and Europe/Canada (Harris, 1999). The second pertains to education outcomes for adolescents who are Chinese, Filipino, Mexican, other Hispanic, or Black (Kao, 1999). These groups were studied because sample sizes in the available data sets were large enough to provide the basis for drawing relatable conclusions. Results are presented comparing these groups overall and also controlling for socioeconomic status (SES), that is, for parent education and family income.

Beginning with health, results based on a health problems index indicate that the number of health problems increases from the first generation to the second generation, and number of health problems increases further between the second and third and later generations. This is the classic pattern of the immigrant paradox, because well-being deteriorates with each successive generation. The same pattern is found for all groups studied, with the exception only of children with Puerto Rican origins and only when controlling for SES, insofar as they did not experience worsening health between second and the third and later generations.[1] It is particularly striking that both before and after controlling for SES, the first generation of most immigrant groups has fewer health problems than third and later generation Whites. But the number of groups experiencing health worse than Whites increases by the second generation and still further by the third and later generations, when only the Chinese are slightly healthier than Whites.

Additional results reflect the extent to which groups are reported to have fair or poor health. Most groups experience poorer health from the first to the second generation and still poorer health in the third and later generations. The exceptions are children with origins in Mexico and Cuba between the second generation and the third and later generations, and those with origins in China and Europe/Canada between the first and second generations. Consistent with the immigrant paradox, obesity increases for most groups between the first and the second generation and between the second and the third and later generations. It is noteworthy that the second and third and later generations for most groups are more likely than Whites in native-born families to be obese, controlling for SES.

For a fourth health indicator, asthma, deterioration occurs from the first to the second to the third and later generations for all groups, excepting only Europe/Canada between the first and second generations. Both before and after controlling for SES, most groups also are less likely than Whites in native-born families to have asthma during the first and second generations but more likely than the White group to have asthma during the third and later generations.

A final health indicator is missing school because of a health or emotional problem. The immigrant paradox holds true for this indicator, controlling for SES, across all three generations for Cuba, China and other Asia, and Europe/Canada and across two generations for the other groups. It does not hold between the first and second generations for Central/South America, Philippines, and Afro-Caribbean, and between the second and third and later generations for Mexico and Puerto Rico.

Turning to risk behaviors among adolescents, both before and after controlling for SES, it is almost universally the case that the proportions ever having sex increase from one generation to the next. Most first- and second-generation immigrant adolescent groups are, controlling for SES, less likely than Whites in native-born families to have ever had sex, whereas most third and later generation groups are more likely than the White native group to have

---

[1]Puerto Ricans are not immigrants because they are U.S. citizens by birth. But this study, and our new ACS analysis, assesses changes between the first generation born in Puerto Rico, the second generation born on the mainland with at least one parent born in Puerto Rico, and the third and later generations who are children born on the mainland with both parents born on the mainland. Puerto Ricans are Spanish speakers, and although they are U.S. citizens by birth, their migration to the U.S. mainland mirrors in important respects that of many other immigrant groups.

ever had sex. Use of controlled substances is based on an index with five items, indicating whether the adolescents ever use cigarettes, alcohol, chewing tobacco, marijuana, or hard drugs, such as inhalants, cocaine, or other illegal drugs. The immigrant paradox holds true, both before and after controlling for SES, for five groups (Mexico, Cuba, Central and South America, China, and other Asians) across all three generations, and for the Philippines and the Afro-Caribbean group across two generations. The immigrant paradox holds regarding substance use for Puerto Rico and Europe/Canada across at least two generations when SES is not controlled, but they experience little change across generations controlling for SES. Also controlling for SES, for all groups and all generations, except third and later generation Cubans, substance use is lower for immigrant groups than for native Whites.

Delinquency in this study is measured using an index with 11 delinquent or illegal behaviors, including painting graffiti, damaging property, shoplifting, running away from home, stealing a car, selling drugs, and burglary. The immigrant paradox holds true regarding delinquency, both before and after controlling for SES, for most groups across the first and second generations but not across the second and third generations. Delinquency rates often change little between the second generation and the third and later generations. The first generation of nearly all groups is less likely than Whites in native-born families, both before and after controlling for SES, to have engaged in delinquent behaviors, but there is more variability in this pattern across the second and later generations.

Violence is measured with an index consisting of nine items reflecting adolescent reports of violent behavior and use of weapons, including fighting, having pulled a knife or gun on someone, having shot or stabbed someone, or having used a weapon in a fight. The pattern across generations is generally consistent, particularly controlling for SES. For all groups except China, controlling for SES, violence increases between the first and second generation, with little change between the second and the third and later generations. For the Mexican-origin group the immigrant paradox holds true across all the generations.

The index of risk behaviors combines indicators for ever having had sex, having in engaged in four or more delinquent acts, having engaged in three or more acts of violence, and having used three or more controlled substances. Thus, this index focuses on adolescents with very high levels of risk behavior. The pattern of results for this index is consistent with the immigrant paradox. Both before and after controlling for SES, risk behaviors increase for nearly every group from the first, to the second, and to the third and later generations. The only exceptions are Japan between the first and second generation, not controlling for SES, and the Philippines, controlling for SES, with no change between the second generation and the third and later generations. Thus, the first generation is least likely to engage in risky behaviors. In addition, every first-generation group, both before and after controlling for SES, is less likely than the native White group to engage in risky behaviors. This is also true for the second-generation and later generation groups.

This study also reports one education-related indicator, whether the adolescent has learning difficulties. This is measured by asking parents whether the adolescent has a specific learning disability, including difficulties with attention or dyslexia, and whether the adolescent received any type of special service with the past 12 months. With and without SES controls, for six or seven of the nine comparisons across the first and second generations, the first generation is least likely to report having learning difficulties, and for six or seven of the nine comparisons across the second and the third and later generations, the third and later generation is most likely to report having learning difficulties. Thus, the immigrant paradox is quite clear in most of these results. In addition, for 22 of the 26 results not controlling for SES and for 25 of the 26 results controlling for SES, children of immigrants across all generations are less likely than Whites in native-born families to be reported as having learning difficulties.

Another study commissioned by the National Academies/Institute of Medicine (Kao, 1999) presented three indicators of education outcomes: grades, standardized math scores, and standardized reading scores. Among the smaller number of groups in this study, not controlling for SES, grades either changed little or declined across generations; controlling for parent's education and family income, results indicate that children with origins in China and Mexico experienced declining grades across all three generations. The same pattern held true across the second and third generation for those with origins in Philippines and across the first and second generations for other Hispanics and Blacks. These findings are generally consistent with the immigrant paradox.

Turning to math, not controlling for SES, test scores rose somewhat and then fell between the first and second generation and then between the second and third generation for Chinese and Filipino adolescents but changed little across generations for Mexican and other Hispanic adolescents. Controlling for SES, Mexican and Black adolescents experienced the immigrant paradox across all three generations, with math test scores declining from the first, to the second, to the third and later generations. For those with origins in China and other Hispanics, however, controlling for SES, math test scores improved between the first and second generations and then declined with the third and later generations. Among adolescents with Philippine origins, controlling for SES, the pattern was the opposite of the immigrant paradox, with math test scores increasing from the first, to the second generation and then further for the third and later generations. It also is important to note that for children with origins in Mexico as well as other Hispanics and Blacks, math test scores for every generation were lower than for Whites in native-born families, controlling for SES. This also was the case for third and later generation Chinese-origin children and first-generation Philippine-origin children.

Results for reading test scores were generally similar to math test score results for Chinese, other Hispanic, and Black children, with declining reading test scores across all generations for Blacks and across the second and the third and later generations for Chinese and other Hispanic adolescents. But the pattern was reversed for Filipino and Mexican adolescents, who instead experienced increases in reading test scores across the first, second, and third and later generations, both with and without controls for SES. Similar to the results for math test scores, controlling for SES, all generations of children with origins in Mexico and other Hispanics and Blacks had lower reading scores than Whites in native-born families, and this was also the case for first and third and later generation children with origins in China, and first generation children with Philippine origins.

Many of these results are consistent with the immigrant paradox. Declining test scores across the generations for some groups, and in particular, the test scores among children with origins in Mexico, other Hispanics, and Blacks that are lower for all generations than for native-born Whites, raise serious concerns for these children and pose important challenges for education policies and programs.

Overall, the results from the work of Harris (1999) and Kao (1999) presented here indicate that across most groups and most generations, the immigrant paradox holds true for physical health, risky behaviors, and some educational outcomes. Thus, children in newly immigrated families often fare comparatively well, both before and after controlling for SES, but declines in well-being that occur across generations are troubling. The third and later generations represent the long-term future of America. These declines in well-being across generations do not reflect well on the success of public policies for children. In addition, by many measures and for many groups, the first and second generations show special strengths given the challenges that they face, faring better than Whites in native-born families, but the third and later generation fares worse than Whites in native-born families. Finally, especially with regard to education indicators for large groups, namely those with origins in Mexico, other Hispanics, and Blacks, all generations perform more poorly, controlling for SES, than Whites in native-born families.

Beyond these issues arising from this analysis of the immigrant paradox, the earlier results from the ACS also indicate that many immigrant groups, as well third and later generation racial–ethnic minorities, live in families with comparatively low SES, that is, with comparatively low parental education and family income. This means that many children, particularly those with origins in Mexico, other Hispanics, and Blacks, are placed in double jeopardy because they live in comparatively low SES families and because they also experience comparatively low education outcomes even after controlling for SES. These challenges give particular urgency to the question of what public policies and programs can be pursued to help assure the well-being and success of children in immigrant and other racial–ethnic minority families.

PUBLIC POLICY RECOMMENDATIONS: LANGUAGE, EDUCATION, HEALTH, INCOME, AND IMMIGRANT ENFORCEMENT

In the short run, when immigrants first arrive in the United States, many have limited English skills. For these children and families, it is important that education, health, social service, and justice system organizations have the capacity to reach out to them in their heritage language. This will increase the success of these organizations in serving their entire client population. This also involves developing cultural sensitivity and cultural competence among workers in these organizations who are responsible for speaking to and working with immigrant families and children. This is important because access to services is important; even though many children in immigrant families fare comparatively well, many do not.

In the longer run, immigrants and their children learn English. To ensure that this occurs as rapidly and effectively as possible, programs that provide English language training should be expanded, and there is a need to develop effective two-generation family literacy programs that foster not only speaking but also reading and writing. These programs could help parents in immigrant families improve their capacity to provide economic support for the families while also fostering children's development. As we have seen, more English fluency in the parents has been accompanied by more optimal environments and outcomes for children.

In addition, a recent longitudinal study in the United States and a recent cross-national study of 13 countries including the United States suggest the following. Adolescents who have fluency in the both their parents' heritage language and the language of the settlement society and who identify with and participate in the cultures of both the society of origin and the society of settlement adjust more successfully than do those with other acculturation profiles (Portes & Rumbaut, 2001; Sam, Vedder, Ward, & Horenczyk, 2006; Suárez-Orozco & Suárez-Orozco, 1995, 2001). Measures of adjustment in these various studies include higher self-esteem, higher education and occupation expectations, higher academic achievement, and lower levels of mental health problems (e.g., anxiety, depression, and psychosomatic symptoms) as well as higher satisfaction with life and lower levels of antisocial behavior. These results suggest the value of programs that foster bilingual fluency in both English and the parents' heritage language for optimum development among children of immigrants. By maintaining the heritage language, children of immigrants can communicate effectively with parents and other family members, which can help to provide safeguards as children acculturate.

Research indicates that it is not essential for teachers to be fluently bilingual. For example, even when prekindergarten through Grade 3 teachers have no experience with a child's first language, they can introduce English to young ELLs and also adopt teaching practices that support home language development. Teachers who encourage the families of children to talk, read, and sing with the child in the parents' heritage language and to use their heritage language in everyday activities will foster the child's first language development even as the child is learning English (Espinosa, 2007, 2008).

Research shows that children who learn English after their home language is established, which is typically around age 3, can add a second language during the prekindergarten and early school years and that these bilingual skills lead to long-term cognitive, cultural, and economic advantages. It has also been found that a dual language approach to teaching is effective for ELLs while not having negative consequences for other children. In fact, dual language programs are effective not only for improving the academic achievements of English language learner students but also for providing benefits to native English speakers, as reflected in standardized test scores and reports by parents, teachers, and school administrators (Espinosa, 2007, 2008).

Access to early education programs is essential to ensure that the youngest children in immigrant families have the opportunity to develop their potential to become integrated, effective, and productive members of American society. Yet access to early education programs is limited for key immigrant groups (Hernandez, Denton, & Macartney, in press). Children in Mexican-origin families as well as those in immigrant families from Central America and Indochina are especially likely to have low rates of enrollment in prekindergarten or nursery school. One plausible reason sometimes cited, particularly for Hispanic immigrants, is that these cultures are more familistic and may prefer child care to be provided at home by parents or other relatives or in more intimate, culturally similar home care instead of by nonrelatives in formal settings. However, alternative socioeconomic barriers (money, transportation) can limit enrollment as well.

Early education programs may cost more than immigrant parents can afford to pay, or the number of openings available locally may be too small to meet the demand, or they may not have access to transportation essential to reach more distant early education programs. Although federal and state governments have policies that are intended to reduce or eliminate such difficulties for poor families, these policies are underfunded. Also, available programs may lack heritage language outreach, or they may lack teachers with a minimal capacity to speak to a child in the heritage language. In addition, parents with limited educational attainments may not know how to access early education programs, or they may not be aware that these programs are necessary for subsequent school success for their children.

A recent study has estimated the extent to which enrollment gaps separating White native-born children, on the one hand, from immigrant or racial–ethnic minority children, on the other, can be accounted for by socioeconomic barriers or cultural preferences (Hernandez et al., in press). For children in immigrant and native Mexican families, as well as children in Central American and Indochinese immigrant families, the results indicate that socioeconomic barriers can account for at least half and perhaps all of the enrollment gap separating them from Whites in native families, whereas most estimates indicate that cultural influences play a comparatively small role in accounting for the gaps in low prekindergarten or nursery school enrollment for these groups.

These results may be surprising in view of the low enrollment rates in the United States for children with origins in Mexico, but they are consistent with the strong commitment to early education in contemporary Mexico, where universal enrollment at age 3 became a national requirement in the 2008–2009 school year (though it is not yet fully implemented; Organisation for Economic Co-operation and Development, 2006). In fact, in 2005, 81% of children age 4 in Mexico were enrolled in preschool, substantially more than the 71% enrolled in preschool at age 4 among native-born Whites in U.S. families in 2004 (Yoshikawa et al., 2006). Given that preschool is less costly in Mexico than in the United States, and given that poverty for the Mexican immigrant group in the United States is quite high, it is not surprising that the proportion of the immigrant Mexican group enrolled in the United States at 55% is substantially lower than the 81% enrolled in Mexico.

In sum, familistic cultural values are sometimes cited to explain lower early education enrollment among immigrants, but the research described here shows socioeconomic barriers can account for at least 50%, and for some groups perhaps all, of the gap. Public policies to support early education could be expanded to reduce or eliminate enrollment gaps due to these barriers.

It also is important to focus on the other end of the educational pipeline, high school graduation. Among young adults, there is a marked distinction between first-generation immigrants born abroad and the second generation born in the United States because many immigrants arrive as adolescents or young adults with very limited education. Second-generation Mexican-origin youth are about as likely as the third and later generations to graduate from high school, at 77% to 79%. But among the first generation, only 40% are high school graduates. Many of these immigrants should not be viewed as high school dropouts because many never entered the U.S. education system. Thus, education policy must address two very different populations, children for whom the education system has failed and adolescents and young adults who have never been touched by the U.S. education system.

Good health is important for children to succeed in school and in life, but many children are not covered by health insurance, despite the fact that the State Children's Health Insurance Program (SCHIP) was created in 1997, almost 15 years ago. Results from the Census Bureau's Current Population Survey, combining the years 2001–2005, indicate that 1 in 6 Mexican-origin children in native-born families (17%) are not covered by health insurance. This rises to almost one third (32%) for children in Mexican-origin immigrant groups. Thus, to prevent health deterioration with acculturation, it is important not only to conserve health practices but also to ensure access to health insurance. Among large immigrant groups other than Mexican-origin children in the United States that can be studied with data from the Current Population Survey given available sample sizes, only children with origins in Central America and Haiti include a high proportion not covered by health insurance. For many of these children, public policies to improve access to health care may be essential to successful development and well-being. It is important that these gaps in health insurance coverage be eliminated. One approach to accomplishing this would be the enactment of the Legal Immigrant Children's Health Improvement Act, which would give states the option to provide federally funded SCHIP and Medicaid to low-income, legal immigrant children and pregnant women.

Turning to income, the exclusion of some immigrant parents from eligibility for welfare programs, in particular the Temporary Assistance for Needy Families program, deprives their U.S. citizen children of important public benefits and services. The recent eligibility exclusion rules not only jeopardize the health and development of the children who are not receiving needed services but have an impact on all Americans who stand to benefit from having a healthy and productive labor force in the future. The Earned Income Tax Credit (EITC) should also be expanded to include a larger number of working parents and children as eligible and to increase the monetary value of the benefits for individual families. The 1996 Federal welfare legislation included increased funding for EITC with the aim of encouraging work among low-income persons. With this change, the EITC as of 2004 reduced child poverty by about 2.3%, that is, lifting out of poverty about 1 in 8 children who would otherwise be classified as poor by the official poverty measure. However, the value of the EITC is too low to lift many other children out of poverty, and it has little effect at higher income levels because its value diminishes rapidly at income levels (in 2008) higher than $18,750 for two-parent families and

$15,750 for one-parent families. If eligibility for EITC were extended to include more families and the monetary value were increased for all eligible families, the EITC would become even more effective in improving the lives of children in low-income families, including immigrant families.

Children and parents in working families also would benefit from additional earnings if parents had access to English language classes combined with other job training. Such programs could help reduce the high level of poverty among children in immigrant families.

Finally, during recent years, U.S. Immigration and Customs and Enforcement (ICE) has increased workplace and home raids as a means of enforcing immigration laws. A recent study of three sites found that on average, for every two adults involved there was a child whose parent was arrested (Capps, Castaneda, Chaudry, & Santos, 2007). Two thirds (66%) of the children were American citizens. The detained parent was often the primary breadwinner, leaving children and other family members without their main source of economic support and coping with fear, isolation, and other psychological stresses. On the basis of these and other findings, Capps et al. (2007) recommended ways to minimize harm to children occurring as a result of worksite raids, including the following.

First, Congress should provide oversight to enforcement activities to ensure children are protected. Second, ICE should assume there will always be children affected when adults are arrested in worksite enforcement operations and should develop appropriate policies for the parents' release. Third, ICE should provide detainees with access to counsel and to telephones and should advise them of their right to confer with their country's consular office. Fourth, social services and economic assistance should be provided over a prolonged period of time, until parents are released from detention or their immigration cases are resolved. Fifth, an information clearinghouse should be developed to provide a foundation for developing best practices in service delivery.

A more recent study (Chaudry et al., 2010) provided additional research and recommendations pertaining to ICE raids. There is wide agreement that immigration laws should be enforced, but the manner in which enforcement occurs should not bring harm to children, who often are U.S. citizens.

CONCLUSIONS

Results presented in this chapter indicate that children of immigrants often experience the strengths associated with living in two-parent families that have a strong work ethic and that are putting down deep roots in their local communities. But many children of immigrants live in families constrained by limited parental education, low English skills, and low family incomes. As a consequence, many lack access to early childhood education and health insurance.

Additional results presented here are broadly consistent with the immigrant paradox, indicating that later generations fare less well than earlier generations on a variety of indicators, both before and after controlling for SES. This suggests that immigrant families bring important strengths to America but that their efficacy dissipates over time. So what public policies, programs, and services do we need to support the initial strengths of immigrant families and their children? Immigrant families bring strong a work ethic that needs to be supported by providing appropriate job skills and English language learning; without this assistance, the persistence of living in poverty might lead to the deterioration of outcomes observed in the second and third generations. Higher levels of formal education can also lead to higher incomes and SES. But in the pursuit of formal education, children of immigrants should be able to acculturate at the same time they strengthen their cultural roots and connections with their families and ethnic enclaves. Education policies should emphasize bilingualism and biculturalism as the optimal outcomes for these children. Dual language education is one of the most effective ways of reaching this goal. Supporting community organizations that involve children in traditional cultural practices that reinforce cultural pride and identification is another avenue. Creating bridges between school curriculum and the heritage culture also reinforces these processes.

The sheer number of children in immigrant families means that they will play a major role in sustaining the American economy during the coming decades. This is critical to the well-being of all Americans but especially to the baby boom generation, which will depend for economic support during retirement on the productivity of all American workers, including those who grew up in immigrant families. Policies fostering English and heritage language literacy and fluency for both adults and children, access to effective early and later education and preventive health services, and sufficient family income can foster the development of children in immigrant families and help these children and families achieve their goals, to the benefit of all Americans.

REFERENCES

Annie E. Casey Foundation. (2006). *The Annie E. Casey Foundation 2006 KIDS COUNT DATA BOOK*. Baltimore, MD: Author.

Capps, R., Castaneda, R. M., Chaudry, A., & Santos, R. (2007) *Paying the price: The impact of immigration raids on America's children*. Washington, DC: National Council of La Raza.

Capps, R., Kenny, G., & Fix, M. (2003). *Health insurance coverage of children in mixed-status immigrant families* (Snapshots of America's Children, No. 12). Washington, DC: The Urban Institute.

Chaudry, A., Capps, R., Pedroza, J. M., Castaneda, R. M., Santos, R., & Scott, M. M. (2010). *Facing our future: Children in the aftermath of immigration enforcement.* Washington, DC: The Urban Institute.

Cherlin, A. J. (1999). Going to extremes: Family structure, children's well-being, and social sciences. *Demography, 36*(4), 421–428. doi:10.2307/2648081

Citro, C. F., & Michael, R. T. (Eds.). (1995). *Measuring poverty: A new approach.* Washington, DC: National Academy Press.

Espinosa, L. M. (2007). English-language learners as they enter school. In R. C. Pianta, M. J. Cox, & K. L. Snow (Eds.), *School readiness and the transition to kindergarten in the era of accountability* (pp. 175–195). Baltimore, MD: Brookes.

Espinosa, L. M. (2008, January). *Challenging common myths about young English language learners* (FCD Policy Brief, Advancing PK-3, No. 8). New York, NY: Foundation for Child Development.

Fix, M., & Passel, J. (1999). *Trends in noncitizens' and citizens' use of public benefits following welfare reform: 1994–97.* Washington, DC: The Urban Institute.

Fix, M., & Zimmerman, W. (1995). When should immigrants receive benefits? In I. V. Sawhill (Ed.), *Welfare reform: An analysis of the issues.* Washington, D.C.: The Urban Institute. Available at http://www.urban.org/url.cfm?ID=306620

Harris, K. M. (1999). The health status and risk behaviors of adolescents in immigrant families. In D. J. Hernandez (Ed.), *Children of immigrants: Health, adjustment, and public assistance* (pp. 286–347). Washington, DC: National Academy Press.

Hernandez, D. J. (Ed.). (1999). *Children of immigrants: Health, adjustment, and public assistance.* Washington, DC: National Academy Press.

Hernandez, D. J., & Charney, E. (Eds.). (1998). *From generation to generation: The health and well-being of children in immigrant families.* Washington, DC: National Academy Press.

Hernandez, D. J., Denton, N. A., & Macartney, S. E. (2007), Child poverty in the U.S.: A new family budget approach with comparison to European countries. In H. Wintersberger, L. Alanen, T. Olk, & J. Qvortrup (Eds.) *COST A19: Children's welfare: Vol. 1. Childhood, generational order and the welfare state: Exploring children's social and economic welfare* (pp. 109–140). Odense: University Press of Southern Denmark.

Hernandez, D. J., Denton, N. A., & Macartney, S. E. (2008). Children in immigrant families: Looking to America's future. *Social Policy Report, 22*(3), 1–24. Available at http://www.srcd.org/

Hernandez, D. J., Denton, N. A., & Macartney, S. (2011). Early childhood education programs: Accounting for low enrollment in immigrant and minority families. In R. Alba & M. C. Waters (Eds.), *The next generation: Immigrant youth in a comparative perspective* (pp. 46–66). New York, NY: New York University Press.

Kao, G. (1999). Psychological well-being and educational achievement among immigrant youth. In D. J. Hernandez (Ed.), *Children of immigrants: Health, adjustment, and public assistance* (pp. 410–477). Washington, DC: National Academy Press.

McLanahan, S., & Sandefur, G. (1994). *Growing up with a single parent: What hurts, what helps*. Cambridge, MA: Harvard University Press.

Organisation for Economic Co-operation and Development. (2006). *Early childhood education and care policy: Country note for Mexico*. Retrieved from http://www.oecd.org/dataoecd/11/39/34429196.pdf

Passel, J. S. (2006, March 7). *Size and characteristics of the unauthorized migrant population in the U.S.* (Pew Hispanic Center Report). Washington, DC: Pew Hispanic Center. Retrieved from http://pewhispanic.org/files/reports/61.pdf

Passel, J. S. (2007, March 28). *Growing share of immigrants choosing naturalization* (Pew Hispanic Center Report). Washington, DC: Pew Hispanic Center. Retrieved from http://pewhispanic.org/files/reports/74.pdf

Portes, A., & Rumbaut, R. G. (2001). *Legacies: The story of the immigrant generation*. Berkeley: University of California Press.

Sam, D. L., Vedder, P., Ward, C., & Horenczyk, G. (2006). Psychological and sociocultural adaptation of immigrant youth. In J. W. Berry, J. S. Phinney, D. L. Sam, & P. Vedder (Eds.), *Immigrant youth in cultural transition: Acculturation identity and adaptation across national contexts* (pp. 117–141). Mahwah, NJ: Erlbaum.

Suárez-Orozco, C., & Suárez-Orozco, M. (1995). *Transformations: Migration, family life, and achievement motivation among Latino adolescents*. Stanford, CA: Stanford University Press.

Suárez-Orozco, C., & Suárez-Orozco, M. (2001). *Children of immigration*. Cambridge, MA: Harvard University Press.

Yoshikawa, H., McCartney, K, Myers, R., Bub, K., Lugo-Gil, J., Knaul, F., & Ramos, M. (2007). *Preschool education in Mexico: Expansion, quality improvement, and curricular reform* (UNICEF Innocenti Research Centre Working Paper). Retrieved from http://www.unicef-irc.org/publications/pdf/iwp_2007_03.pdf

Zimmermann, W., & Tumlin, K. (1999). *Patchwork policies: State assistance for immigrants under welfare reform* (Occasional Paper No. 24). Washington, DC: The Urban Institute.

2

HISTORICAL ORIGINS OF THE IMMIGRANT PARADOX FOR MEXICAN AMERICAN STUDENTS: THE CULTURAL INTEGRATION HYPOTHESIS

RAYMOND BURIEL

This chapter analyzes the origins of the immigrant student paradox for Mexican Americans by tracing its roots to the historically self-selected nature of Mexican immigration. The *immigrant student paradox* refers to the better than expected academic and behavioral outcomes for children of immigrants relative to their later generation peers. It is argued that the *cultural integration hypothesis*, first put forth in 1984, explains the immigrant student paradox for Mexican Americans. This hypothesis holds that Mexican immigrant culture represents a unique segment of Mexican culture that is selective with respect to occupational, educational, and psychological characteristics conducive to success in the United States. These traits tend to erode over generations in the United States because of negative acculturating experiences. Biculturalism is proposed as an adaptation strategy to maintain immigrant Mexican culture while simultaneously selectively acculturating to positive aspects of American culture.

EVOLUTION OF THE CULTURAL INTEGRATION HYPOTHESIS

In 1984, I wrote a chapter for the second edition of the book *Chicano Psychology* (Martinez & Mendoza, 1984) challenging the prevailing behavioral

37

science view that the educational and social problems of Mexican Americans were due to their culture. At the time, the "culture damaging" or "culture deprivation" view was a convenient catchall for explaining the problems of Mexican Americans and other ethnic minorities in the United States. In contrast, my review of the literature in the areas of economic mobility, education, and delinquency revealed that Mexican Americans who were more thoroughly integrated into their immigrant Mexican culture were the most successful members of their group. I described this as "the seemingly paradoxical hypothesis that integration with traditional Mexican-American culture fosters healthy sociocultural adjustment to mainstream American society" (Buriel, 1984, p. 95). I viewed immigrant Mexican culture as the traditional or original culture brought to the United States by highly self-selected immigrants. Because of damaging acculturating influences, this traditional culture changed over time and became more characteristic of the cultural orientation of later generation Mexican Americans. Nevertheless, on the basis of the evidence I presented, I argued that retention of the original immigrant culture by later generation Mexican Americans was conducive to their success. This was possible through the development of biculturalism, which preserved aspects of traditional immigrant Mexican American culture, such as Spanish fluency, while simultaneously allowing for the acquisition of Euro American cultural competencies. Biculturalism allowed individuals to retain the achievement-oriented aspects of their immigrant culture and to express them in prescribed ways using Euro American culture, such as English fluency. Bicultural development is more likely in the first and second generations because immigrant parents who can provide a firsthand traditional cultural upbringing raise the children in these two groups. These children also develop Euro American cultural competencies in school. Because third-generation children are not raised by immigrant parents, the traditional Mexican cultural upbringing may be lacking in their socialization, and they become more acculturated to Euro American culture (Buriel, 1993a). Without the reinforcement and protection of immigrant culture, these children may become more susceptible to society's negative stereotypes of their group and the high-risk behaviors of their peers, which can diminish their chances for educational success.

At the root of the cultural integration hypothesis, which can help explain the immigrant student paradox, is the self-selected nature of Mexican immigrants. Historically, the achievement-oriented nature of immigrants to the United States has been dismissed because of the prevailing assumptions that immigrant cultures are inferior to mainstream American culture and that assimilation is the only pathway to success for immigrants and their children. In the case of Mexican Americans, this assumption received early spurious support based on the results of methodologically flawed studies that failed to control for within-group diversity related to generation and culture. This chapter briefly reviews the history of the "culture damaging" view of immigrants in the United States and the research approaches that seemed to support this perspective for Mexican Americans. The chapter also describes some of the early research leading up to the cultural integration hypothesis and the self-selected nature of Mexican immigrants. The chapter concludes with a discussion of how adherence to immigrant culture is conducive to the success of children from immigrant families.

In response to the tidal waves of immigration from eastern and southern Europe between 1892 and 1915, the prevailing social and educational policy of the United States was to "Americanize" the children of immigrants. This view is strikingly captured in the recommendations of E. P. Cubberley, a noted educator of the time, for whom Cubberley Hall at Stanford University was named. According to Cubberley, the goals of public education should be the eradication of ethnic cultures and the implantation of an American consciousness and culture:

> Everywhere these people settle in groups or settlements, and . . . set up their national manners, customs, and observances. Our task is to break up these groups and settlements, to assimilate and amalgamate these people as part of our American race, and to implant in their children, as far as can be done, the Anglo-Saxon conception of righteousness, law and order, and our popular government, and to awaken in them a reverence for our democratic institutions and for those things in our national life which we as a people hold to be of abiding worth. (Cubberley, 1909, pp. 15–16)

The educational and social policies that promoted Americanization were premised on the assumptions that ethnic cultures were inherently inferior and that Anglo-Saxon American culture was morally and intellectually superior (Ramirez & Castañeda, 1974). The struggles of immigrant families to adapt to life in the United States were described by Gordon (1964) as "pressure-cooker assimilation." Within two generations, these "old" immigrants replaced their ethnic cultures with an American culture and melted into the mainstream. Moreover, the educational, economic, social, and political achievements of the descendants of these "old" immigrants have become the standard that is held up for "new" immigrants from Asia and Latin America to emulate as markers of successful adaptation to life in the United States. As in the past, the prescribed pathway to successful adaptation is through cultural assimilation. However, as the chapters of this book indicate, becoming more "American" may be associated with developmental risks. In fact, the paradox is that the least acculturated immigrants and their children often experience more successful outcomes than their more Americanized, later generation peers.

Until 1970, the decennial census collected data about parents' nativity in order to track the economic and educational gains made by successive generations of the descendants of the "old" immigrants. After the gains of the descendants of "old" immigrants appeared to level out, the decennial census quit collecting data on nativity. The accumulation of data seemed to indicate that gains were made between the first, second, and third generations, as these descendants of "old" immigrants shed their ethnic heritages and increasingly replaced them with an American consciousness and culture. Within the past 3 decades, as immigration from Asia and Latin America has swelled, fears have arisen that these "new" immigrants and their children are resisting assimilation. Pat Buchanan, a former presidential candidate and advisor to President Nixon, wrote a best-selling book, titled *The Decline of the West* (2002), in which he argued that American culture is on the verge of extinction because of immigration from Mexico. He wrote that these immigrants' loyalty to Mexico, their refusal to learn English, and their slow pace of acculturation are bringing down the United States. According to Buchanan, Mexican immigrants need to cut ties with Mexico and become "American" if they want to succeed in this country. Many educators also support the assimilationist position when they refer to Mexican-descent students as being "at risk," a term that replaced being "culturally disadvantaged." Embedded in these views and terminology surrounding Mexican immigrants and their children are the same assumptions that prevailed about "old" immigrants, namely, the inferiority of immigrant cultures and the superiority of American culture and the need for a speedy acculturation. The social ethos of these assumptions is reflected in "English-only" laws in many parts of the country, the dismantling of bilingual education in many states, and the attempt to deny public education to the children of undocumented immigrants (Proposition 187 in California; *Text of Proposition*, 1994, p. 1).

The assimilationist position would have some credence if it were shown that in fact Americanized Mexican Americans are the most successful members of their group. However, the immigrant student paradox challenges this view. Unfortunately, Americanization ideology is so entrenched and unquestioned in our society that it has drawn attention away from the unexpected successes of recent immigrants and their children and the decline of later generation Latinos who appear to be more Americanized.

How did the view of an inferior Mexican culture and a superior American culture take hold in the behavioral science literature and lead to the promotion of assimilation to North American culture for Mexican American immigrants and their descendants? I believe that the answer lies in early two-group studies that sought to document racial and cultural differences between Mexican Americans and Euro Americans in a variety of areas. Most notable was the area of intelligence testing in the 1930s that compared these two groups without taking into account issues of English language proficiency and culturally biased test instruments (Sánchez, 1932, 1934). These early studies concluded that the group differences observed in intelligence were genetic or racial in nature. These interpretations were anchored in the dominant paradigms of those times in the social sciences and in society in general whereby racial and ethnic group differences were attributed solely to genetic influences. Later, culture replaced race/ethnicity as the main causal explanation for differences between Mexican Americans and Euro Americans. During the 1960s and 1970s, it was typical for the behavioral science literature to refer to Mexican Americans (as well as African Americans and Puerto Ricans) as being "culturally disadvantaged." In fact, important social policies of the era, such as Head Start, were based on the assumption that Mexican American and African American children needed early preschool intervention to overcome the disadvantaging effects of their home cultures. Thus, cultural deprivation became a convenient explanation for high rates of Mexican American poverty (Kuvlesky & Patella, 1971), high school dropouts (Demos, 1962), and juvenile delinquency (Heller, 1966).

Many similar investigations followed (Padilla & Ruiz, 1973) that relied on a two-group study design. These studies were conceptually and methodologically flawed because they equated ethnicity with culture and failed to take into account important within-group differences such as generation, language, and degree of cultural involvement. In many comparisons the groups also differed in socioeconomic status. On the assumption that all Mexican Americans are alike, researchers compared randomly drawn or convenient samples of Mexican Americans and Euro Americans and concluded that any differences between the groups were due to culture. This is the fallacy of equating ethnicity with culture. Although all Mexican Americans may share a common Mexican ancestry, they do not share the same culture to the same degree. Methodological flaws involved a failure to take into account important within-group differences among Mexican Americans that are related to positive developmental outcomes. Random samples were drawn because that was thought to yield representative groups, which is considered sound methodological practice. However, without a further breakdown of characteristics of the sample, important within-group differences were masked. Some of these within-group differences, such as generation, have now been shown to have a positive effect on developmental outcomes but in unexpected directions, hence the immigrant paradox. For example, until 1980, a random sample of Mexican American children would have yielded 13% first generation, 30% second generation, and 57% third generation (Fry & Passel, 2009). Given what we know today about the immigrant student paradox, the disproportionately high number of third-generation students could have masked positive test results for first- and second-generation children when the scores of all children were averaged and compared with a Euro American sample.

The reliance on two-group studies tended to define Mexican Americans in the behavioral sciences literature only in relation to Euro Americans rather than themselves. Thus, when some investigators began submitting their research for publication using only Mexican American samples, to show the importance of within-group factors, journal reviewers often criticized them for not having a Euro American "control group." That practice perpetuated the use of a "gold standard" of Euro Americans and the deficient status of everybody else.

EARLY EVIDENCE OF ECONOMIC AND
OCCUPATIONAL MOBILITY AMONG
MEXICAN AMERICANS FROM IMMIGRANT FAMILIES

Despite the preponderance of two-group studies, there were early, isolated investigations of Mexican Americans that looked solely within the group. These studies tended to present the strengths of Mexican Americans and their culture. The earliest of these investigations was the anthropological work of Manuel Gamio (1931), who conducted life-history interviews to study the adaptation of Mexican immigrants and Mexican Americans in the United States. His sample included working adult men and women. Although most had little formal education, they were described as "articulate, introspective, perceptive, philosophical, and cognizant of historical, social, economic, and political factors affecting their lives" (Ramirez, 1983, p. 44). Many expressed the desire for a better life for their children, which included more schooling in the United States. In 1970, the first national study of Mexican Americans gave a glimpse of important within-group differences related to the immigrant paradox (Grebler, Moore, & Guzman, 1970). The study was conducted between 1965 and 1966 and was based on interviews with nearly 1,200 adults in San Antonio, Texas, and Los Angeles, California, as well as census data for 1960. Generational analyses of the census data compared the incomes of first-, second-, and third-generation men between the ages of 35 and 44 years living in the southwest. Although the median incomes of the three generations were relatively low, there was a substantial increase (21%) in income between foreign-born ($3,682) and second-generation ($4,664) Mexican Americans. The third generation, however, had a median income ($4,454) that was lower than the second generation's. Analyses of the 1970 census data by Chiswick (1979) revealed an even more dramatic picture of economic downward mobility among Mexican Americans from nonimmigrant homes. After controlling for years of schooling and labor market experience, weeks worked, marital status, area of residence, country of birth, and years living in the United States, Chiswick found the earnings of second-generation men to be 5% to 9% greater than those of their third-generation counterparts. Even more interesting was the finding that after about 15 years of U.S. residence, the earnings of Mexican immigrants equaled that of Mexican Americans born in this country. As noted earlier, the U.S. Census Bureau stopped collecting relevant nativity data after 1970, thereby making it difficult to conduct future generational analyses of the type reported in 1970 and 1980, which is a real scientific loss.

Two early ethnographic studies exploring the occupational mobility of Mexican-descent women living in the United States yielded findings consistent with the cultural integration hypothesis. In the first of these investigations, Melville (1980) classified the social mobility aspirations of 47 women (31 foreign born and 16 native born) living in Houston, Texas. Using extensive interviews and observations, she classified 14 women in her sample as having high upwardly mobile aspirations. Of these 14 women, 12 were immigrants and two were U.S. born. In other words, only 12.5% of the women born in the United States held upwardly mobile aspirations compared with approximately 39% of the Mexican-born women. Another ethnographic study by Gandara (1982) examined the family histories of 17 high-achieving Mexican American women who were originally from lower socioeconomic backgrounds. All of the women had law degrees, medical degrees, or doctoral degrees. Her findings revealed that

> the majority of these women had not assimilated very much into North-American culture with respect to status variables. Almost all were Catholic, most were from large families (M = 5.5 children), most were bilingual or spoke only Spanish at home (77%), and most were first generation (70%). (p. 172)

At the time, I noted that Gandara's study was important for three reasons. First, it focused attention on the achievements of Mexican Americans rather than their failure, which was a big departure from the culture-damaging perspective of that era. Second, it helped draw attention to the fact that many women of Mexican descent have careers outside the home. Finally, it provided support for the cultural integration hypothesis.

EARLY EDUCATION STUDIES SUPPORTING
THE CULTURAL INTEGRATION HYPOTHESIS

The previously cited study by Grebler et al. (1970) also examined educational attainment of first-, second-, and third-generation Mexican Americans using data from the 1960 U.S. census. Their analyses looked at years of schooling completed by persons between the ages of 14 and 24 years. Overall, the schooling of Mexican Americans at that time was relatively low. Nevertheless, whereas fewer first-generation immigrants completed high school (8.1%), more from the second generation completed high school (16.1%)

than from the third generation (14.0%). However, slightly more first-generation individuals completed some college (4.3%) than those from the third generation (4.0%), and the second generation was the highest (4.5%) in this category of educational attainment. Recently, Tellez and Ortiz (2008) re-interviewed 684 of the nearly 1,200 participants from Grebler et al.'s original survey along with 758 of their children. The inclusion of the original participants' children made for a longitudinal and intergeneration design capable of tracking the educational mobility of immigrants and their children between the years 1960 and 2000. Tellez and Ortiz conducted several different analyses to examine the effects of multiple variables on years of schooling completed. Their final multivariate analysis controlled for family income, parents' marital status and education, language usage, public or private school attendance, gender, neighborhood characteristics, and other variables associated with years of education. The results of their final analysis showed that immigrant children who came to the United States at a young age with their parents, often referred to as the *1.5 generation*, had the most years of schooling (13.3). There was no statistical difference in years of schooling completed between the second generation and the *2.5 generation* (those who came from families with at least one immigrant parent; 13.1 and 13.2, respectively). However, all three of these groups had significantly more years of education than the third and fourth generation, who did not differ from each other (13.0 and 12.5, respectively; Tellez & Ortiz, 2008). The results of this study indicate a decline in years of schooling completed between children of foreign-born parentage and native-born parentage. I reviewed several other studies in my earlier chapter (Buriel, 1984) that support Tellez and Ortiz's findings.

One important way Mexican Americans remain integrated with immigrant culture is through the use of the Spanish language on a regular basis. Spanish usage and fluency permit greater contact and more complex involvement with recent immigrants and a sharing of their values and aspirations. Within immigrant families, Spanish language usage can also facilitate the intergenerational transmission of cultural values and promote better parent–child communication and relationships that can be beneficial to students' academic success. In both immigrant and native-born families, the retention of Spanish contributes to children's bilingualism, which is associated with a cognitive style characterized by greater flexibility and abstract thinking (see Chapter 7, this volume). Thus, among native-born Mexican Americans, bilingualism may conserve and reinforce for them aspects of immigrant culture and simultaneously promote a cognitive style related to school achievement. This was shown in early studies with populations ranging from first-graders to college students. Henderson and Merrit (1968) investigated the environmental backgrounds of Mexican American first-graders who had been identified through various tests as having either high or low potential for future academic success.

In addition to scoring higher on several environmental predictor variables, the high-potential children also scored significantly higher than the low-potential group on a test of Spanish vocabulary. This finding led the researchers to conclude that the "data seem to refute the common assumption that children from families that are 'most Mexican' in their behavior and outlook will have the most difficulty in school" (p. 105). A follow-up study of these same children 3 years later, at the end of third grade, confirmed that the high-potential Spanish-speaking children performed better academically than their low-potential English-monolingual peers (Henderson, 1972).

Because of its national scope, the High School and Beyond study conducted by the National Opinion Research Center (Nielsen & Fernandez, 1981) was one of the first investigations to create awareness of a large-scale immigrant student paradox. The national sample of 58,728 high school students included 1,068 sophomores and 1,204 seniors of Mexican descent. All students provided information on family background variables, including language usage and years of U.S. residence. In addition, they completed achievement-related tests, including educational aspirations, math and reading achievement, and English vocabulary. Results showed that for both sophomores and seniors, Spanish usage was related to lower scores on all four achievement measures. However, Spanish proficiency was positively related to higher aspirations for both classes and also to higher math and vocabulary scores for seniors. Speaking Spanish, per se, may not be as indicative of cultural integration as Spanish proficiency because the latter reflects greater command of the language and cognitive ability. The extra effort put into being proficient in Spanish among adolescents may reflect a desire to remain closely connected to the mainstream of Mexican immigrant culture and to their families. In line with other studies, Nielsen and Fernandez (1981) also found that for both sophomores and seniors, achievement decreased in all four areas as length of U.S. residence increased. In their explanation of these findings, they hinted at the role of selective immigration, stating that "since those families with higher status are more likely to be able to marshal the resources necessary for immigration, they also bring with them a constellation of attributes which tend to encourage high academic achievement" (p. 72). Nielsen and Fernandez did not offer an explanation of the achievement-oriented attributes associated with Mexican immigrants.

Two early investigations with Mexican-descent college students also support the important role of Spanish language retention in students' achievement. In the earliest of these studies, Long and Padilla (cited in Ramirez, 1971) investigated the bilingual antecedents of academic success among Spanish-surnamed graduate students at the University of New Mexico in Albuquerque. They found that 94% of the students successfully completing their graduate programs were raised in Spanish–English bilingual homes and that most of the unsuccessful students came from homes where only English was spoken.

Long and Padilla concluded that bilingual students may have been better able to interact effectively with Spanish-speaking members of their ethnic group as well as Euro Americans, thus making them better adjusted members of both groups. Another college-age study by García (1981), in Texas, investigated the effects of students' cultural maintenance on their academic performance. Mexican American students from 13 colleges and universities were sampled on a variety of family background, social–psychological, and achievement variables. Using multivariate analyses, García found that being proficient in Spanish and coming from a Spanish-dominant home were positively associated with better grades.

Early studies in the area of educational achievement for Mexican Americans reflect two dominant trends. First, earlier generation students from immigrant homes outperform later generation students. Second, students fluent in Spanish, regardless of nativity, perform better academically across grade levels ranging from first grade, high school, and through college and graduate school. Spanish fluency may permit greater involvement with immigrants and their culture as well as successful adaptation to communities where both Spanish and English are dominant languages. We also know that later research has identified various cognitive advantages of being bilingual (see Chapter 7, this volume), so these advantages might represent direct pathways to better schooling outcomes.

THE DISASSOCIATION OF MEXICAN IMMIGRANT CULTURE FROM DELINQUENCY AND CRIME

Noninvolvement in criminal and delinquent behavior by immigrants and their children can be viewed as an indirect indicator of successful adjustment to U.S. society. As we have seen, a strong work ethic and going to school are two common characteristics of immigrants. These same characteristics also represent two widely acknowledged deterrents to crime. People who work and go to school are perhaps too busy to commit crimes, and they generally hold values that are in line with society's rules for maintaining social order. Nevertheless, a popular misconception is that immigrants cause increases in crime. The frequent juxtaposition of the words *crime*, *Mexican*, and *immigrants* in the press and other popular media has created an imaginary causal link between these three elements that historically predates the Mexican American War of 1846 (Buriel, 1984; Butcher & Piehl, 1998; McWilliams, 1968; Woll, 1977). Gangs in particular have drawn the media's attention, with headlines such as "Culture and Crime Play Role in Gangs," which appeared in the *Los Angeles Times* in an article on Mexican American youths (Culture and Crime Play Role in Gangs, 1979). The title of the article implicates Mexican culture as the cause of gang behavior. Yet, a rigorous empirical investigation by Moore (1978) of the formation of Los Angeles' earliest gangs showed that of a total of 209 males who belonged to these gangs between 1945 and 1960, only three were born in Mexico. More recent scholarship on Mexican American gangs and delinquency has concluded that prejudice, segregation, cultural loss, and acculturative stress are most responsible for these behaviors (Buriel, Calzada, & Vasquez, 1982; Moore, 1978, 1991; Samaniego & Gonzalez, 1999; Vigil, 1988, 2007).

The perceived association of Mexican immigrants and criminal behavior was most vividly demonstrated in 1994 in California with the passage of Proposition 187, which was put forth as the "Save Our State" initiative. Proposition 187 sought to deny undocumented immigrants and their children access to public services, including education. Although Proposition 187 was declared unconstitutional, its sentiments endure in spite of the fact that many large-scale studies challenge the association between immigrants and increases in crime. For example, Butcher and Piehl (1998) used national data from the Uniform Crime Reports and the Current Population Surveys to analyze the relationship between immigration into 43 metropolitan areas and those areas' crime rate. A secondary analysis focused on young immigrants, who are most likely to belong to gangs, using the National Longitudinal Survey of Youth. The results showed that cities with high levels of immigrants tend to have high crime rates but that there is no relationship between changes in crime and changes in immigration. Moreover, evidence from the National Longitudinal Survey of Youth analysis showed that young immigrants are less likely to commit crime than their native-born counterparts (Butcher & Piehl, 1998). Unfortunately, in areas with increased immigration rates, immigrants are often the victims of crime, which links immigrants to crime without taking into account their victimization. Immigrants might be reluctant to report these crimes because they do not want to be involved with law enforcement authorities, so the crimes might go undetected.

In a recent book on high-achieving undocumented Latino high school and college students, Perez (2009) presented a summary of four current large-scale studies showing significantly less crime activity among immigrants relative to the rest of society. Perez made a good point in noting that many of the reported crimes of immigrants are civil infractions involving violations of U.S. immigration law and not criminal acts. Thus, despite current legislative efforts to criminalize Latino immigrants, such as Arizona's SB 1070, the fact remains that the vast majority of Latino immigrants and their children (documented or not) are busy pursuing their "American dream" through legitimate pathways such as occupational mobility, academic success, and service in the U.S. military.

SELF-SELECTION FACTORS AND
MEXICAN IMMIGRANT CULTURE

A major tenet of the cultural integration hypothesis is that the culture of Mexican immigrants arises from the self-selection factors that distinguish immigrants from their compatriots who do not immigrate. In a sense, immigrants are not typical Mexicans, because if they were they would have remained in Mexico as is typical of the majority of Mexicans. Instead, they have voluntarily decided to leave their country, home, and family in search of greater opportunities in the United States. Moreover, they are aware they may face prejudice, discrimination, and a limited ability to communicate because they do not speak English. The desire for change, even in the face of great sacrifices and risks, distinguishes Mexican immigrants from those who do not immigrate.[1]

Occupational Background

An enduring stereotype depicts Mexican immigrants as illiterate *campesinos* from impoverished rural backgrounds who come to the United States primarily to do farm work. Such a view is fueled by a simplistic *push–pull* model of immigration that postulates the greatest "push" to immigrate comes from the most deprived sectors of Mexican society, and these immigrants are "pulled" to the sector of greatest need in the United States, namely farm work. Moreover, this northward movement is assumed to follow the lines of least resistance, thereby predicting more immigration by people living closest to the border than those in the interior of Mexico. Years of immigration studies debunk the assumptions of the push–pull model for Mexican immigrants. The research shows that Mexican immigration has historically originated from a few interior states that are not the poorest in Mexico and involves mostly the urban working class rather than the poorest rural *campesinos*. A longitudinal study of Mexican immigration by Portes and Bach (1985) found that the primary source of Mexican immigration lies in the progressively oriented mainstream of Mexican society. These are people working in skilled and semiskilled occupations who believe their labor will yield more rewards in the United

---

[1]For the most part, Mexican immigrants have been characterized as "economic" immigrants because their primary motivation for leaving Mexico has been to improve their economic and social standard of living. The current drug wars in Mexico may be motivating some Mexicans to come to the United States for reasons of personal safety. However, there are no reliable statistics on this possible alteration in the Mexican immigrant stream. Nevertheless, the drug war situation in Mexico may increasingly come to resemble the plight of Latino immigrants from countries such as El Salvador and Guatemala who left their homelands in the recent past to escape the life-threatening risks of wars in their countries. Immigrants from these Central American countries, and their U.S.-born children, have contributed positively to the immigrant paradox.

States. Because the most destitute seldom have the financial resources to arrange passage to the United States, the border crossing is undertaken mostly by a "middling" stratum (Portes & Bach, 1985) caught up in an upwardly mobile current of opportunity seekers headed to *El Norte*.

Educational Background

Historically, Mexican immigrants have completed more years of schooling prior to immigrating than the prevailing national average for the entire Mexican population. An early study (Portes, 1979) of 806 undocumented male Mexican immigrants, ages 18 to 60, found that 65% had completed elementary school and 32% had completed some secondary schooling. By contrast, the Mexican national average at the time was 31% completing elementary school and 15% some secondary school. An interesting aside was that the fathers of these immigrants, who went to school decades earlier, also had 3.5 more years of schooling than the Mexican population of their same age (Portes & Bach, 1985). This indicates that immigrant families have traditionally placed a high value on education. It is not surprising, therefore, that most adult immigrants report better education for their children as one of their primary motives for coming to the United States (Cornelius, Chavez, & Castro, 1982; Gamio, 1931). A recent report (Suro, 2005) indicated that self-selection in terms of education continues today. A one-of-a-kind survey of Mexican immigrants applying for identity cards (*matrícula consular*) at Mexican consulates in the United States collected extensive demographic information about the participants, including level of education. The education level of the immigrants was then compared with the current national data for Mexico. Three times as many immigrants had completed high school compared with the Mexican population (22% and 7%, respectively; Suro, 2005). Although the high school completion rate of these immigrants is not high by U.S. standards, it nevertheless reflects the value they placed on education considering the limited schooling resources in their homeland and competing pressures to leave school early in order to work.

The self-selected nature of immigrant parents' education in Mexico benefits their own children's education in the United States through the assistance they can give them with schoolwork and the educational expectations they hold for them. In an earlier work (Buriel, 1987), I noted that parents with 6 or more years of schooling in Mexico have well-developed cognitive skills they can transmit to their children. I found that fathers' schooling in Mexico was positively related to the math achievement of their 1.5-generation junior high school children in the United States. In addition, mothers' education in Mexico was positively related to the reading achievement of their second-generation junior high school children. (It should be noted that a sixth-grade education in Mexico is more academically advanced than in the United States owing to necessity of providing children with as many basic skills as possible before they exit school early to join the labor market.) I also found that Mexican immigrant parents expected more schooling for their children than their native-born counterparts. When asked about the highest level of schooling they expected for their children, immigrant parents typically responded "graduate from a 4-year college," whereas native-born parents responded "attend a 2-year community college," a value that might contribute to the immigrant paradox.

Gonzales, in Chapter 11 of this volume, notes that as a result of the Immigration Reform and Control Act of 1986, the nature of immigration from Mexico changed to include more women and children. The available evidence indicates that despite this shift, the educational selectivity of Mexican immigrants persists. Salgado de Snyder (1994) found that since the mid-1970s and throughout the 1980s, the migration of Mexican women increased considerably. Most of these women came from large Mexican cities, and their educational level was higher than the Mexican national average. Feliciano (2005) examined the educational selectivity of Mexican immigrants from 1960 to 2000, using databases of the United Nations Educational, Scientific, and Cultural Organization and census data from the United States and Mexico. She found that across this 40-year span was a pattern of strong positive selection: "Migrants consistently averaged over one more year of schooling than Mexican nonmigrants" (p. 55).[2]

Because most Mexican immigrant parents have not attended schools in the United States, they may not be as aware as their native-born counterparts of the negative schooling conditions their children face. Using their own experience in Mexico as a frame of reference, they exhort their children to take advantage of the educational opportunities they did not have, in spite of the often-troubling realities at their children's schools. These children are poised to succeed when caring teachers take note of their schooling engagement and give them special attention to surmount the difficulties they encounter. Native-born parents' firsthand experience with the U.S. educational system, on the other hand, may have tempered their expectations about their own educations and in turn may diminish the expectations they hold for their children's educations.

---

[2]Another way in which immigration has changed since the 1980s is that there are now more indigenous Mexicans who represent a larger percentage of immigration to the United States. Despite their Mexican origins, these "new" immigrants are different from their nonindigenous "mestizo" counterparts. Many speak indigenous languages and do not know Spanish, and they are often poorer than their mestizo counterparts. As yet, there is no research examining the immigrant paradox with this growing indigenous population in the United States.

Psychological Factors

Anecdotal evidence suggests Mexican immigrants bring with them psychological characteristics conducive to success in the United States. The first is deferred gratification, which is expressed in the potential immigrants' ability to carefully regulate their spending as they save enough money to transact their passage to the United States, which currently ranges from $3,000 to $5,000. Even more deferred gratification is evident in the ability of cash-strapped immigrants to send remittances home on a regular basis. A second characteristic is risk taking, which arises from the fact that there are no guarantees that their $3,000 to $5,000 hard-earned investment to cross the border will be successful. If they are successful, as most are, risk taking may continue to operate in their adaptation to U.S. society as they venture into becoming small business owners, self-employed entrepreneurs, and home buyers. Immigrants' financial investment and commitment to their adopted homeland is reflected in their relatively high rates of homeownership. Nationally, slightly more than half (55%) of the children of immigrants live in homes owned by their parents compared with 70% of children of native-born parents, a difference of only 15% (Hernandez, Denton, & Macartney, 2008). These differences are reversed in some parts of the country. In California, more Latino immigrants own their own homes than third-generation members of their group, another fact supporting the immigrant paradox.

Empirical evidence documenting self-selected psychological factors associated with Mexican immigrants comes from an early study by Fromm and Maccoby (1970). Their study is unique because it assessed personality factors of individuals prior to immigration and compared them with characteristics of others from the same setting who did not immigrate. Fromm and Maccoby conducted an intensive community study of a population ($N = 406$) living in the central region of Mexico in order to test hypotheses regarding the universality of Fromm's theory of "social character." According to Fromm, there are a limited number of social characters or personality types, which through careful examination can be identified throughout the world. Mexico was selected as one of the geographic research sites to test Fromm's theory. Factor analysis of an assortment of measures yielded three dominant social characters in the community being investigated. These social characters and their associated personality traits are as follows:

1. *Receptive-Passive:* Individuals in this group are fatalistic, submissive, and idealize authority. *e*
2. *Productive-Hoarding:* This group is characterized by independence, formality, responsibility, and democratic decision making.

The hoarding of ideas. Hoarding ideas and deciding what is best.

3. *Productive-Exploitive:* The members in this group believe in progress, change, making new opportunities, mobility, and individualism.

Because of funding discontinuities, 10 years elapsed between the time the data were collected and the time they were analyzed, during which some individuals from the community immigrated to the United States. This made it possible to examine a possible relationship between social character and immigration. Fromm and Maccoby (1970) reported a significant correlation ($r = .35$) between having a Productive social character (Nos. 2 and 3 in their list) and immigrating to the United States. Migrating from the community to other parts of Mexico was unrelated to social character, indicating that movement to the United States was uniquely related to social character rather than a more general tendency to seek change. Fromm and Maccoby therefore concluded that coming to the United States, compared with moving within Mexico to seek change, "is, in psychological terms the much bolder and more ambitious of the two decisions" (p.136). Therefore, from the perspective of Fromm and Maccoby's theoretical model, it can be said that Mexican immigrants come from the ranks of the most productive sectors of the Mexican population. Gamio's (1931) ethnographic study 30 years earlier and Suro's (2005) survey 35 years later strongly suggest a similar conclusion. Fromm and Maccoby found that adults with productive social characters also had children with the same personality traits. This suggests that immigrant parents are likely to instill through socialization their same productive social charters in their U.S.-born children.

THE CULTURAL INTEGRATION HYPOTHESIS AND BEYOND: BICULTURALISM

The cultural integration hypothesis holds that Mexican immigrant culture is highly selective in nature and conducive to upwardly mobile change. This imparts to immigrants a sense of optimism and resilience. In addition, prior to immigration, potential immigrants grow up in Mexico surrounded by a familiar culture and supportive social environment. They therefore are likely to arrive in the United States with favorable self-concepts that act as buffers against the deleterious effects of prejudice and discrimination they face in this country. In an early study, Dworkin (1965) found that foreign-born Mexican American adults held more favorable views of themselves than their native-born counterparts. A later study with first-, second-, and third-generation Mexican American adolescents (Buriel & Vasquez, 1982) examined their agreement to positive and negative stereotypes of their ethnic group and compared their responses with those of Euro Americans of the same age. All three generations were higher in their rejection of negative stereotypes of their group than Euro Americans. However, third-generation and Euro American youths rejected positive stereotypes of Mexican Americans (e.g., hardworking, scientific, education minded) at a significantly higher rate than first- and second-generation adolescents. That is, adolescents from immigrant homes were more likely to believe positive characteristics about their ethnic group, which is due perhaps to the more positive self-concepts held by their parents, suggesting another mechanism behind the immigrant paradox. On the basis of a frame of reference developed in Mexico, immigrant parents can offer positive perspectives that debunk the negative stereotypes that their children hear about members of their group. However, because third and later generation children have parents with frames of reference developed in the United States, they may be at greater risk for internalizing self-defeating images of Mexican Americans that have the potential to become self-fulfilling prophecies. Unidirectional acculturation, whereby individuals acculturate toward American culture and away from Mexican immigrant culture, may strip them of the values conducive to success and expose them to less positive images of themselves and their ethnic group. Biculturalism instead might provide buffers against these negative influences.

In addition to values conducive to success and favorable self-concepts, immigrant Mexican culture is also associated with several family-life characteristics that can contribute to children's well-being. Beginning at birth, Mexican and other Latina immigrant mothers have healthier babies than the general U.S. population, a phenomenon known as the *Latina immigrant paradox* (Hayes-Bautista, 2004). Immigrant children are more likely to grow up in two-parent families (see Chapter 1, this volume). Although more children in immigrant families live below a "basic budget poverty baseline" than those in native-born families, more children with parents from Mexico (92%) have working fathers (Hernandez et al., 2008). These fathers represent the working poor who model productive behaviors for their children, and who often send remittances to Mexico in spite of their financial situation. These fathers also emphasize the need for a better education so their children can be economically mobile. Early research has also shown that Mexican immigrant couples experience greater marital satisfaction (Casas & Ortiz, 1985), are more socially supportive of each other (de Anda, 1984), and are in greater agreement about child rearing than their native-born peers (Buriel, 1993b). Relative to native-born parents, Mexican immigrant parents stress greater self-reliance, productive use of time, and early assumption of responsibility in their child-rearing orientations (Buriel, 1993b). This helps prepare children for the adultlike roles often assigned to them in order to help the family in its adjustment to U.S. society. For example, many children of immigrants serve as interpreters and translators between their parents and English-speaking professionals in many institutional settings, including schools, medical offices, banks, and businesses.

Children in this role are referred to as *language brokers*. Although language brokering can be stressful, it is also positively associated with greater social self-efficacy, higher academic performance, and more biculturalism among Latino adolescents (Buriel, Perez, DeMent, Chavez, & Moran, 1998; Dorner, Orellana, & Li-Grining, 2007).

Integration with immigrant Mexican culture is most often associated with children growing up in homes where parents are immigrants to the United States (Buriel, 1993a). It is more difficult to sustain this integration in homes where parents are native born because of their life-long exposure to American acculturating influences. Unidirectional acculturation simultaneously weakens children's integration with immigrant Mexican culture and their close ties with their families and exposes them to both the positive and negative aspects of American culture. Among the positive aspects are the English language and the social competencies necessary for successful adaptation to U.S. society. Among the negative aspects are (a) the internalization of self-defeating stereotypes regarding Mexican Americans that abound in many sectors of U.S. society, such as the media, schools, and national politics, and (b) during adolescence, the adoption of a myriad of high-risk behaviors that get in the way of academic success (unprotected sex, early pregnancy, juvenile delinquency, substance abuse, etc.).

The immigrant student paradox is significant not only because of the extraordinary achievements of children from immigrant homes but also because their achievements are contrasted against the declining achievements of third- and later generation children of Mexican descent. As the chapters in book indicate, such declines are usually associated with greater unidirectional Americanization. Tellez and Ortiz (2008) argued that prevalent negative stereotypes regarding the academic abilities of Mexican Americans results in children being *racialized* or "sorted into the social hierarchy based on the meanings that members of society give to presumed physical and cultural characteristics" (Tellez & Ortiz, 2008, p. 131). This results in lower teacher expectations and tracking of Mexican-descent students into less challenging curriculums on the basis of their perceived race, most likely accounting for decreasing educational achievement from the third generation onward. Racialization also negatively impacts the identity formation of third- and later generation Mexican Americans. According to Macias (2006), the identities of some Mexican-descent children from nonimmigrant homes are strongly constrained and determined more by perceptions and expectations of the majority than their subjective sense of group membership. For some third-generation Mexican Americans, the combination of their Chicano or Mexican American identity and low Spanish ability places them on the margins, "not Mexican enough to be accepted as a fellow ethnic among immigrants, yet not Anglo enough to be accepted as a casually engaged non-ethnic" (Macias,

2006, pp. 112–113). As a result, many third-generation Mexican Americans must deal with the reality that people perceive them as "Mexican" even when they do not exhibit the traits typically associated with this group, such as being foreign born and speaking Spanish. In contrast to the "assignment errors" (Macias, 2006) experienced by the third generation, Tellez and Ortiz (2008) contended that

> the second generation's schooling advantage derives from their resistance to assimilation and their ability to mobilize ethnicity as a positive resource to escape the disadvantages wrought on them by public schools. . . . By contrast, the third generation no longer benefits from immigrant optimism and the cultural protections against discrimination offered by the second generation's immigrant family. (pp. 104–105)

There are indications, however, that through bidirectional acculturation, integration with immigrant Mexican culture can extend beyond the second generation, with predictable positive results, because of the development of biculturalism. Bidirectional acculturation involves retention and reinforcement of immigrant Mexican culture while simultaneously acculturating to the positive aspects of American culture. The result is a bicultural adaptation strategy that enables individuals to meet the positive expectations of American culture without sacrificing the empowering aspects of immigrant Mexican culture.

An early study (Landsman et al., 1992) involving 510 Mexican American high school students from the first, second, and third generation provides support for the academic advantages of biculturalism. Students of each generation were divided into high and low bicultural groups on the basis of responses to a biculturalism scale and were compared on their academic grades and hours spent on homework. Results showed that within each generation group, high biculturals had higher grades and spent more time on homework. As noted earlier, Spanish language proficiency can serve as a marker for the retention of immigrant Mexican culture because it permits access to immigrant populations and a sharing of their values and aspirations. Portes and Rumbaut (2001) found that fluent bilingualism improved self-esteem over time and resulted in higher academic ambitions. A recent study by Kim and Chao (2009) found that higher reading and writing skills in Spanish were significant positive predictors of school effort for Mexican American students from the first to the third generation. *School effort* was defined as hours spent studying per week, completing assignments, and attentiveness in class.

In addition to being bilingual, bicultural individuals have been shown to express more cognitive flexibility (Hong, Morris, Chiu, & Benet-Martinez, 2000), lower levels of depression, and greater feelings of self-worth than their more monocultural peers (Birman, 1998; Miranda & Umhoefer, 1998). A positive association between biculturalism and academic performance has also been consistently reported in the literature (Buriel et al., 1998; LaFromboise, Coleman, & Gerton, 1993).

CONCLUSION

Many Mexican Americans live in environments that place dual cultural demands on them—Mexican and American. On the one hand, they are faced with elders who remain monolingual Spanish and steady streams of Mexican immigrants who expect them to speak Spanish and be familiar with Mexican culture. Failure to do so can bring ridicule and shame (Ochoa, 2004). On the other hand, they must acculturate to American culture in order to competently interact with Euro Americans in many settings having implications for their success in this country, such as schools and places of employment. Success in these important settings can be motivated by integration with immigrant Mexican culture and facilitated through selective acculturation to American culture. Therefore, the most advantageous formula for success for Mexican Americans of all generations may be through the development of biculturalism.

REFERENCES

Birman, D. (1998). Biculturalism and perceived competence in Latino immigrant adolescents. *American Journal of Community Psychology, 26*, 335–354. doi:10.1023/A:1022101219563

Buchanan, P. J. (2002). *The death of the West: How dying populations and immigrant invasions imperil our country and civilization*. New York, NY: St. Martin's Press.

Buriel, R. (1984). Integration with traditional Mexican-American culture and sociocultural adjustment. In J. L. Martinez & R. H. Mendoza (Eds.), *Chicano psychology* (2nd ed., pp. 95–130). New York, NY: Academic Press.

Buriel, R. (1987). *Academic performance of foreign- and native-born Mexican Americans: A comparison of first-, second-, and third-generation students and parents* (Report: Inter-University Program for Latino Research). Austin: University of Texas.

Buriel, R. (1993a). Acculturation, respect for cultural differences, and biculturalism among three generations of Mexican American and Euro American school children. *The Journal of Genetic Psychology, 154*, 531–543. doi:10.1080/00221325.1993.9914751

Buriel, R. (1993b). Childrearing orientations in Mexican American families: The influence of generation and sociocultural factors. *Journal of Marriage and the Family, 55*, 987–1000. doi:10.2307/352778

Buriel, R., Calzada, S., & Vasquez, R. (1982). The relationship of traditional Mexican American culture to adjustment and delinquency among three generations of

Mexican American male adolescents. *Hispanic Journal of Behavioral Sciences, 4,* 41–55. doi:10.1177/07399863820041003

Buriel, R., & Vasquez, R. (1982). Stereotypes of Mexican descent persons: Attitudes of three generations of Mexican Americans and Anglo-American adolescents. *Journal of Cross-Cultural Psychology, 13,* 59–70. doi:10.1177/0022022182131006

Buriel, R., Perez, W., DeMent, T., Chavez, D. V., & Moran, V. R. (1998). The relationship of language brokering to academic performance, biculturalism and self-efficacy among Latino adolescents. *Hispanic Journal of Behavioral Sciences, 20,* 283–297. doi:10.1177/07399863980203001

Butcher, K. F., & Piehl, A. M. (1998). Cross-city evidence on the relationship between immigration and crime. *Journal of Policy Analysis and Management, 17,* 457–493. doi:10.1002/(SICI)1520-6688(199822)17:3<457::AID-PAM4>3.0.CO;2-F

Casas, J. M., & Ortiz, S. (1985). Exploring the applicability of the dyadic adjustment scale for assessing level of marital adjustment with Mexican Americans. *Journal of Marriage and the Family, 47,* 1023–1027. doi:10.2307/352346

Chiswick, B. R. (1979). The economic progress of immigrants: Some apparently universal patterns. In W. Fellner (Ed.), *Contemporary economic problems* (pp. 357–399). Washington, DC: American Enterprise Institute.

Cornelius, W. A., Chavez, L. R., & Castro, J. G. (1982). *Mexican immigrants in southern California: A summary of current knowledge* (Working Papers in U.S.–Mexican Studies, No. 36). La Jolla, CA: Center for U.S.–Mexican Studies, University of California, San Diego.

Cubberley, E. P. (1909). *Changing conceptions of education.* Boston, MA: Houghton.

Culture and crime play role in gangs. (1979). *Los Angeles Times,* p. 1.

de Anda, D. (1984). Informal support networks of Hispanic mothers: A comparison across age groups. *Journal of Social Service Research, 7,* 89–105. doi:10.1300/J079v07n03_07

Demos, G. D. (1962). Attitudes of Mexican-American and Anglo-American groups toward education. *The Journal of Social Psychology, 57,* 249–256. doi:10.1080/00224545.1962.9710923

Dorner, L. M., Orellana, M. F., & Li-Grining, C. P. (2007). "I helped my mom," and it helped me: Translating the skills of language brokers into improved standardized test scores. *American Journal of Education, 113,* 451–478. doi:10.1086/512740

Dworkin, A. G. (1965). Stereotypes and self-images held by native-born and foreign-born Mexican Americans. *Sociology and Social Research, 49,* 214–224.

Feliciano, C. (2008). *Unequal origins: Immigrant selection and the education of the second generation.* El Paso, TX: LFB Scholarly Publishing.

Fromm, E., & Maccoby, M. (1970). *Social character in a Mexican village.* Englewood Cliffs, NJ: Prentice-Hall.

Fry, R., & Passel, J. S. (2009). *Latino children: A majority are U.S.-born offspring of immigrants* (Report: Pew Hispanic Center). Washington, DC: Pew Research Center.

Gamio, M. (1931). *The Mexican immigrant: His life-story*. Chicago, IL: University of Chicago Press.

Gandara, P. (1982). Passing through the eye of the needle: High-achieving Chicanas. *Hispanic Journal of Behavioral Sciences, 4*, 167–179. doi:10.1177/07399863820 042003

García, H. D. C. (1981). *Bilingualism, confidence, and college achievement* (Rep. No. 381). Baltimore, MD: Center for Social Organization of Schools, Johns Hopkins University.

Gordon, M. M. (1964). *Assimilation in American life: The role of race, religion and national origins*. London, England, and New York, NY: Oxford University Press.

Grebler, L., Moore, J. W., & Guzman, R. C. (1970). *The Mexican American people*. New York, NY: The Free Press.

Hayes-Bautista, D. (2004). *La nueva California*. Berkeley: University of California Press.

Heller, C. (1966). *Mexican-American youth: Forgotten youth at the crossroads*. New York, NY: Random House.

Henderson, R. W. (1972). Environmental predictors of academic performance of disadvantaged Mexican-American children. *Journal of Consulting and Clinical Psychology, 38*, 297. doi:10.1037/h0032642

Henderson, R. W., & Merrit, C. G. (1968). Environmental backgrounds of Mexican American children with different potentials for school success. *The Journal of Social Psychology, 75*, 101–106. doi:10.1080/00224545.1968.9712478

Hernandez, D. J., Denton, N. A., & Macartney, S. E. (2008). *Children in immigrant families: Looking to America's future* (Social Policy Report). Ann Arbor, MI: Society for Research in Child Development.

Hong, Y.-Y., Morris, M. W., Chiu, C.-Y., & Benet-Martinez, V. (2000). Multicultural minds: A dynamic constructivist approach to culture and cognition. *American Psychologist, 55*, 709–720. doi:10.1037/0003-066X.55.7.709

Kim, S. Y., & Chao, R. K. (2009). Heritage language fluency, ethnic identity, and school effort of immigrant Chinese and Mexican adolescents. *Cultural Diversity and Ethnic Minority Psychology, 15*, 27–37. doi:10.1037/a0013052

Kuvlesky, W. P., & Patella, V. M. (1971). Degree of ethnicity and aspirations for upward mobility among Mexican American youth. *Journal of Vocational Behavior, 1*, 231–244. doi:10.1016/0001-8791(71)90024-8

LaFromboise, T., Coleman, H. L. K., & Gerton, J. (1993). Psychological impact of biculturalism: Evidence and theory. *Psychological Bulletin, 114*, 395–412. doi:10.1037/0033-2909.114.3.395

Landsman, M. A., Padilla, A. M., Leiderman, P. H., Clark, C., Ritter, P., & Dornbusch, S. (1992). *Biculturalism and academic achievement among Asian and Hispanic adolescents*. Unpublished manuscript, School of Education, Stanford University, Stanford, CA.

Macias, T. (2006). *Mestizo in America: Generations of Mexican ethnicity in the suburban southwest*. Tucson: The University of Arizona Press.

Martinez, J. L., & Mendoza, R. H. (Eds.). (1984). *Chicano psychology* (2nd ed.). New York, NY: Academic Press.

McWilliams, C. (1968). *North from Mexico*. New York, NY: Greenwood Press.

Melville, M. B. (1980). Selective acculturation of female Mexican migrants. In M. B. Melville (Ed.), *Twice a minority: Mexican American women* (pp. 155–163). St. Louis, MO: Mosby.

Miranda, A. O., & Umhoefer, D. L. (1998). Depression and social interest differences between Latinos in dissimilar acculturation stages. *Journal of Mental Health Counseling, 20*, 159–171.

Moore, J. W. (1978). *Homeboys*. Philadelphia, PA: Temple University Press.

Moore, J. W. (1991). *Going down to the barrio: Homeboys and homegirls in change*. Philadelphia, PA: Temple University Press.

Nielsen, F., & Fernandez, R. M. (1981). *Hispanic students in American high schools: Background characteristics and achievement*. Washington, DC: National Center for Education Statistics.

Ochoa, G. A. (2004). *Becoming neighbors in a Mexican American community: Power, conflict, and solidarity*. Austin: University of Texas Press.

Padilla, A. M., & Ruiz, R. E. (1973). *Latino mental health: A review of the literature*. Rockville, MD: National Institute of Mental Health.

Perez, W. (2009). *We ARE Americans : Undocumented students pursuing the American dream*. Sterling, VA: Stylus.

Portes, A. (1979). Illegal immigration and the international system: Lessons from recent legal Mexican immigration to the United States. *Social Problems, 26*, 425–438. doi:10.1525/sp.1979.26.4.03a00070

Portes, A., & Bach, R. L. (1985). *Latin journey: Cuban and Mexican immigration in the United States*. Berkeley: University of California Press.

Portes, A., & Rumbaut, R. (2001). *Legacies: The story of the immigrant second generation*. Berkeley: University of California Press.

Ramirez, M. (1971). The relationship of acculturation to educational achievement and psychological adjustment in Chicano children and adolescents: A review of the literature. *El Grito: A Journal of Contemporary Mexican-American Thought, 4*, 21–28.

Ramirez, M. (1983). *Psychology of the Americas: Mestizo perspectives on personality and mental health*. New York, NY: Pergamon Press.

Ramirez, M., & Castañeda, A. (1974). *Cultural democracy, bicognitive development, and education*. New York, NY: Academic Press.

Salgado de Snyder, V. N. (1994). Mexican women, mental health, and migration: Those who go and those who stay behind. In R. G. Malgady & O. Rodriguez (Eds.), *Theoretical and conceptual issues in Hispanic mental health* (pp. 114–139). Malabar, FL: Krieger.

Sánchez, G. I. (1932). Group differences and Spanish-speaking children—A critical review. *Journal of Applied Psychology, 16*, 549–558. doi:10.1037/h0072844

Sánchez, G. I. (1934). Bilingualism and mental measures: A word of caution. *Journal of Applied Psychology, 18,* 765–772.

Samaniego, R. Y., & Gonzalez, N. A. (1999). Multiple mediators of the effects of acculturation status on delinquency for Mexican American adolescents. *American Journal of Community Psychology, 27,* 189–210. doi:10.1023/A:1022883601126

Suro, R. (2005). *Survey of Mexican migrants: Part one. Attitudes about immigration and major demographic characteristics.* Washington, DC: Pew Research Center.

Tellez, E. E., & Ortiz, V. (2008). *Generations of exclusion: Mexican Americans, assimilation, and race.* New York, NY: Russell Sage Foundation.

Text of proposition. (1994). Retrieved from http://www.apsu.edu/files/read/calprop text187.pdf

Vigil, J. D. (1988). *Barrio gangs.* Austin: University of Texas Press.

Vigil, J. D. (2007). *The projects: Gang and non-gang families in East Los Angeles.* Austin: University of Texas Press.

Woll, A. L. (1977). *The Latin image in American film.* Los Angeles, CA: UCLA Latin American Publications.

3

STUDYING THE IMMIGRANT PARADOX IN THE MEXICAN-ORIGIN POPULATION

ROBERT CROSNOE

[handwritten: Can use in literature review!] ✓

Mexico-origin families make up the biggest segment of the immigrant population of the United States, and as a group, they have high rates of socioeconomic disadvantage that block social mobility across generations. For these reasons, the children of Mexican immigrants provide a valuable lens through which to examine the *immigrant paradox*—the phenomenon in which more assimilated immigrants are less successful at navigating life in the United States than newly arrived immigrants. The most consistent aspect of the paradox in this group is its inconsistency. Indeed, its presence and magnitude varies considerably depending on the point of comparison, the stage of development considered, the domain of interest, and the degree of attention to socioeconomic circumstances. Drawing on nationally representative data on American youth and evidence from ethnographic work, this chapter documents how the Mexican-born and U.S.-born children of Mexican immigrants fare, relative to their native White, African American, and Latino/a peers, on aspects of

[handwritten margin note: comparison between Mexican born + US Born]

Support for the research discussed in this chapter came from young scholar fellowships from the Foundation for Child Development and the William T. Grant Foundation and from National Institute of Child Health and Human Development Grants R01 HD055359 (PI: Robert Crosnoe) and R24 HD042849 (PI: Mark Hayward).

adjustment and functioning. In general, the immigrant paradox is most likely to be found in high school (vs. earlier stages), when looking at social behavior (vs. test performance), and when family socioeconomic status (SES) is held constant. Such patterns are relevant to major policy aims, including public assistance programs and early educational intervention.

Reflecting my interdisciplinary background in sociology of education, social demography, and developmental psychology, I have spent the past several years conducting research on the Mexican immigrant population in the United States that views the developmental trajectories of the children of Mexican immigrants against the backdrop of the socioeconomic and racial–ethnic stratification systems that structure their parents' lives in this country (Crosnoe, 2006b). Not surprisingly, then, my take on the immigrant paradox is that we can learn just as much from identifying where it does not apply as from identifying where it does apply. In the spirit of studying a general rule through its exceptions, therefore, this chapter covers issues of diversity, heterogeneity, and inconsistency in the immigrant paradox in the largest and most visible immigrant population in the United States: Mexican-origin families. It draws on quantitative and qualitative analyses to sketch out how evidence for and conclusions about the immigrant paradox can fluctuate according to the comparison group used, the life stage being studied, the developmental domain of interest, and the degree to which family SES is taken into account. These fluctuations are crucial to theoretical understanding of the immigrant paradox as well as to policy interventions targeting immigrant youth.

THE IMMIGRANT PARADOX

The evidence that has been reported of the immigrant paradox in health, education, behavior, and general well-being has had a substantial influence on the ways in which social and behavioral scientists conceptualize and study immigration, assimilation, and acculturation and, perhaps, has led to a prevailing view that the immigrant paradox is the norm (Cavanagh, 2007; Driscoll, 1999; Frisbie, Forbes, & Hummer, 1998; Glick & White, 2003; Gordon-Larsen, Harris, Ward, & Popkin, 2003; Hirschman, 2001; Kao, 1999). Yet closer inspection of this evidence reveals that researchers often mean different things when they use the immigrant paradox vocabulary and that, indeed, the immigrant paradox is far from a generalized phenomenon. Instead, it holds for some groups and not for others, a pattern that has led to the emergence of new theoretical perspectives on immigrant youth. Segmented assimilation is one example. This perspective contends that the interplay of sending (i.e., home country) and receiving (i.e., United States) contexts of immigration can lead to highly variable outcomes of assimilation across generations, positive for some groups and negative for others. Thus, both immigrant paradox and *immigrant risk*—instances in which newly arrived immigrants are less successful at navigating life in the United States than more assimilated immigrants—can occur depending on the segment of the population considered (Portes & Zhou, 2008).

When looking at Mexican immigrant families, the majority of immigrants in the United States (Hernandez, Denton, & Macartney, 2008), the best answer to the question "Is there an immigrant paradox?" is, "It depends." To be more specific, it depends on what the point of comparison is. The immigrant paradox is more likely to be observed when the focus is on generational differences within the population (i.e., the children of Mexican immigrants compared with the children of native-born Mexican Americans) or on "downward" comparisons with highly disadvantaged nonimmigrant groups (i.e., the children of Mexican immigrants compared with the children of native-born African Americans) than when the focus is on "upward" comparisons with highly advantaged nonimmigrant groups (i.e., the children of Mexican immigrants compared with the children of native-born Whites). Thus, looking across all three types of comparisons and then integrating the results of these comparisons is probably the best way to determine the degree to which the immigrant paradox is truly characteristic of the Mexican immigrant population or if is instead more localized.

- Most studies take on a "downward" comparison (immigrant MA vs. AM) or "upward" comparison (MA vs. White) with lack of research looking within the group (M vs MA)

A QUESTION OF STAGE

Most of the scientific research on immigrant youth in the United States has focused on adolescents rather than children. Yet, different developmental stages provide different lenses through which to view some phenomena. Thus, our understanding of the immigrant paradox is still incomplete. Fortunately, the adolescent-specific nature of research on immigrant youth is changing because of several factors, including increasing evidence that early childhood interventions provide a great deal of leverage in efforts to reduce population-level disparities in adolescent and adult outcomes (Heckman, 2006), external supports for research specifically on young immigrant children (e.g., the Foundation for Child Development Changing Faces of America's Children program; see http://www.fcd-us.org), and the availability of new public use data with ample representation of immigrant families (e.g., the Birth and Kindergarten cohorts of the Early Childhood Longitudinal Study; see http://nces.ed.gov/ECLS/ as well as Chapters 4 and 7 in this volume). Consequently, tracking the immigrant paradox across stages of development and/or stages of schooling is now possible, and the results of such comparisons are telling.

National Patterns of Academic Achievement

Looking at academic patterns across stages is a good starting point because of the long span of formal schooling in the United States as well as the importance of schooling outcomes for long-term trajectories in the global economy (Goldin & Katz, 2009). Within the broad domain of achievement, math achievement is particularly useful for cross-stage comparisons involving immigrants because math is a consistently important, stratified, and hierarchically organized subject in American schools, one with powerful effects on eventual educational attainment. It also may be less dependent on language skills (Adelman, 2006; Goldenberg, 2008).

Figure 3.1 presents information about how young people who participated in the National Educational Longitudinal Study (NELS), a nationally representative study of a cohort of American eighth-graders, scored on standardized math tests from 1988 (when they were in eighth grade) through 1992 (when the majority were in 12th grade). The growth curve analyses that produced these results did not take into account any other factors besides race–ethnicity, immigration status, and school location. In other words, they did not control for SES.

The 10,908 NELS youth who were the native-born children of native-born White parents (hereafter, *third-plus generation*) clearly scored higher on math tests than others and then increased their advantage over time, whereas the 1,511 third-plus-generation African Americans clearly scored lower and

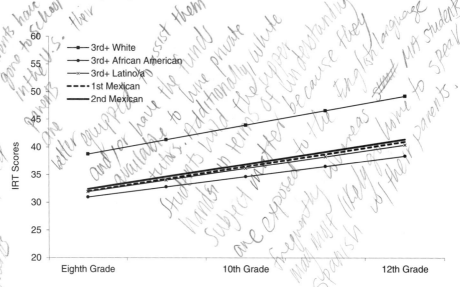

Figure 3.1. Trajectories of math achievement in secondary school. Data from the National Education Longitudinal Study. IRT = Item Response Theory; 3rd+ = third generation and later; 1st = first generation; 2nd = second generation.

lost ground over time. The three Latino/a subgroups clustered in between these two ends. By the end of the time frame, the 427 NELS youth who were the American-born children of Mexican-born parents (hereafter, *second generation*) had significantly higher math test scores, on average, than their third-plus-generation Latino/a peers (*n* = 1,173, of whom a substantial number were likely of Mexican origins). The 163 Mexican-born children of Mexican-born parents (hereafter, *first generation*) were not significantly different in their math test score performance than the second-generation Mexican immigrants or the third-plus-generation Latinos/as.

Figure 3.2 presents the elementary school comparison for these math achievement trajectories. These results came from analyses of young people who participated in the Early Childhood Longitudinal Study—Kindergarten Cohort (ECLS-K; see http://nces.ed.gov/ecls/), a nationally representative study of a cohort of American kindergartners. They took standardized math tests from 1999 (when they were in the spring semester of kindergarten) through 2004 (when the majority were in fifth grade). Again, these patterns controlled for school location but not SES.

Similar to NELS, the 6,188 third-plus-generation Whites scored higher on math tests, increasingly so, than other children. The remaining results, however, differed from NELS. The next highest scoring group was the 979 third-plus-generation Latinos/as, who also increased their advantage over the non-White groups over time. The Mexican-origin children and third-plus-generation African Americans (*n* = 1,223) started off in a similar low position,

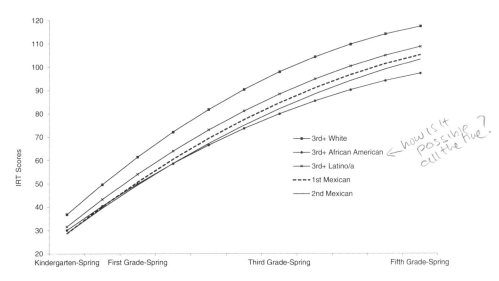

Figure 3.2. Trajectories of math achievement in elementary school. Data from Early Childhood Longitudinal Study—Kindergarten Cohort. IRT = Item Response Theory; 3rd+ = third generation and later; 1st = first generation; 2nd = second generation.

but the first-generation ($n = 81$) and second-generation ($n = 626$) Mexican children eventually pulled ahead.

Looking across stages of schooling, therefore, revealed evidence of the immigrant paradox when comparing children from Mexican immigrant families with third-plus-generation African Americans in both elementary and secondary school and when comparing second-generation Mexican Americans with third-plus-generation Latinos/as in secondary school only. Yet, we saw no evidence of the immigrant paradox when comparing first- and second-generation Mexican children with each other in either stage of schooling or when comparing first-generation Mexican Americans with third-plus-generation Latinos/as in elementary school. Finally, we saw evidence of something entirely different—what we can refer to as the *immigrant risk* —when comparing children from Mexican immigrant families with third-plus-generation Whites in either stage of schooling and with third-plus-generation Latinos/as in elementary school only.

Points of Discussion About Stage

Although neither stage of schooling examined presented a clear picture of the immigrant paradox in achievement, the evidence was much more consistent for secondary school. Indeed, the immigrant risk model held more strongly for the elementary school students. In addition to the potential problems with focusing exclusively on math test scores as a marker of achievement, these cross-stage differences could reflect several things.

First, specific sampling issues could be at work. For example, NELS excluded English language learners, but ECLS-K did not (it did allow them to take Spanish versions of the math tests if necessary). Considering that English language learners tend to come from more disadvantaged backgrounds and have more trouble in school (Callahan, 2005), these sampling issues likely made the immigrant subsamples of NELS more selective than those in ECLS-K, thereby contributing to the appearance of an immigrant paradox.

Second, sampling issues could be more general (i.e., issues extending beyond these two data sets). For example, the nature of compulsory schooling laws in the United States means that secondary school data sets will be more subject to attrition and dropout biases than data sets on earlier stages of schooling. Given that Mexican immigrant youth have higher dropout rates than other adolescents, secondary school samples likely have more selective subsamples of these youth that would bias comparisons. Moreover, Mexican immigrants who arrive in the United States as teenagers might not even enroll in school at all, further exacerbating those biases (Fry, 2003; Oropesa & Landale, 2009).

Third, differences in achievement disparities across stages of schooling might reflect a real developmental or educational trend, not just specific or general sampling issues. If the patterns from Figures 3.1 and 3.2 were to persist even after these sampling issues were addressed, that would be evidence that Mexican immigrant youth adapt to the educational system as they move through it, even if the schools they attend are often of lower quality (Crosnoe, 2006b).

All three scenarios are plausible explanations for why the immigrant paradox appears more likely to occur in secondary school than in elementary school—at least in the specific case of math achievement tests. The challenge is to determine which one matters the most and, therefore, the degree to which the immigrant paradox is a real phenomenon that is stage specific.

A QUESTION OF DOMAIN

Although the importance of educational attainment to socioeconomic attainment is at a historic high (Goldin & Katz, 2009), academic factors are not the sole criteria for assessing the current and future prospects of immigrant youth in the U.S. Indeed, the immigrant paradox can play out in many domains of socioemotional functioning that correlate with positive developmental outcomes. Disparities related to immigration in these domains are important in their own right but also help to shed light on disparities in educational and socioeconomic attainment (Crosnoe, 2006a). Thus, adjudicating between the immigrant paradox and immigrant risk models in health, social competence, and general behavior and comparing the results to the educational domain is necessary. In doing so in the remainder of this chapter, I focus on elementary school, given evidence that nonacademic factors play a bigger role in group disparities in academic outcomes in the early stages of schooling than in later stages (Entwisle & Alexander, 2002).

National Patterns of General Adjustment and Functioning

In ECLS-K, teachers rated children on several domains of behavior in every year of data collection. Figure 3.3 presents trends in teachers' ratings of children on a 4-point scale gauging their observations of fighting, aggression, and other dimensions of acting out in class. In line with past research (e.g., Downey & Pribesh, 2004), teachers consistently rated third-plus-generation African Americans as exhibiting these externalizing behaviors over time, followed by third-plus-generation Latinos/as, and then third-plus-generation Whites. The children from Mexican immigrant families demonstrated different longitudinal patterns. First-generation children started school with teacher ratings similar to third-plus-generation Latinos/as, but their ratings declined over time so that by fifth grade, they were rated by teachers as exhibiting the lowest level of externalizing behaviors of all groups. Second-generation

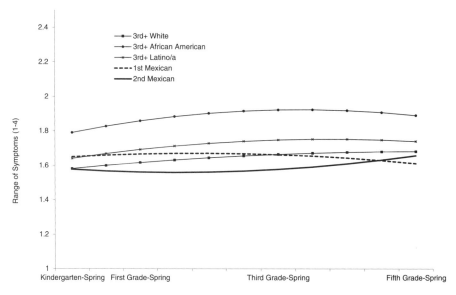

Figure 3.3. Trajectories of teacher-reported externalizing behaviors in elementary school. Data from Early Childhood Longitudinal Study—Kindergarten Cohort; 3rd+ = third generation and later; 1st = first generation; 2nd = second generation.

children followed the opposite trajectory. Worth noting, however, is that children from Mexican immigrant families had generally low levels of externalizing behaviors and more closely resembled third-plus-generation White children than children from other minority groups, a pattern echoed in Chapter 4 of this volume in analyses focusing on all Latino/a immigrants in ECLS-K.

Although not presented in a figure, the longitudinal patterns for teacher ratings of social competence (e.g., observations of friendliness, cooperation) and work habits (e.g., being on task) in school were similar to those for externalizing behaviors. Mexican-origin children started school with ratings in between groups on the more favorable (third-plus-generation Whites) and less favorable (third-plus-generation African Americans) ends, but over time they were rated in increasingly favorable ways by teachers relative to other groups. By the end of elementary school, therefore, they tended to most resemble the third-plus-generation Whites. This pattern was especially true of first-generation Mexican immigrant children, who were eventually rated by teachers as having the most social competence and best work habits of all groups.

Figure 3.4 presents over-time trends in parents' ratings (on a 5-point scale) of the general health of their children. The observed patterns of global health ratings differed sharply from the trends in teacher ratings of general adjustment and functioning in school. At the start of elementary school, Mex-

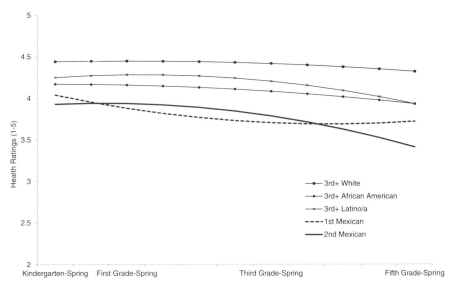

Figure 3.4. Trajectories of parent-rated health in elementary school. Data from Early Childhood Longitudinal Study—Kindergarten Cohort; 3rd+ = third generation and later; 1st = first generation; 2nd = second generation.

ican immigrant parents rated their children (whether U.S.-born or not) lower on global health than third-plus-generation White, Latino/a, and African American parents. Because the ratings of Mexican immigrant parents of U.S.-born children decreased more sharply than those of other parents over time, the differences observed at the beginning of elementary school were more pronounced by the end. Because the ratings of Mexican-born children of Mexican immigrant parents eventually plateaued, their relative position among the five focal groups did not suffer as badly as that of the U.S.-born children of Mexican immigrant parents, although they still ranked near the bottom. One caveat to these findings is that past evidence suggests that Mexican American parents are more likely to rate their children lower on scales of global health than on scales of actual health problems (Mendoza & Dixon, 1999), so the possibility of reporter bias exists.

The longer that children from Mexican immigrant families stayed in school, the better their general behavior at school looked, in relative terms, to their teachers, but the worse their health looked, again relatively speaking, to their parents. Furthermore, both orthogonal patterns appeared to be more pronounced for Mexican-born children than U.S.-born children of Mexican origins. The domain of school-based socioemotional behavior, therefore, presents fairly consistent evidence of the immigrant paradox, but the immigrant risk model holds when the focus shifts to health.

Points of Discussion About Domain

On the basis of the ECLS-K patterns just described, similar patterns reported in Chapter 4 in this volume for the Latino/a population more generally, and other examinations of disparities related to immigration in socioemotional adjustment and health (Crosnoe, 2006a; Harker, 2001), I will make a speculative conclusion as a suggestion for future research. Perhaps immigrant risk is more likely than the immigrant paradox in domains of child development that are a direct function of institutional systems in the United States (e.g., health care, public education) and, as such, are more subject to stratification in these systems. Children's connections to formal organizations and institutions, therefore, may be a venue in which the protective cultural forces that create the immigrant paradox in other domains are counteracted by differential treatment, discrimination, and other forces that contribute to immigrant risk.

This conclusion relates to the ample discussion among scholars about the cultural traditions in the Mexican immigrant population that could conceivably factor into processes of risk or protection. For example, the well-documented values of familism and *educación* in Mexican culture, both of which emphasize decorum and interpersonal respect for elders, may lead children from Mexican immigrant families to be better behaved in school and to be viewed as socially adjusted by adults, including their teachers (Arcia, Reyes-Blanes, & Vazquez-Montilla, 2000; Reese, Balzano, Gallimore, & Goldberg, 1995; Valenzuela, 1999). On the one hand, this is clearly an advantage they have over other children. Yet, the provocative work of Lareau (2004) has documented how socioeconomically advantaged parents give their children a competitive edge in school by teaching them how to demand attention and work the system. Thus, what seems like a clear developmental positive in general could be less positive for them in specific institutional settings, especially as they grow older and leave elementary school.

Indeed, I witnessed this dualism of positive socioemotional behavior in an ethnographic study I did in a school in Texas that had a sizeable representation of Mexican-origin students. The teachers in the school found Mexican-origin youth to be easy students and generally considered them a pleasure to have in the classroom, but they also often interpreted their docility as evidence that they were unmotivated (Crosnoe, 2011).

A QUESTION OF INTERSECTION

A key tenet of the segmented assimilation perspective is that immigrant outcomes are, in part, dependent on the sectors of American society that immigrants enter (Portes & Zhou, 2008). In line with this perspective, Mexican migration cannot be adequately understood without attention to the ways that it intersects with the socioeconomic stratification system of the United States.

National Patterns Adjusted by Family Socioeconomic Status

The starkness of the intersection between migration and socioeconomic stratification is apparent in ECLS-K. Of the children with Mexican immigrant parents, more than 80% came from families in which the annual income was less than 185% of the federal poverty threshold. Moreover, the modal level of parent education in this group was less than a high school degree. Both of the statistics were significantly below what was seen in all other groups in the sample.

As when looking at other migration streams, the socioeconomic circumstances of Mexican immigrants complicate analyses of the immigrant paradox. Controlling for parent income, education, and occupation has an enormous impact on all achievement, socioemotional, and health patterns discussed so far, even more so when language use is also taken into account (note that more than 85% of the children of Mexican immigrants in ECLS-K lived in households in which English was not the dominant language, similar to census patterns reported in Chapter 1 and echoing the distributions reported in Chapter 7 in this volume on monolingual and bilingual families by national origin and generation status). For achievement, controlling for SES revealed that children from Mexican immigrant families (both generations in secondary school, first generation in elementary school) were indistinguishable from third-plus-generation Whites and were higher achievers than all other groups. Thus, controlling for SES strengthened the immigrant paradox in secondary school and weakened immigrant risk in elementary school. Once family SES was taken into account, the immigrant paradox patterns in all teacher-rated socioemotional behaviors also grew more pronounced, with the children of Mexican immigrants rated much higher by teachers over time than their peers from other groups. The only domain in which family SES did not have a sizeable impact was health. Regardless of family SES, the children of Mexican immigrants (especially children born in the United States themselves) had lower levels of parent-reported health. ← scared to report! Think it will be louled down upon in their culture

Points of Discussion About Intersection

That taking into account the socioeconomic circumstances of Mexican immigrant families produces or strengthens the immigrant paradox and/or washes out or waters down immigrant risk is not new information. These patterns are evident in many published research reports, including several chapters in this volume (e.g., Chapters 4 and 7, this volume). Yet, critical discussion of the practical importance of these patterns is lacking.

To be more specific, we need to ask and answer the question, "What does it mean, in the 'real world,' to control for SES?" SES-controlled patterns indicate that within any given socioeconomic strata, children from Mexican immigrant families are doing better than or similar to third-plus-generation White children. This is statistical language that scholars speak and understand, and such procedures are standard practice. Yet, in the United States, the Mexican immigrant population is so disadvantaged in socioeconomic terms that matching Mexican immigrant children and their White peers across the socioeconomic distribution is difficult. Moving past the low end of the distribution, for example, cell sizes for Mexican immigrants become sparser and more selective. One could be concerned, therefore, that focusing on evidence of the immigrant paradox that only emerges from analyses that control for family SES may be somewhat misleading from a policy perspective, even if it is statistically feasible and useful for the sake of data analysis.

In other words, the message coming out of the scientific literature that immigrant children are doing well, even better than nonimmigrant youth, may suggest that immigrant children do not need policy attention and intervention—when in reality, many segments of the immigrant population (e.g., children from Mexican immigrant families) do. Their marginalization and disenfranchisement may be a function of SES, but they still need help and support. This possibility, of course, is countered by the value of SES-controlled comparisons. Results indicating that within groups defined by race–ethnicity and social class, immigrant youth tend to do better than others highlight the often unnoticed strengths and successes of immigrant populations in an era in which immigration (and immigration policy) is being hotly debated. Controlling for SES in statistical analyses, therefore, may be both productive and counterproductive, depending on the context of the discussion (e.g., theoretical, applied). As a result, social and behavioral scientists need to be more critical of the findings that they disseminate on immigrant paradox and risk.

CONCLUSION

As discussed in the opening of this chapter, thinking about the immigrant paradox as group, period, and context specific and dependent on the comparison group is a useful method for better understanding it. What is found when exploring diversity is that often, variability within and across pockets of society speaks to the problems of mistranslations or mismatches between the worlds that immigrants are trying to bridge. This variability, therefore, can lead to refinement of our understanding of assimilation, incorporation, and acculturation as well as the role of development in these processes. In the immigrant paradox, for example, immigrants are protected from some clear disadvantages posed by American society and culture that would be especially problematic for them given their tenuous socioeconomic positions that preceded or resulted from their migration. In immigrant risk, however, immigrant status itself becomes a disadvantaged social status, so that double stratification occurs.

On the applied level, this discussion of variability in the immigrant paradox in the Mexican immigrant population also speaks to major policy debates. First, the aspect of family SES that had the biggest impact on immigration-related patterns in NELS and ECLS-K was parent education. This finding echoes a substantial literature on the salutary impact on socioeconomically disadvantaged children of investing in their parents', especially their mothers', education as well as recent policy goals of the Obama administration to support the continuing education of low-income women (Crosnoe & Kalil, 2010; Kalil & Crosnoe, 2009). As already reported, the level of parent education in ECLS-K was quite low among Mexican immigrants, but a fifth of Mexican immigrant women returned to school when their children entered school themselves. Second, one of the major child-focused policy initiatives in recent years has been the push for early educational investments in socioeconomically disadvantaged children, especially those from racial–ethnic minority groups, so that their levels of school readiness will be improved (Heckman, 2006). In ECLS-K, however, only 11% of first-generation Mexican children and 17% of second-generation Mexican children attended preschool before entering the formal educational system. Improving access to and uptake in preschool enrollment in this population, therefore, would seem to be a necessity. Yet in doing so, we need to be concerned not just with numbers but also with quality. Getting more children from Mexican immigrant families into preschool will not do any good if the preschools that they are attending or the elementary schools into which they transition from preschool are of low quality (Fuller, 2007).

In this chapter, I have done more to raise questions about the immigrant paradox than I have to provide answers about it. I think that this reflects the current state of our understanding of the immigrant paradox. It is an important concept with real policy implications, and so discussion and debate about it is healthy. We just need to recognize that what we do not know or understand about the immigrant paradox still outweighs what we do know, a recognition that lays out a research agenda for the future. Being able to make multiple comparisons—by generation, national origin, age, and stage of schooling—for multiple outcomes within the same source of data is crucial. Using the Children of Immigrants Longitudinal Study (Portes & Rumbaut, 2001) and the Longitudinal Immigration Student Adaptation Study (Suárez-Orozco, Rhodes, & Milburn, 2009) as models, we need a large, representative, and longitudinal study of immigrant youth that can be broken down by national or regional origin with sufficient cell size coverage; that follows children from the prekindergarten years through secondary school, collects data on achievement, health, and general development; and carefully tracks attrition out of the sample over time while allowing for statistical adjustments for attrition bias and follows any students who leave the educational system. Although the expense of such an enterprise will be great, the timing could not be better: Immigration is set to dominate the public and political discourse in the United States in the years to come.

REFERENCES

Adelman, C. (2006). *The toolbox revisited: Paths to degree completion from high school through college.* Washington, DC: U.S. Department of Education.

Arcia, E., Reyes-Blanes, M., & Vazquez-Montilla, E. (2000). Constructions and reconstructions: Latino parents' values for children. *Journal of Child and Family Studies, 9,* 333–350. doi:10.1023/A:1026444507343

Callahan, R. M. (2005). Tracking and high school English learners: Limiting opportunity to learn. *American Educational Research Journal, 42*(2), 305–328. doi:10.3102/00028312042002305

Cavanagh, S. (2007). Drinking as a product of assimilation: Immigration from Mexico, peer networks, and adolescent alcohol use. *Sociological Perspectives, 50,* 393–416. doi:10.1525/sop.2007.50.3.393

Crosnoe, R. (2006a). Health and the education of children from race/ethnic minority and immigrant Families. *Journal of Health and Social Behavior, 47,* 77–93. doi:10.1177/002214650604700106

Crosnoe, R. (2006b). *Mexican roots, American schools: Helping Mexican immigrant children succeed.* Palo Alto, CA: Stanford University Press.

Crosnoe, R. (2011). *Fitting in, standing out: Navigating the social challenges of high school to get an education.* New York, NY: Cambridge University Press.

Crosnoe, R., & Kalil, A. (2010). Educational progress and parenting among Mexican immigrant mothers of young children. *Journal of Marriage and Family, 72,* 976–990. doi:10.1111/j.1741-3737.2010.00743.x

Driscoll, A. K. (1999). Risk of high school dropout among immigrant and native Hispanic youth. *The International Migration Review, 33,* 857–876. doi:10.2307/2547355

Downey, D. B., & Pribesh, S. (2004). When race matters: Teachers' evaluations of students' classroom behavior. *Sociology of Education, 77,* 267–282. doi:10.1177/003804070407700401

Entwisle, D. R., & Alexander, K. L. (2002). The first grade transition in life course perspective. In J. Mortimer & M. Shanahan (Eds.), *Handbook of the life course* (pp. 229–250). New York, NY: Kluwer Academic/Plenum.

Frisbie, W. P., Forbes, D., & Hummer, R. A. (1998). Hispanic pregnancy outcomes: Additional evidence. *Social Science Quarterly, 79,* 149–169.

Fry, R. (2003). *Hispanic youth dropping out of U.S. high schools: Measuring the challenge.* Washington, DC: Pew Hispanic Center.

Fuller, B. (2007). *Standardized childhood: The political and cultural struggle over early education.* Palo Alto, CA: Stanford University Press.

Glick, J. E., & White, M. J. (2003). The academic trajectories of immigrant youths: Analysis within and across cohorts. *Demography, 40,* 759–783. doi:10.1353/dem.2003.0034

Goldenberg, C. (2008). Teaching English language learners: What the research does—and does not—say. *American Educator.* Retrieved from http://www.aft.org/pubs-reports/american_educator/issues/ summer08/goldenberg.pdf

Goldin, C., & Katz, L. (2009). *The race between technology and education.* Cambridge, MA: Harvard University Press.

Gordon-Larsen, P., Harris, K., Ward, D., & Popkin, B. (2003). Acculturation and overweight-related behaviors among Hispanic immigrants to the US: The National Longitudinal Study of Adolescent Health. *Social Science & Medicine, 57,* 2023–2034. doi:10.1016/S0277-9536(03)00072-8

Harker, K. (2001). Immigrant generation, assimilation, and adolescent psychological well-being. *Social Forces, 79,* 969–1004. doi:10.1353/sof.2001.0010

Heckman, J. J. (2006, June 30). Skill formation and the economics of investing in disadvantaged children. *Science, 312,*1900–1902. doi:10.1126/science.1128898

Hernandez, D. J., Denton, N. A., & Macartney, S. E. (2008). *Children in immigrant families: Looking to America's future* (Social Policy Report). Ann Arbor, MI: Society for Research in Child Development.

Hirschman, C. (2001). The educational enrollment of immigrant youth: A test of the segmented-assimilation hypothesis. *Demography, 38,* 317–336. doi:10.1353/dem.2001.0028

Kalil, A., & Crosnoe, R. (2009). Two generations of educational progress in Latin American immigrant families in the U.S. In E. L. Grigorenko & R. Takanishi (Eds.), *Immigration, diversity, and education* (pp. 188–204). New York, NY: Routledge/Taylor & Francis.

Kao, G. (1999). Psychological well-being and educational achievement among immigrant youth. In D. J. Hernandez (Ed.), *Children of immigrants: Health, adjustment, and public assistance* (pp. 410–477). Washington, DC: National Academy Press.

Lareau, A. (2004). *Unequal childhoods: Class, race, and family life.* Berkeley: University of California Press.

Mendoza, F. S., & Dixon, L. B. (1999). The health and nutritional status of immigrant Hispanic children. In D. J. Hernandez (Ed.), *Children of immigrants: Health, adjustment, and public assistance* (pp. 187–243). Washington, DC: National Academy Press.

Oropesa, R. S., & Landale, N. (2009). Why do immigrant youths who never enroll in U.S. schools matter? School enrollment among Mexicans and non-Hispanic Whites. *Sociology of Education, 82,* 240–266. doi:10.1177/003804070908200303

Portes, A., & Rumbaut, R. G. (2001). *Legacies: The story of the immigrant second generation*. Berkeley: University of California Press.

Portes, A., & Zhou, M. (2008). The new second generation: Segmented assimilation and its variants. In D. Grusky (Ed.), *Social stratification: Class, race, and gender in sociological perspective* (pp. 658–669). Boulder, CO: Westview.

Reese, L., Balzano, S., Gallimore, R., & Goldberg, C. (1995). The concept of *educación:* Latino family values and American schooling. *International Journal of Educational Research, 23,* 57–81. doi:10.1016/0883-0355(95)93535-4

Suárez-Orozco, C., Rhodes, J., & Milburn, M. (2009). Unraveling the immigrant paradox: Academic engagement and disengagement among recently arrived immigrant youth. *Youth & Society, 41,* 151–185. doi:10.1177/0044118X09333647

Valenzuela, A. (1999). *Subtractive schooling: U.S. Mexican youth and the politics of caring.* Albany: State University of New York Press.

II

BEHAVIOR AND HEALTH OUTCOMES ACROSS GENERATIONS

4

BEHAVIORAL OUTCOMES IN EARLY CHILDHOOD: IMMIGRANT PARADOX OR DISADVANTAGE?

KRISTIN TURNEY AND GRACE KAO

Immigrant children and children of immigrants—those born in the United States with at least one parent born abroad—are an important and growing demographic group in the United States. Indeed, immigrants or children of immigrants make up almost one quarter of the school-aged population (O'Hare, 2004). The majority of these children are racial minorities; more than three quarters of all foreign-born individuals in the United States are from Latin America or Asia. Similarly, immigrant status is an important feature of some racial and ethnic minority groups; approximately 60% of Hispanic children and 90% of Asian children were born outside of the United States or have at least one parent born outside of the United States (Zhou, 1997). This group of children has captured the attention of scholars across a wide range of disciplines, most of whom find that these children have increasingly diverse developmental outcomes (Rumbaut & Portes, 2001).

As documented elsewhere in this volume, a growing body of literature provides support for an *immigrant paradox* in a wide range of outcomes throughout

Kristin Turney's work on this project was supported by the Robert Wood Johnson Foundation Health & Society Scholars Program.

the life course. The immigrant paradox posits that despite having fewer socioeconomic resources, a lack of English proficiency, and the marginalization and isolation that accompanies being a new arrival to the United States, immigrants and their children exhibit resilience and sometimes outperform their native-born counterparts. Some researchers, for instance, have found that immigrant groups experience favorable health outcomes despite socioeconomic disadvantages (Markides & Coreil, 1986; Palloni & Morenoff, 2001). Others have found that children of immigrants have better academic achievement and attainment than children of native-born parents (see, e.g., Chapter 2, this volume).

Despite this growing body of literature that lends credence to the immigrant paradox, the time in the life course at which the paradox emerges is unclear. [Additionally, although much interest in studying the paradox has focused on academic outcomes among children, adolescents, and young adults, we know very little about whether the immigrant paradox applies to behavioral outcomes among children, particularly young children.] To fill this stark gap in the literature, this chapter explores the extent of the immigrant paradox in the life course by focusing on one set of outcomes in early childhood: children's behavioral outcomes, reported by their parents and teachers during first grade. ← Why are they only looking at 1st grade. Can be biased or non-relevant because young children are still under the control of their parents it is not until middle school-like that students make their own choices based off education.

Understanding disparities in young children's behavior is crucial because both theoretical perspectives and empirical research suggest that behavior in early childhood is linked to divergent trajectories throughout the life course (Caspi, Bem, & Elder, 1989; Entwisle & Alexander, 1989; Hofstra, Van der Ende, & Verhulst, 2000; McLeod & Kaiser, 2004). Advantages and disadvantages accumulate over time; children who fall behind their counterparts in early childhood are at risk for disadvantaged outcomes in later childhood, adolescence, and adulthood. Greater behavior problems in childhood, for example, are associated with a lower likelihood of graduating from high school (McLeod & Kaiser, 2004). Externalizing behavior problems in childhood can have long-term consequences, with individuals who exhibit problem behaviors in childhood reporting lower psychological well-being, less kin support, and lower quality intimate relationships in adulthood (Knoester, 2003; Moffitt, Caspi, Harrington, & Milne, 2002).

As described in this chapter, we used data from the Early Childhood Longitudinal Study—Kindergarten Cohort (ECLS-K) to examine variation in both parent- and teacher-reported behavioral outcomes by race and immigrant status. We explored the immigrant paradox in two ways. First, we compared outcomes of minority immigrant children with those of their native-born White counterparts. Second, we compared outcomes of minority immigrant

The reason this is true is because when people label or perceive you in one way you start believing it is true and continue it, but if you tell the same student you see potential in him/her they tend to aspire to big goals for their future.

Teachers need to be trained in what to say and not say in front of students.

We consider both race and ethnicity. We use the term *race* for ease of discussion, but it is important to note, in particular, that Hispanics do not comprise a separate race group.

children with those of native-born children of the same race. Additionally, when multivariate analyses provided evidence of an immigrant paradox, we examined the extent to which characteristics of the family environment—including family structure, cultural interactions between parents and children, and speaking a non-English language at home—may explain the advantages experienced by immigrant children. Our focus on behavioral outcomes allowed us to bypass one limitation of examining academic achievement among immigrant children with the ECLS-K. In these data, some language-minority children were excluded from the academic readiness assessments. In kindergarten, about 15% of the sample took the Oral Language Development Scale test, and about half of those tested (41% of the children who spoke Spanish and 62% of the children who spoke another language) had inadequate English skills to take the assessments in English (Rock & Pollack, 2002). All parents and teachers, regardless of children's language minority status, were asked about children's behavior.

BACKGROUND

Variation in Behavioral Outcomes Among Minority Immigrant Children

Behavioral problems in early childhood are not evenly distributed across the population. A large body of research suggests that Black and Hispanic children, compared with their White counterparts, have more behavioral problems in childhood (Crosnoe, 2006; McLeod & Nonnemaker, 2000). Many, although not all, of these racial disparities can be explained by differences in socioeconomic status (SES) because Blacks and Hispanics, on average, have fewer socioeconomic resources than Whites (Achenbach, Howell, Quay, & Conners, 1991). Indeed, SES is one of the most stable, consistent predictors of children's behavior (Gerard & Buehler, 1999). Family income and parental educational attainment are inversely and independently associated with young children's behavior (Duncan, Brooks-Gunn, & Klebanov, 1994; Lee & Burkam, 2002; Strohschein, McDonough, Monette, & Shao 2005; Yeung, Linver, & Brooks-Gunn, 2002).

With regard to variation in behavior by immigrant status, the evidence is less straightforward. Some research on adolescents suggests that immigrant children and children of immigrants have more behavioral problems than their counterparts with native-born parents (Schwartz, Pantin, Prado, Sullivan, & Szapocznik, 2005). Problem behaviors may result from a lack of resources, cultural barriers, or linguistic obstacles. However, other research, consistent with the immigrant paradox, has found that some groups of immigrant children have favorable behavioral outcomes (Beiser, Hou, Hyman, & Tousignant,

2002; Crosnoe, 2006; Fuligni, 1998; Harker, 2001; Jutte, Burgos, Mendoza, Ford, & Huffman, 2003; Valenzuela, 1999). Using data from the ECLS-K, for example, Crosnoe (2006) found that Hispanic and Asian immigrant children and children of immigrants, according to their teachers, had better behavior at the beginning of kindergarten than their native-born White counterparts.

Explaining the Immigrant Paradox

The immigrant paradox may be explained by a host of contextual factors, including the neighborhoods in which immigrant children reside and the schools that they attend. In addition, characteristics of the family environment may be protective for children of immigrants. There is some evidence, for example, that the deinstitutionalization of marriage that has swept across the United States has affected immigrant children less than their native-born peers (Cherlin, 2004; Landale & Oropesa, 2007). Given the high marriage and low divorce rates among Asians, living with married parents is more common among Asian immigrant children than other minority immigrant groups (Walton & Takeuchi, 2010). By and large, children with married parents have favorable behavioral outcomes, compared with their counterparts in single-parent families (Carlson & Corcoran, 2001; Sigle-Rushton & McLanahan, 2004), and it may be that this advantage contributes to the immigrant paradox. In addition, cultural discussions between parents and children may be another aspect of the family environment that explains the immigrant paradox. Immigrant parents are more likely than native-born parents to discuss children's racial and ethnic heritage with them (Hughes et al., 2006). Given that parenting behaviors are strongly linked to children's outcomes (Amato & Fowler, 2002; Koblinsky, Kuvalanka, & Randolph, 2006; Simons, Whitbeck, Beaman, & Conger, 1994), it follows that these discussions about racial and ethnic heritage are also positively correlated with children's outcomes (Hughes et al., 2006). Finally, the fact that immigrant children are more likely than native-born children to speak multiple languages at home may be a protective factor because bilingualism is linked to favorable behavior (Han, 2010). Though these characteristics of the family environment—family structure, cultural discussions between parents and children, and speaking a non-English language at home—are not exhaustive of all familial factors that may be protective for immigrant children, they provide a useful starting point for understanding the mechanisms underlying the immigrant paradox.

Additional Correlates of Children's Behavior

Behavioral outcomes in early childhood are correlated with a host of additional characteristics that we accounted for in our multivariate analyses.

In addition to socioeconomic resources such as education or income, parental employment—particularly maternal employment—is protective for children's behavior (Bianchi, 2000). Children with older mothers have fewer behavioral problems than their counterparts with younger mothers (Furstenberg, 2003), and children with siblings may learn important social interaction skills from these siblings (Downey & Condron, 2004). Children's characteristics are also important. Male children generally have more behavior problems, particularly externalizing behaviors, than female children (Robinson et al., 2008), and children's age is also correlated with behavior (Alink et al., 2006).

Research Questions

On the basis of theoretical expectations and prior empirical research, we address three research questions in this chapter. First, to what extent do minority immigrant children, compared with their native-born White counterparts, exhibit evidence of an immigrant paradox in parent- and teacher-reported behavioral outcomes in first grade? Second, is there evidence of an immigrant paradox in terms of behavioral outcomes among minority immigrant children, compared with native-born children of their same race? Finally, when the immigrant paradox exists, to what extent do characteristics of the family environment explain this paradox?

DATA AND METHODS

Data Source

We used data from the ECLS-K, a study conducted by the National Center of Education Statistics (NCES) that comprises a nationally representative sample of children who began kindergarten during the 1998–1999 school year.[2] These data were collected in a multistage sampling frame in which students were nested within about 1,000 schools in 100 counties. These data were collected at multiple points in time: the beginning of kindergarten, the end of kindergarten, the beginning of first grade (though for only a subsample of children), the end of first grade, third grade, fifth grade, and eighth grade. Data were collected from children's parents and schools and, beginning when they were in third grade, the children themselves. The original sample included more than 22,000 students in approximately 3,500 classrooms in 1,280 schools, though children have been lost to nonresponse and attrition.

---

[2]Comprehensive documentation is available from the NCES website (http://nces.ed.gov/).

These data are particularly well suited to answer our research questions about the immigrant paradox in early childhood behaviors. To begin with, children's behaviors were documented by reports from both parents and teachers. Because parents and teachers observe children in two different settings, at home and in school, examining both sets of reports is advantageous for documenting a complete picture of behavior in early childhood. These data are also valuable because they contain an oversample of children of immigrant parents. To our knowledge, the ECLS-K provides data from the only nationally representative sample of young children that includes a large enough number of immigrant children to make meaningful comparisons between native- and foreign-born children by race.

Key Variables

Children's Behavior

Our outcomes of interest are the children's scores on the Social Rating Scale, a series of questions administered to both parents and teachers during the spring of the children's first grade. We focused on first grade because of both substantive and practical reasons. We were interested in behavior during early childhood because of its link to later well-being, and this is one of the few waves when both parents and teachers were asked about children's behaviors. Parents and teachers were asked how often children exhibited particular skills and behaviors using the following scale: never (1); occasionally or sometimes (2); regularly but not all of the time (3); and most of the time (4). Thus, values for each outcome variable range from 1 to 4. Respondents were also given the opportunity to report that they had no opportunity to observe a particular behavior, and these observations were coded as missing and thus excluded from our analyses. The scales administered to parents and teachers captured similar constructs, with parent reports measuring behavior observed at home and teacher reports measuring behavior observed at school (Rock & Pollack, 2002).

We examined three parent-reported outcomes: social interaction, sad/lonely behaviors, and impulsive/overactive behaviors. The Social Interaction scale includes three items that measure children's interactions with peers and adults ($\alpha = 0.70$). The Sad/Lonely Behaviors scale includes four items about children's acceptance by others, sadness, loneliness, and self-esteem ($\alpha = 0.60$), and the Impulsive/Overactive Behaviors scale taps children's impulsivity and activity level ($\alpha = 0.46$). For Social Interaction, higher values indicate more favorable behaviors. The opposite is true of Sad/Lonely Behaviors and Impulsive/Overactive Behaviors; higher values indicate more behavioral problems (Rock & Pollack, 2002).

In addition, we examined three outcomes reported by teachers: interpersonal skills, internalizing problem behaviors, and externalizing problem behaviors. The Interpersonal Skills scale includes five items that rate the children's skills in (a) forming and maintaining friendships; (b) getting along with people who are different; (c) comforting or helping others; (d) expressing feelings, ideas, and opinions in positive ways; and (e) showing sensitivity to others' feelings ($\alpha = 0.89$). Internalizing and externalizing problem behaviors reflect behaviors that might interfere with the learning process and with the children's abilities to interact positively in the classroom. The Internalizing Problem Behaviors scale includes four items that assess anxiety, sadness, loneliness, and self-esteem ($\alpha = 0.80$). The Externalizing Problem Behaviors scale includes five items that assess how often children argue, fight, get angry, act impulsively, and disturb ongoing activities ($\alpha = 0.90$; Rock & Pollack, 2002).[3] Higher values on the Interpersonal Skills Scale indicate more favorable behaviors, and higher internalizing and externalizing problem behaviors indicate worse behaviors.

Race and Immigrant Status

Children's race and immigrant status is represented by the following dummy variables: non-Hispanic White native-born (reference category), non-Hispanic White foreign-born, non-Hispanic Black native-born, non-Hispanic Black foreign-born, Hispanic native-born, Hispanic foreign-born, non-Hispanic Asian native-born, non-Hispanic Asian foreign-born, non-Hispanic other race native-born, and non-Hispanic other race foreign-born.[4] Because the children were still very young, we categorized them by the race of the mother. Because mothers usually serve as primary decision makers in early childhood, we believe that mothers' backgrounds are more influential in determining children's outcomes than children's race (see Turney & Kao, 2009b).[5]

We also categorized children on the basis of the immigrant status of their mother, which was first collected during the fourth wave of data collection, when children were at the end of first grade.[6] We did this for two reasons. First, because all children in the sample had to reside in the United States by kindergarten entry, there were few first-generation children in the sample (about 2%

---

[3]Unfortunately, we cannot examine the reliability of these measures by race. For proprietary reasons, NCES does not release the individual measures that comprise the composite measures of behavior.

[4]Because some race groups are too small to analyze separately, we combined the following children into an "other" race category: Hawaiian/Pacific Islander, American Indian/Alaska Native, and non-Hispanic multiracial.

[5]In supplemental analyses not presented, we substituted child's race for mother's race. The findings were substantively similar, though stronger, when child's race was used.

[6]Parent respondents were asked where the child's father was born, though this information was not collected until children were in third grade. Substantial attrition occurred between first grade, when information was available for mother's immigrant status, and third grade. In addition, there was substantial item-level missing data on paternal country of birth. Thus, we used mother's country of birth.

of children were born outside the United States). Additionally, there were few meaningful differences between first- and second-generation children. The first-generation experience among youth is one that is defined by the transition from one educational system to another. First-generation youth (as well as first-generation adults) are commonly described as living in two worlds, or not knowing whether they are ethnic or American. This modal description of first-generation youth does not apply to our sample because, by design, every foreign-born student had already arrived in the United States by the time they entered kindergarten. These children had not experienced schooling elsewhere, and their age may have precluded them from experiencing the stressful and disruptive transition associated with migration. Descriptive analyses also showed no substantive differences in parent- and teacher-reported behavioral outcomes of first- and second-generation children.[7] Thus, consistent with our previous work and the work of others (Crosnoe, 2006; Turney & Kao, 2009a; Turney & Kao, 2009b), we focused on differences between children born to immigrant mothers and children born to native-born mothers. Thus, throughout this chapter, the terms *foreign-born* or *immigrant* refer to mothers rather than the children themselves.

Characteristics of the Family Environment

Our multivariate analyses included characteristics of the family environment that may explain the immigrant paradox. To begin with, family structure is represented by the following dummy variables: married (reference category), separated, divorced, widowed, and never married. Additionally, we examined three indicators that capture cultural interactions between parents and children. Parents reported how often the following occurred (1 = *never*, 2 = *almost never*, 3 = *several times a year*, 4 = *several times a month*, 5 = *several times a week or more*): someone in family talks with child about his or her ethnic or racial heritage; someone in family talks with child about family's religious beliefs or traditions; and someone in family participates in special cultural events or traditions connected with racial or ethnic background.[8] Finally, we included a dummy variable indicating that a non-English language is spoken at home. All of these family characteristics were measured at the second wave of data collection, when children were completing kindergarten, so that they are exogenous from the dependent variables that were measured in first grade.

---

[7]White first- and second-generation children provided one exception to this, although the pattern was not consistent across outcomes. White first-generation children, compared with their second-generation counterparts, had more parent-reported sad/lonely behaviors and fewer teacher-reported internalizing behavior problems.

[8]These three variables were moderately correlated ($\alpha = 0.58$). Because they are conceptually distinct items, we did not create an index.

Covariates

The multivariate analyses included numerous covariates that prior research has found associated with children's behavioral outcomes. In most cases, the covariates were measured the year preceding the measurement of behaviors. To begin with, our multivariate analyses included several controls for family SES during the child's kindergarten year. The ECLS-K data includes a five-category composite SES measure that takes into account mother's education, father's education, mother's occupational prestige, father's occupational prestige, and household income. Each of these five categories was standardized to have a mean of 0 and a standard deviation of 1. The composite measure is an average of the available categories because some children had fewer than five available categories because of an absent parent (NCES, 2001).[9] Additionally, we included dummy variables for mother's and father's employment status: full-time (reference category), part-time (working fewer than 35 hours per week), and not employed.

The multivariate analyses controlled for additional demographic characteristics of parents and children. We included the age of the parent respondent, a continuous variable that ranges from 19 to 80 years, measured in kindergarten. Number of children in the household (including the focal child), also measured in kindergarten, is a continuous variable that ranges from 1 to 11. A dummy variable indicates child gender (1 = *male*, 0 = *female*). We controlled for child age at the time the behavioral outcomes were measured (end of first grade), which is a continuous variable that ranges from 72 to 96 months. Finally, a dummy variable indicates the parent respondent's relationship to the child (1 = *mother*, 0 = *not mother*). In about 95% of observations, the parent respondent at the end of first grade is the child's mother.

Analytic Sample

For analyses that examined parent-reported behavioral outcomes, the analytic sample included 12,974 children. We first deleted observations missing data on maternal race (n = 2,898), as well as additional observations missing data on maternal immigrant status (n = 1,675). We then deleted additional cases that were missing data on parent-reported behavioral outcomes in first grade (n = 101). Our strategy for constructing the analytic sample for analyses that examined teacher-reported behavioral outcomes was similar; instead of deleting observations missing parent-reported behaviors, we deleted observations missing teacher-reported behaviors (n = 1,833) for an analytic sample of

---

[9]We substituted the individual indicators of SES for composite SES in supplemental analyses not presented and found the results were substantively similar.

11,242 children. The two analytic samples did not differ significantly on children's behaviors or observable demographic characteristics.

However, children in both analytic samples were, on average, more advantaged than the full sample ($p < .05$). Those in the analytic samples had better interpersonal skills and fewer externalizing behaviors. Additionally, those in the analytic samples had higher composite SES than those in the full sample. Parent respondents were older, more likely to be married, and less likely to speak a non-English language at home. It is important to note that the race and immigrant composition of the analytic and full samples were not significantly different.

Analytic Plan

We used ordinary least squares (OLS) regression to estimate the association between race and immigrant status and children's behavioral outcomes in first grade. We examine descriptive statistics in Tables 4.1 and 4.2. Tables 4.3 and 4.4 display estimates for parent- and teacher-reported outcomes, respectively. We estimated three models for each parent- and teacher-reported outcome. In both Tables 4.3 and 4.4, our key independent variables, dummy variables indicating race and immigrant status, are included in each model. The first model, in addition to race and immigrant status, included the composite SES measure. In the second model, we also included the following variables: mother's employment status, father's employment status, respondent's age, number of children in household, child gender, child age, and respondent relationship to child. In the final model, we examined how characteristics of the family environment may mediate race and immigrant differences in children's outcomes. These characteristics included family structure, cultural interactions between parents and children, and speaking a language other than English at home.

As shown in Tables 4.3 and 4.4, the reference category was native-born White children, and thus, these analyses did not examine differences between native- and foreign-born children of the same race. Table 4.5 shows the results of our analyses by racial subgroups to estimate children's behavioral outcomes as a function of immigrant status. These analyses directly compared native-born children in each racial category with foreign-born children of the same racial category (i.e., native-born Hispanics with foreign-born Hispanics). The first set of models included a dummy variable for immigrant status and the composite indicator of SES, and the second set of models added the additional demographic characteristics included in the second set of models in Tables 4.3 and 4.4.

Few observations within the analytic sample were missing data on the covariates, and we used the *ice* (imputation by chained equations) command in Stata to impute missing data (Royston, 2004). We used 10 data sets and, in the imputation model, included variables related to the research questions or to the likelihood of being missing (Allison, 2002).[10] Because of nonrandom attrition over time and the complex stratified random sampling design, our multivariate analyses used weights constructed by NCES. All analyses also used the accompanying strata and primary sampling unit variables.

Description of Sample

We present descriptive statistics for the analytic sample in Table 4.1. Native-born White children were more than three fifths (62%) of the sample. Native-born Black children were the next largest group, about 12% of the sample. About 6% of children were native-born Hispanics, and 9% were foreign-born Hispanics. Asian native- and foreign-born children made up, respectively, 1% and 4% of the sample. About 12% of both children's mothers and fathers did not have a high school diploma or GED, and more than one fourth of mothers (26%) and one third of fathers (32%) were college graduates. Fewer than half of mothers (46%) and more than nine tenths of fathers (92%) were working full-time. Parent respondents were, on average, 34 years old, and the majority of them (75%) were married.

RESULTS

Bivariate Evidence of an Immigrant Paradox in Behavioral Outcomes

Table 4.2 presents the means of parent- and teacher-reported behavioral outcomes by race and immigrant status. We used analysis of variance with pairwise tests with Bonferroni corrections for multiple comparisons. By and large, these descriptive results demonstrate little evidence of an immigrant paradox with respect to parent-reported behavioral outcomes. One exception to this general pattern is for White foreign-born children, who had slightly more favorable impulsive/overactive behaviors than White native-born children (1.82, compared with 1.74, $p < .05$).

Instead of demonstrating evidence of an immigrant paradox, these bivariate findings provide support for an immigrant *disadvantage* in behavioral outcomes reported by parents. This is particularly true of social interaction, where all groups of immigrant children had less favorable scores than native-

---

[10]Analyses that used listwise deletion produced substantively similar estimates.

TABLE 4.1
Descriptive Statistics of Variables Used in Analyses

Variable	M	SD	Minimum	Maximum
Parent-reported behavior (4)				
Social interaction	3.40	0.54	1.00	4.00
Sad/lonely behaviors	1.54	0.39	1.00	4.00
Impulsive/overactive behaviors	1.85	0.66	1.00	4.00
Teacher-reported behavior (4)				
Interpersonal skills	3.12	0.64	1.00	4.00
Internalizing behaviors	1.58	0.51	1.00	4.00
Externalizing behaviors	1.64	0.63	1.00	4.00
Race and immigrant status (1)				
White native-born	0.62	—	0.00	1.00
White foreign-born	0.03	—	0.00	1.00
Black native-born	0.12	—	0.00	1.00
Black foreign-born	0.01	—	0.00	1.00
Hispanic native-born	0.06	—	0.00	1.00
Hispanic foreign-born	0.09	—	0.00	1.00
Asian native-born	0.01	—	0.00	1.00
Asian foreign-born	0.04	—	0.00	1.00
Other race native-born	0.03	—	0.00	1.00
Other race foreign-born	0.01	—	0.00	1.00
Family characteristics				
Family structure (2)				
Married	0.75	—	0.00	1.00
Separated	0.04	—	0.00	1.00
Divorced	0.08	—	0.00	1.00
Widowed	0.01	—	0.00	1.00
Never married	0.12	—	0.00	1.00
Family discusses ethnic or racial heritage (2)	2.71	1.24	1.00	5.00
Family discusses religious beliefs or traditions (2)	3.90	1.20	1.00	5.00
Family participates in cultural events or traditions (2)	2.24	1.10	1.00	5.00
Non-English language spoken at home (2)	0.12	—	0.00	1.00
Additional demographic characteristics				
Composite socioeconomic status (1)	0.08	0.80	−4.75	2.75
Log of household income (1)	10.58	0.97	0.00	13.82
Mother's occupational prestige (1)	30.07	22.53	0.00	77.50
Father's occupational prestige (1)	33.65	20.75	0.00	77.50
Mother's education (1)				
Less than high school	0.12	—	0.00	1.00
High school diploma or GED	0.29	—	0.00	1.00
Some college	0.33	—	0.00	1.00
College degree or higher	0.26	—	0.00	1.00

TABLE 4.1
Descriptive Statistics of Variables Used in Analyses   *(Continued)*

Variable	M	SD	Minimum	Maximum
Father's education (1)				
Less than high school	0.12	—	0.00	1.00
High school diploma or GED	0.30	—	0.00	1.00
Some college	0.26	—	0.00	1.00
College degree or higher	0.32	—	0.00	1.00
Mother's employment status (1)				
Full-time	0.46	—	0.00	1.00
Part-time	0.23	—	0.00	1.00
Not employed	0.32	—	0.00	1.00
Father's employment status (1)				
Full-time	0.92	—	0.00	1.00
Part-time	0.03	—	0.00	1.00
Not employed	0.05	—	0.00	1.00
Mother's age (1)	33.68	6.38	19.00	80.00
Number of children in household (1)	1.75	1.04	1.00	11.00
Respondent not mother (4)	0.05	—	0.00	1.00
Male (1)	0.51	—	0.00	1.00
Age (4)	86.86	4.22	72.00	96.00

Note. N = 12,974. Numbers in parentheses refer to waves of data collection: 1 = first wave of data collection (fall of kindergarten); 2 = second wave of data collection (spring of kindergarten); 4 = fourth wave of data collection (spring of first grade). Descriptive statistics presented were calculated with analytic sample predicting parent-reported outcomes.

born White children. For example, native-born White children had social interaction scores of 3.47 compared with 3.10 ($p < .001$) for their foreign-born Hispanic peers and 3.20 ($p < .001$) for their foreign-born Asian peers. Additionally, Asian foreign-born children had more sad/lonely behaviors than native-born White children (1.58 compared with 1.53, $p < .05$), and other race foreign-born children had more impulsive/overactive behaviors (2.10 compared with 1.74, $p < .001$). It is important to note, though, that Hispanic foreign-born and Asian foreign-born children had sad/lonely and impulsive/overactive behaviors similar to those of their native-born White counterparts.

The bivariate results of teacher-reported outcomes provide evidence for both an immigrant paradox and an immigrant disadvantage in early childhood behavior. To begin with, Asian foreign-born children displayed some evidence of an immigrant paradox. On average, their teachers reported they had more favorable internalizing (1.48 compared with 0.58, $p < .001$) and externalizing behaviors (1.47 compared with 1.61, $p < .001$) than native-born White children, and their interpersonal skills were comparable. On the other hand, foreign-born Hispanic children and foreign-born other race children had less favorable interpersonal skills than native-born Whites.

TABLE 4.2

Unweighted Descriptive Statistics of Key Variables, by Race and Immigrant Status

Variable	White		Black		Hispanic		Asian		Other race	
	NB	FB	NB	FB	NB	FB	NB	FB	NB	FB
Parent-reported behavior										
Social interaction	3.47	3.37***	3.40***	3.28***	3.38***	3.10***	3.32**	3.20***	3.40**	3.15***
Sad/lonely behaviors	1.53	1.56	1.55	1.59	1.52	1.52	1.53	1.58	1.55	1.65**
Impulsive/overactive behaviors	1.82	1.74*	2.05***	1.83	1.87*	1.85	1.82	1.79	1.95***	2.10***
Teacher-reported behavior										
Interpersonal skills	3.16	3.15	2.93***	3.19	3.11*	3.11*	3.22	3.19	2.97***	3.02*
Internalizing behaviors	1.58	1.58	1.64***	1.60	1.61	1.56	1.49	1.48***	1.67***	1.53
Externalizing behaviors	1.61	1.59	1.86***	1.66	1.66	1.58	1.49	1.47***	1.77***	1.60
Family characteristics										
Family structure										
Married	0.82	0.86	0.35***	0.65***	0.69***	0.75***	0.87	0.90***	0.55***	0.79
Separated	0.03	0.03	0.09***	0.07*	0.06***	0.05***	0.04	0.01***	0.08***	0.07
Divorced	0.08	0.07	0.09	0.07	0.09	0.05***	0.04	0.03***	0.10	0.10
Widowed	0.01	0.01	0.01	0.01	0.01	0.01	0.01	0.01	0.01	0.01
Never married	0.06	0.04	0.46***	0.21***	0.15***	0.14***	0.04	0.06	0.26***	0.03
Family discusses ethnic or racial heritage	2.37	3.21***	3.25***	3.17***	3.17***	3.29***	3.46***	3.49***	3.38***	3.47***
Family discusses religious beliefs or traditions	3.90	3.90	3.93	3.88	3.92	4.05***	3.55**	3.66***	3.80	3.74
Family participates in cultural events or traditions	2.04	2.67***	2.52***	2.75***	2.45***	2.40***	2.82***	2.93***	2.73***	2.78***
Non-English language spoken at home	0.01	0.24***	0.00	0.12***	0.22***	0.80***	1.32***	0.58***	0.01	0.29***
N	8,054	324	1,509	108	745	1,156	106	536	344	92

Note. Asterisks reflect analysis of variance with pairwise tests with Bonferroni corrections for multiple comparisons. Asterisks compare all race and immigrant groups to children of native-born White mothers. Sample sizes for each race and immigrant group reflect sample sizes for analytic sample predicting parent-reported outcomes. NB = native-born; FB = foreign-born.

*p < .05. **p < .01. ***p < .001.

Given that these descriptives suggest at least some evidence of an immigrant paradox in early childhood behavior, our multivariate analyses tested the idea that these advantages may be explained by characteristics of the family environment such as family structure, cultural interactions between parents and children, and speaking a language other than English at home. In Table 4.2, we present descriptive statistics of these family-level characteristics by race and immigrant status.

As expected, foreign-born Asian children were more likely than native-born Whites to live with married parents (90% compared with 82%, $p < .001$). Hispanic foreign-born children, on the other hand, were less likely to live with married parents (75% compared with 82%, $p < .001$) and more likely to live with never married parents (14% compared with 6%, $p < .001$). Additionally, there were stark group differences with respect to cultural interactions. Compared with native-born Whites, all groups were more likely to discuss ethnic or racial heritage with their children and to participate in cultural events or traditions. The pattern was less consistent for discussions of religious beliefs or traditions, with Hispanic foreign-born parents more likely and Asian foreign-born parents less likely to report this than White native-born parents. Finally, consistent with expectations, all minority immigrant groups were more likely than native-born White children to speak a language other than English at home. About 80% of Hispanic foreign-born children and 58% of Asian foreign-born children spoke a non-English language at home compared with only 1% of native-born White children. Taken together, these descriptives suggest strong differences in the family environment of native-born White children and minority immigrant children.

Estimating Parent-Reported Behavioral Outcomes

The bivariate results presented in Table 4.2 provide evidence for both an immigrant paradox and an immigrant disadvantage in behavioral outcomes. However, it is possible these bivariate associations are spurious and instead the result of other factors associated with minority immigrant status or children's behavior, such as SES or child gender. Thus, to better isolate the relationship between race and immigrant status and children's behavior, we estimated this association in Table 4.3, taking into account a host of demographic characteristics of the parent and child.

The first set of models in Table 4.3, which includes the composite indicator of SES, shows findings generally consistent with the bivariate results. Most groups of minority immigrant parents, compared with native-born White parents, reported less favorable behaviors in their children. However, there is some evidence of an immigrant paradox. Net of SES, Hispanic foreign-born children had fewer sad/lonely (-0.05, $p < .01$) and impulsive/

TABLE 4.3
Ordinary-Least-Squares Regression Models Predicting Parent-Reported Behavior

Variable	Social interaction			Sad/lonely behaviors			Impulsive/overactive behaviors		
	Model 1	Model 2	Model 3	Model 1	Model 2	Model 3	Model 1	Model 2	Model 3
Race and immigrant status									
White native-born (reference)	—	—	—	—	—	—	—	—	—
White foreign-born	-0.12**	-0.11**	-0.10**	0.03	0.02	0.01	-0.09*	-0.09*	-0.09*
	(0.04)	(0.04)	(0.04)	(0.03)	(0.03)	(0.03)	(0.04)	(0.04)	(0.04)
Black native-born	-0.04*	-0.05*	-0.06***	-0.01	-0.01	-0.03^	0.11***	0.10***	0.07*
	(0.02)	(0.02)	(0.02)	(0.02)	(0.02)	(0.03)	(0.03)	(0.03)	(0.03)
Black foreign-born	-0.20**	-0.19*	-0.20*	0.02	0.02	0.01	-0.01	-0.03	-0.03
	(0.08)	(0.08)	(0.08)	(0.05)	(0.05)	(0.17)	(0.09)	(0.09)	(0.09)
Hispanic native-born	0.01	0.01	0.01	-0.04^	-0.04^	-0.05*	-0.02	-0.03	-0.03
	(0.03)	(0.03)	(0.03)	(0.02)	(0.02)	(0.02)	(0.04)	(0.04)	(0.04)
Hispanic foreign-born	-0.33***	-0.32***	-0.24***	-0.05*	-0.05**	-0.07**	-0.10***	-0.10***	-0.09*
	(0.02)	(0.02)	(0.03)	(0.02)	(0.02)	(0.03)	(0.03)	(0.03)	(0.04)
Asian native-born	-0.21**	-0.19*	-0.18	0.02	0.02	0.01	-0.01	-0.03	-0.02
	(0.08)	(0.08)	(0.08)	(0.04)	(0.04)	(0.04)	(0.06)	(0.06)	(0.06)
Asian foreign-born	-0.27***	-0.25***	-0.19***	0.03	0.02	-0.01	-0.04	-0.04	-0.04
	(0.04)	(0.04)	(0.04)	(0.02)	(0.02)	(0.02)	(0.04)	(0.04)	(0.04)
Other race native-born	-0.01	0.01	-0.03	-0.01	-0.01	-0.02	0.04	0.02	0.01
	(0.04)	(0.04)	(0.04)	(0.03)	(0.03)	(0.03)	(0.05)	(0.05)	(0.05)
Other race foreign-born	-0.34**	-0.31**	-0.31**	0.09^	0.09^	0.07	0.23*	0.20*	0.21*
	(0.10)	(0.10)	(0.10)	(0.05)	(0.05)	(0.05)	(0.09)	(0.09)	(0.09)

Family structure

Married	—	—	—						
Separated			-0.01 (0.03)			0.08** (0.03)			0.10* (0.05)
Divorced			0.01 (0.02)			0.03^ (0.02)			0.10** (0.03)
Widowed			0.07 (0.08)			0.07^ (0.04)			0.18^ (0.10)
Never married			-0.06* (0.02)			0.06*** (0.02)			0.14*** (0.03)
Family discusses ethnic or racial heritage			0.02*** (0.01)			0.01 (0.01)			-0.01 (0.01)
Family discusses religious beliefs or traditions			0.03*** (0.01)			-0.01 (0.01)			-0.02* (0.01)
Family participates in cultural events or traditions			0.01 (0.01)			0.01 (0.01)			-0.01 (0.01)
Non-English language spoken at home			-0.15*** (0.03)			0.03 (0.02)			0.01 (0.04)
Constant	3.450	3.370	3.245	1.549	1.468	1.446	1.883	2.088	2.120
R^2	.055	.067	.081	.005	.006	.011	.034	.052	.060
N	12,974	12,974	12,974	12,974	12,974	12,974	12,974	12,974	12,974

Note. Analyses weighted to account for sampling design. Robust standard errors are in parentheses. Model 1 includes a composite indicator of socioeconomic status (SES) that comprises the following: household income (log), mother's occupational prestige, father's occupational prestige, mother's education, and father's education. Models 2 and 3 include composite SES, mother's employment status, father's employment status, mother's age, number of children in household, respondent not mother, child is male, and child age (in months).
^p < .10. *p < .05. **p < .01. ***p < 0.01.

overactive (-0.10, $p < .001$) behaviors than their native-born White counterparts. Evidence for the paradox among Hispanic foreign-born children persists in the second set of models because taking into account additional demographic characteristics does little to alter the behavioral advantages experienced by these children.

To explain the immigrant paradox among Hispanics, we included characteristics of the family environment in the final set of models. Taking into account family structure, cultural interactions, and speaking a non-English language at home does not explain the Hispanic paradox in sad/lonely behaviors. On the other hand, these characteristics substantially attenuate the Hispanic immigrant advantage in impulsive/overactive behaviors (-0.09, $p < .05$). In supplemental analyses, we find that cultural interactions between parents and children most substantially mediate this paradox.

Though the multivariate analyses provide some evidence of an immigrant paradox in parent-reported behavioral outcomes—especially among Hispanic foreign-born children—they provide much greater evidence for disparities in behavioral outcomes among both minority and immigrant children. For example, the final set of models indicates that nearly all groups of children—with the exception of Hispanic native-born children and other race native-born children—had worse social interaction than native-born White children. Black native-born children and other race foreign-born children, on average, had disadvantaged impulsive/overactive behaviors. White foreign-born children, compared with their White native-born counterparts, had fewer impulsive/overactive behaviors.

As expected, characteristics of the family environment were linked to children's behaviors. Children with separated or never married parents generally had worse behavior than their counterparts with married parents. More frequent discussions of religious beliefs or traditions was linked to better social interaction and fewer impulsive/overactive behaviors, and frequent discussions of ethnic or racial heritage was associated with better social interaction. Children did not experience behavioral benefits from speaking a non-English language at home. Instead, this was associated with worse social interaction. Though not included in the tables, the additional covariates worked as expected. Higher SES, for example, was associated with more favorable behaviors in children, and children with younger mothers had worse behaviors. Male children had less favorable social interaction and impulsive/overactive behaviors than their female counterparts.

Estimating Teacher-Reported Behavioral Outcomes

An examination of teacher-reported behavior provided more consistent evidence of an immigrant paradox in behavioral outcomes. Though the first set of models in Table 4.4 provided no evidence of an immigrant paradox in interpersonal skills, these models did provide strong evidence of an immigrant paradox in internalizing and externalizing behaviors. This immigrant paradox persisted in both the second and third set of models. In the final model, Hispanic foreign-born children had more favorable internalizing (-0.10, $p < .01$) and externalizing (-0.07, $p < .10$) behaviors than their White native-born counterparts. Asian foreign-born children also had more favorable internalizing (-0.13, $p < .01$) and externalizing (-0.13, $p < .01$) behaviors.

Teachers' reports of children's behaviors, compared with parents' reports, provided less evidence of an immigrant disadvantage in behavior. In fact, foreign-born children were not disadvantaged across any of the three teacher-reported outcomes; they had either similar or better interpersonal skills, internalizing behaviors, and externalizing behaviors. On the other hand, some groups of native-born minorities experienced systematic disparities compared with their native-born White counterparts. Both native-born Black and other race children had worse interpersonal skills and externalizing behaviors. Similar to the models predicting parent-reported behaviors, the additional covariates worked as expected.

Within-Race Comparisons of Parent- and Teacher-Reported Behavioral Outcomes

Comparing outcomes of immigrant children with those of native-born White children, as we did in the prior analyses, is a common method of examining inequalities between groups. This approach, however, may miss important within-race comparisons (i.e., we did not estimate differences between native- and foreign-born Hispanics). Within-race comparisons, as opposed to comparing all groups to native-born Whites, may better approximate acculturation and thus be a more effective way to document the immigrant paradox. Thus, as shown in Table 4.5, we estimated parent- and teacher-reported behavioral outcomes separately for each of the five race groups in our data: White, Black, Hispanic, Asian, and other race. Turning first to parent-reported outcomes, there was no evidence of an immigrant paradox when foreign-born children were compared with native-born children of the same race. In fact, with the exception of Asian children, there was instead evidence of an immigrant disadvantage in social interaction. For example, in the final model that included all covariates, Hispanic foreign-born children had worse social interaction than their native-born counterparts, according to their parents (-0.28, $p < .001$). With respect to sad/lonely and impulsive/overactive behaviors, there were few differences between native- and foreign-born children of the same racial group. White foreign-born children had fewer impulsive/overactive behaviors than their White native-born counterparts (-0.09, $p < .05$), and there

TABLE 4.4
Ordinary-Least-Squares Regression Models Predicting Teacher-Reported Behavior

Variable	Interpersonal skills			Internalizing behaviors			Externalizing behaviors		
	Model 1	Model 2	Model 3	Model 1	Model 2	Model 3	Model 1	Model 2	Model 3
Race and immigrant status									
White native-born (reference)									
White foreign-born	−0.01	−0.02	−0.02	−0.07	−0.05	−0.02	0.01	0.01	−0.05
	(0.04)	(0.05)	(0.05)	(0.04)	(0.04)	(0.04)	(0.04)	(0.04)	(0.04)
Black native-born	−0.18***	−0.16***	−0.13***	0.20***	0.18***	−0.03	0.02	0.01	0.14***
	(0.02)	(0.02)	(0.03)	(0.03)	(0.03)	(0.02)	(0.02)	(0.02)	(0.03)
Black foreign-born	−0.06	−0.03	−0.01	0.06	0.03	0.01	0.05	0.03	0.01
	(0.09)	(0.09)	(0.09)	(0.09)	(0.10)	(0.06)	(0.06)	(0.06)	(0.09)
Hispanic native-born	−0.02	−0.01	−0.01	0.01	−0.01	−0.04	−0.02	−0.02	−0.01
	(0.04)	(0.03)	(0.04)	(0.03)	(0.03)	(0.03)	(0.03)	(0.03)	(0.03)
Hispanic foreign-born	0.05^	0.05^	0.05	−0.09***	−0.08**	−0.10**	−0.08**	−0.08**	−0.07^
	(0.03)	(0.03)	(0.04)	(0.03)	(0.03)	(0.04)	(0.02)	(0.02)	(0.04)
Asian native-born	0.03	0.06	0.06	−0.12*	−0.15*	−0.11*	−0.09^	−0.10*	−0.15*
	(0.07)	(0.08)	(0.08)	(0.06)	(0.06)	(0.05)	(0.05)	(0.05)	(0.06)
Asian foreign-born	0.02	0.03	0.04	−0.14**	−0.13**	−0.13**	−0.10**	−0.10**	−0.13**
	(0.04)	(0.04)	(0.05)	(0.04)	(0.04)	(0.04)	(0.03)	(0.03)	(0.05)
Other race native-born	−0.14**	−0.12**	−0.10*	0.12**	0.12**	−0.01	0.03	0.02	0.10*
	(0.05)	(0.05)	(0.05)	(0.04)	(0.04)	(0.04)	(0.04)	(0.04)	(0.04)
Other race foreign-born	−0.08	−0.04	−0.04	0.01	−0.02	−0.10^	−0.06	−0.08	−0.01
	(0.09)	(0.09)	(0.09)	(0.09)	(0.08)	(0.06)	(0.06)	(0.06)	(0.08)

	(1)	(2)	(3)	(4)	(5)	(6)	(7)	(8)	(9)
Family structure									
Married			—			—			—
Separated			−0.08*			0.18***			0.11**
			(0.04)			(0.04)			(0.04)
Divorced			−0.09**			0.09***			0.10**
			(0.03)			(0.02)			(0.03)
Widowed			0.11			−0.09			−0.10
			(0.09)			(0.09)			(0.09)
Never married			−0.11***			0.06**			0.11***
			(0.03)			(0.02)			(0.03)
Family discusses ethnic or racial heritage			0.01			0.01			−0.01
			(0.01)			(0.01)			(0.01)
Family discusses religious beliefs or traditions			0.01*			−0.01*			−0.01
			(0.01)			(0.01)			(0.01)
Family participates in cultural events or traditions			−0.01			0.01			−0.01
			(0.01)			(0.01)			(0.01)
Non-English language spoken at home			−0.02			0.04			−0.01
			(0.04)			(0.03)			(0.04)
Constant	3.133	2.598	2.605	1.631	2.015	1.821	1.599	1.850	1.996
R^2	0.034	0.081	0.086	0.029	0.081	0.026	0.014	0.018	0.086
N	11,242	11,242	11,242	11,242	11,242	11,242	11,242	11,242	11,242

Note. Analyses weighted to account for sampling design. Robust standard errors are in parentheses. Model 1 includes a composite indicator of socioeconomic status (SES) that comprises the following: household income (log), mother's occupational prestige, father's occupational prestige, mother's education, and father's education. Models 2 and 3 include composite SES, mother's employment status, father's employment status, mother's age, number of children in household, respondent not mother, child is male, and child age (in months).

^$p < .10$. *$p < .05$. **$p < .01$. ***$p < .001$.

TABLE 4.5
Ordinary-Least-Squares Regression Models for Foreign-Born Coefficient
Predicting Parent- and Teacher-Reported Behavior, by Race

| | Parent-reported | | | | | |
| | Social interaction | | Sad/lonely behaviors | | Impulsive/overactive behaviors | |
Variable	Model 1	Model 2	Model 1	Model 2	Model 1	Model 2
White	−0.11**	−0.10**	0.02	0.02	−0.09*	−0.09*
(n = 8,378)	(0.04)	(0.04)	(0.03)	(0.03)	(0.04)	(0.04)
Black	−0.16*	−0.16*	0.03	0.03	−0.10	−0.10
(n = 1,617)	(0.08)	(0.08)	(0.06)	(0.06)	(0.09)	(0.09)
Hispanic	−0.29***	−0.28***	−0.02	−0.02	−0.07	−0.07
(n = 1,901)	(0.10)	(0.04)	(0.03)	(0.03)	(0.04)	(0.04)
Asian	−0.04	−0.03	0.01	−0.01	0.01	0.02
(n = 642)	(0.09)	(0.09)	(0.05)	(0.05)	(0.07)	(0.07)
Other race	−0.33**	−0.26**	0.09	0.08	0.18^	0.19^
(n = 436)	(0.10)	(0.10)	(0.05)	(0.06)	(0.10)	(0.10)

| | Teacher-reported | | | | | |
| | Interpersonal skills | | Internalizing behaviors | | Externalizing behaviors | |
	Model 1	Model 2	Model 1	Model 2	Model 1	Model 2
White	−0.01	−0.02	0.01	−0.01	−0.06	−0.05
(n = 7,360)	(0.04)	(0.05)	(0.04)	(0.04)	(0.04)	(0.04)
Black	0.12	0.14	0.02	0.01	−0.16	−0.16
(n = 1,371)	(0.09)	(0.09)	(0.06)	(0.06)	(0.10)	(0.10)
Hispanic	0.07	0.06	−0.06^	−0.07^	−0.09*	−0.08*
(n = 1,571)	(0.04)	(0.04)	(0.04)	(0.04)	(0.04)	(0.04)
Asian	−0.02	−0.04	0.01	0.01	0.01	0.02
(n = 555)	(0.08)	(0.08)	(0.06)	(0.06)	(0.07)	(0.07)
Other race	0.06	0.09	−0.11	−0.10	−0.11	−0.12
(n = 385)	(0.10)	(0.10)	(0.07)	(0.07)	(0.10)	(0.09)

Note. Analyses weighted to account for sampling design. Robust standard errors are in parentheses. Model 1 includes a composite indicator of socioeconomic status (SES) that comprises the following: household income (log), mother's occupational prestige, father's occupational prestige, mother's education, and father's education. Model 2 includes composite SES, mother's employment status, father's employment status, mother's age, number of children in household, respondent not mother, child is male, and child age (in months).
^$p < .10$. *$p < .05$. **$p < .01$. ***$p < .001$.

is some evidence that other race foreign-born children had more impulsive/ overactive behaviors (0.19, $p < .10$)

According to teachers' reports of children's behaviors, there was some evidence of an immigrant paradox for Hispanic children. In the final model, Hispanic foreign-born children, compared with Hispanic native-born children, had marginally better internalizing (−0.07, $p < .10$) and externalizing (−0.08,

$p < .05$) behaviors. In supplemental analyses not presented, we found that characteristics of the family environment did not explain this paradox.

DISCUSSION

In the analyses presented in this chapter, we used data from the ECLS-K, a nationally representative sample of children who were in kindergarten during the 1998–1999 school year, to examine the immigrant paradox—the proposition that immigrants, despite having fewer socioeconomic resources, have more favorable outcomes than their native-born counterparts—in parent- and teacher-reported behavior in early childhood. Overall, our multivariate analyses have provided some evidence for an immigrant paradox but suggest that the salience of the immigrant paradox depends on several factors, including race, outcome, and comparison group.

To begin with, we found much greater support for an immigrant paradox in teacher-reported behavior than parent-reported behavior. We found evidence of a Hispanic immigrant paradox in teacher-reported internalizing and externalizing behaviors, both when compared with native-born Whites and native-born Hispanics. With respect to Asian children, we found evidence of an immigrant paradox in teacher-reported internalizing and externalizing behaviors when these children were compared with native-born Whites but not when compared with native-born children of the same race. In addition, a Hispanic immigrant paradox existed for parent-reported sad/lonely and impulsive/overactive behaviors but only when foreign-born Hispanics were compared with native-born Whites. The differences in parent- and teacher-reported outcomes may have been an artifact of the greater measurement error in the parent-reported outcomes (alphas ranged from 0.46 to 0.70 for the three parent-reported outcomes and from 0.80 to 0.90 for the three teacher-reported outcomes).

On the other hand, the differential evidence of an immigrant paradox, depending on whether parents or teachers were reporting on children's behaviors, may represent two sides of the same coin. Immigrant parents are likely to be worried about their own integration into American life, and they may be more sensitive to their own children's difficulties in interacting with other children. Immigrant parents may also have different expectations of their children than native-born parents. These children, who are viewed by their parents as being less integrated with their peers, may be quiet and less disruptive in the classroom; hence, teachers may report more favorable behavioral outcomes. Additionally, teachers are likely comparing the focal child with the rest of their students, whereas parents may be comparing the focal child with their other children or with the children of their friends. These patterns suggest the possibility that teachers may view immigrant children favorably and document the importance of relying on multiple reporters of children's behaviors. It is also possible that children behave differently at home than they do at school. Our secondary data do not allow us to explore this possibility, though the use of ethnographic examinations of this possibility is an important direction for future research.

Though we found some support for the immigrant paradox in early childhood behavior, we also found evidence of an immigrant disadvantage, particularly when parents were reporting on their children's behaviors. Across the board, immigrant parents were more likely than native-born White parents to report poor social interaction skills in their children. Except among Asian children, these findings persisted when foreign-born children were compared with native-born children of their own race. Immigrant parents perceived their children to lack social interaction skills, which may have precluded these parents from encouraging their children to get involved in extracurricular activities that may have enhanced their interaction skills. If such children indeed experience difficulty with social interaction, extracurricular activities or programs targeted specifically to young immigrant children may be one way to reduce such differentials. We also found that other race foreign-born parents, compared with White native-born parents, were more likely to report sad/lonely behaviors in their children. When teachers reported on children's behaviors, however, there was no evidence of an immigrant disadvantage.

With one exception, we found that characteristics of the family environment—family structure, cultural discussions, and speaking a non-English language at home—did not explain the immigrant paradox. Though there were important racial differences in family environment, many of which put immigrant children at an advantage, these characteristics did little to explain the paradox. The one exception was in parent-reported impulsive/overactive behaviors among Hispanics—here, the immigrant paradox was nearly accounted for by differences in family environment. Thus, for Hispanic children, the family may be an important point for early intervention. Overall, though, for immigrant children in first grade, characteristics of the family environment were not as strongly predictive of behavioral outcomes as prior research suggested would be true for native-born White children (Carlson & Corcoran, 2001). It may also be that our indicators of family environment did not capture the intricate family dynamics that may have explained the immigrant paradox. Our cursory measure of family structure, for example, lumped together children of single parents and children with cohabiting parents, even though prior research has shown that children fare better when raised by unmarried cohabiting parents than by single parents (Smock, 2000). We also did not take into account relationship quality between parents, an important predictor of child well-being (Amato, Loomis, & Booth, 1995; Cummings & Davies, 2002). Future research should pay attention to these and other indicators of the family environment to examine systematic differences between native- and foreign-born families as well as the effects of these differences on child well-being.

There are additional limitations. First, though we took into account both race and immigrant status, we did not take into account ethnicity or country of origin. There may be ethnic differences in children's behavior, as well as the family environments they grow up in, and this is an important direction for future research. The low validity of the parent-reported behaviors is another limitation. Additionally, as is the case with nearly all observational data, our analyses likely suffered from unobserved heterogeneity. Our multivariate analyses controlled for a host of characteristics that may be associated with children's behavior, but we were unable to account for some factors such as peer group influences or neighborhood characteristics. In particular, our estimation of teacher-reported behaviors would be strengthened by taking into account characteristics of the teachers or schools (i.e., teachers' race, teachers' years of experience, percentage of foreign-born children in schools); though this was beyond the scope of our analyses, it is an important direction for future research. Finally, it is important to remember that our analytic samples are more advantaged than the full sample of children, which may bias our estimates of children's behaviors in complex ways.

Despite these limitations, our analyses extend prior research on child well-being in elementary school. We used nationally representative data to examine the immigrant paradox in parent and teacher reports of children's behavior in first grade. We have added to a growing body of literature examining outcomes of children of immigrants and have found evidence of both an immigrant paradox and an immigrant disadvantage in early childhood behavior. The heterogeneity in the experiences of minority immigrant children is manifested early in the life course and may be linked to different cultural experiences in the family's country of origin or differential resources before and after the family arrives in the United States. In other words, it is oversimplistic to think that children from immigrant families uniformly fare better or worse than those from native-born families no matter what outcome we consider. What is clear is that immigrant youth may experience advantages in some indicators of well-being but disparities in other indicators. For children of immigrants (and immigrant adults), perhaps the most difficult part of the migration experience is the social isolation they face. If immigrant children are indeed less socially integrated in kindergarten, then researchers and policymakers alike should examine how schools can do more to welcome these children and their parents.

REFERENCES

Achenbach, T. M., Howell, C. T., Quay, H. C., & Conners, C. K. (1991). National survey of problems and competencies among four- to sixteen-year-olds: Parents' reports for normative and clinical samples. *Monographs of the Society for Research in Child Development, 56*(3), v–120. doi:10.2307/1166156

Alink, L. R. A., Mesman, J., van Zeijl, J., Stolk, M. N., Juffer, F., Koot, H. M., . . . van IJzendoorn, M. H. (2006). The early childhood aggression curve: Development of physical aggression in 10- to 50-month-old children. *Child Development, 77,* 954–966. doi:10.1111/j.1467-8624.2006.00912.x

Allison, P. (2002). *Missing data.* New York, NY: Sage.

Amato, P. R., & Fowler, F. (2002). Parenting practices, child adjustment, and family diversity. *Journal of Marriage & the Family, 64,* 703–716. doi:10.1111/j.1741-3737.2002.00703.x

Amato, P., Loomis, L. S., & Booth, A. (1995). Parental divorce, marital conflict, and offspring well-being during early adulthood. *Social Forces, 73,* 895–915. doi:10.2307/2580551

Beiser, M., Hou, F., Hyman, I., & Tousignant, M. (2002). Poverty, family process, and the mental health of immigrant children in Canada. *American Journal of Public Health, 92,* 220–227. doi:10.2105/AJPH.92.2.220

Bianchi, S. M. (2000). Maternal employment and time with children: Dramatic change or surprising continuity? *Demography, 37,* 401–414. doi:10.1353/dem.2000.0001

Carlson, M. J., & Corcoran, M. E. (2001). Family structure and children's behavioral outcomes. *Journal of Marriage & the Family, 63,* 779–792. doi:10.1111/j.1741-3737.2001.00779.x

Caspi, A., Bem, D. J., & Elder, G. H. (1989). Continuities and consequences of interactional styles across the life course. *Journal of Personality, 57,* 375–406. doi:10.1111/j.1467-6494.1989.tb00487.x

Cherlin, A. (2004). The deinstitutionalization of American marriage. *Journal of Marriage & the Family, 66,* 848–861. doi:10.1111/j.0022-2445.2004.00058.x

Crosnoe, R. (2006). Health and the education of children from race/ethnic minority and immigrant families. *Journal of Health and Social Behavior, 47,* 77–93. doi:10.1177/002214650604700106

Cummings, E. M., & Davies, P. T. (2002). Effects of marital conflict on children: Recent advances and emerging themes in process-oriented research. *Journal of Child Psychology and Psychiatry, 43,* 31–63. doi:10.1111/1469-7610.00003

Downey, D. B., & Condron, D. J. (2004). Playing well with others in kindergarten: The benefits of siblings at home. *Journal of Marriage & the Family, 66,* 333–350. doi:10.1111/j.1741-3737.2004.00024.x

Duncan, G. J., Brooks-Gunn, J., & Klebanov, P. K. (1994). Economic deprivation and early childhood development. *Child Development, 65,* 296–318. doi:10.2307/1131385

Entwisle, D. R., & Alexander, K. L. 1989. Early schooling as a "critical period" phenomenon. In K. Namboodiri & R. G. Corwin (Eds.), *Sociology of education and socialization* (pp. 27–55). Greenwich, CT: JAI Press.

Fuligni, A. J. (1998). The adjustment of children from immigrant families. *Current Directions in Psychological Science, 7,* 99–103. doi:10.1111/1467-8721.ep10774731

Furstenberg. F. F. (2003). Teenage childbearing as a public issue and private concern. *Annual Review of Sociology, 29,* 23–39. doi:10.1146/annurev.soc.29.010202.100205

Gerard, J. M., & Buehler, C. (1999). Multiple risk factors in the family environment and youth problem behaviors. *Journal of Marriage & the Family, 61,* 343–361. doi:10.2307/353753

Han, W.-J. (2010). Bilingualism and socioemotional well-being. *Children and Youth Services Review, 32,* 720–731. doi:10.1016/j.childyouth.2010.01.009

Harker, K. (2001). Immigrant generation, assimilation, and adolescent psychological well-being. *Social Forces, 79,* 969–1004. doi:10.1353/sof.2001.0010

Hofstra, M. B., Van der Ende, J., & Verhulst, F. C. (2000). Continuity and change of psychopathology from childhood into adulthood: A 14-year follow-up study. *Journal of the American Academy of Child and Adolescent Psychiatry, 39,* 850–858. doi:10.1097/00004583-200007000-00013

Hughes, D., Rodriguez, J., Smith, E. P., Johnson, D. J., Stevenson, H. C., & Spicer, P. (2006). parents' ethnic-racial socialization practices: A review of research and directions for future study. *Developmental Psychology, 42,* 747–770. doi:10.1037/0012-1649.42.5.747

Jutte, D. P., Burgos, A., Mendoza, F., Ford, C. B., & Huffman, L. C. (2003). Use of the Pediatric Symptom Checklist in a low-income, Mexican American population. *Archives of Pediatrics & Adolescent Medicine, 157,* 1169–1176. doi:10.1001/archpedi.157.12.1169

Knoester, C. (2003). Implications of childhood externalizing problems for young adults. *Journal of Marriage & the Family, 65,* 1073–1080. doi:10.1111/j.1741-3737.2003.01073.x

Koblinsky, S. A., Kuvalanka, K. A., & Randolph, S. M. (2006). Social skills and behavior problems of urban, African American preschoolers: Role of parenting practices, family conflict, and maternal depression. *American Journal of Orthopsychiatry, 76,* 554–563. doi:10.1037/0002-9432.76.4.554

Landale, N. S., & Oropesa, R. S. (2007). Hispanic families: Stability and change. *Annual Review of Sociology, 33,* 381–405. doi:10.1146/annurev.soc.33.040406.131655

Lee, V. E., & Burkam, D. T. (2002). *Inequality at the starting gate: Social background differences in achievement as children begin school.* Washington, DC: Economic Policy Institute.

Markides, K. S., & Coreil, J. (1986). The health of Hispanics in the southwestern United States: An epidemiological paradox. *Public Health Reports, 101,* 253–265.

McLeod, J., & Kaiser, K. (2004). Childhood emotional and behavioral problems and educational attainment. *American Sociological Review, 69*(5), 636–658. doi:10.1177/000312240406900502

McLeod, J. D., & Nonnemaker, J. M. (2000). Poverty and child emotional and behavioral problems: Racial/ethnic differences in processes and effects. *Journal of Health and Social Behavior, 41,* 137–161. doi:10.2307/2676302

Moffitt, T. E., Caspi, A., Harrington, H., & Milne, B. J. (2002). Males on the life-course-persistent and adolescence-limited antisocial pathways: Follow-up at age 26 years. *Development and Psychopathology, 14,* 179–207. doi:10.1017/S0954579402001104

National Center for Education Statistics. (2001). *User's manual for the ECLS-K base year public-use data files and electronic codebook* (NCES 2001-029 Revised). Washington, DC: U.S. Department of Education.

O'Hare, W. P. (2004). *Trends in the well-being of America's children.* New York, NY, and Washington, DC: Russell Sage Foundation & Population Reference Bureau.

Palloni, A., & Morenoff, J. (2001). Interpreting the paradoxical in the Hispanic paradox: Demographic and epidemiological approaches. *Annals of the New York Academy of Sciences, 954,* 140–174. doi:10.1111/j.1749-6632.2001.tb02751.x

Robinson, M., Oddy, W. H., Li, J., Kendall, G. E., de Klerk, N. H., Silburn, S. R., . . . Mattes, E. (2008). Pre- and postnatal influences on preschool mental health: A large-scale cohort study. *Journal of Child Psychology and Psychiatry, 49,* 1118–1128. doi:10.1111/j.1469-7610.2008.01955.x

Rock, D. A., & Pollack, J. M. (2002). *Early childhood longitudinal study—Kindergarten class of 1998–99 (ECLS-K), psychometric report for kindergarten through first grade* (Working Paper No. 2002-05). Washington, DC: U.S. Department of Education, National Center for Education Statistics.

Royston, P. (2004). Multiple imputation of missing values. *Stata Journal, 4,* 227–241.

Rumbaut, R. G., & Portes, A. (2001). *Ethnicities: Children of immigrants in America.* Berkeley: University of California Press.

Schwartz, S. J., Pantin, H., Prado, G., Sullivan, S., & Szapocznik, J. (2005). Family functioning, identity, and problem behavior in Hispanic immigrant early adolescents. *The Journal of Early Adolescence, 25,* 392–420. doi:10.1177/0272431605279843

Sigle-Rushton, W., & McLanahan, S. (2004). Father absence and child well-being: A critical review. In D. P. Moynihan, T. M. Smeeding, & L. Rainwater (Eds.), *The future of the family* (pp. 116–155). New York, NY: Russell Sage Foundation.

Simons, R. L., Whitbeck, L. B., Beaman, J., & Conger, R. D. (1994). The impact of mothers' parenting, involvement by nonresidential fathers, and parental conflict on the adjustment of adolescent children. *Journal of Marriage & the Family, 56,* 356–374. doi:10.2307/353105

Smock, P. J. (2000). Cohabitation in the United States: An appraisal of research themes, findings, and implications. *Annual Review of Sociology, 26,* 1–20. doi:10.1146/annurev.soc.26.1.1

Strohschein, L., McDonough, P., Monette, G., & Shao, Q. (2005). Marital transitions and mental health: Are there gender differences in the short-term effects of marital status change? *Social Science & Medicine, 61*, 2293–2303. doi:10.1016/j.socscimed.2005.07.020

Turney, K., & Kao, G. (2009a). Assessing the private safety net: Perceptions of social support among minority immigrant parents. *The Sociological Quarterly, 50*, 666–692. doi:10.1111/j.1533-8525.2009.01157.x

Turney, K., & Kao, G. (2009b). Barriers to school involvement: Are immigrant parents disadvantaged? *The Journal of Educational Research, 102*, 257–271. doi:10.3200/JOER.102.4.257-271

Valenzuela, A. (1999). *Subtractive schooling: U.S.-Mexican youth and the politics of caring.* Albany: SUNY Press.

Walton, E., & Takeuchi, D. T. (2010). Family structure, family processes, and well-being among Asian Americans: Considering gender and nativity. *Journal of Family Issues, 31*, 301–332. doi:10.1177/0192513X09350873

Yeung, W. J., Linver, M. R., & Brooks-Gunn, J. (2002). How money matters for young children's development: Parental investment and family processes. *Child Development, 73*, 1861–1879. doi:10.1111/1467-8624.t01-1-00511

Zhou, M. (1997). Growing up American: The challenge confronting immigrant children and children of immigrants. *Annual Review of Sociology, 23*, 63–95. doi:10.1146/annurev.soc.23.1.63

5

EXPLORING THE IMMIGRANT PARADOX IN ADOLESCENT SEXUALITY: AN ECOLOGICAL PERSPECTIVE

MARCELA RAFFAELLI, HYEYOUNG KANG, AND TRISTAN GUARINI

[Adolescents in the United States are more likely than teens in other industrialized nations to experience unplanned pregnancies, teen births, and sexually transmitted infections as a result of risky sexual behaviors (e.g., early sexual initiation, unprotected sex; Guttmacher Institute, 2002). In many non-Western nations, including the Asian and Latin American nations from which most current U.S. immigrants originate, adolescent sexual involvement (especially among girls) has traditionally been uncommon or occurred in the context of marriage (e.g., Blum & Mmari, 2005). Thus, immigrant adolescents are typically confronted with the challenge of negotiating sexuality in a very different context than their (or their parents') home country.]

[This chapter examines whether an immigrant paradox is evident for adolescent sexual behavior.] The *immigrant paradox* refers to the phenomenon whereby later immigrant generation (or increased acculturation) is associated with worsening outcomes despite decreases in objective risk factors (e.g., improvements in socioeconomic status and English fluency)] The immigrant

Manuscript preparation was supported in part by a USDA National Institute of Food and Agriculture Hatch Grant to Marcela Raffaelli (Project No. 600108-793000-793323).

paradox has been documented in a variety of outcomes, including substance use, mental health, and education (for review, see Schwartz, Unger, Zamboanga, & Szapocznik, 2010). There is accumulating evidence that sexual behavior also changes across immigrant generations or with time in the United States in ways consistent with the paradox (e.g., Abraído-Lanza, Armbrister, Flórez, & Aguirre, 2006). Our chapter builds on this work in several key ways.

Research generally supports the existence of an immigrant paradox in sexual behavior (e.g., Choi, 2008; Harris, 1999; McDonald, Manlove, & Ikramullah, 2009; Trejos-Castillo & Vazonyi, 2009). Because studies have examined different types of sexual outcomes and a variety of immigration-related variables, however, it is difficult to draw firm conclusions from this body of work. Therefore, we begin by presenting analyses of national data to determine if the immigrant paradox is evident for adolescent sexual behavior. Moreover, prior research has focused on describing the paradox rather than identifying mechanisms and processes that may account for the observed changes. Thus, we devote the second part of the chapter to considering possible explanations for the results. We present an integrated ecological model that includes potential explanatory factors accounting for immigration-related changes in sexual behavior and use it to structure a review of the existing literature. Throughout the chapter, we focus on Asians and Latinos, who make up more than three quarters of the current foreign-born population in the United States (Larsen, 2004) and who have been the focus of most research with immigrant families. Given space constraints, we do not consider the experiences of sexual-minority youth (see Russell & Truong, 2001).

IS THE IMMIGRANT PARADOX EVIDENT FOR ADOLESCENT SEXUAL BEHAVIOR?

The immigrant paradox would predict that adolescents who are first-generation immigrants (or less acculturated) will engage in less sexual risk behavior than their later generation (or more acculturated) counterparts, despite higher levels of poverty and other demographic risks (e.g., Schwartz et al., 2010). Because prior research has used different methods and yielded conflicting results, we conducted analyses of data from the National Longitudinal Study of Adolescent Health (Add Health). Add Health involved a nationally representative sample of 90,000 in-school U.S. adolescents (Grades 7–12 at Wave I); Asian and Latin American respondents were over-sampled. About 12,000 students also completed in-home interviews that assessed sexual behavior (Harris et al., 2009).

[handwritten margin notes: "many Harris - oversampled Asians X 12,000 students completed survey at home"]

Building on earlier descriptive work (e.g., Harris, 1999), we used Add Health Wave I data provided by Latinos ($N = 3,162$) and Asian Americans ($N = 1,403$) to examine differences across immigrant generations in three sexual behaviors: ever had sexual intercourse (yes–no), age at first sexual intercourse (in years, among those who had ever had sex), and use of birth control at first sexual intercourse (yes–no). Given prior work suggesting that the age at which a young person migrated affects their cultural adaptation (e.g., Rumbaut, 1997), we categorized immigration generation as 1 (foreign born, came to United States at age 13 or older), 1.5 (foreign born, moved to United States before age 13), 2 (U.S. born with at least one foreign-born parent), or 3 (U.S. born with U.S.-born parents). Because prior work on sexuality has shown that gender is a major factor in shaping young people's experience (e.g., Crockett, Raffaelli, & Moilanen, 2003; Diamond & Savin-Williams, 2009), analyses were conducted separately for girls and boys. Multivariate regressions were conducted to evaluate the effect of immigrant generation on the three sexual behaviors while controlling for age, parental education, family income, and family structure (single- vs. two-parent households). However, because of small cell sizes in analyses limited to adolescents who reported having had intercourse (i.e., mean age at first intercourse and birth control use), regression results are only reported for analyses of lifetime sexual intercourse.

Among Asian American boys (Table 5.1), those from later immigrant generations had higher rates of sexual intercourse, an earlier age at first intercourse, and increased use of birth control at first intercourse. For example, fewer than one quarter of first-generation boys had ever had sexual inter-

They may not of had to complete the remainder questions maybe just follow ups for other students

TABLE 5.1
Descriptive Results: Sexual Behavior of Asian American Adolescents by Gender and Generation (G)

Variable	Asian American boys ($n = 673$)				Asian American girls ($n = 730$)			
	G1	G1.5	G2	G3	G1	G1.5	G2	G3
Ever had sex (% yes)	22.0	27.2	23.5	30.9	20.3	18.6	33.3	35.8
Mean age of first sex (years)[a]	16.25	15.86	15.20	14.91	17	15.87	15.45	14.98
Birth control with first sex (% yes)[a]	20.0	49.1	49.2	54.3	64.3	70.3	55.4	59.2

[a]Among those who have ever had sex (boys = 182, girls = 188).

TABLE 5.2
Logistic Regressions Predicting Lifetime Sexual Intercourse Among Asian American Adolescents

	Asian American boys				Asian American girls			
Generation	β	SE	Wald	Exp(β)	β	SE	Wald	Exp(β)
1	−2.07*	0.92	5.04	1.26	−2.99**	0.90	10.97	0.50
1.5	−0.93	0.52	3.18	0.40	−1.45**	0.48	9.11	0.23
2	−0.53	0.44	1.44	0.59	−0.81	0.45	3.22	0.44
Step 2 χ^{2a}	6.95				18.41***			
Model χ^{2b}	43.01**				50.20***			
Nagelkerke R^2	0.25				0.29			

Note. Third generation is the reference group. Statistics are from Step 2 of the model; control variables entered at Step 1 (age, parent education, family income, and family structure) were omitted for ease of presentation.
$^a df = 3.$ $^b df = 7.$
*$p < .05.$ **$p < .01.$

⅓ had sex 3rd generation

course compared with nearly one third of third-generation boys. Results of logistic regression analyses (Table 5.2) indicate that first-generation Asian American boys were 87.4% less likely to have had sexual intercourse than third-generation boys, with 1.5- and second-generation boys not differing from those in the third generation. Age at first intercourse showed a linear decline across generation, and birth control use at first intercourse increased from the first to the third generation (Table 5.1).

A different pattern emerged for Asian American girls. About one fifth of both first- and 1.5-generation girls reported ever having sexual intercourse, compared with two thirds of those in the second and third generations (Table 5.1). Logistic regression analyses showed that first-generation girls were 95.0% and 1.5-generation girls 76.6% less likely than their third-generation counterparts to have engaged in sexual intercourse; second- and third-generation girls did not differ (Table 5.2). Similar to their male counterparts (Table 5.1), Asian American girls demonstrated a linear decrease in age at first intercourse across immigrant generations, but the pattern for birth control use was less clear cut (perhaps because of the limited number of girls reporting intercourse across generation groups). ← under-reported

Among Latino boys, generational differences in ever having intercourse, age of sexual initiation, and birth control use at first intercourse were observed (Table 5.3). Results of the logistic regression analysis (Table 5.4) indicate that first-generation Latino boys were 71.6% less likely than third-generation boys to have had sexual intercourse, but those in the 1.5 and second generations were not significantly different from their third-generation counterparts. As shown in Table 5.3, Latino boys' age at first intercourse decreased, and birth control use at first intercourse increased, across immigrant generations.

TABLE 5.3
Descriptive Results: Sexual Behavior of Latino Adolescents by Gender and Generation (G)

Variable	Latino boys (n = 1,631)				Latina girls (n = 1,601)			
	G1	G1.5	G2	G3	G1	G1.5	G2	G3
Ever had sex (% yes)	39.7	47.1	45.2	48.0	30.0	29.1	34.3	39.3
Mean age at first sex (years)[a]	15.96	14.60	14.90	14.34	16.95	15.81	15.64	15.03
Birth control at first sex (% yes)[a]	50.0	54.1	57.5	60.5	61.9	51.3	52.0	57.5

[a]Among those who have ever had sex (boys = 753, girls = 559).

Similar to Asian American girls, both first- and 1.5-generation Latinas were significantly less likely to report having sexual intercourse than their third-generation counterparts (Table 5.4). First-generation Latinas had the highest age of first intercourse, with declines in each subsequent generation (Table 5.3). The pattern for birth control use was different from other behaviors (Table 5.3). First- and third-generation Latinas had higher levels of birth control use than 1.5- and second-generation Latinas.

These findings provide support for the immigrant paradox in sexual behavior. Among both Asian American and Latino youth, those in the first (and in some cases 1.5) generation were less likely to have sexual intercourse and to wait longer to begin having intercourse than their U.S.-born counterparts. The overall result is that third-generation Latinos of both genders and Asian American girls had similar or higher rates of sexual involvement when

TABLE 5.4
Logistic Regressions Predicting Lifetime Sexual Intercourse Among Latino Adolescents

Generation	Latino boys				Latina girls			
	β	SE	Wald	Exp(β)	β	SE	Wald	Exp(β)
1	−1.26*	0.57	4.95	0.28	−2.93**	1.06	7.60	0.53
1.5	−0.36	0.24	2.21	0.70	−0.80**	0.29	7.37	0.45
2	−0.23	0.19	1.42	0.80	−.29	0.21	2.04	0.75
Step 2 χ^{2a}	6.94				19.72***			
Model χ^{2b}	110.35***				82.41***			
Nagelkerke R^2	0.19				0.16			

Note. Third generation is the reference group. Control variables entered at Step 1 (age, parent education, family income, and family structure) were omitted for ease of presentation.
[a]$df = 3$. [b]$df = 7$.
*$p < .05$. **$p < .01$

compared with non-Hispanic White teens (36.7% of European American Add Health respondents reported ever having intercourse). Average age at first intercourse among third-generation Latinos and Asian Americans was also similar to the age reported by non-Hispanic White Add Health respondents (14.8 years). Changes in birth control were less consistent, but regardless of ethnic background or gender, third-generation youth were less likely to use birth control at first sex than European American teens (67.1%). The net result of these changes is that youth from later immigrant generations were more likely to engage in sexual risk behavior than more recent immigrants.

In light of the evidence from our analysis and prior research (e.g., Choi, 2008; Harris, 1999; McDonald et al., 2009; Trejos-Castillo & Vazsonyi, 2009) that the immigrant paradox exists for sexual behavior among Asian American and Latino adolescents, we turn next to identifying theoretically grounded explanations for this phenomenon.

EXPLAINING THE IMMIGRANT PARADOX IN ADOLESCENT SEXUAL BEHAVIOR

In this section, we provide a brief overview of theories of adolescent sexuality, describe an integrative model of adolescent sexuality, and apply the model to the literature on the sexuality of Latino and Asian American adolescents from different immigrant generations. Our goal is to provide a conceptual framework that can be used to guide future work exploring the sexuality of Latino and Asian American immigrants and their descendants in the United States.

General Theories of Sexuality

Sexuality research in the United States has been described as fragmented across disciplines and largely risk focused (e.g., Di Mauro, 1997). The fragmentation is evident in the diversity of approaches used to frame studies of adult sexual behavior, which predate the study of adolescent sexuality (e.g., DeLamater & Hyde, 2004; Harvey, Wenzel, & Sprecher, 2004; Rossi, 1994). Sexuality research has examined physiological aspects of human sexual functioning, clinical aspects of sexuality, sexuality in close relationships, sexual risk behaviors (particularly with respect to HIV/AIDS), and (more recently) normative sexuality across the life course.

Research on adolescent sexuality is more narrowly focused than the adult literature, with most studies describing antecedents and correlates of a small set of sexual behaviors associated with problematic outcomes. This reflects the fact that until recently it was extremely difficult to obtain funding to conduct research on normative aspects of adolescent sexuality (Gardner & Wilcox, 1993). As a result, most research has been conducted from a problem-oriented perspective (Diamond, 2006) and—aside from specific topics like gender identity and pubertal maturation—has neglected noncoital sexual development (Crockett et al. 2003; Diamond & Savin-Williams, 2009). Research on adolescent sexuality has increased in recent years with the advent of national data sets that allow systematic research in large samples of U.S. adolescents. At the same time, greater acceptance of teen sexuality has allowed in-depth explorations of how adolescents make sense of their emerging sexuality (see volumes edited by Crouter & Booth, 2006; Florsheim, 2003; Furman, Brown, & Feiring, 1997; Shulman & Collins, 1997). This literature has identified multiple factors associated with adolescent sexual behavior.

An Integrative Ecological Model of Adolescent Sexuality

In an effort to synthesize the voluminous research findings, scholars have proposed a variety of integrative models of adolescent sexuality (e.g., Crockett et al., 2003; Diamond & Savin-Williams, 2009). To our knowledge, research with immigrant adolescents has not been framed using comprehensive perspectives similar to those developed for studying general populations of adolescents. Instead, Afable-Munsuz and Brindis (2006) identified two theories used to guide most studies of Latino youth sexuality. One theory suggests that the stress of acculturation increases vulnerability to risky behavior (including sexual risk taking), and the other highlights changes in cultural beliefs and values (e.g., gender norms) as a key mechanism underlying acculturation-related changes in sexual behavior. However, 12 of the 17 studies reviewed by these authors did not directly measure these theoretically identified variables but instead relied on proxy measures of acculturation (e.g., language, generation, time in the United States).

When discussing changes in sexual behavior due to immigrant generation and/or acculturation, scholars have highlighted the need for research that examines underlying mechanisms and processes (e.g., Abraído-Lanza et al., 2006). For example, if differences in sexual behavior across immigrant generations are due to changes in gender role beliefs or sexual permissiveness, it is important to measure these intervening variables directly. Moreover, recent theoretical advances indicate that this research must take into account the fact that attitudes and behaviors are shaped not only by the host culture (i.e., acculturation) but also by the heritage culture (i.e., enculturation; Gonzales, Fabrett, & Knight, 2009). There is increasing evidence that developing a bicultural sense of self—one that balances the host and heritage culture—may result in optimal outcomes among ethnically diverse youth in multicultural contexts (Gonzales et al., 2009; Schwartz et al., 2010). Unfortunately,

large-scale national studies do not typically measure culturally relevant factors known to influence sexual behavior (e.g., attitudes and values related to
gender and sexuality) along with variables reflecting the immigrant experience (e.g., immigrant status, acculturative stress). Instead, these data sets
include proxy variables like generation of immigration or language use that
do not reflect mechanisms and pathways that may account for changes in sexual behavior across immigrant generations (e.g., McLoyd, 2004; Zane & Mak,
2003). Ultimately, this limits the move from describing changes in sexual
behavior across immigrant generations to identifying the mechanism underlying those changes (e.g., Guilamo-Ramos, Jaccard, Pena, & Goldberg, 2005;
McDonald et al., 2009; Santelli, Abraido-Lanza, & Melnikas, 2009).

To advance the research agenda on immigrant sexuality, we present
an integrative model adapted from a model of adolescent sexual health
proposed by Tolman, Striepe, and Harmon (2003). Tolman et al. drew on
Bronfenbrenner's bioecological theory (e.g., Bronfenbrenner & Morris,
1998) to identify factors that affect adolescent sexuality and position them
within a set of nested domains representing different ecological levels (individual characteristics, romantic relationships, other social relationships, and
sociocultural or sociopolitical factors).

APPLYING THE INTEGRATIVE ECOLOGICAL MODEL
TO IMMIGRANT ADOLESCENTS

Figure 5.1 depicts our version of the integrative ecological model, adapted
to reflect factors relevant to immigrant adolescents. Given the complexity of this
model, an empirical test is beyond the scope of this chapter. Instead, we use this
model to organize a review of the literature, paying particular attention to how
factors at each ecological level change across immigrant generations or with
increased acculturation. Because gender is a key aspect of adolescent sexuality,
gender-related findings are described whenever possible. In addition, because the
experiences of immigrants and their descendants are conditioned by structural
components that may operate indirectly on sexual behavior (e.g., socioeconomic
opportunities; see Brindis, Wolfe, McCarter, Ball, & Starbuck-Morales, 1995;
Lara, Gamboa, Kahramanian, Morales, & Hayes Bautista, 2005), we also report
on whether these types of variables were included in analyses.

Individual Factors

The individual occupies the innermost circle of the model. Variables in
this domain include attitudes, values, and beliefs (e.g., sexual self-concept,
sexual comfort, permissiveness, self-efficacy, sexual knowledge) as well as

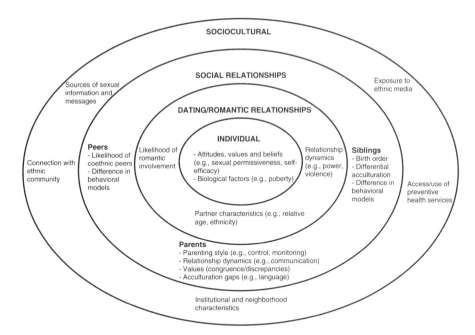

Figure 5.1. Integrative ecological model of immigrant adolescent sexuality. From "Gender Matters: Constructing a Model of Adolescent Sexual Health," by D. L. Tolman, M. I. Striepe, and T. Harmon, 2003, *Journal of Sex Research, 40,* p. 8. Copyright 2003 by Taylor & Francis. Adapted with permission.

biological factors (e.g., pubertal timing and genetic influences). Because of a lack of research on immigration-related differences in biological factors, we focus on individual variables reflecting sexuality-related attitudes, values, and beliefs.

Studies with Asian Americans indicate that increased acculturation is associated with a decline in sexual conservatism (see Okazaki, 2002). For example, among Chinese college students in the United States, acculturation was positively associated with permissive attitudes toward premarital sexual involvement (Huang & Uba, 1992). Canadian-born Asians and long-term immigrants had more liberal sexual attitudes and higher levels of sexual knowledge than recent Asian immigrants (Meston, Trapnell, & Gorzalka, 1998). In a study that examined multiple predictors of teenage girls' expectations regarding various sexual transitions, U.S.-born Asian sixth- to eighth-grade girls did not differ from those born outside the United States on measures of sexual intentions or desired age at first birth but perceived a higher likelihood of a nonmarital birth (East, 1998).

There is a similar pattern of acculturation associated with increasingly liberal sexual attitudes among Latino youth. For example, among 16- to 22-year-old Latinos, endorsement of sexual values related to gender role norms declined with acculturation, with gender differences evident for some dimensions (Deardorff, Tschann, & Flores, 2008). Among Mexican American high school students, an internal health locus of control was associated with stronger identification with the majority U.S. culture or with a bicultural orientation (Guinn, 1998). Together, these findings indicate that acculturation may be associated with increased sexual empowerment. In contrast, East (1998) reported that Latina adolescents born in the United States reported lower desired ages for first birth and perceived a higher likelihood of having a child outside of marriage than those born outside the United States; among teens born in Mexico, time in the United States was associated with increases in girls' predictions that they would experience a nonmarital birth. These apparently discrepant findings may reflect the same underlying dynamic: Decreased sexual conservatism associated with acculturation may result in an increased likelihood that adolescents will have sex and also view a nonmarital birth as acceptable.

In summary, individual-level factors such as sexual attitudes and values change across immigrant generations in ways that may explain observed shifts in sexual behavior described in the first part of this chapter. For example, there is evidence that young people from later generations or who are more acculturated hold more permissive sexual attitudes than those from early generations or who are less acculturated. However, the limited research in this area makes it difficult to draw conclusions about how specific variables are associated with different sexual behaviors. Most important, research is needed to establish whether attitudes and values actually mediate associations between immigrant generation and sexual behaviors. One study reported that attitudes toward sexuality (e.g., importance of waiting until marriage to have sex) were stronger predictors of Latina adolescents' sexual activity than immigrant generation (Jimenez, Potts, & Jimenez, 2002); this finding awaits replication in representative samples of Latino and Asian American adolescents.

Romantic Relationships

Relationships represent primary contexts in which young people explore their sexuality. Key variables identified by Tolman et al. (2003) include partner characteristics, power dynamics, and communication. There is emerging evidence that these aspects of romantic relationships change across immigrant generations in ways that may explain the immigrant paradox.

In one Add Health study, the likelihood of being in a romantic relationship increased with immigrant generation for both genders (King & Harris, 2007). In addition, first-generation girls were less likely than later generation girls to have met their partner's parents, told others they were a couple, or thought of themselves as a couple. Other analyses indicate that foreign-born and U.S.-born Chinese adolescents were equally likely to be romantically involved—about 32%—whereas such involvement was likely for 58% of European American adolescents (Kuo & St. Lawrence, 2006). These different findings highlight the value of conducting within-group analyses.

In terms of partner characteristics, first-generation adolescents are more likely to date within their racial–ethnic group than are later generation adolescents (King & Harris, 2007). For example, among Latina respondents in the National Survey of Family Growth, those who completed the interview in Spanish (vs. English) were less likely to report a first sexual relationship with a non-Latino partner (King & Bratter, 2007). Among Chinese college students in the United States, those who dated European Americans were more sexually experienced (Huang & Uba, 1992). Partner age is another important predictor of sexual involvement; in general, girls with older partners engage in higher levels of sexual risk behavior (e.g., Vanoss Marín, Coyle, Gómez, Carvajal, & Kirby, 2000). Regardless of ethnicity, foreign-born girls were more likely than U.S.-born girls to have a first sexual partner who was at least 3 years older (Manlove, Ryan, & Franzetta, 2007). In a multiethnic sample of 10- to 13-year-olds, lower linguistic acculturation was associated with having a boyfriend or girlfriend 2 or more years older (Vanoss Marín et al., 2000). Little is known about how other aspects of relationships are associated with immigration-related factors. One study reported that immigrant Latina girls were at reduced risk for lifetime experiences of dating violence compared with their nonimmigrant counterparts, but immigrant status was not protective for Asian girls (Silverman, Decker, & Raj, 2007).

Taken together, results from multiple national studies indicate that both the likelihood of adolescents being in a relationship and their partners' characteristics change across immigrant generation and with acculturation. These changes in romantic relationships may be linked to the changes in sexual behavior described earlier. For example, youth who date outside their ethnic group are likely to become involved with partners whose sexual expectations and experiences differ from those found within their family and home culture (e.g., European American peers who are more likely to be sexually active) and thus may engage in sexual activity. However, we were unable to identify studies that examined whether changes in relationships accounted for the immigrant paradox in sexual behavior. It is also unclear whether relationship qualities (e.g., communication, relative power) also change across immigrant generations. Finally, the extent to which dating behavior reflects individual preferences—as opposed to parental limits or peer influence—among youth in different immigrant generations has not been considered (King & Harris, 2007; Raffaelli & Ontai, 2001). Additional work is needed to gain a full picture of Asian and Latino adolescents' romantic and sexual relationships and to explore how immigration-related changes in these relationships are associated with changing sexual behavior.

Social Relationships

Within the model proposed by Tolman et al. (2003), social relationships can afford emotional, social, and informational support. We next examine how relationships identified in the adolescent sexuality literature change across immigration generations or with acculturation.

Parents

Parents are thought to influence adolescent sexuality in a variety of ways, including the extent to which they monitor and control their children and communicate their sexual values and attitudes as well as through the overall quality of the parent–child relationship. Parenting behaviors in these areas, which reflect culturally based belief systems, change across successive generations in the United States, although findings vary for specific parenting dimensions.

Among Latinos, parental socialization practices have been described as shifting from emphasizing interdependence and parental control to promoting individualism and child autonomy (e.g., Buriel, 1993; Grau, Azmitia, & Quattlebaum, 2009), which may afford adolescents opportunities for sexual involvement. However, empirical studies of acculturation-related changes in parenting have yielded conflicting results. In multivariate Add Health analyses, U.S.-born mothers of Mexican descent were more likely to be described by adolescents as permissive (vs. authoritative) than immigrant Mexican mothers (Driscoll, Russell, & Crockett, 2008). In contrast, Mexican immigrants to the United States and Mexican Americans reported higher levels of authoritarian parenting than their counterparts in Mexico—that is, parents in Mexico were *less* strict than their U.S. counterparts (Varela et al., 2004). Therefore, authoritarian parenting, which emphasizes obedience and power assertion, may represent immigrant parents' reaction to ecological demands (e.g., discrimination, fear for adolescents' safety in impoverished or high crime neighborhoods). This possibility is supported by a study finding no differences between first- and second-generation Latino adolescents' reports of maternal behavior (including monitoring and support) after controlling for age, gender, family structure, socioeconomic status, and length of residence in the United States (Trejos-Castillo & Vazsonyi, 2009).

Among Asian Americans, different findings have emerged for distinct aspects of parent–child relationships. Some studies have suggested that parenting becomes more authoritative across generation. For example, Taiwanese American mothers reported less parental control than mothers in

Taiwan (Chiu, 1987), and more acculturated Asian American parents were described as more accepting of premarital sex than less acculturated parents (J. L. Kim & Ward, 2007). However, in another study, Chinese immigrant youth disclosed more to their mothers than did second-generation teens (Yau, Tasopoulos-Chan, & Smetana, 2009). Among Add Health participants, Asian adolescents' reports of attachment to parents did not differ by birthplace or home language use (Hahm, Lahiff, & Guterman, 2003). These somewhat contradictory findings may result from a lack of attention to other features of the parent–child relationship or to the cultural heterogeneity of the populations studied.

The differential pace of cultural adaptation between parents and children has been identified as a salient factor in immigrant families (e.g., Kwak, 2003; Phinney, Ong, & Madden, 2000). Acculturation discrepancies and parent–child challenges have been linked in multiple Latino groups (Brook, Whiteman, Balka, Win, & Gursen, 1997; Gil & Vega, 1996). Findings are less consistent for Asian Americans (e.g., Fuligni, 1998; Phinney, Kim-Jo, Osorio, & Vilhjalmsdottir, 2005), but in one study, a greater acculturation discrepancy between Chinese immigrant parents and their adolescent children was associated with lower levels of inductive reasoning, monitoring, and child-reported supportive parenting (S. Y. Kim, Chen, Li, Huang, & Moon, 2009). Differential acculturation has not been examined as a possible factor in adolescents' sexual behavior, but parent–child language discrepancies are known to affect family communication (Kang, Okazaki, Abelmann, Kim-Prieto, & Lan, 2010; Tseng & Fuligni, 2000). It may be particularly difficult for children and parents to discuss sexuality because of differences in values and beliefs (Le & Kato, 2006). Among Filipino Americans, youth acculturation and a greater language gap were associated with lower levels of parent–adolescent communication about sex (Chung et al., 2007). Similarly, Asian American college students with a language discrepancy in the home received less information about sex from their mothers than those without a language discrepancy (J. L. Kim & Ward, 2007).

Differential parental expectations for sons and daughters are also important to consider. For example, Latino parents tend to grant less autonomy to, and place more responsibilities on, daughters than sons (Buriel, 1993; Domenech Rodríguez, Donovick, & Crowley, 2009). Similarly, Asian American women reported that compared with their brothers, they had more restrictions placed on their social lives by parents (J. L. Kim, 2009). In terms of sexuality, gendered parental expectations have been found for Latinos (Raffaelli & Iturbide, 2009) and Asians (J. L. Kim, 2009). However, little is known about changes in gender-related expectations across immigrant generations or the implications of these changes for adolescent sexuality.

In summary, generational changes have been reported in at least some aspects of parent–child relationship dynamics that are likely relevant to adolescent sexuality. To date, however, little is known about how these changes are actually related to adolescent sexuality. Moreover, given indications that some changes in parenting may be reactions to immigration—rather than reflecting cultural beliefs—it is critical that future studies consider characteristics of the broader ecological settings in which immigrant families are embedded.

Siblings

There is evidence from the developmental literature that siblings influence each others' sexuality, particularly older siblings who may serve as models for sexual behavior and childbearing (for review, see East, 2009). Despite a strong emphasis on family relations in the literature on ethnic minority and immigrant families (e.g., Cauce & Domenech Rodríguez, 2002; Zhou, 1997), studies that have a primary focus on siblings are rare. Instead, immigration scholars have focused on limited aspects of sibling relationships (e.g., caretaking, impact of family separation; see Suárez-Orozco & Suárez-Orozco, 2001; Valenzuela, 1999).

One study showed that sibling birth order was associated with level of acculturation such that older siblings in Korean American and Vietnamese American families were more likely to identify with the family's ethnic culture and consequently play a role as disciplinarians to their younger, more assimilated siblings (Pyke, 2005). In Mexican and Mexican American families, siblings reported more conflicts when fathers were born in the United States (vs. Mexico) and spent less time together as a dyad when either parent was U.S. born; no differences emerged for sibling intimacy (Updegraff, McHale, Whiteman, Thayer, & Delgado, 2005). Little other information is available about sibling relationships in immigrant families, how these relationships change across immigrant generations or with acculturation, and the resulting impact on sexual behavior.

Peers

In the United States, the peer group provides an important socialization context for adolescents. Peers are thought to affect sexuality through their actual and perceived behavior and adherence to conventional norms and values. It has been suggested that immigrant youth may turn to peers (rather than family members) for informational and emotional support (e.g., Cavanagh, 2007). National studies are now yielding information about the structure and characteristics of peer groups across immigrant generations.

Among Add Health respondents, the likelihood of having a best friend from the same panethnic group (e.g., Asian or Latino) or nationality decreased from the first to the third generation (Kao & Joyner, 2006); analyses controlled for demographics and school composition. Similar results were found in a multisite international study (Phinney, Berry, Vedder, & Liebkind, 2006). Thus (similar to findings for romantic relationships), early generation youth are more likely than later generation youth to interact with co-ethnic peers. Analysis of social network data from Add Health also revealed that the friends of first-generation Mexican Americans were less likely to engage in "party culture" behaviors (e.g., drinking, smoking) than those of second- or third-generation youth (Cavanagh, 2007). Thus, youth from later immigrant generations appear to have friends who not only differ in cultural background but also provide different behavioral models than friends of those in earlier generations.

In summary, it is evident that many aspects of social relationships change across immigrant generations or with acculturation in ways that may shed light on the immigrant paradox in sexual behavior. For example, decreased parental control and increased contact with peers from different backgrounds may provide adolescents with opportunities and models for sexual exploration. Again, however, the extent to which changes in social relationships are associated with immigrant adolescents' sexual behavior remains largely unexplored.

Sociocultural Factors

The outermost layer of the ecology is the sociocultural context, representing macrolevel forces that affect individuals' everyday lives indirectly. Factors operating at this level include institutions that provide young people with information (e.g., school-based sex education programs), health care (e.g., teen clinics), and messages regarding sexuality (e.g., religious leaders) as well as the political systems that shape these institutions (e.g., policies regarding funding of comprehensive sex education). Next, we provide examples of how macrolevel factors may be associated with the immigrant paradox in adolescent sexual behavior.

There is ample evidence that immigrant generation/acculturation is associated with greater access to, and use of, preventive health services because of increased insurance coverage and comfort with the U.S. medical system (Loue, 1998). This shift may account for increased use of birth control among Asian American and Latino boys (although it is unclear why a similar increase is not observed among girls in these groups). Another example of how sociocultural forces shape individual behavior is that immigrant groups may preserve key aspects of their home culture through ethnic enclaves and institutions (Zhou, 1997). For example, ethnic churches play a critical role in Korean immigrant communities by providing various services (e.g., religious services, educational resources), social networks, and the maintenance of ethnic ties (Chong, 1998; Zhou & Kim, 2006). Ethnic churches also contribute to the construction and reinforcement of ethnic identity among second-generation Korean American youth (Chong, 1998), which may foster biculturalism. As noted earlier, there is emerging evidence that being bicultural may protect youth from becoming involved in problem behaviors (Gonzales et al., 2009; Schwartz et al., 2010). Thus, ethnic enclaves and institutions may affect sexual behavior indirectly by influencing young people's social networks, activities, and identities.

Entertainment media also represent a potent source of socialization regarding sexuality (Pardun, L'Engle, & Brown, 2005; Ward, 2003). With the advent of satellite and Internet media, immigrants and their children have unprecedented access to programs from their home countries. Researchers have begun to explore immigrant teens' media use and the influence of media on their sexual attitudes. For example, Rivadeneyra and Ward (2005) reported that Latino adolescents (71% of whom were second generation) watched both Spanish and English TV, and exposure to specific genres was associated with differential gender role attitudes among girls. In multivariate analyses, level of exposure to specific types of media (Spanish prime time comedies, English talk shows) were stronger predictors than acculturation of traditional gender role attitudes. These findings support the notion that media use might mediate the association between acculturation and sexuality through its influence on young people's sexual attitudes and values. Future research is needed to examine this possibility.

The sociocultural domain represents an important but largely unexplored area for future research on the sexuality of immigrant youth. The Add Health data set, which was designed to allow multilevel analyses, provides unique opportunities for explorations of macro influences on adolescent behavior, including schools and neighborhoods. This work would undoubtedly shed light on mechanisms underlying the immigrant paradox in adolescent sexual behavior.

CONCLUSIONS

This chapter has addressed two main topics. First, we asked whether Latino and Asian American adolescents from distinct immigrant generations show differences in various sexual behaviors that are consistent with the immigrant paradox. Our answer was yes: Analyses of national data revealed a general pattern for increased sexual involvement and sexual risk behavior across immigrant generations. Second, we proposed an integrative ecological framework that can be used to conceptualize possible mechanisms that may underlie these observed generation differences and applied the framework to the existing literature. Taken as a whole, this work has implications for research, practice, and policy.

Our analysis of the Add Health data identified a number of future research directions. One issue is the value of considering age at immigration, which has been identified as an important factor (e.g., Rumbaut, 1997) but has seldom been explored in sexuality research. Our results indicate that among male adolescents, the 1.5 generation (foreign-born youth who arrived in the U.S. before age 13) was similar to the second and third generations, but among female adolescents, the first and 1.5 generation were more similar. These findings may reflect the fact that girls in immigrant families typically experience stronger gender-related socialization and stricter parental controls than their male peers (e.g., J. L. Kim, 2009; Raffaelli & Iturbide, 2009). The findings may also reflect gender differences in pubertal timing.[1] Because girls start to mature an average of 1.5 years earlier than boys (Sun et al., 2002), many girls in the 1.5 generation will have gone through puberty in their home country, whereas many boys in the 1.5 generation will enter puberty after arrival in the United States. Additional research on biological influences, including immigration-related influences on pubertal status and timing, is clearly warranted (Irwin, 2005).

A second issue is the importance of considering subethnic group differences. Because of data limitations, we collapsed across national origin groups rather than presenting detailed information on specific Asian (e.g., Chinese, Korean) and Latino (e.g., Mexican, Puerto Rican) subgroups. It is important to note, however, that these panethnic groups are not monolithic. For example, despite sharing common values (e.g., collectivistic orientation, emphasis on education, sexual reticence; J. L. Kim & Ward, 2007; Okazaki, 2002), Asian subgroups (particularly East and South Asians) differ considerably in sexual attitudes and behaviors. They also differ in ways that may be linked to acculturation processes, such as historical connections between their home countries and the United States, timing of immigration, and socioeconomic situation (Choi, 2008). Future research on adolescent sexuality should take these factors into account.

There is an urgent need for research that moves from describing generational differences in sexual behavior to identifying factors that account for them. To further this endeavor, we have presented an integrative model incorporating factors that have been identified as important influences on

---

[1]We thank Amy Marks for bringing this possibility to our attention.

adolescent sexuality and have reviewed the literature on immigration-related changes in these factors. In doing so, we have identified numerous opportunities for future research examining how changes at various levels of the ecology may account for the immigrant paradox in sexual behavior. Findings from prior studies provide initial support for various aspects of the proposed conceptual model, but additional work is needed to provide a comprehensive test of the model. This work will be challenging, because studies examining different pieces of the model have typically been conducted separately, and thus existing data sets do not include all the factors in the model. Thus, a test of the overall model will require either new data collection or the analysis of multiple data sets.

It is important to note that although levels of the model have been discussed separately, it is important to consider cross-level effects. For example, ethnic and generational makeup of peer groups have been linked to romantic relationship characteristics among adolescents of different immigrant generations (King & Harris, 2007), and one study showed that individual values and partner preferences espoused by Latina adolescents were influenced by their perceptions of maternal dating approval (Guilamo-Ramos et al., 2009). Similarly, cultural values operate at multiple levels. For example, in most Asian cultures, sexuality is viewed as a private matter (S. Y. Kim & Wong, 2002), which may contribute to reticence on sexual matters in multiple domains, including parent–child communication (Lau, Markham, Lin, Flores, & Chacko, 2009) and health-seeking behavior (Okazaki, 2002). It is also important to recognize that sexuality does not develop in a vacuum—at the same time that youth are negotiating their emerging sexuality, they are also pursuing developmental tasks in other arenas of life (e.g., education, careers). Therefore, future research should examine cross-domain effects.

In closing, we draw on our review of the literature to offer initial recommendations for policy and practice. One general finding is the variability among immigrant adolescents due to ethnic group, gender, and age at migration. Because of this, practitioners and policymakers must develop a nuanced understanding of the immigrant populations they work with and avoid one-size-fits-all approaches. Our review also identified potential protective factors that could be the focus of interventions and policies. For example, there is evidence that adolescents who are strongly attached to both their home culture (i.e., enculturated) and the host culture (i.e., acculturated) are less likely to become involved in problem behaviors (Gonzales et al., 2009; Schwartz et al., 2010). Therefore, promoting biculturalism through after-school programs, ethnic organizations, or policies that support cultural maintenance could ultimately promote the sexual health of immigrant youth. Moreover, warm and supportive parent–child relationships are potent protective factors, yet many immigrant families experience challenges due to language discrepancies. Policies that support bilingualism in immigrant children and their parents could help ameliorate some of these difficulties.

Given high rates of recent and current immigration into the United States, issues of cultural adaptation and change will remain salient for theorists, researchers, and practitioners working on issues of adolescent sexuality. We believe that developing and testing theoretically grounded integrative models represents a fruitful approach to building our understanding of immigration-related changes in sexuality and sexual behavior. We hope that this chapter contributes to this important endeavor.

REFERENCES

Abraído-Lanza, A. F., Armbrister, A. N., Flórez, K. R., & Aguirre, A. N. (2006). Toward a theory-driven model of acculturation in public health research. *American Journal of Public Health*, 96, 1342–1346. doi:10.2105/AJPH.2005.064980

Afable-Munsuz, A., & Brindis, C. D. (2006). Acculturation and the sexual and reproductive health of Latino youth in the United States: A literature review. *Perspectives on Sexual and Reproductive Health*, 38, 208–219. doi:10.1363/3820806

Blum, R. W., & Mmari, K. N. (2005). *Risk and protective factors affecting adolescent reproductive health in developing countries*. Baltimore, MD: Johns Hopkins Bloomberg School of Public Health. Available at http://whqlibdoc.who.int/publications/2005/9241593652_eng.pdf

Brindis, C., Wolfe, A. L., McCarter, V., Ball, S., & Starbuck-Morales, S. (1995). The association between immigrant status and risk-behavior pattern in Latino adolescents. *Journal of Adolescent Health*, 17, 99–105. doi:10.1016/1054-139X(94)00101-J

Bronfenbrenner, U., & Morris, P. A. (1998). The ecology of developmental processes. In W. Damon (Series Ed.) & R. M. Lerner (Volume Ed), *Handbook of child psychology: Theoretical models of human development* (Vol. 1, pp. 993–1028). New York, NY: Wiley.

Brook, J. S., Whiteman, M., Balka, E. B., Win, P. E., & Gursen, M. D. (1997). African-American and Puerto Rican drug use: A longitudinal study. *Journal of the American Academy of Child & Adolescent Psychiatry*, 36, 1260–1268. doi:10.1097/00004583-199709000-00019

Buriel, R. (1993). Childrearing orientations in Mexican American families: The influence of generation and sociocultural factors. *Journal of Marriage & the Family*, 55, 987–1000. doi:10.2307/352778

Cauce, A. M., & Domenech Rodríguez, M. D. (2002). Latino families: Myth and realities. In. J. M. Contreras, K. A. Kerns, & A. M. Neal-Barnett (Eds.), *Latino children and families in the United States: Current research and future directions* (pp. 3–25). Westport, CT: Praeger.

Cavanagh, S. E. (2007). Peers, drinking, and the assimilation of Mexican American youth. *Sociological Perspectives, 50*, 393–416. doi:10.1525/sop.2007.50.3.393

Chiu, L. H. (1987). Child-rearing attitudes of Chinese, Chinese-American, and Anglo-American mothers. *International Journal of Psychology, 22*, 409–419. doi:10.1080/00207598708246782

Choi, Y. (2008). Diversity within: Subgroup differences of youth problem behaviors among Asian Pacific Islander American Adolescents. *Journal of Community Psychology, 36*, 352–370. doi:10.1002/jcop.20196

Chong, K. (1998). What it means to be Christian: The role of religion in the construction of ethnic identity and boundary among second-generation Korean Americans. *Sociology of Religion, 59*, 259–286. doi:10.2307/3711911

Chung, P. J., Travis, R., Kilpatrick, S., Elliott, M., Lui, C., Khandwala, S., . . . Schuster, M. A. (2007). Acculturation and parent-adolescent communication about sex in Filipino-American families: A community-based participatory research study. *Journal of Adolescent Health, 40*, 543–550. doi:10.1016/j.jadohealth.2007.01.004

Crockett, L. J., Raffaelli, M., & Moilanen, K. (2003). Adolescent sexuality: Behavior and meaning. In G. R. Adams & M. Berzonsky (Eds.), *Handbook of adolescence* (pp. 371–392). Malden, MA: Blackwell.

Crouter, A. C., & Booth, A. (Eds.). (2006). *Romance and sex in adolescence and emerging adulthood: Risks and opportunities.* Mahwah, NJ: Erlbaum.

Deardorff, J., Tschann, J., & Flores, E. (2008). Sexual values among Latino youth: Measurement development using a culturally based approach. *Cultural Diversity and Ethnic Minority Psychology, 14*, 138–146. doi:10.1037/1099-9809.14.2.138

DeLamater, J., & Hyde, J. S. (2004). Conceptual and theoretical issues in studying sexuality in close relationships. In J. H. Harvey, A. Wenzel, & S. Sprecher (Eds.), *The handbook of sexuality in close relationships* (pp. 7–30). Mahwah, NJ: Erlbaum.

Di Mauro, D. (1997). Sexuality research in the United States. In J. Bancroft (Ed.), *Researching sexual behavior: Methodological issues* (pp. 3–8). Bloomington: Indiana University Press.

Diamond, L. M. (2006). Introduction: In search of good sexual-developmental pathways for adolescent girls. *New Directions for Child and Adolescent Development, 2006*, 1–7. doi:10.1002/cd.158

Diamond, L. M., & Savin-Williams, R. C. (2009). Adolescent sexuality. In R. M. Lerner & L. Steinberg (Eds.), *Handbook of adolescent psychology: Vol. 1. Individual bases of adolescent development* (pp. 479–523). Hoboken, NJ: Wiley.

Domenech Rodríguez, M. M., Donovick, M. R., & Crowley, S. L. (2009). Parenting styles in a cultural context: Observations of "protective parenting" in first generation Latinos. *Family Process, 48*, 195–210. doi:10.1111/j.1545-5300.2009.01277.x

Driscoll, A. K., Russell, S., & Crockett, L. (2008). Parenting styles and youth well-being across immigrant generations. *Journal of Family Issues, 29*, 185–209. doi:10.1177/0192513X07307843

East, P. L. (1998). Racial and ethnic differences in girls' sexual, marital, and birth expectations. *Journal of Marriage & the Family, 60*, 150–162. doi:10.2307/353448

East, P. L. (2009). Adolescents' relationships with siblings. In R. M. Lerner & L. Steinberg (Eds.), *Handbook of adolescent psychology: Vol. 2. Contextual influences on adolescent development* (pp. 43–73). Hoboken, NJ: Wiley.

Florsheim, P. (Ed.). (2003). *Adolescent romantic relations and sexual behavior: Theory, research, and practical implications*. Mahwah, NJ: Erlbaum.

Fuligni, A. J. (1998). Authority, autonomy, and parent–adolescent conflict and cohesion: A study of adolescents from Mexican, Chinese, Filipino, and European backgrounds. *Developmental Psychology, 34*, 782–792. doi:10.1037/0012-1649.34.4.782

Furman, W., Brown, B. B., & Feiring, C. (Eds.). (1997). *The development of romantic relationships in adolescence*. New York, NY: Cambridge University Press.

Gardner, W., & Wilcox, B. L. (1993). Political intervention in scientific peer review: Research on adolescent sexual behavior. *American Psychologist, 48*, 972–983. doi:10.1037/0003-066X.48.9.972

Gil, A. G., & Vega, W. A. (1996). Two different worlds: Acculturative stress and personal adjustment among Hispanic adolescent boys. *Journal of Social and Personal Relationships, 13*, 435–456. doi:10.1177/0265407596133008

Gonzales, N. A., Fabrett, F. C., & Knight, G. P. (2009). Acculturation, enculturation, and the psychosocial adaptation of Latino youth. In F. A. Villarruel, G. Carlo, J. M. Contreras, & M. Azmitia (Eds.), *Handbook of U.S. Latino psychology: Developmental and community based perspectives* (pp. 115–134). Thousand Oaks, CA: Sage.

Grau, J. M., Azmitia, M., & Quattlebaum, J. (2009). Latino families: Parenting, relational, and developmental processes. In F. A. Villarruel, G. Carlo, J. M. Contreras, & M. Azmitia (Eds.), *Handbook of U.S. Latino psychology: Developmental and community based perspectives* (pp. 153–169). Thousand Oaks, CA: Sage.

Guilamo-Ramos, V., Bouris, A., Jaccard, J., Lesesne, C., Gonzalez, B., & Kalogerogiannis, K. (2009). Family mediators of acculturation and adolescent sexual behavior among Latino youth. *The Journal of Primary Prevention, 30*, 395–419. doi:10.1007/s10935-009-0180-1

Guilamo-Ramos, V., Jaccard, J., Pena, J., & Goldberg, V. (2005). Acculturation-related variables, sexual initiation, and subsequent sexual behavior among Puerto Rican, Mexican, and Cuban youth. *Health Psychology, 24*, 88–95. doi:10.1037/0278-6133.24.1.88

Guinn, B. (1998). Acculturation and health locus of control among Mexican American adolescents. *Hispanic Journal of Behavioral Sciences, 20*, 492–499. doi:10.1177/07399863980204006

Guttmacher Institute. (2002). *Facts in brief: Teenagers' sexual and reproductive health*. New York, NY: Author.

Hahm, H. C., Lahiff, M., & Guterman, N. B. (2003). Acculturation and parental attachment in Asian-American adolescents' alcohol use. *Journal of Adolescent Health, 33*, 119–129. doi:10.1016/S1054-139X(03)00058-2

Harris, K. M. (1999). The health status and risk behaviors of adolescents in immigrant families. In D. J. Hernandez (Ed.), *Children of immigrants: Health, adjustment, and public assistance* (pp. 286–347). Washington, DC: National Academy Press.

Harris, K. M., Halpern, C. T., Whitsel, E., Hussey, J., Tabor, J., Entzel, P., & Udry J. R. (2009). *The National Longitudinal Study of Adolescent Health: Research design*. Available at http://www.cpc.unc.edu/projects/addhealth/design

Harvey, J. H., Wenzel, A., & Sprecher, S. (Eds.). (2004). *The handbook of sexuality in close relationships*. Mahwah, NJ: Erlbaum.

Huang, K., & Uba, L. (1992). Premarital sexual behavior among Chinese college students in the United States. *Archives of Sexual Behavior, 21*, 227–240. doi:10.1007/BF01542994

Irwin, C. E. (2005). Pubertal timing: Is there any new news? [Editorial]. *Journal of Adolescent Health, 37*, 343–344. doi:10.1016/j.jadohealth.2005.08.014

Jimenez, J., Potts, M. K., & Jimenez, D. R. (2002). Reproductive attitudes and behavior among Latina adolescents. *Journal of Ethnic & Cultural Diversity in Social Work, 11*, 221–249. doi:10.1300/J051v11n03_04

Kang, H., Okazaki, S., Abelmann, N., Kim-Prieto, C., & Lan, S. (2010). Redeeming immigrant parents: How Korean American emerging adults reinterpret their childhood. *Journal of Adolescent Research, 25*, 441–464. doi:10.1177/0743558410361371

Kao, G., & Joyner, G. (2006). Do Hispanic and Asian Adolescents practice panethnicity in friendship choices? *Social Science Quarterly, 87*, 972–992. doi:10.1111/j.1540-6237.2006.00411.x

Kim, J. L. (2009). Asian American women's retrospective reports of their sexual socialization. *Psychology of Women Quarterly, 33*, 334–350. doi:10.1111/j.1471-6402.2009.01505.x

Kim, J. L., & Ward, L. M. (2007). Silence speaks volumes: Parental sexual communication among Asian American emerging adults. *Journal of Adolescent Research, 22*, 3–31. doi:10.1177/0743558406294916

Kim, S. Y., Chen, Q., Li, J., Huang, X., & Moon, U. J. (2009). Parent–child acculturation, parenting, and adolescent depressive symptoms in Chinese immigrant families. *Journal of Family Psychology, 23*, 426–437. doi:10.1037/a0016019

Kim, S. Y., & Wong, V. T. (2002). Assessing Asian and Asian American parenting: A review of the literature. In K. S. Kurasaki, S. Okazaki, & S. Sue (Eds.), *Asian American mental health: Assessment theories and methods* (pp. 185–201). New York, NY: Plenum Press.

King, R. B., & Bratter, J. L. (2007). A path toward interracial marriage: Women's first partners and husbands across racial lines. *The Sociological Quarterly, 48*, 343–369. doi:10.1111/j.1533-8525.2007.00081.x

King, R. B., & Harris, K. M. (2007). Romantic relationships among immigrant adolescents. *The International Migration Review, 41*, 344–370. doi:10.1111/j.1747-7379.2007.00071.x

Kuo, W. H., & St. Lawrence, J. (2006). Sexual behavior and self-reported sexually transmitted diseases (STDs): Comparison between White and Chinese American young people. *Culture, Health & Sexuality, 8*, 335–349. doi:10.1080/13691050600784518

Kwak, K. (2003). Adolescents and their parents: A review of intergenerational family relations for immigrant and non-immigrant families. *Human Development, 46*, 115–136. doi:10.1159/000068581

Lara, M., Gamboa, C., Kahramanian, M. I., Morales, L. S., & Hayes Bautista, D. E. (2005). Acculturation and Latino health in the United States: A review of the literature and its sociopolitical context. *Annual Review of Public Health, 26*, 367–397. doi:10.1146/annurev.publhealth.26.021304.144615

Larsen, L. J. (2004, August). *The foreign-born population in the United States: 2003* (Current Population Reports, P20-551). Washington, DC: U.S. Census Bureau. Available at http://www.census.gov/prod/2004pubs/p20-551.pdf

Lau, M., Markham, C., Lin, H., Flores, G., & Chacko, M. (2009). Dating and sexual attitudes in Asian American adolescents. *Journal of Adolescent Research, 24*, 91–113. doi:10.1177/0743558408328439

Le, T. N., & Kato, T. (2006). The role of peer, parents, and culture in risky sexual behavior for Cambodian and Lao/Mien adolescents. *Journal of Adolescent Health, 38*, 288–296. doi:10.1016/j.jadohealth.2004.12.005

Loue, S. (Ed.). (1998). *Handbook of immigrant health.* New York, NY: Plenum Press.

Manlove, J. S., Ryan, S., & Franzetta, K. (2007). Risk and protective factors associated with the transition to a first sexual relationship with an older partner. *Journal of Adolescent Health, 40*, 135–143. doi:10.1016/j.jadohealth.2006.09.003

McDonald, J. A., Manlove, J., & Ikramullah, E. N. (2009). Immigration measures and reproductive health among Hispanic youth: Findings from the National Longitudinal Survey of Youth, 1997-2003. *Journal of Adolescent Health, 44*, 14–24. doi:10.1016/j.jadohealth.2008.08.001

McLoyd, V. C. (2004). Linking race and ethnicity to culture: Steps along the road from inference to hypothesis testing. *Human Development, 47*, 185–191. doi:10.1159/000077990

Meston, C., Trapnell, P., & Gorzalka, B. (1998). Ethnic, gender, and length-of-residency influences on sexual knowledge and attitudes. *Journal of Sex Research, 35*, 176–188. doi:10.1080/00224499809551931

Okazaki, S. (2002). Influences of culture on Asian Americans' sexuality. *Journal of Sex Research, 39*, 34–41. doi:10.1080/00224490209552117

Pardun, C. J., L'Engle, K. L., & Brown, J. D. (2005). Linking exposure to outcomes: Early adolescents' consumption of sexual content in six media. *Mass Communication & Society, 8*, 75–91. doi:10.1207/s15327825mcs0802_1

Phinney, J. S., Berry, J. W., Vedder, P., & Liebkind, K. (2006). The acculturation experience: Attitudes, identities and behaviors of immigrant youth. In J. W.

Berry, J. S. Phinney, D. L. Sam, & P. Vedder (Eds.), *Immigrant youth in cultural transition: Acculturation, identity, and adaptation across national contexts* (pp. 71–116). Mahwah, NJ: Erlbaum.

Phinney, J. S., Kim-Jo, T., Osorio, S., & Vilhjalmsdottir, P. (2005). Autonomy and relatedness in adolescent-parent disagreements: Ethnic and developmental factors. *Journal of Adolescent Research, 20,* 8–39. doi:10.1177/0743558404271237

Phinney, J. S., Ong, A., & Madden, T. (2000). Cultural values and intergenerational value discrepancies in immigrant and non-immigrant families. *Child Development, 71,* 528–539. doi:10.1111/1467-8624.00162

Pyke, K. (2005). "Generational deserters" and "Black sheep": Acculturative differences among siblings in Asian immigrant families. *Journal of Family Issues, 26,* 491–517. doi:10.1177/0192513X04273578

Raffaelli, M., & Iturbide, M. I. (2009). Sexuality and sexual risk behaviors among Latino adolescents and young adults. In F. A. Villarruel, G. Carlo, J. M. Contreras, & M. Azmitia (Eds.), *Handbook of U.S. Latino psychology: Developmental and community based perspectives* (pp. 399–414). Thousand Oaks, CA: Sage.

Raffaelli, M., & Ontai, L. L. (2001). "She's 16 years old and there's boys calling over to the house": An exploratory study of sexual socialization in Latino families. *Culture, Health & Sexuality, 3,* 295–310. doi:10.1080/13691050152484722

Rivadeneyra, R., & Ward, L. M. (2005). From *Ally McBeal* to *Sábado Gigante:* Contributions of television viewing to the gender role attitudes of Latino adolescents. *Journal of Adolescent Research, 20,* 453–475. doi:10.1177/0743558405274871

Rossi, A. S. (Ed.). (1994). *Sexuality across the life course.* Chicago, IL: University of Chicago Press.

Rumbaut, R. G. (1997). Ties that bind: Immigration and immigrant families in the United States. In A. Booth, A. C. Crouter, & N. Landale (Eds.), *Immigration and the family: Research and policy on U.S. immigrants* (pp. 3–46). Mahwah, NJ: Erlbaum.

Russell, S. T., & Truong, N. L. (2001). Adolescent sexual orientation, race and ethnicity, and school environments: A national study of sexual minority youth of color. In K. K. Kumashiro (Ed.), *Troubling intersections of race and sexuality: Queer students of color and anti-oppressive education* (pp. 113–130). Lanham, MD: Rowman & Littlefield.

Santelli, J. S., Abraido-Lanza, A. F., & Melnikas, A. J. (2009). Editorial: Migration, acculturation, and sexual and reproductive health of Latino adolescents. *Journal of Adolescent Health, 44,* 3–4. doi:10.1016/j.jadohealth.2008.10.135

Schwartz, S. J., Unger, J. B., Zamboanga, B. L., & Szapocznik, J. (2010). Rethinking the concept of acculturation: Implications for theory and research. *American Psychologist, 65,* 237–251. doi:10.1037/a0019330

Shulman, S., & Collins, W. A. (Eds.). (1997). *Romantic relationships in adolescence: Developmental perspectives.* San Francisco, CA: Jossey-Bass.

Silverman, J. G., Decker, M. R., & Raj, A. (2007). Immigration-based disparities in adolescent girls' vulnerability to dating violence. *Maternal and Child Health Journal, 11,* 37–43. doi:10.1007/s10995-006-0130-y

Suárez-Orozco, C., & Suárez-Orozco, M. M. (2001). *Children of immigration.* Cambridge, MA: Harvard University Press.

Sun, S. S., Schubert, C. M., Chumlea, W. C., Roche, A. F., Kulin, H. E., Lee, P. A., . . . Ryan, A. S. (2002). National estimates of the timing of sexual maturation and racial differences among U.S. children. *Pediatrics, 110,* 911–919. doi:10.1542/peds.110.5.911

Tolman, D. L., Striepe, M. I., & Harmon, T. (2003). Gender matters: Constructing a model of adolescent sexual health. *Journal of Sex Research, 40,* 4–12. doi:10.1080/00224490309552162

Trejos-Castillo, E., & Vazsonyi, A. T. (2009). Risky sexual behaviors in first and second generation Hispanic immigrant youth. *Journal of Youth and Adolescence, 38,* 719–731. doi:10.1007/s10964-008-9369-5

Tseng, V., & Fuligni, A. J. (2000). Parent-adolescent language use and relationships among immigrant families with East Asian, Filipino, and Latin American backgrounds. *Journal of Marriage & the Family, 62,* 465–476. doi:10.1111/j.1741-3737.2000.00465.x

Updegraff, K. A., McHale, S. M., Whiteman, S. D., Thayer, S. M., & Delgado, M. Y. (2005). Adolescent sibling relationships in Mexican American families: Exploring the role of familism. *Journal of Family Psychology, 19,* 512–522. doi:10.1037/0893-3200.19.4.512

Valenzuela, A. (1999). Gender roles and settlement activities among children and their immigrant families. *American Behavioral Scientist, 42,* 720–742. doi:10.1177/0002764299042004009

Vanoss Marín, B., Coyle, K. K., Gómez, C. A., Carvajal, S. C., & Kirby, D. B. (2000). Older boyfriends and girlfriends increase risk of sexual initiation in young adolescents. *Journal of Adolescent Health, 27,* 409–418. doi:10.1016/S1054-139X(00)00097-5

Varela, R. E., Vernberg, E. M., Sanchez-Sosa, J., Riveros, A., Mitchell, M., & Mashunkashey, J. (2004). Parenting style of Mexican, Mexican American, and Caucasian-non-Hispanic families: Social context and cultural influences. *Journal of Family Psychology, 18,* 651–657. doi:10.1037/0893-3200.18.4.651

Ward, L. M. (2003). Understanding the role of entertainment media in the sexual socialization of American youth: A review of empirical research. *Developmental Review, 23,* 347–388. doi:10.1016/S0273-2297(03)00013-3

Yau, J. P., Tasopoulos-Chan, M., & Smetana, J. (2009). Disclosure to parents about everyday activities among American adolescents from Mexican, Chinese, and European backgrounds. *Child Development, 80,* 1481–1498. doi:10.1111/j.1467-8624.2009.01346.x

Zane, N., & Mak, W. (2003). Major approaches to the measurement of acculturation among ethnic minority populations: A content analysis and an alternative empirical strategy. In K. M. Chun, P. B. Organista, & G. Marín (Eds.), *Acculturation: Advances in theory, measurement, and applied research* (pp. 39–60). Washington, DC: American Psychological Association. doi:10.1037/10472-005

Zhou, M. (1997). Growing up American: The challenge confronting immigrant children and children of immigrants. *Annual Review of Sociology, 23*, 63–95. doi:10.1146/annurev.soc.23.1.63

Zhou, M., & Kim, S. S. (2006). Community forces, social capital, and educational achievement: The case of supplementary education in the Chinese and Korean immigrant communities. *Harvard Educational Review, 76*, 1–29.

6

IMMIGRANT GENERATIONAL STATUS AND DELINQUENCY IN ADOLESCENCE: SEGMENTED ASSIMILATION AND RACIAL–ETHNIC DIFFERENCES

HOAN N. BUI

[Handwritten margin notes: ✱ Research in the 20th century suggest that immigrants and their children are involved in lots of crimes. Additionally, research suggests that if immigrant assimilate to their host culture faster there will be more positive outcomes for these groups. ✱ Resettlement time and assimilation predict crime amongst immigrants and their children? ← Very old research, sounds bias!!]

Research on the relationship between immigration and crime has been conducted since the early 20th century in response to public concerns about negative impacts of immigration on society. Immigrants and their children were perceived as disproportionately engaging in criminal activity. Theories of crime and delinquency developed in the first half of the 20th century suggest direct or indirect links of the crime problem to adverse social conditions in the resettlement community and immigrants' unsuccessful adaptation (Miller, 1958; Sellin, 1938; Shaw & McKay, 1942). These theories reflect early assimilation perspective that assumes a positive impact of assimilation, the necessity of assimilation for upward mobility, and the linear relationship between resettlement time and assimilation (Gordon, 1964). Empirical

This research used data from Add Health, a program project directed by Kathleen Mullan Harris and designed by J. Richard Udry, Peter S. Bearman, and Kathleen Mullan Harris at the University of North Carolina at Chapel Hill and funded by Eunice Kennedy Shriver National Institute of Child Health and Human Development Grant P01-HD31921, with cooperative funding from 23 other federal agencies and foundations. Special acknowledgment is due Ronald R. Rindfuss and Barbara Entwisle for assistance in the original design. Information on how to obtain the Add Health data files is available on the Add Health website (http://www.cpc.unc.edu/addhealth). No direct support was received from Grant P01-HD31921 for this analysis.

research has challenged this perspective and has shown that the foreign born, compared with their native-born counterparts, have had lower levels of crime involvement and have been less likely to engage in risk behavior (Butcher & Piehl, 2005; Harris, 1998; Immigration Commission, 1911; National Commission on Law Observance and Enforcement, 1932; Rumbaut, 1999, 2005b). These research findings, which are often called the *immigrant paradox*, suggest negative effects of assimilation. Prior studies that explored the relationship between immigration and crime, however, often failed to make comparisons across racial–ethnic groups. Consequently, the role of race–ethnicity in adaptation experiences and outcomes has not been well understood. Limited research on the immigration–delinquency link has indicated no generational differences in delinquency among some social groups for different types of offenses (Bui, 2005). This raises the question of the universal negative effects of assimilation on delinquency. The present study addresses this question by examining self-reported delinquency to determine the immigrant paradox in delinquency across racial–ethnic groups and to identify factors that may contribute to racial–ethnic differences in the relationship between immigration status and delinquency.

CONCEPTUAL FRAMEWORK

Assimilation perspectives have been used to understand the immigration–crime link. The classic model of assimilation emphasizes the benefits of assimilation for upward social mobility (Gordon, 1964), but the recent assimilation perspective (or acculturation perspective) suggests negative impacts of assimilation on behavior through the process of acculturation (Rumbaut, 1999). As the first step of assimilation, acculturation occurs on a number of dimensions, including the incorporation of the language, cultural beliefs, values, and behavior of the host society (Berry, 1980). Acculturation may facilitate delinquency through its negative effects on family relationships, peer pressure, and education. It has been argued that acculturation to American culture often challenges the immigrants' traditional hierarchical parent–child relations and other cultural mandates by which children are to submit to parental authority and control (Lin & Liu, 1993). Because children typically acculturate more rapidly than their parents, the controlling role of parents can diminish when acculturated children adopt values and beliefs that are in conflict with those of their parents, who tend to experience acculturation at a slower pace (Rumbaut, 2005a; Szapocznik & Kurtines, 1993). Acculturated youths are also seen as more susceptible to peer pressure because they tend to spend more time with friends and engage in activities outside the home than less acculturated youths (Rueschenberg

& Buriel, 1989). Increasing values of peer friendship can distance youths from the family, diminish the family bond, and make the task of parental monitoring and supervision more difficult and less effective. Negative effects of acculturation on education are also reflected in the erosion of educational aspiration and achievement among second- and third-generation adolescents (Fuligni, 1997; Rumbaut, 2005a). A lack of family relationships, peer pressure, and low levels of academic involvement and achievement can facilitate delinquency (Hirschi, 1969).

More recent scholarship suggests that the effect of assimilation is not always positive or negative (Zhou & Bankston, 2006). Rather, the assimilation process is segmented to produce various outcomes. The segmented assimilation perspective emphasizes the social context of immigration resettlement as an important factor in the life experiences of the second generation and suggests that assimilation outcomes depend on the characteristics of the social sectors into which particular immigrant groups assimilate (Portes & Zhou, 1993). One path of assimilation facilitates the integration of immigrants and their children into the White middle class, whereas another path can lead to permanent poverty and assimilation to the underclass. Portes and Zhou (1993) identified the social contexts that create risks to downward assimilation. First, racial–ethnic prejudice and discrimination can make skin color, physical features, and different culture barriers to social integration and upward mobility for particular immigrant groups. Second, the concentration of immigrant households in inner-city neighborhoods can expose second-generation children to the adversarial subculture that marginalized native-born youths have developed to cope with their own difficult situations. Assimilation into this subculture can block parental expectations and plans for intergenerational mobility. The third contextual source of vulnerability is the absence of mobility ladders for new immigrants and their children reflected in a lack of well-paying and stable jobs for unskilled or semiskilled persons as a result of globalization and the deindustrialization of the U.S. economy.

Downward assimilation can create a great risk for crime and delinquency. In the United States, race and class tend to overlap and facilitate social isolation and residential segregation (Massey & Denton, 1993). Race and class segregation create a concentration of poverty, intensify social isolation of low-income individuals, and lead to social disorganization, which in turn facilitates crime and delinquency (Massey & Denton, 1993; Sampson & Wilson, 1995; Shihadeh & Shrum, 2004). Race and class segregations also contribute to delinquency through children's negative school experiences, which are determined in large part by family socioeconomic status (Rumbaut, 2005a). When schools are segregated by students' socioeconomic status, they differ in teacher quality, staffing ratios, school climate, and teachers' expectations, which are associated with students' academic achievement and dropout rates (McNeal, 1997; Pong, 1998;

Rumberger & Willms, 1992). Empirical research has shown positive relationships among poor academic performance, dropping out, and delinquency (Cernkovich & Giordano, 1992; Maguin & Loeber, 1996).

A combination of acculturation and segmented assimilation perspectives can be useful for understanding racial and ethnic differences in the relationship between immigration status and delinquency. First-generation youths can have lower levels of delinquency because a lack of acculturation can help maintain stronger family attachment and stricter parental control, thus protecting them from negative influences from outside the home, including deviant subcultures and peer pressure (Lee, 1998; Rueschenberg & Buriel, 1989). In addition, high levels of academic performance among first-generation children, which are associated with higher aspiration among immigrant parents for their children's education and children's greater effort on education, can also prevent delinquency (Fuligni, 1997; Kao & Tienda, 1995; Rumbaut, 1999). Among the second and later generations, poor school quality, negative school outcomes, and criminogenic environments that are associated with low socioeconomic status will facilitate delinquency when acculturation reduces family attachment, decreases parental control, and increases peer associations.

In short, the literature suggests that assimilation tends to occur at the second and later generations and can produce positive or negative outcomes, depending on the social context of assimilation. Race–ethnicity and social class are major factors that determine the social sectors into which immigrants' children are assimilated and subsequent adaptation outcomes. Because race–ethnicity and social class tend to overlap (Massey & Denton, 1993), I hypothesized in this study that the immigrant paradox in delinquency does not exist for all racial–ethnic groups, and groups that possess fewer economic and social resources will experience higher levels of delinquency among the second and later generations.

METHOD

Sample and Data

Data for the present study were collected by the National Longitudinal Study of Adolescent Health (Add Health). The Add Health project used a complex sampling design, which included stratification (based on regions) and clustering (based on schools), to select a nationally representative and probability-based sample of students from Grades 7 through 12 in the United States. A school-based design was used to sample high schools and feeder middle schools across the country. Students from these schools (a total of 132 schools) formed the sample for the In-School data with more than 90,000 cases. A sample of these students were selected to participate in the In-Home data collection phase. In-Home data were collected through face-to-face interviews conducted at home with selected students and their parents or parent figures. Contextual data, which were created with information from the 1990 U.S. census and other data sources, include characteristics of students' residential locations. The present study used In-Home data (Wave I) collected between September 1994 and December 1995 combined with contextual data (Wave I). The original sample included 20,745 students. After cases with age values above 20 years old and cases with missing values on weights, racial–ethnic identification, and immigration status were eliminated, 18,036 cases remained in the study for data analysis. The ages of student respondents ranged from 12 to 20, with a mean of 16.7 years. Males accounted for 49% of the sample ($n = 8,838$); non-Hispanic Whites (hereafter Whites) 52.7% ($n = 9,503$), non-Hispanic Blacks (hereafter Blacks) 21.6% ($n = 3,893$), Asians 7% ($n = 1,265$); Hispanics 17.3% ($n = 3,116$), and students with other racial–ethnic identifications 1.4% ($n = 259$). Regarding immigration status, the first generation accounted for 8% of the sample ($n = 1,454$), second generation 15.2% ($n = 2,736$), and third and later generations 76.2% ($n = 13,846$). Table 6.1 summarizes the distribution of immigration status by racial–ethnic identification.

Variables

Consistent with acculturation and segmented assimilation frameworks, seven groups of variables were used for data analysis, including outcome variables, five groups of independent variables (immigration status, family background, family relationships, school experience, and neighborhood context), and control variables (demographic characteristics). Principal-component factor and scale reliability analyses were conducted to determine scale items for scale (or composite) variables. The results of factorial analysis (not shown)

TABLE 6.1
Immigration Status by Race and Ethnicity

Racial group	First generation n (%)	Second generation n (%)	Third generation n (%)	Total n (%)
Non-Hispanic White	64 (4.4)	544 (19.9)	8,895 (64.2)	9,503 (52.7)
Non-Hispanic Black	75 (5.2)	234 (8.6)	3,584 (25.9)	3,893 (21.6)
Asian	557 (38.3)	499 (18.2)	209 (1.5)	1,265 (7.0)
Hispanic	721 (49.6)	1,384 (50.6)	1,011 (7.3)	3,116 (17.3)
Other	37 (2.5)	75 (1.7)	147 (1.1)	259 (1.4)
Total	1,454 (100)	2,736 (100)	13,846 (100)	18,036 (100)

indicated that scale items for each scale variable loaded on a common factor with loadings greater than .45 and that all scale variables had internal consistency values (Cronbach's alphas) greater than .60.

Outcome Variables

Because of differences in offense nature and motivation, self-reported delinquency was measured by two separate variables. The scale of Violent Delinquency consists of seven items asking if a student engaged in the following acts within 12 months prior to the interview: (a) used or threatened with a weapon, (b) took part in a group fight, (c) took part in a serious physical fight, (d) seriously injured someone, (e) got into a physical fight, (f) pulled a knife or gun on someone, (g) shot or stabbed someone. The first four items have four response categories (0 = *never*; 1= *1 or 2 times*; 2 = *3 or 4 times*; 3 = *5 or more times*), and the last three items have three response categories (0 = *never*; 1 = *once*; 2 = *more than once*). The actual total score of violent delinquency ranges from 0 to 18, with an alpha value of .786. The scale of property delinquency includes seven items asking if a student engaged in the following behavior within 12 months prior to the interview: (a) burglarized a building, (b) stole something worth less than $50; (c) stole something worth more than $50; (d) damaged property; (e) shoplifted; (f) stole a car; (g) sold drugs. Each scale item has four response categories (0 = *never*; 1 = *1 or 2 times*; 2 = *3 or 4 times*; 3 = *5 or more times*). The actual total score of property delinquency ranges from 0 to 21, with an alpha value of .767.

Independent and Control Variables

Immigration status has been used as a measure of assimilation and acculturation (Isralowitz, 2004; Nagasawa, Qian, & Wong, 2001). Although assimilation varies among individuals, first-generation youths, as a group, tend to experience a lower level of assimilation than those in later generations (Buriel, Calzada, &Vasquez, 1982). Consistent with immigration literature (Portes, 1996; Rumbaut, 1998) and the U.S. Census Bureau (2001), a student's immigration status is defined by his or her birthplace and those of his or her parents. The first generation includes foreign-born students with both foreign-born parents; the second generation American-born students with at least one foreign-born parent, and the third and later generation American-born students with both American-born parents (for convenience, this group is referred as the *third-plus generation*). Family background was measured in the present study by three separate variables, including family structure, family's annual income, and parents' education. Measures of family relationships focus on the importance of family attachment, parental supervision, and parent–child conflicts. School experience was measured by academic performance (grade point average [GPA] for math, science, English, and history), attachment to school, commitment to school, and troubles at school. Measures of neighborhood context emphasize the concentration of disadvantage (poverty, unemployment, reliance on public assistance, and female head of family), neighborhood incivility (problem of drugs and trash), and exposure to violence. Age, sex, and race–ethnicity are control variables.

For comparison purposes, I created a variable representing Immigration Status × Race–Ethnicity, with three generations for each racial–ethnic group and the "other" category (a total of 13 categories). Missing values were handled in several ways. For categorical variables, a missing category was created for missing-value cases. Because the missing-value category is of little interest for the study, statistics for the missing category are not reported. Missing values for interval variables were handled in two ways, depending on the proportion of missing values. Family income had the greatest proportion of cases with missing values (27%), followed by academic performance for English, math, science, and history (5%–15%). On the basis of the assumption that incomes and academic performance vary with immigration status and race–ethnicity, missing values in household incomes and academic performance were imputed with the predicted marginal means from regression for 13 Immigration Generation × Race–Ethnicity categories. For income, observed household incomes were regressed on family structure, parents' immigration status, race–ethnicity, education, and work status as well as urbanicity; for academic performance, observed grades were regressed on family incomes, parents' education, and students' immigration status and race–ethnicity. For other interval variables, because the number of cases with missing values was small (less than 2%), mean replacement was applied and correspondent dichotomous variables (missing vs. nonmissing) were included in data analysis to check the bias of mean replacement.[1] For other interval variables (with fewer than 2% missing-value cases), mean replacement was applied, and correspondent dichotomous variables (missing vs. nonmissing) were included in data analysis to check the bias of mean replacement. Results of data analysis (not reported) indicated that the coefficients for the missing and nonmissing variables were not significant, meaning that mean replacements did not cause bias to the estimates. (See Appendix 6.1 for variable description and measurement.)

---

[1]Multiple imputation is not feasible for complex sampling designed data like Add Health because of a lack of programs for multiple imputation that can take into account sampling errors caused by the complex sampling design.

Add Health data have three weights, including poststratification weight, which is based on region (West, Midwest, South, and Northeast); cluster weight, which is based on schools; and grand sample weight. All three weights are included in the data analysis. To adjust sampling errors caused by the complex sampling design, a special statistical software package, SPSS for complex sample design, was used for statistical analysis.

Bivariate Analysis

Table 6.2 summarizes the results of one-way analysis of variance (for interval variables) and cross-tab analysis (for categorical variables) used to determine bivariate relationships of immigration status with delinquency as well as other independent and control variables. For each racial–ethnic group, the first generation served as the reference; natural log transformation was applied to the delinquency variables to adjust their skewed distributions. The results show that generational differences in delinquency exist in most of the racial–ethnic groups. Consistent with acculturation perspective, second- and third-plus-generation Whites and Hispanics as well as third-plus-generation Blacks have significantly higher levels of violent delinquency than their first-generation counterparts (because the "other" category is not an interest of the present study, statistics pertaining to this group are not reported). Similarly, second-generation Whites and Asians as well as second- and third-plus-generation Blacks and Hispanics have significantly higher levels of property delinquency than their first-generation counterparts. Contrary to the acculturation perspective, there are no significant differences in violent delinquency among Asians in all three generations and between first- and second-generation Blacks; for property delinquency, no significant differences exist between the first and third generations for Whites and Asians.

Bivariate relationships of generation status with independent and control variables also vary across racial–ethnic groups. Compared with their first-generation counterparts, second- and third-plus-generation Blacks, Asians, and Hispanics are significantly younger. For family background, there are no generational differences in family structure for Blacks and Whites, but third-plus-generation Asians and Hispanics are significantly less likely to report living with two biological parents (hereafter *two-parent families*). There are also no generational differences in family income for Whites and Blacks, but second- and third-plus-generation Asians and Hispanics have significantly higher levels of family income. Second- and/or third-plus-generation Whites, Blacks, and Asians have lower levels of parents' education, but third-plus-generation Hispanics have a higher level of parents' education. Regarding

TABLE 6.2
Descriptive Statistics: Racial–Ethnic Groups by Generations

Variable	Non-Hispanic White			Non-Hispanic Black			Asian			Hispanic		
	1	2	3	1	2	3	1	2	3	1	2	3
Violent delinquency	0.36	0.55*	0.57**	0.46	0.64	0.84**	0.45	0.55	0.41	0.56	0.78***	0.86***
Property delinquency	0.34	0.53*	0.50	0.26	0.55**	0.45*	0.49	0.66*	0.51	0.36	0.69***	0.67***
Age	16.28	15.83	15.90	17.34	16.28**	16.12**	16.45	15.91*	15.67*	16.61	15.84*	15.85*
Male (%)	54.00	53.00	51.20	58.00	48.60	49.10	48.10	50.10	54.60	47.90	49.50	53.90
Two bio parents (%)	59.20	57.20	58.00	27.20	24.00	28.00	74.70	77.10	55.60***	56.10	58.60	41.40***
Family income	44.41	53.69	49.30	33.78	32.30	30.87	37.95	58.05**	55.55***	22.01	31.90***	40.15***
Parents' college (%)	30.60	17.80*	14.30**	16.00	11.40	5.40***	28.20	29.10	16.70*	2.60	3.50	6.30*
Parental control	1.95	1.82	1.81	1.72	1.38	1.47	1.88	1.98	2.16	2.41	2.25	1.89**
Family attachment	15.97	15.18	15.16	14.42	13.68	13.57	14.96	14.66	15.87*	15.78	15.23*	15.36
Parent–child conflicts (%)	32.30	36.80	39.10	25.00	26.00	31.40	36.10	38.70	29.20*	29.10	41.80***	39.30**
Grade point average	3.13	2.91	2.88*	2.76	2.75	2.57*	3.27	3.08***	2.87***	2.65	2.62	2.66
Troubles in school	2.97	4.34***	4.33***	3.67	4.03	4.13	3.32	3.70	3.94*	3.28	3.91**	4.51***
School attachment	18.22	18.19	18.67	19.06	17.94	18.08	18.92	18.83	18.34	19.33	18.19***	18.43***
School commitment	9.29	8.62**	8.58***	9.42	8.64***	8.47***	9.21	9.31	9.08	8.02	8.11	8.17
Concentrated disadvantage	0.22	0.25	0.28*	0.48	0.50	0.67*	0.31	0.23*	0.27	0.51	0.48	0.38***
Neighborhood incivility	3.93	4.41***	4.49***	5.03	4.90	5.44	4.25	4.16	4.27	4.58	4.64	4.90*
Exposure to violence	0.07	0.12	0.09	0.25	0.31	0.29	0.11	0.17	0.04*	0.20	0.29***	0.27

Note. First generation is used as the reference. Statistics are means if not indicated otherwise. Measures of violent and property delinquency are logged. 1 = first generation; 2 = second generation; 3 = third generation.
*p < .05. *p < .01. ***p < .001.

family relationships, there are no generational differences for Whites and Blacks, but second- and/or third-plus-generation Hispanics experienced a significantly lower level of parental control and family attachment and a higher level of parent–child conflict. Inconsistent with the acculturation perspective, second- and third-plus-generation Asians reported a significantly higher level of family attachment and a lower level of parent–child conflict.

For school experience, there is no generational difference in academic performance (measured by GPA) for Hispanics, but third-plus-generation Whites and Blacks as well as second- and third-plus-generation Asians have significantly lower academic performance than their first-generation counterparts; second- and/or third-plus-generation Whites, Hispanics, and Asians also experienced higher levels of troubles in school. In addition, second- and third-plus-generation Hispanics, Blacks, and Whites reported significantly lower levels of school attachment or school commitment. Regarding neighborhood context, third-plus-generation Whites and Blacks experienced higher levels, and second-generation Asians and third-plus-generation Hispanics lower levels, of concentrated disadvantage than their first-generation counterparts. There were no generational differences in neighborhood incivility for Blacks and Asians and no generational differences in exposure to violence for Whites and Blacks, but second- and third-plus-generation Whites as well as third-plus-generation Hispanics reported higher levels of neighborhood incivility; second- and third-plus-generation Hispanics reported a higher level, but third-plus-generation Asians a lower level, of exposure to violence. In the next section, I describe how multivariate analysis was used to determine how racial and ethnic differences in family background, family relationship, school experience, and neighborhood context contribute to racial–ethnic disparity in the relationship between immigration status and delinquency.

Multivariate Analysis

General linear models (GLM) with hierarchical analysis (Jang, 2002) were used to determine generational differences in delinquency and factors contributing to these differences. For each racial/ethnic group, the first generation was used as reference. For each type of delinquency, six models of hierarchical regression were created. The initial model (Model 1), which included the outcome variable (delinquency), immigration status, and control variables, was used to determine the relationship between immigration status and delinquency while demographic characteristics (age and sex) were accounted for. Next, four groups of variables measuring family background (Model 2), family relationships (Model 3), school experience (Model 4), and neighborhood context (Model 5) were alternatively included to assess the contribution of each group of variables to generational differences in delinquency for each racial–ethnic group. Finally, the full model (Model 6) was used to estimate the sole effect of each independent variable while the effects of other variables in the model were taken into account.

Violent Delinquency

Table 6.3 presents the parameter estimates (coefficients) from GLM for violent delinquency. The initial model (Model 1) indicates that when age and sex are accounted for, there are no differences in violent delinquency

TABLE 6.3
General Linear Model: Parameter Estimates for Violent Delinquency

Variable	Model					
	1	2	3	4	5	6
Non-Hispanic White						
Second generation	.17	.15	.12	.04	.12	.01
Third generation	.20*	.17*	.14	.08	.16	.00
Non-Hispanic Black						
Second generation	.20	.18	.13	.08	.14	−.01
Third generation	.39**	.36**	.33*	.23	.33*	.14
Asian						
Second generation	.08	.09	.05	.03	.04	.02
Third generation	−.09	−.12	−.07	−.17*	−.05	−.16
Hispanic						
Second generation	.21***	.21***	.13**	.14***	.13***	.04
Third generation	.26***	.26***	.21***	.20***	.19***	.10*
Age	−.03***	−.03***	−.04***	−.04***	−.03***	−.05***
Male	.38***	.39***	.42***	.32***	.34***	.31***
Family income		−.00**				−.00
Two biological parents		−.14***				−.05*
Parents' college degree		−.18***				−.09***
Parental control			−.01			−.00
Family attachment			−.03***			−.01**
Conflict with parents			.27***			.15***
Grade point average				−.11***		−.09***
Troubles in school				.06***		.04***
School attachment				−.02***		−.01**
School commitment				−.03***		−.02***
Neighborhood incivility					.04***	.02***
Concentrated disadvantage					−.03	−.01
Exposure to violence					.60***	.50***
R^2	.09	.11	.15	.20	.20	.30

Note. First generation was used as the reference group. Violent delinquency was logged. Model 1 = demographic; Model 2 = family background; Model 3 = family relationships; Model 4 = school experience; Model 6 = full model.
*$p < .05$. **$p < .01$. ***$p < .001$.

between the first and second generations for Whites and Blacks, but third-plus-generation Whites and Blacks have significantly higher levels of violent delinquency than their first-generation counterparts (the coefficient for third-generation Whites = .20, $t = 2.35$, $p = .02$; the coefficient for third-generation Blacks = .39, $t = 2.84$, $p > .00$). Second- and third-plus-generation Hispanics also have significantly higher levels of violent delinquency (the coefficient for second-generation Hispanics = .21, $t = 4.47$, $p < .00$; the coefficient for third-generation Hispanics = .26, $t = 5.01$, $p < .00$). However, there is no significant generational difference in violent delinquency among Asians. The results in Models 2, 3, 4 and 5 indicate that most of the family background, family relationship, school experience, and neighborhood context variables, except parental control and concentrated disadvantage, are significantly associated with violent delinquency. Age, family income, family structure, parents' education, family attachment, GPA, school attachment, and school commitment are negatively associated with violent delinquency, but being male, conflicts with parent, troubles in school, neighborhood incivility, and exposure to violence are positively associated with violent delinquency. The full model (Model 6) indicates no significant generational differences in violent delinquency for Whites, Blacks, and Asians, but third-plus-generation Hispanics have a significantly higher level of violent delinquency than their first-generation counterparts, suggesting that all independent and control variables only partially explain generational differences in violent delinquency among Hispanics (the coefficient for third-generation Hispanics reduces 62% in Model 6 and remains significant). Most family background, family relationship, school experience, and neighborhood context variables remain significant, except for family income, parental control, and concentrated disadvantage, which are not significant predictors for violent delinquency.

Additional analyses (results are not shown) were performed to examine the relationship of violent delinquency with each independent variable and its contribution to generational differences in violent delinquency for each racial–ethnic group. Results of multivariate and bivariate analyses (Table 6.2) indicate that not all independent variables have significant relationships with violent delinquency, and their contributions to generational differences in delinquency also vary across racial–ethnic groups. For Whites, lower levels of parents' education, academic performance, and commitment to school as well as higher levels of school troubles, concentration of disadvantage, and neighborhood incivility apparently contributed to a higher level of violent delinquency among the third-plus generation,[2] with school variables contributing

---

[2]Separate analysis shows that concentrated disadvantage is significantly and positively associated with violent delinquency for Whites, but it is significantly and negatively associated with property delinquency for Hispanics.

the most (the coefficient for third-generation Whites decreases 99% in Model 6 and becomes insignificant). For Blacks, lower levels of parents' education, academic performance, and school commitment apparently contribute to higher levels of violent delinquency among the third-plus generation, with the most contribution also coming from school variables (the coefficient for third-plus-generation Blacks decreases 64% in Model 6 and becomes insignificant). Among Asians, lower academic performance but more school troubles apparently contribute to violent delinquency among the third-plus generation, which already has a low level of delinquency, because controlling these variables further lowers violent delinquency among the third-plus generation (the coefficient for third-plus-generation Asians in Model 4 decreases 90% and becomes significant). For Hispanics, lower levels of family and school attachment but higher levels of parent–child conflict, school troubles, neighborhood incivility, and exposure to violence apparently contribute to higher levels of violent delinquency among the second generation and partially contribute to higher levels of violent delinquency among the third-plus generation (in Model 6, the coefficient for second-generation Hispanics decreases 81% and becomes insignificant; the coefficient for third-plus-generation Hispanics decreases 52% but remains significant).

Property Delinquency

Table 6.4 reports the parameter estimates (coefficients) from GLM for property delinquency. The initial model (Model 1) shows that after age and sex are taken into account, there is no generational difference in property delinquency among Whites, but second- and third-plus-generation Blacks and Hispanics as well as second-generation Asians have significantly higher levels of property delinquency than their first-generation counterparts (the coefficient for second-generation Blacks = .31, $t = 2.82$, $p < .00$; the coefficient for third-generation Blacks = .22, $t = 2.52$, $p = .03$; the coefficient for second-generation Hispanics = .33, $t = 7.55$, $p < .00$; the coefficient for third-generation Hispanics = .30, $t = .6.19$, $p < .00$; the coefficient for second-generation Asians = .16, $t = 2.11$, $p = .04$). The results in Models 2, 3, 4, and 5 indicate that except for parent's education, family income, and school commitment, most of the variables measuring family background, family relationship, school experience, and neighborhood context are significantly associated with property delinquency. Family structure, parental control, family attachment, academic performance, and school attachment are negatively associated with property delinquency, but conflict with parents, troubles in school, neighborhood incivility, and exposure to violence are positively associated with property delinquency. Concentrated disadvantage is negatively associated with property delinquency in an unexpected direction. Perhaps neighborhoods

TABLE 6.4
General Linear Model: Parameter Estimates for Property Delinquency

Variable	Model 1	2	3	4	5	6
Non-Hispanic White						
Second generation	.19	.18	.12	.07	.17	.01
Third generation	.17	.16	.09	.04	.16	−.01
Non-Hispanic Black						
Second generation	.31**	.29**	.27*	.26*	.28*	.18
Third generation	.22*	.21*	.18*	.14	.23*	.12
Asian						
Second generation	.16*	.16*	.13	.12	.12	−.00
Third generation	−.01	−.04	.01	−.08	−.00	−.11
Hispanic						
Second generation	.33***	.33***	.24***	.25***	.27***	.17***
Third generation	.30***	.27***	.22***	.20***	.23***	.13**
Age	.00	.00	−.02***	−.01	−.00	−.02***
Male	.21***	.22***	.25***	.16***	.19***	.17***
Family income		.00				−.00*
Two biological parents		−.12***				−.02
Parents' college degree		−.02				.03
Parental control			−.02***			−.02**
Family attachment			−.04***			−.02***
Conflict with parents			.25***			.16***
Grade point average				−.06***		−.05***
Troubles in school				.07***		.06***
School attachment				−.02***		−.01**
School commitment				−.01		−.01
Neighborhood incivility					.02***	.01
Concentrated disadvantage					−.15***	−.13***
Exposure to violence					.40***	.32***
R^2	.03	.04	.11	.15	.09	.21

Note. First generation was used as the reference group. Property delinquency was logged. Model 1= demographic; Model 2 = family background; Model 3 = family relationship; Model 4 = school experience; Model 6 = full model.
$*p < .05.$ $**p < .01.$ $***p < .001.$

that experience high levels of concentrated disadvantage (measured by poverty, unemployment, reliance on public assistance, and female head of family) are too poor to have valuable property to attract potential offenders. The full model (Model 6) shows no significant generational differences in property delinquency for Whites, Blacks, and Asians, but it shows that second- and third-plus-generation Hispanics have significantly higher levels of property delinquency than their first-generation counterparts. This suggests that all independent and control variables only partially contribute to generational differences in property delinquency among Hispanics (in Model 6, the coefficients for second- and third-plus-generation Hispanics are reduced 48% and 57% but remain significant). Parents' education and school commitment are not significant predictors; age, parental control, family attachment, GPA, school attachment, and concentration of disadvantage are negatively associated with property delinquency, but being male, parent–child conflicts, and troubles in school are positively associated with property delinquency. The coefficients for family structure and neighborhood incivility become insignificant, but the coefficient for family income becomes significant, suggesting the interaction of these variables with family background, family relationships, school experience, and neighborhood context variables.

Similar to the case of violent delinquency, additional analyses (results are not shown) were performed to examine the relationship of property delinquency with each independent variable and its contribution to generational differences in property delinquency for each racial–ethnic group. Results of multivariate and bivariate analyses (Table 6.2) indicate that the contribution of independent variables to generational differences in property delinquency vary across racial–ethnic groups. For Blacks, lower levels of parents' education, academic performance, and commitment to school apparently contribute to higher levels of property delinquency among the second and third-plus generations, with school variables contributing the most (in Model 6, the coefficients for second-generation and third-plus-generation Blacks decrease 42% and 45% and become insignificant). Among Asians, lower academic performance and concentration of disadvantage apparently explain a higher level of property delinquency among the second generation (the coefficient for second-generation Asians decreases 99% in Model 6 and becomes insignificant). For Hispanics, a lower proportion of two-parent families and lower levels of parental control, family attachment, school attachment, and concentrated disadvantage but higher levels of parent–child conflict, trouble in school, neighborhood incivility, and exposure to violence partially explain higher levels of property delinquency among the second and third-plus generation (in Model 6, the coefficients for second-generation and third-plus-generation Hispanics reduce 48% and 57% and remain significant).

DISCUSSION AND CONCLUSION

In summary, data analysis indicates that higher levels of delinquency among second- and/or third-generation Whites, Blacks, and Asians are largely explained by higher levels of negative school experiences and lower levels of parents' education. For Hispanics, higher levels of negative family and school experiences as well as negative neighborhood conditions contribute to higher levels of delinquency among the second and third generations. These findings suggest that the immigrant paradox in delinquency and factors contributing to it vary with racial–ethnic groups, reflecting group differences in the pattern of immigration and resettlement experiences. For Hispanics, factors that contribute to the immigrant paradox in delinquency are likely a result of disadvantaged social conditions experienced by Hispanic immigrants. Often coming to the United States as farm workers or manual laborers, immigrants from Mexico and Latin America tend to have a low level of education; fewer than half (44%) of Latino immigrants have completed high school, and only 10% have college educations (Portes & Rumbaut, 2006). In addition, the immigration category of most Latino immigrants (temporary working visa, family reunification, or undocumented immigrant) often makes them ineligible for government assistance. Data from the study show that the proportions of first- and second-generation Hispanics in the study who have two parents with college degrees (2.6% and 3.5% respectively) are much lower than those among their Asian and White counterparts (17.8%–30.6%). Although the proportion of third-plus-generation Hispanics having both parents with college degrees (6.3%) is higher than among their first- and second-generation counterparts, this proportion is still much lower than among third-plus-generation Asians and Whites (16.7% and 14.3% respectively).

A very low level of parents' education among first-generation Hispanics and a lack of government assistance for disadvantaged Hispanic immigrants can serve as a starting point for a cycle of downward mobility that negatively affects later generations. Research has consistently shown the association between family socioeconomic status, school quality, neighborhood environment, and children's academic achievement (Han, 2006; Pong & Hao, 2007; Portes & Hao, 2004; Portes & MacLeod, 1999; Ryabov & Van Hook, 2007). Family background may not affect academic performance of first-generation children because more homework hours and high expectations for children's education among immigrant parents may compensate for their disadvantaged socioeconomic situations, but educational achievement among the second and third generations is heavily influenced by family socioeconomic status (e.g., parents' education, occupation, and income) and the average socioeconomic level of their schools (Caplan, Choy, & Whitmore, 1992; Kao & Tienda, 1995; Portes & MacLeod, 1996; Rumbaut, 2005a). Because socioeconomic status determines residential locations and school quality, Hispanic immigrants have been found to reside in the worst neighborhoods, and their children attend the most segregated schools under the worst conditions (Crosnoe, 2005, 2006; Pong & Hao, 2007). These negative conditions may explain high levels of trouble in school and less commitment to education among second- and third-generation Hispanics, which in turn are associated with high levels of delinquency. Negative neighborhood conditions may further contribute to delinquency problems because gang and vice activities in slums can facilitate dropping out among underachievers, who are likely to be the target of gang membership recruitment and lured into deviant and illegal activities. A relatively lower level of concentration of disadvantage experienced by third-plus-generation Hispanics (M = .38) may not help because it is still much higher than that experienced by their Asian and White counterparts (Ms = .28 and .27). A lower level of concentration of disadvantage, but not low enough to change the community social conditions, may be associated with more delinquency because such situations offer more valuable targets for property crime. In addition, children's poor academic performance and parent–child gaps in acculturation can increase parent–child conflicts, reduce family attachment, and facilitate delinquency among second- and third-plus-generation Hispanics.

The experience of Blacks with the immigrant paradox in delinquency also reflects the social disadvantage experienced by this group. Indeed, data from the study indicate that third-generation Blacks experience a significantly higher level of concentration of disadvantage than their first- and second-generation counterparts, who also experience higher levels of negative neighborhood conditions than Whites and Asians. The negative neighborhood conditions experienced by Blacks reflect a pattern of racial segregation and discrimination rooted in American history and can have strong implications for delinquency (Hacker, 1992). Because neighborhood characteristics are related to school quality, a very high level of concentration of disadvantage experienced by third-generation Blacks can be associated with lower levels of academic performance and school commitment in this group, which in turn are related to delinquency. In addition, criminogenic elements, including adults' criminal activity and gangs, that are often found in disorganized neighborhoods also facilitate delinquency (Shaw & McKay, 1942). A study of life experience of Blacks in U.S. inner-city neighborhoods indicated that high levels of concentration of disadvantage can lead to social isolation and the development of an alternative subculture that emphasizes violence as an adaptation to severe economic and cultural deprivations (Anderson, 1994). A relatively high level of parents' education among first- and second-generation Blacks can be beneficial for children's academic performance under negative neighborhood conditions because parents with high levels of education can positively influence children's education by serving as role models, monitoring children's learning progress, or tutoring and helping with homework (Portes & MacLeod, 1999). A much lower level of parents' education among the third-plus generations can contribute children's negative school experience (e.g., lower academic performance and less commitment to school). The existence of the immigrant paradox in property delinquency but not in violent delinquency among second-generation Blacks suggests the importance of school commitment in preventing property delinquency because a lower level of school commitment among the second generation can be associated with a significantly higher level of property delinquency.

A lack of immigrant paradox in delinquency among Whites and Asians is likely a result of their immigration patterns and relatively advantageous situations. The overall educational achievement among Asian immigrants, with 80% having completed high school and more than 40% having a college education, is higher than the U.S. average; among European, Canadian, and Australian immigrants, 77% have completed high school and 29% have some college education, which is similar to the U.S. average (Portes & Rumbaut, 2006). Immigrants from Asia, Africa, Europe, and Canada are much more likely than those from Mexico and Latin America to arrive in the United States under the professional emigration category and earn higher incomes. A high level of parents' education among first-generation White and Asian immigrants and a lack of racial–ethnic prejudice and discrimination experienced by White immigrants can facilitate intergenerational upward mobility and integration into the middle class. More financial resources can prevent delinquency through better residential locations and thus better schools and education for children. In addition, a high level of education among parents may also facilitate their own acculturation and prevent parent–child conflicts resulting from the acculturation gap between parents and children. This may explain why third-plus-generation Asians experience higher family incomes, a higher level of family attachment, a lower level of parent–child conflict, and a much lower level of exposure to violence than their first- and second-generation counterparts. Because family background (e.g., parents' education, occupation, and income) can affect residential locations and children's education, a lower level of parents' education experienced by third-plus-generation Whites may lead to more negative school experience and worse neighborhood conditions, which in turn contribute to a higher level of violent delinquency. Second-generation Whites also have a lower level of parents' education, but it may not be low enough to affect neighborhood conditions and thus children's education and delinquency. Higher levels of negative neighborhood conditions (concentration of disadvantage and neighborhood incivility) among second- and third-plus-generation Whites may not contribute to a higher level of property delinquency because households located in areas with a high level of concentrated disadvantage may be too poor to offer opportunities for property crime, and youth who experience high levels of economic and cultural deprivation but have neither legal nor illegal opportunities for property crime may engage in more violence (e.g., group fighting) to express their frustration or to deal with boredom (Cloward & Ohlin, 1960).

In conclusion, the study supports a segmented assimilation perspective and suggests the significance of immigrants' socioeconomic characteristics and the social conditions of the host communities in shaping their adaptation process and outcomes. Findings from the study have important implications for social policy to address the immigrant paradox in delinquency. Support and assistance for disadvantaged first-generation immigrants to improve their socioeconomic conditions (e.g., higher levels of education, occupation status, and incomes) are necessary for facilitating their reintegration into mainstream society and preventing delinquent behavior among their children. In addition, promoting biculturalism in immigrant communities can be beneficial because bicultural children can draw resources from both the immigrant community and mainstream society to benefit their education (Feliciano, 2001). In addition, biculturalism can prevent family conflicts resulting from the gaps in acculturation between parents and children and help children of immigrants maintain close relationships with families. Close family relationships and good education are both preventive factors for delinquency (Hirschi, 1969). Because neighborhood and school effects are prominent during adolescence when children are most susceptible to influence outside the home (Pong & Hao, 2007), it is important to improve safety conditions and the quality of schools in disadvantaged communities where new immigrants often reside to increase their chance for successful integration. Long-term policy should address the problem of residential and school segregation resulting from race and class inequality and aim toward giving children of economically disadvantaged and minority immigrants an equal opportunity for good education and safe environment for appropriate personal development.

Despite important findings and policy implications, the present study has several limitations. The study lacks variables that directly measure acculturation, assimilation, and racial–ethnic prejudice, which might provide additional explanations for generational differences in delinquency among Hispanics. In addition, because data analysis focuses on four broad racial–ethnic groups, the findings cannot reflect within-group diversities. The poorest Asian groups, such as Cambodians and Laotians, may not have the same successful outcomes experienced by Chinese, Filipino, Korean, or South Asian Americans. Similarly, Cuban Americans may not face the same hardships experienced by Mexican or Dominican Americans. Finally, because of a lack of information distinguishing voluntary immigrants from involuntary immigrants who had been transported to the United States as slaves, third-plus-generation Blacks may include descendants of former slaves whose life circumstances must be different from those of recent immigrants. Because half of the generational differences in delinquency among Hispanics still remain unexplained, more research is needed to improve understanding of factors contributing to generational differences in delinquency among Hispanics and other discrete groups.

APPENDIX 6.1: VARIABLE DESCRIPTIONS

Variable	Description
Outcome variables	
Violent Delinquency (scale)	Four items: used or threatened with a weapon; took part in a group fight; took part in a serious physical fight; seriously injured someone (0 = *never;* 1 = *1 or 2 times;* 2 = *3 or 4 times;* 3 = *5 or more times*) Three items: got into a physical fight; pulled a knife or gun on someone; shot or stabbed someone (0 = *never;* 1 = *once;* 2 = *more than once*). Range = 0–18; α = .786.
Property Delinquency (Scale)	Seven items: burglary; stealing things < $50; stealing things > $50; vandalism; shoplifting; stealing a car; selling drugs (0 = *never;* 1 = *1 or 2 times* ; 2 = *3 or 4 times;* 3 = *5 or more times*). Range = 0–21; α = .767.
Independent variables	
Generation status	First generation = foreign born with both foreign-born parents Second generation = U.S. born with at least one foreign-born parent Third generation = U.S. born with both U.S.-born parents
Family structure	1 = two biological parents; 2 = other types of parent
Parent's education	1 = both parents with college degrees; 2 = other
Family income	Family's annual income in thousand dollars
Family attachment (scale)	Four items: people in the family are understanding; people in the family have fun together; the family pays attention to the respondent; the respondent wants to leave home (0 = *not at all;* 1 = *very little;* 2 = *somewhat;* 3 = *quite a bit;* 4 = *very much*). Range = 0–16; α = .75.
Parental Control (scale)	Seven items: parents control weekend curfew; friends; clothing; TV time; TV programs; weekday bedtime; diet (0 = *no;* 1= *yes*). Range = 0–7; α = .61.
Parent–child conflicts	Argue with parents (yes/no)
Academic performance	Grade point average of four majors: English, math, sciences, and history. Range = 1–4.
School attachment (scale)	Five items: the respondent feels close to people at school; close to school; happy at school; safe in school; teachers' fairness (1 = *strongly disagree;* 2 = *disagree;* 3 = *neither;* 4 = *agree;* 5 = *strongly agree*). Range = 5–25; α = .76.
School commitment	A combination of 2 items: (a) the respondent wants to attend college and (b) how likely the respondent will attend college (1 = *very low;* 2 = *somewhat low;* 3 = *neutral;* 4 = *somewhat high;* 5 = *very high*). Range = 2–10
Trouble in school(scale)	Four items: trouble getting along with teacher; trouble in paying attention; trouble in getting homework done; trouble with other students (0 = *never;* 1 = *just a few times;* 2 = *about once a week;* 3 = *almost every day;* 4 = *every day*). Range = 0–16; α = .69.

Variable	Description
Neighborhood Incivility (scale)	Three items: problem of trash; problem of drugs; want to leave the neighborhood because of these problems (0 = *not a problem/not at all;* 1= *a small problem/some;* 2 = *a big problem/very much*). Range = 0–6; α = .67.
Concentrated Disadvantage (scale)	Four items: proportion of single-mom households with children; proportion of families with incomes below poverty level; proportion of families receiving public assistance; unemployment rate. Range (standardized) = 1.09–6.56; α =.89.
Exposure to violence	How often the respondent sees shooting or stabbing of persons (0 = *never;* 1 = *once;* 2 = *more than once*).
Control variables	
Age	Age in years. Range 12–20.
Sex	Male; female.
Race–ethnicity	Non-Hispanic White (White); non-Hispanic Black (Black); Asian; Hispanic; Other

REFERENCES

Anderson, E. (1994, May). The code of the streets. *Atlantic Monthly, 273,* 81–94.

Berry, J. V. (1980). Acculturation as varieties of adaptation. In A. M. Padilla (Ed.), *Acculturation: Theory, models, and some new findings* (pp. 207–236). Boulder, CO: Westview.

Bui, H. N. (2005). Immigration and self-reported delinquency: The interplay of immigration generations, gender, race, and ethnicity. *Journal of Criminal Justice, 28,* 71–99.

Buriel, R., Calzada, S., & Vasquez, R. (1982). The relationship of traditional Mexican American culture to adjustment and delinquency among three generations of Mexican American male adolescents. *Hispanic Journal of Behavioral Sciences, 4,* 41–55. doi:10.1177/07399863820041003

Butcher, K. F., & Piehl, A. M. (2005). *Why are immigrants' incarceration rates so low? Evidence on selective immigration, deterrence, and deportation* (Working Paper No. 2005-19). Chicago, IL: Federal Reserve Bank of Chicago.

Caplan, N., Choy, M. H., & Whitmore, J. K. (1992). Indochinese refugee families and academic achievement. *Scientific American, 266,* 36–42. doi:10.1038/scientificamerican0292-36

Cernkovich, S., & Giordano, P. C. (1992). School bonding, race, and delinquency. *Criminology, 30,* 261–291. doi:10.1111/j.1745-9125.1992.tb01105.x

Cloward, R., & Ohlin, L. (1960). *Delinquency and opportunity: A theory of delinquent gangs.* New York, NY: Free Press.

Crosnoe, R. (2005). The diverse experiences of Hispanic students in the American educational system. *Sociological Forum, 20,* 561–588.doi: 10.1007/s11206-005-9058-z

Crosnoe, R. (2006). *Mexican roots, American schools: Helping immigrant children suc-ceed*. Palo Alto, CA: Stanford University Press.

Feliciano, C. (2001). The benefit of biculturalism: Exposure to immigrant culture and dropping out among Asian and Latino Youths. *Social Science Quarterly, 82,* 865–879. doi:10.1111/0038-4941.00064

Fuligni, A. J. (1997). The academic achievement of adolescents from immigrant fam-ilies: The roles of family background, attitudes, and behavior. *Child Development, 68,* 351–363. doi:10.1111/j.1467-8624.1997.tb01944.x

Gordon, M. (1964). *Assimilation in American life: The role of race, religion, and national origin*. New York, NY: Oxford University Press.

Hacker, A. (1992). *Two nations: Black and White, separate, hostile, unequal*. New York, NY: Ballentine.

Han, W. J. (2006). Academic achievements of children of immigrant families. *Edu-cational Research Review, 1,* 286–318.

Harris, K. M. (1998). Health status and risk behavior of adolescents in immigrant fam-ilies. In D. Hernandez (Ed.), *Children of immigrants: Health, adjustment, and public assistance* (pp. 286–374). Washington, DC: National Academy Press.

Hirschi, T. (1969). *Causes of delinquency*. Berkeley: University of California Press.

Immigration Commission. (1911). *Report of the Immigration Commission* (S. Rep. No. 61-750, Vol. 36). Washington, DC: U.S. Government Printing Office.

Isralowitz, R. E. (2004). Cultural identification and substance use. *Journal of Social Psychology, 144,* 222–224. doi:10.3200/SOCP.144.2.222

Jang, S. J. (2002). Race, ethnicity, and deviance: A study of Asian and non-Asian ado-lescents in America. *Sociological Forum, 17,* 647–680. doi:10.1023/A:1021081 524775

Kao, T., & Tienda, M. (1995). Optimism and achievement: The educational per-formance of immigrant youth. *Social Science Quarterly, 76,* 1–19.

Lee, Y. H. (1998). Acculturation and delinquent behavior: The case of Korean Amer-ican youths. *International Journal of Comparative and Applied Criminal Justice, 22,* 273–292.

Lin, C., & Liu, W. (1993). Intergenerational relationships among Chinese immigrants from Taiwan. In H. P. McAdoo (Ed.), *Family ethnicity: Strength in diversity* (pp. 271–286). Newbury Park, CA: Sage.

Maguin, E., & Loeber, R. (1996). Academic performance and delinquency. In M. Tonry (Ed.), *Crime and justice: A review of research* (Vol. 20, pp. 145–164). Chicago, IL: University of Chicago Press.

Massey, D. S., & Denton, N. A. (1993). *American apartheid: Segregation and the mak-ing of the underclass*. Cambridge, MA: Harvard University Press.

McNeal, R. B., Jr. (1997). High school dropouts: A closer examination of school effects. *Social Science Quarterly, 78,* 209–222.

Miller, W. (1958). Lower class culture as a generating milieu of gang delinquency. *Journal of Social Issues, 14*: 5–19.

Nagasawa, R., Qian, Z., & Wong, P. (2001). Theory of segmented assimilation and the adoption of marijuana use and delinquent behavior by Asian Pacific youth. *The Sociological Quarterly, 42*, 351–372. doi:10.1111/j.1533-8525.2001.tb02405.x

National Commission on Law Observance and Enforcement. (1932). *Report on crime and the foreign born*. Washington, DC: U.S. Government Printing Office.

Pong, S. I. (1998). The school compositional effect of single-parenthood on 10th grade achievement. *Sociology of Education, 71*, 23–42. doi:10.2307/2673220

Pong, S. I., & Hao, L. (2007). Neighborhood and school factors in the school performance of immigrants' children. *The International Migration Review, 41*, 206–241. doi:10.1111/j.1747-7379.2007.00062.x

Portes, A. (1996). Preface. In A. Portes (Ed.), *The second generation* (pp. ix–x). New York, NY: Russell Sage Foundation.

Portes, A., & Hao, L. (2004). The schooling of children of immigrants: Contextual effects on the educational attainment of the second generation. *Proceedings of the National Academy of Sciences, USA, 101*, 11920–11927.

Portes, A., & MacLeod, D. (1996). Educational progress of children of immigrants: The roles of class, ethnicity, and school contexts. *Sociology of Education, 69*, 255–275. doi:10.2307/2112714

Portes, A., & MacLeod, D. (1999). Educating the second generation: Determinants of academic achievement among children of immigrants in the United States. *Journal of Ethnic and Migration Studies, 25*, 373–396. doi:10.1080/1369183X.1999.9976693

Portes, A., & Rumbaut, R. (2006). *Immigrant America: A portrait*. Berkeley: University of California Press.

Portes, A., & Zhou, M. (1993). The new second generation: Segmented assimilation and its variants. *The Annals of the American Academy of Political and Social Science, 530*, 74–96. doi:10.1177/0002716293530001006

Rueschenberg, E., & Buriel, R. (1989). Mexican American family functioning and acculturation: A family systems perspective. *Hispanic Journal of Behavioral Sciences, 11*, 232–244. doi:10.1177/07399863890113002

Rumbaut, R. (1998). Transformations: The post-immigrant generation in an age of diversity. In L. F. Tomasi (Ed.), *In defense of the alien* (pp. 229–259). New York, NY: Center for Migration Studies.

Rumbaut, R. (1999). Assimilation and its discontents: Ironies and paradoxes. In C. Hirschman, P. Kasinitz, & J. DeWind (Eds.), *The handbook of international migration: The American experience* (pp. 172–195). New York, NY: Russell Sage Foundation.

Rumbaut, R. (2005a). Children of immigrants and their achievement: The roles of family, acculturation, social class, ethnicity, and school contexts. In R. D. Taylor

(Ed.), *Addressing the achievement gap: Theory informing practice* (pp. 23–59). Greenwich, CT: Information Age.

Rumbaut, R. (2005b). Turning points in the transition to adulthood: Determinants of educational attainment, incarceration, and early childbearing among children of immigrants. *Ethnic and Racial Studies, 28*, 1041–1086. doi:10.1080/014 19870500224349

Rumberger, R. W., & Willms, J. D. (1992). The impact of racial and ethnic segregation on the achievement gaps in California high schools. *Educational Evaluation and Policy Analysis, 14*, 377–396.

Rayabov, I., & Van Hook, J. (2007). School segregation and academic achievement among Hispanic children. *Social Science Research, 36*, 767–788. doi:10.1016/j. ssresearch.2006.04.002

Sampson, R. J., & Wilson, W. J. (1995). Toward a theory of race, crime, and urban inequality. In J. Hagan & R. D. Peterson (Eds.), *Crime and inequality* (pp. 37–54). Stanford, CA: Stanford University Press.

Sellin, T. (1938). *Culture conflict and crime.* New York, NY: Social Research Council.

Shaw, C. R., & McKay, H. D. (1942). *Juvenile delinquency in urban areas.* Chicago, IL: University of Chicago Press.

Shihadeh, E., & Shrum, W. (2004). Serious crime in urban neighborhoods: Is there a race effect? *Sociological Spectrum, 24*, 507–533. doi:10.1080/02732170490459502

Szapocznik, J., & Kurtines, W. M. (1993). Family psychology and cultural diversity: Opportunity for theory, research and application. *American Psychologist, 48*, 400–407. doi:10.1037/0003-066X.48.4.400

U.S. Census Bureau. (2001). *Profile of the foreign-born population in the United States: 2000.* Washington, DC: U.S. Department of Commerce.

Zhou, M., & Bankston, C. L., III. (2006). Delinquency and acculturation in the twenty-first century: A decade's change in a Vietnamese American community. In R. Martinez Jr. & A. Valenzuela Jr. (Eds.), *Immigration and crime: Race, ethnicity, and violence* (pp. 117–139). New York, NY: New York University Press.

III

FAMILY AND COMMUNITY FACTORS AFFECTING ACADEMIC OUTCOMES

7

BILINGUALISM AND ACADEMIC ACHIEVEMENT: DOES GENERATION STATUS MAKE A DIFFERENCE?

WEN-JUI HAN

In recent decades in the United States, the concentration of immigration from Latin American and Asian countries has led to a significant increase in the use of non-English languages at home. By 2050, more than half the growth rate of the school-aged population is projected to be made up of children of immigrants (Passel & Cohn, 2008). As more English-language-learner (ELL) students are entering school systems across the country, educators and researchers are seeking ways to alleviate these students' academic woes and improve their school performance. To date, most policies and programs have focused on English-only instruction as the optimal method of improving ELL students' academic achievement (Zehler et al., 2003).

Over the past 20 years, researchers have become intrigued by the *immigrant paradox:* Immigrants and early generation children (foreign-born and children of foreign-born parents) generally do well in American society despite having few economic resources and having to navigate a new culture and language, but this success is often not sustained by later generations (Rumbaut,

I gratefully acknowledge support from the Foundation for Child Development PK-3 Initiative and the Columbia University Diversity Research Fellowship.

161

1994). As children in later generations become more removed from their parents' native culture, they often lose touch with some of that culture's protective aspects, including the sometimes high value placed on education and familial respect. Moreover, to the detriment of these children, with each subsequent generation they become increasingly reluctant to speak their family's native language (Rumbaut, 1994). Studies have demonstrated the benefits of bilingual fluency, linking it to various positive academic outcomes (Golash-Boza, 2005; Portes & Hao, 1998, 2002, 2004; Portes & McLeod, 1999), higher self-esteem (Portes & Hao, 2002), and stronger family cohesion (Portes & Hao, 2002; Tseng & Fuligni, 2000). Researchers have largely attributed bilingualism's positive effects to its relationship with greater cognitive flexibility and abstract thinking skills (Bialystok, 1988; Rumbaut, 1995; Willig, 1985) and to the positive "cultural capital" bilingual children can access in their families and communities (Bankston & Zhou, 1995; Portes & Rumbaut, 2006; Portes & Zhou, 1993; Rumberger & Larson, 1998). Studies by Andrew Fuligni and colleagues (e.g., Fuligni, 1997, 1998; Fuligni & Flook, 2005; Tseng & Fuligni, 2000) add contextual support to the importance of speaking the same language as one's parents and grandparents. These studies show how this language congruence may enhance parent–child communication and relationships and how this improved relationship and communication could impact children's motivation to succeed academically. These findings challenge the popular belief that for children of immigrant backgrounds, a rapid shift to monolingual English fluency is best for their well-being.

In practice, many studies have shown the successful use of bilingual education to promote ELL students' academic performance (Christian, Howard, & Loeb, 2000; Christian, Montone, Lindholm, & Carranza, 1997; Lindholm-Leary, 2001). For example, in a large-scale study, Collier and Thomas (2004) analyzed 700,000 student records and found that only those children who received strong grade-level cognitive and academic support in both their first and second languages for many years were succeeding at the end of high school (e.g., achieving as well as, if not better than, their "mainstream" native-English-speaking [NES] peers). Bilingually schooled students, after 4 to 7 years of such instruction, outperformed in all subjects their mainstream NES peers who were educated monolingually in English. Collier and Thomas also showed that bilingual education may put ELL students on a positive academic trajectory to narrow and eventually close their initial academic gap with their mainstream NES peers.

The raw reading and math trajectories from kindergarten to fifth grade for the children analyzed in the present study indeed reveal a paradoxical pattern. In general, first- and second-generation children with non-English language backgrounds (i.e., they are not English monolingual) exhibited notably better reading and math scores as well as faster trajectories in reading and math scores relative to their third-or-later-generation peers; thus, third-or-later-generation children who are not English monolingual tend to fall behind over time relative to their first- and second-generation peers. The question is then what factors might account for these diverging academic trajectories by generation and language group. Is this a natural process (e.g., regression to the mean), or do environments play a role?

Two conceptual frameworks may help explain the paradox: the ecological systems theory (Bronfenbrenner, 2005) and an integrative model of child development put forward by García Coll and her colleagues (1996). Using the microsystems specified in the ecological perspective, children of immigrants being able to speak the mother tongue with their parents and grandparents represents an important intergenerational interaction that is assumed to be beneficial to parent–child communication and relationships, which, in turn, enhances children's well-being (Fuligni & Flook, 2005). How may this then be applied to the interactions between children and larger environments? The integrative model of child development (García Coll et al., 1996) explicitly identifies the interrelationships between adaptive culture (e.g., traditions and cultural legacies, acculturation) and the larger environment (e.g., schools) and how such interactions may shape children's cognitive and socioemotional well-being. Applying this framework, we can assume that children's non-English language backgrounds represent adaptive culture, which involves both risks and benefits for children growing up in the United States. On one hand, a non-English language may be discouraged by the larger society (e.g., schools) because it is not the supported dominant culture. If this is the case, children may be vulnerable to "failure feedback" from teachers and peers that may, in turn, result in decreased confidence in their abilities or future success and negative educational trajectories, particularly in the early and middle-school years (Eccles, 1999). On the other hand, if the larger environment (e.g., schools) supports children's non-English language background, then the benefits of being accepted can operate a strong force in increasing children's confidence in their abilities and thus, in turn, their academic achievement and socioemotional well-being.

To examine the immigrant paradox and to add to the knowledge about the relationship between language backgrounds and the academic trajectories of children during their early school years, we used a large, contemporary longitudinal data set, the Early Childhood Longitudinal Survey—Kindergarten Cohort (ECLS-K). In recent decades, researchers have used well-designed quantitative cross-sectional studies with small, local samples to study the academic achievement of children with various language backgrounds at one point in time (e.g., Portes & Hao, 1998; Rumbaut, 1994). Other researchers have used similar qualitative data sets to examine the longitudinal process of children's learning experiences. Much solid empirical evidence shows how children of immigrants perform academically in their middle-school years (e.g., Rumbaut, 1994). Still lacking, however, is solid empirical evidence regarding how a national sample of children with various language backgrounds might perform during their early school years from a longitudinal lens. The current study fills this knowledge gap by following children over the first 5 years of formal schooling, using generation status to examine immigrant paradox patterns and determine how non-English language usage (as a proxy for cultural capital) may moderate the paradox pattern.

This chapter focuses on Latin American and Asian ethnic groups, the most rapidly growing ethnic groups in the United States. Children from these groups often do not speak English at home. However, previous studies have found that youths of the second generation and beyond tend not to preserve their parents' linguistic heritage (Portes & Hao, 1998). For these reasons, this study centers on how generation status and English (or non-English) proficiency might be related to children's academic performance. Building on previous research on bilingualism (Portes & Hao, 1998, 2002, 2004) as well as on effective-school literature (Rutter & Maughan, 2002), this study uses models that control for a large set of child, family, and school characteristics in order to examine the possible connection between degrees of bilingualism and children's academic trajectories during early school years.

METHOD

Data

This study used data from the ECLS-K, a large cohort of children who entered kindergarten in the 1998–1999 school year and who were followed longitudinally through eighth grade. Children were drawn randomly via a multistage probability design from a nationally representative sample of roughly 1,000 U.S. public and private schools, with an average of more than 20 children per school ($N = 21,260$ in the fall of kindergarten in 1998 and $N = 11,820$ in the spring of fifth grade in 2004). The ECLS-K collected detailed information on children's language proficiency on school entry and the language spoken between the parent and child at home, making the ECLS-K the only national data set able to evaluate the relationship between children's language backgrounds during their early school years and their developmental trajectories.

To restrict the analysis only to children from Latin American and Asian backgrounds as well as to native-born non-Hispanic Whites, 4,160 children with family roots in other regions or who identified themselves as non-Hispanic Black, multiracial, or of an unlisted race–ethnicity were excluded. Additionally, the present sample includes only children who provided information about their home language, resulting in a study sample of 16,360 children. Of these, 58% were non-Hispanic White, 14% of the children spoke a language other than English at home, and about half of the children were male.

Measures

Academic Performance

The ECLS-K assessed language use, literacy (in the reading assessment), and mathematics in fall and spring of kindergarten and in the spring of first, third, and fifth grades. The reading assessment included questions designed to measure basic skills (e.g., letter and word recognition), receptive vocabulary, and comprehension (listening to and understanding words in context). The mathematics assessment measured skills in conceptual and procedural knowledge and problem solving. The reliability of the assessments is high, ranging from 0.88 to 0.97 from kindergarten to fifth grade (hereafter, K to 5).

Direct assessments of reading and mathematics competence were collected in one-on-one testing sessions using an item response theory (IRT) approach. A brief language screening (the Oral Language Developmental Scale [OLDS]) was given in the fall of kindergarten to 15% of children who were identified by teachers or school records as having a non-English language background. Approximately 59%, or 1,360, of these children (8% of the overall sample) scored below the cutoff point and were given only the mathematics assessments that year. By first grade, this number was down to 340, with 85% of these children's families originating from Mexico, 10% from other Latin American countries, and 5% from Asian countries. Beginning in third grade, the OLDS was no longer administered, and all children were assessed in English. All English- and Spanish-speaking students (but not students speaking other languages) were administered the math assessment in all grades regardless of their language ability.

Standardized t tests ($M = 50$, $SD = 10$) were used to examine reading and math outcomes via a transformed measure of the IRT scale score. This norm-referenced score represents children's abilities relative to their average peers nationwide (i.e., children who entered kindergarten in fall 1998), and a change in mean t scores over time reflects a change in relative ability, which is the focus of this chapter.

Immigrant Generation Status and Race–Ethnicity

Both the mother and the father reported whether she or he was born in the United States, whether the child was born in the United States, and the country of origin if born outside the United States. Children were coded as *immigrant* if they had at least one foreign-born parent, as *first-generation immigrant* if they were not born in the United States and had at least one foreign-born parent, and as *second-generation immigrant* if they were born in the United States but had at least one foreign-born parent. Ten Latin American countries, Spanish-speaking Caribbean countries, and Asian regions were categorized: Puerto Rico,[1] Central America (e.g., Costa Rica, El Salvador), South America (e.g., Argentina, Brazil), the Dominican Republic, Mexico, Cuba, East Asia (e.g., China, Japan), Vietnam/Thailand/Cambodia/Laos, other Southeast Asia (e.g., Indonesia, Malaysia, Philippines), and India. Hereafter, *Latin America* is used to represent both Latin American and Spanish-speaking Caribbean countries for simplicity. Approximately 12% of the study sample children were identified as children of immigrants originating from either Latin American or Asian regions. More than 60% of these children originated from Latin America, with the majority originating from Mexico. About 5% of children originating from Latin American regions and 6% originating from Asian regions were first-generation immigrants; the corresponding numbers for second-generation are 42% (Latino) and 61% (Asian), respectively, and 53% (Latino) and 32% (Asian), respectively, for third or later generation. For native-born children (both child and parents born in the United States), race–ethnicity was divided into three groups: non-Hispanic White, Hispanic, and Asian. Non-Hispanic Whites made up two-thirds of the total current analyzed sample. A total of 2,020 Latino and 490 Asian children were identified as third or later generation (hereafter, *third generation*).

Language Group

Children's language status was measured by the combination of the language they spoke at home and their English proficiency as measured at school entry. For the home language, the ECLS-K collected information in the fall of kindergarten on four directions of language interaction between the parents and child: mother's language spoken to child, father's language spoken to child, child's language spoken to mother, and child's language spoken to father. Each of these four interaction pairs consists of four possible language-use patterns: never, sometimes, often, or very often speaks the native language. The second part of the determination of children's language status comes from their English proficiency at school entry, as determined by whether they were administered and passed the OLDS (Duncan & De Avila, 2000). This mea-

---

[1] It is important to note that although children from Puerto Rico were also identified as first- or second-generation immigrants if they themselves or their parent(s) were not born on the U.S. mainland, these children are U.S. citizens. However, this chapter acknowledges the importance of the geographical and cultural differences between children from Puerto Rico and those born on the U.S. mainland and thus separates them in the analyses.

sure was combined with children's language use at home with the mother to create five dummy variables that represent children's language status. *English monolingual* children were defined as those who never spoke a non-English language to their parents and either did not need to take the OLDS or passed it at kindergarten entry. Children who sometimes spoke a non-English language to their parents and either did not need to take the OLDS or passed the test at kindergarten entry were defined as *English-dominant bilingual*. Children who often or very often spoke non-English to their parents and either did not need to take the OLDS test or passed it by the end of kindergarten were defined as *fluent bilingual*. Children who sometimes, often, or very often spoke non-English to their parents and passed the OLDS at the end of first grade were defined as *non-English-dominant bilingual*. Children who did not pass the OLDS by the end of first grade were defined as *non-English monolingual* no matter how often they spoken non-English at home. Tables 7.1 and 7.2 present the distribution of language groups by generation status and country of origin. Table 7.1 includes first and second generation, and Table 7.2 includes third generation.

Larger School Setting

Borrowing from a large body of effective-school literature (e.g., Rutter & Maughan, 2002), a total of 14 variables that represent five constructs (i.e., English as second language instruction and services, school resources, student learning environment, supportive teaching environment, and school safety) were used to evaluate the school environment. For details, please see Han and Bridglall (2009).

Child and Family Characteristics

Time-invariant variables collected in the fall of the kindergarten year included child's gender, birth weight, attendance in center-based care before kindergarten, parents' marital status at birth, and parental education (mother or father, whichever was higher). Time-variant variables were collected at all interview points and included the presence of siblings in the household, the number of people under age 18 in the household, living in a single-parent family, family socioeconomic status (calculated from family income, parental education, and occupation), parental educational expectations, home environment, parental school involvement, region (e.g., Northeast), and location of residence (i.e., city, suburban, or rural).

Empirical Strategy

Rates of missing data were generally less than 4% for the demographic and family characteristics. Rates were higher for school factors but generally below

TABLE 7.1
Percentage Distribution by Generation Status and Language Group Among First and Second Generation

Origin	First generation				
	English monolingual	English-dominant bilingual	Fluent bilingual	Non-English-dominant bilingual	Non-English monolingual
Latin American origins and native-born Hispanic (n = 1,760)					
Puerto Rico (n = 100)	1.25	3.75	7.50	0.00	0.00
Central America (n = 190)	0.61	0.00	2.42	2.42	0.61
South America (n = 200)	1.14	2.27	5.68	2.27	1.70
Dominican Republic (n = 70)	0.00	1.67	1.67	5.00	0.00
Mexico (n = 1140)	0.10	0.20	4.33	3.15	3.44
Cuba (n = 60)	0.00	3.70	5.56	0.00	1.85
Asian origins and native-born Asian (n = 1,030)					
East Asia (n = 250)	1.52	1.52	4.55	2.02	0.51
Thailand/Vietnam/ Cambodia/Laos (n = 320)	0.00	0.41	1.22	0.82	0.41
Other Southeast Asia (n = 330)	3.11	3.11	3.81	1.04	0.69
India (n = 130)	5.00	5.00	7.00	1.00	0.00

TABLE 7.2
Percentage Distribution by Language Group Among Native-Born Children

Racial–ethnic group	Language group				
	English monolingual	English-dominant bilingual	Fluent bilingual	Non-English-dominant bilingual	Non-English monolingual
Non-Hispanic White (n = 11,060)	98.53	1.17	0.30	0.00	0.00
Hispanic (n = 2,020)	61.03	21.51	9.81	3.15	2.43
Asian (n = 490)	36.46	12.50	19.27	14.58	2.60

English monolingual	English-dominant bilingual	Fluent bilingual	Non-English-dominant bilingual	Non-English monolingual
Second generation				

English monolingual	English-dominant bilingual	Fluent bilingual	Non-English-dominant bilingual	Non-English monolingual
Latin American origins and native-born Hispanic ($n = 1,760$)				
23.75	32.50	18.75	10.00	2.50
21.21	13.94	26.67	23.64	8.48
29.55	20.45	30.11	5.11	1.70
5.00	21.67	41.67	18.33	5.00
6.49	11.90	30.09	19.08	21.24
24.07	27.78	29.63	7.41	0.00
Asian origins and native-born Asian ($n = 1,030$)				
22.22	17.17	39.39	10.10	1.01
7.76	14.29	42.86	24.08	8.16
44.29	26.99	10.73	4.50	1.73
26.00	27.00	25.00	3.00	1.00

20%. The growth curve modeling used in this analysis handles such unbalanced data well; students did not have to be assessed at all data points to be included in the analysis (Singer & Willett, 2003). Still, multiple imputation (STATA *ice*) was used to handle missing data with five imputed data sets.

Three-level growth curve modeling was used to estimate the associations between generation and language status and children's reading and math trajectories. Analyses were estimated with Level 1 as time (i.e., within-individual effects), Level 2 as individuals (i.e., between-individual and within-school effects), and Level 3 as schools (i.e., between-school effects). With longitudinal data involving five assessment points, children's academic trajectories were estimated to compare the growth rate of each group over time. All continuous variables were centered at their grand mean values, except the dummy variables (e.g., attending public school), so that the reference child represents a realistic scenario (Singer & Willett, 2003). In addition, the variable "time" was centered so that initial status would refer to the fall semester of kindergarten, which is the true starting point. Native-born, non-Hispanic White, English monolingual children (hereafter, *White English monolingual*) were the reference group. For brevity's sake, the estimates for child, family, and school characteristics are not presented.

RESULTS

The raw data (not shown) of reading and math trajectories from K to 5 for the children in the cohort reveal a paradoxical pattern. The descriptive data (not shown) indicating the differences between children of varying language and generational status shed light on this pattern. Specifically, by children's language background within ethnic groups, the raw data (not shown) suggest that among Latino children, English monolinguals and to a lesser extent English-dominant bilinguals and fluent bilinguals were better off than Latinos who spoke less English on a number of sociodemographic variables (e.g., family socioeconomic status), their parents' involvement in their schooling, and school characteristics. In the Asian group, non-English monolingual children had the most disadvantaged characteristics. Overall, non-English monolingual children were more likely to be of Central American, Dominican, Mexican, or Thai/Vietnamese/Cambodian/Laotian descent. These trends were generally true within each generation. A few notable differences, however, are that third-generation Latino and Asian children were more likely to have mothers unmarried at birth than their first- and second-generation peers. Parents of first-generation children were more likely to have higher educational expectations and to foster stronger family routines (e.g., bedtime, taking part in culture-related activities) than parents of second and third generations. These descriptive differences indicate that first- and to a certain degree second-generation children showed rather strong ties to their native culture and values.

The multilevel results discussed here assess children's academic trajectories from K to 5. Table 7.3 presents the reading and math results for the Latino group (the two left columns) and the Asian group (the two right columns). For both groups, approximately half of the variation in reading scores is attributable to differences among children and 22% to differences among schools; about half of the variation in math scores is attributable to differences among children and 21% to differences among schools. In addition, the average White English monolingual child's reading score was nonzero ($b = 51.85, p < .001$, for models focusing on Latinos and $b = 51.86$, $p < .001$, for Asians) and had a strong positive slope ($b = 0.17, p < .001$, for models focusing on Latinos and

TABLE 7.3
Growth-Curve Results of Academic Achievements From Kindergarten to Fifth-Grade

Language group	Latin American origins and native-born Hispanic		Asian origins and native-born Asian	
	Reading	Math	Reading	Math
Fixed effects				
Intercept	51.85 (0.08)***	53.18 (0.08)***	51.86 (0.08)***	53.23 (0.08)***
First generation				
English monolingual	-2.49 (1.06)*	-2.49 (1.06)*	-1.63 (0.91)	-2.20 (1.02)*
English-dominant bilingual	-1.66 (1.97)	-3.20 (1.98)	2.02 (1.74)	-1.95 (1.96)
Fluent bilingual	-2.66 (1.22)*	-5.15 (1.24)***	0.83 (1.49)	-0.26 (1.70)
Non-English-dominant bilingual	-1.69 (1.46)	-5.34 (1.48)**	-5.46 (2.41)*	-6.41 (2.70)
Non-English monolingual	-4.67 (1.46)***	-6.27 (1.48)***	-10.28 (3.98)**	-12.30 (4.45)**
Second generation				
English monolingual	-1.10 (0.87)	-3.65 (0.90)***	0.20 (0.90)	-0.92 (1.06)
English-dominant bilingual	-0.82 (0.96)	-3.20 (0.99)***	1.62 (1.02)	-1.30 (1.19)
Fluent bilingual	-2.29 (1.54)	-4.65 (0.94)***	-0.63 (0.99)	-3.50 (1.17)**
Non-English-dominant bilingual	-3.98 (0.96)***	-9.53 (0.99)***	-6.85 (1.16)***	-9.11 (1.18)***
Non-English monolingual	-4.73 (0.99)***	-9.37 (1.02)***	-8.07 (1.72)***	-9.35 (1.73)***
Third generation				
English-dominant bilingual	-0.74 (0.42)	-1.36 (0.47)*	-1.01 (0.71)	-1.11 (0.71)
Fluent bilingual	-1.11 (0.67)	-3.40 (0.67)**	-2.08 (1.01)	-2.98 (0.80)**
Non-English-dominant bilingual	-4.79 (1.30)***	-9.74 (1.30)***	-9.40 (1.52)***	-12.12 (1.51)***
Non-English monolingual	-4.20 (1.50)**	-9.89 (1.50)***	-10.07 (3.51)***	-15.26 (3.48)***
Rate of change				
Intercept	0.17 (0.02)***	-0.29 (0.02)***	0.16 (0.02)***	-0.32 (0.02)***
First generation				
English monolingual	-0.18 (0.35)	0.07 (0.33)	0.08 (0.29)	0.20 (0.28)
English-dominant bilingual	0.57 (0.62)	0.70 (0.59)	-0.36 (0.53)	0.79 (0.50)
Fluent bilingual	0.57 (0.30)	1.33 (0.29)***	-0.04 (0.41)	0.66 (0.39)
Non-English-dominant bilingual	-0.17 (0.39)	1.00 (0.37)**	0.50 (0.75)	0.72 (0.71)

(continues)

TABLE 7.3
Growth-Curve Results of Academic Achievements From Kindergarten to Fifth-Grade (Continued)

Language group	Latin American origins and native-born Hispanic		Asian origins and native-born Asian	
	Reading	Math	Reading	Math
Rate of change				
Non-English monolingual	0.39 (0.40)	0.89 (0.38)*	2.48 (1.30)	1.76 (1.23)
Second generation				
English monolingual	0.35 (0.15)*	0.77 (0.15)***	-0.08 (0.15)	0.47 (0.14)***
English-dominant bilingual	0.28 (0.17)	0.58 (0.16)***	-0.59 (0.19)**	0.40 (0.18)*
Fluent bilingual	0.54 (0.12)***	1.12 (0.12)***	0.07 (0.15)	0.98 (0.14)***
Non-English-dominant bilingual	0.36 (0.16)*	1.52 (0.15)***	0.07 (0.25)	1.57 (0.24)***
Non-English monolingual	-0.01 (0.17)	1.11 (0.16)***	-1.02 (0.49)*	0.07 (0.46)
Third generation				
English-dominant bilingual	0.04 (0.14)	0.27 (0.13)*	0.25 (0.21)	0.19 (0.20)
Fluent bilingual	-0.11 (0.22)	0.47 (0.21)*	0.34 (0.24)	0.92 (0.23)***
Non-English-dominant bilingual	0.40 (0.43)	1.64 (0.41)***	0.49 (0.48)	2.16 (0.46)***
Non-English monolingual	0.08 (0.49)	1.30 (0.47)**	0.59 (1.16)	3.07 (1.10)**
Variance components				
Within-person	20.39 (0.28)***	19.16 (0.27)***	20.04 (0.30)***	18.84 (0.29)***
Level 2: Between person				
In initial status	27.73 (0.69)***	29.68 (0.69)***	28.62 (0.78)***	29.32 (0.76)***
In rate of change	1.03 (0.08)***	0.59 (0.07)***	1.09 (0.08)***	0.58 (0.08)***
Covariance	-0.25***	-0.15**	-0.30***	-0.62 (0.20)***
Level 3: Between school				
In initial status	3.11 (0.82)***	2.75 (1.11)*	3.31 (1.05)***	2.55 (0.46)***
In rate of change	0.18 (0.09)	0.21 (0.12)	0.20 (0.08)*	0.20 (0.10)*
Covariance	-0.64***	-0.50***	-0.67***	-2.27 (0.45)***
R^2	.2388	.2321	.2036	.1945

Note. Standard errors are in parentheses. Models also control for children's country of origin (Puerto Rico, Central America, South America, Dominican Republic, Mexico, Cuba, and native-born Hispanic, with native-born non-Hispanic White English monolingual as the reference group). Model 2 also controls for child's characteristics: being a boy, low birth weight, and attending center-based care before kindergarten; family's characteristics: mother married at birth, having siblings present, number of family members under age 18 at home, family's socioeconomic status, and living in single-parent family; and parental educational practices and home environment: parental educational expectations, parental participating in school events, home learning activities, and region and location of residence.

$b = 0.16$, $p < .001$, for Asians), indicating an increase through the grades relative to non-White peers. The average White English monolingual child's math score was nonzero ($b = 53.18$, $p < .001$, for models focusing on Latinos and $b = 53.23$, $p < .001$, for Asians) with a strong negative slope ($b = -0.29$, $p < .001$, for models focusing on Latinos and $b = -0.32$, $p < .001$, for Asians), indicating a decrease through the grades relative to their non-White peers.

Reading Results for Latino Children

As shown in Table 7.3, after controlling for all child, family, and school characteristics, compared with White English monolingual children, children with significantly lower reading scores fell into the following groups: Non-English monolingual children, no matter their generation status; second- and third-generation children categorized as Non-English-dominant bilingual; and first-generation English monolingual and fluent bilingual children. It is important to note that only second-generation English monolingual, fluent bilingual, and non-English-dominant bilingual children had significantly faster growth rates (steeper slopes) from K to 5 compared with White English monolingual children. For example, White English monolingual children averaged 51.85 on their reading scores in the fall of kindergarten compared with second-generation fluent bilingual children, whose scores averaged 49.56. With a slope of 0.17, the reading score for White English monolingual children at the spring of fifth grade was 52.53 [51.85 + (0.17*4)], whereas it was 52.40 [49.56 + (0.17 + 0.54)*4] for second-generation fluent bilingual children. Seemingly illustrative of the immigrant paradox, first-generation children who were not English monolingual were doing as well as, if not better than, their second-generation peers, whereas third-generation children were lagging behind their peers.

Math Results for Latino Children

With the exception of children in the first-generation English-dominant bilingual group, children in all language and generation status groups had a significantly lower average math score at school entry compared with the children in the White English monolingual group. Whereas the math trajectory of the White English monolingual children decreased at a significant rate from K to 5, the math trajectory of all other groups except first-generation English monolingual and English-dominant bilinguals increased at a significant rate during the same period. Thus, for example, White English monolingual children had an average math score of 53.18 at the start of kindergarten compared with 48.03 for first-generation fluent bilingual children; the former group had an average math score of 52.02 in the spring of fifth grade compared with 52.19

for the latter. Echoing the immigrant paradox phenomenon, first-generation children who were not English monolingual were doing as well as, if not better than, their second- and third-generation peers.

Reading Results for Asian Children

As shown in the right two columns of Table 7.3, both non-English-dominant bilingual and non-English monolingual children—no matter their generation status—had significantly lower average reading scores compared with White English monolingual children. Notably, second-generation English-dominant bilingual and non-English monolingual children had a significantly slower growth rate (flatter slope) than White English monolingual children. In addition, in every language group except English monolingual, first-generation children were performing better than their corresponding second- and third-generation peers, once again illustrating the immigrant paradox.

Math Results for Asian Children

The far right column of Table 7.3 shows that on average, second- and third-generation fluent bilingual, non-English-dominant bilingual, and non-English monolingual children had significantly lower math scores compared with White English monolingual children. First-generation English monolingual and non-English monolingual children also had significantly lower math scores. Whereas White English monolingual children had a significantly decreasing rate of change in their math trajectories, all second-generation (except non-English monolingual) and third-generation (except English-dominant bilingual) children had significantly increasing rates of change (steeper slopes). Again, first-generation children had higher math scores on average than their corresponding second- and third-generation peers.

Figures 7.1 and 7.2 show reading and math results, respectively, among native-born children and those of Latin American origin, and Figures 7.3 and 7.4 show reading and math results, respectively, among native-born children and those of Asian origin. These figures illustrate several notable results. First, English-dominant bilingual and fluent bilingual first- and second-generation children were doing as well as, if not better than, White English monolingual children on both reading and math scores by the end of fifth grade. It is important to note that even if first-generation fluent bilingual children lagged behind their English-dominant bilingual and White English monolingual peers at school entry, they caught up with or even surpassed these peers by the end of fifth grade. The results for non-English-dominant bilingual and non-English monolingual children echo similar patterns.

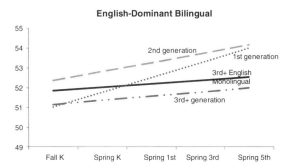

English-Dominant Bilingual

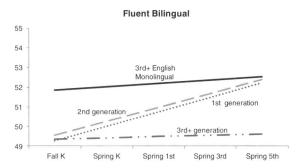

Fluent Bilingual

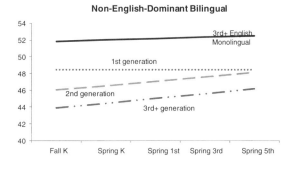

Non-English-Dominant Bilingual

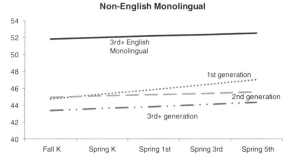

Non-English Monolingual

Figure 7.1. Predicted reading scores among children of Latin American origins and native-born children by language and generation status.

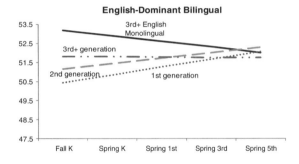

English-Dominant Bilingual

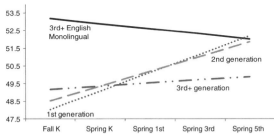

Fluent Bilingual

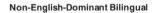

Non-English-Dominant Bilingual

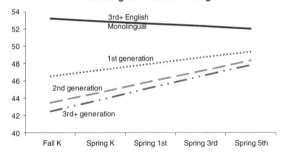

Non-English Monolingual

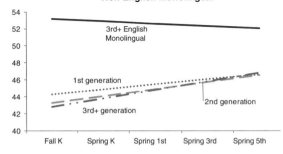

Figure 7.2. Predicted math scores among children of Latin American origins and native-born children by language and generation status.

176   WEN-JUI HAN

English-Dominant Bilingual

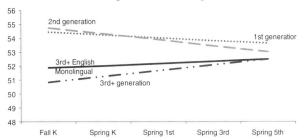

Fluent Bilingual

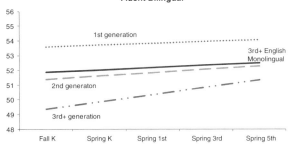

Non-English-Dominant Bilingual

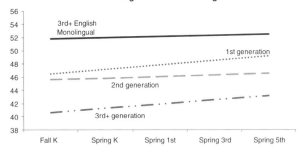

Non-English Monolingual

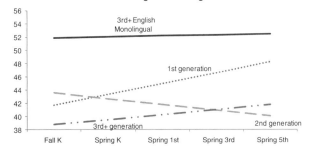

Figure 7.3. Predicted reading scores among children of Asian origins and native-born children by language and generation status.

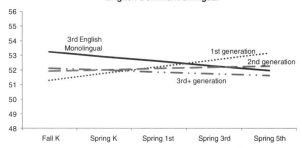

English-Dominant Bilingual

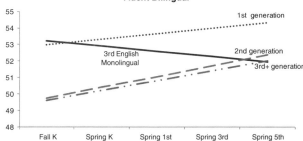

Fluent Bilingual

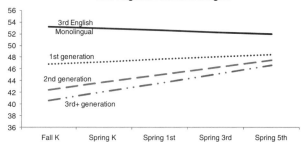

Non-English-Dominant Bilingual

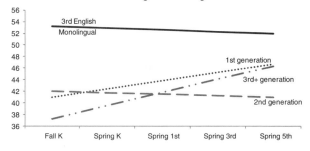

Non-English Monolingual

Figure 7.4. Predicted math scores among children of Asian origins and native-born children by language and generation status.

DISCUSSION AND CONCLUSION

This chapter began with the hypothesis that bilingualism is beneficial to children's learning experiences. A shared language may build a strong connection between parents and children and also may provide children with access to social and cultural capital. Being fluent in the dominant language along with the native one supports the acquisition of skills necessary to perform well in school. This chapter also started with the supposition that generation status might make a difference in children's learning experiences given the intriguing immigrant paradox hypothesis that generation and total assimilation lead to poorer performance. The results shown in this chapter indicate that on average, English-dominant bilingual and fluent bilingual children were performing as well as, if not better than, White English monolingual children. In contrast, non-English-dominant bilingual and non-English monolingual children had significantly lower academic performance on average than English monolingual children at school entry. This was still the case by the end of fifth grade, though in many cases their academic trajectories were steeper than those of English monolingual children. Furthermore, first- and second-generation children who were not English monolingual had similar—and in most cases better—academic performance than their corresponding third-generation peers.

One possible explanation for the better performance of English-dominant bilingual and fluent bilingual children may be that such children have other characteristics that lead to better academic outcomes. The raw data include significant correlations between being in the English-dominant bilingual or fluent bilingual group and being in a family with higher socioeconomic status with two parents who have higher educational expectations. Similarly, being in either of these groups is also significantly correlated with being less likely to attend a public school or a school with a high concentration of poor and minority students. However, the models control for these and other child and family characteristics.

Language fluency coupled with generation status, therefore, may account for some of the estimated differences, potentially an indication of the interplay within microsystems (Bronfenbrenner, 2005). Specifically, previous studies have shown that loss of the mother tongue might compromise children's ties with their parents and their cultural community (Rumbaut, 1994). Studies also have shown that in each subsequent immigrant generation, use of the mother tongue decreases (Portes & Hao, 1998). These two sets of findings suggest that the later generations who use a lesser degree of their parents' native language might not take advantage of the cultural capital offered by their parents and ethnic communities. As a consequence, the parent–child relationship may suffer, which could have implications for children's school performance. The results shown here demonstrate that the first- and second-generation

English-dominant bilingual and fluent bilingual groups had the academic trajectories that allowed them to do as well as or even surpass the "mainstream" children. This is particularly true for first-generation fluent bilingual Asian children, who not only had higher reading and math scores than White English monolingual peers but also had higher reading and math scores than their second-generation English-dominant bilingual peers by the end of fifth grade.

With regard to Latino children, results show a complex interplay between generation status and language background. In other words, the immigrant paradox hypothesis may not be as straightforward as it seems: Both the degree of bilingualism and generation status matter. Specifically, for Latino children with strong English skills (English monolingual, English-dominant bilingual, and fluent bilingual), language background seems to account for more variation in their academic performance than generation status. Among these Latino children, the second generation performed better than their first- and third-generation Latino peers either by having better academic outcomes from the beginning or by having fast-increasing trajectories that allowed them to narrow or even surpass these Latino peers by the end of fifth grade (Figures 7.1 and 7.2). For Latino children with low English language proficiency (non-English-dominant bilingual and non-English monolingual), generation status seems to be more important than language background. Among these Latino children, the first generation performed better than their second- and third-generation Latino peers—a classic immigrant paradox story. If non-English language is a proxy for the extent to which children can benefit from cultural capital (Golash-Boza, 2005), then these first-generation Latino children seemed to benefit from protective cultural capital, allowing them to perform better than their second- and later generation peers.

For Asian children, the immigrant paradox seems more straightforward, as also shown in Chapters 9 and 12 in this volume. Specifically, for all Asian children, no matter their language backgrounds (except for English monolingual), the first-generation students performed better than their second- and third-generation Asian peers by either having better academic scores from the beginning or by having the fast-increasing trajectories to outperform their later generation Asian peers by fifth grade.

In light of these results, the hypotheses of the immigrant paradox and of the positive effects of bilingualism on children's academic success seem to be logical explanations. These results highlight the benefits of being bilingual and how that might foster children's well-being, as echoed in Chapter 10 in this volume. These results also suggest that cultural capital (e.g., high value placed on education and familial respect) may provide important protective factors, particularly for children with weak English proficiency. However, non-English-dominant bilingual and non-English monolingual children lagged behind their White English monolingual peers, suggesting that the importance of language fluency—and a serious lack of English proficiency—cannot be overlooked. These results, which serve as evidence for immigrant risk, indicate that schools could play a larger role in supplying the resources necessary to assist these children with their English proficiency.

Returning to the ecological systems theory and the integrative model of child development, the results on (a) the benefits of being English-dominant bilingual and fluent bilingual and (b) the generally better academic performance of first- and second-generation children than their third-generation peers highlight the complex interplay among individuals, families, and larger environments. Specifically, the immigrant paradox applies to most of the children from immigrant families despite their language backgrounds. However, only immigrant children who possess a good handle on two languages seem to thrive. In other words, children who speak both English and the native language well may benefit not only from parent–child communication but also from the acceptance of the larger environment because of their fluency in English. This result emphasizes the dual importance of family and the larger environment (e.g., schools) in shaping children's academic achievement. In particular, despite their parents' encouragement, children may not have the motivation to speak their parents' language if few of their peers and teachers speak the language or if they are not given the opportunity to use it at school. On the other hand, it is important for schools to provide the opportunity for children who speak limited English at home to gain English proficiency. Although these two issues seem contradictory, the message is the same: Children's developmental experience and trajectories, particularly for ELL children, do not depend solely on family background—school environment is important as well.

The bottom-line message is that first- and second-generation children were doing as well as, if not better than, their third-generation peers. First- and second-generation fluent bilingual children were doing even better, with their academic performance surpassing that of native-born non-Hispanic White English monolingual children by the end of fifth grade. Child and family characteristics explained some of these observable differences by generational and language status, as did school environment, but these factors do not explain all the differences. This study also highlights that both the immigrant paradox and immigrant risk must be considered when examining young children of immigrants, particularly during their early school years, as asserted in Chapter 3 of this volume.

Caution nonetheless should be noted. First, despite the large overall sample size offered by the national ECLS-K data set, the sample size for some groups of children was in fact very small, rendering the estimates less reliable and thus calling for tentative interpretations. These groups include all Asian non-English monolingual children, no matter their generation status. Second, although some differences were found between first- and second-generation children in terms of their academic performance and trajectories, in most cases these differences were not statistically significant enough to allow the claim that first-generation children were doing better than their second-generation peers. If anything, our results show that first- and second-generation children were doing better than their corresponding third-generation peers. As Crosnoe (Chapter 3, this volume) points out, using only academic achievement data from early school years may not provide a clear and consistent portrayal of children's immigrant paradox stories.

Furthermore, bilingualism is not an easy concept to capture. For children of immigrants, being bilingual represents a source of culture, identity, and strength. Bilingualism is also important to immigrant parents because it allows children to maintain close ties to their family and to preserve the family's culture into the next generation. Despite using ECLS-K data for both children and parents, the present analyses were clearly not able to fully explain the effects of bilingualism. However, this chapter offers a first step toward understanding the environmental forces that influence children of different generations and specific ethnic backgrounds.

REFERENCES

Bankston, C. L., III, & Zhou, M. (1995). Effects of minority-language literacy on the academic achievement of Vietnamese youths in New Orleans. *Sociology of Education*, 68(1), 1–17. doi:10.2307/2112760

Bialystok, E. (1988). Levels of bilingualism and levels of linguistic awareness. *Developmental Psychology*, 24, 560–567. doi:10.1037/0012-1649.24.4.560

Bronfenbrenner, U. (Ed.). (2005). *Making human beings human: Bioecological perspectives on human development*. Thousand Oaks, CA: Sage.

Christian, D., Howard, E. R., & Loeb, M. I. (2000). Bilingualism for all: Two-way immersion education in the United States. *Theory Into Practice*, 39, 258–266.

Christian, D., Montone, C., Lindholm, K., & Carranza, I. (1997). *Profiles in two-way immersion Education*. McHenry, IL: Delta Systems.

Collier, V. P., & Thomas, W. P. (2004). The astounding effectiveness of dual language education for all. *NABE Journal of Research and Practice*, 2(1), 1–20.

Duncan, S. E., & De Avila, E. A. (2000). *PreLAS 2000 examiner's manual, English forms C and D*. Monterey, CA: CTB/McGraw-Hill.

Eccles, J. S. (1999). The development of children ages 6–14. *The Future of Children*, 9(2), 30–44. doi:10.2307/1602703

Fuligni, A. J. (1997). The academic achievement of adolescents from immigrant families: The roles of family background, attitudes, and behavior. *Child Development*, 68, 351–363.

Fuligni, A. J. (1998). Parental authority, adolescent autonomy, and parent–adolescent relationships: A study of adolescents from Mexican, Chinese, Filipino, and European backgrounds. *Developmental Psychology, 34,* 782–792. doi:10.1037/0012-1649.34.4.782

Fuligni, A. J., & Flook, L. (2005). A social identity approach to ethnic differences in family relationships during adolescence. In R. Kail (Ed.), *Advances in child development and behavior* (Vol. 33, pp. 125–152). New York, NY: Academic Press.

García Coll, C., Lamberty, G., Jenkins, R., McAdoo, H. P., Crnic, K., Wasik, B. H., & García, H. V. (1996). An integrative model for the study of developmental competencies in minority children. *Child Development, 67*(5), 1891–1914. doi:10.2307/1131600

Golash-Boza, T. (2005). Assessing the advantages of bilingualism for the children of immigrants. *The International Migration Review, 39,* 721–753. doi:10.1111/j.1747-7379.2005.tb00286.x

Han, W.-J., & Bridglall, B. (2009). Assessing school supports for ELL students using the ECLS-K. *Early Childhood Research Quarterly, 24,* 445–462. doi:10.1016/j.ecresq.2009.08.003.

Lindholm-Leary, K. (2001). *Dual-language education.* Clevedon, England: Multilingual Matters.

Passel, J., & Cohn, D. (2008). *U.S. population projections: 2005–2050.* Washington, DC: Pew Hispanic Center. Retrieved from http://pewhispanic.org/ files/reports/ 85.pdf

Portes, A., & Hao, L. (1998). E pluribus unum: Bilingualism and loss of language in the second generation. *Sociology of Education, 71,* 269–294. doi:10.2307/2673171

Portes, A., & Hao, L. (2002). The price of uniformity: Language, family and personality adjustment in the immigrant second generation. *Ethnic and Racial Studies, 25,* 889–912. doi:10.1080/0141987022000009368

Portes, A., & Hao, L. (2004). The schooling of children of immigrants: Contextual effects on the educational attainment of the second generation. *Proceedings of the National Academy of Sciences of the United States of America, 101,* 11920–11927. doi:10.1073/pnas.0403418101

Portes, A., & McLeod, D. (1999). Educating the second generation: Determinants of academic achievement among children of immigrants in the United States. *Journal of Ethnic and Migration Studies, 25,* 373–396. doi:10.1080/1369183X.1999.9976693

Portes, A., & Rumbaut, R. G. (2006). *Immigrant America: A portrait.* Berkeley: University of California Press.

Portes, A., & Zhou, M. (1993). The new second generation: Segmented assimilation and its variants. *Annals of the American Academy of Political and Social Science, 530,* 74–96. doi:10.1177/0002716293530001006

Rumbaut, R. G. (1994). The crucible within: Ethnic identity, self-esteem and segmented assimilation among children of immigrants. *The International Migration Review, 28,* 748–794. doi:10.2307/2547157

Rumbaut, R. G. (1995). The new Californians: Comparative research findings on the educational progress of immigrant children. In R. G. Rumbaut & W. A. Cornelius (Eds.), *California's immigrant children: Theory, research, and implications for educational policy* (pp. 17–69). La Jolla: Center for U.S.-Mexican Studies, University of California, San Diego.

Rumberger, R., & Larson, K. A. (1998). Toward explaining differences in educational achievement among Mexican American language-minority students. *Sociology of Education, 71,* 68–92.

Rutter, M., & Maughan, B. (2002). School effectiveness findings, 1979–2002. *Journal of School Psychology, 40,* 451–475. doi:10.1016/S0022-4405(02)00124-3

Singer, J. D., & Willett, J. B. (2003). *Applied longitudinal data analysis: Modeling change and event occurrence.* New York, NY: Oxford University Press.

Tseng, V., & Fuligni, A. J. (2000). Parent–adolescent language use and relationships among immigrant families with East Asian, Filipino, and Latin American backgrounds. *Journal of Marriage & the Family, 62,* 465–476. doi:10.1111/j.1741-3737.2000.00465.x

Willig, A. C. (1985). A meta-analysis of selected studies on the effectiveness of bilingual education. *Review of Educational Research, 55,* 269–317.

Zehler, A. M., Fleischman, H. L., Hopstock, P. J., Stephenson, T. G., Pendzick, M. L., & Sapru, S. (2003). *Descriptive study of services to LEP students and LEP students with disabilities: Vol. I* (Research Report). Washington, DC: Office of English Language Acquisition, Language Enhancement and Academic Achievement of Limited English Proficient Students, U.S. Department of Education.

8

AN IMMIGRANT ADVANTAGE IN THE EARLY SCHOOL TRAJECTORIES OF LATINO PRESCHOOLERS FROM LOW-INCOME IMMIGRANT FAMILIES

NATALIA PALACIOS

The significant rise in immigration that took place at the end of the 20th century and continues into the 21st has resulted in demographic shifts in the composition of the United States and of elementary schools in particular (see Chapter 1, this volume). These changes call attention to the academic achievement and potential of Latino immigrant children, particularly because these children are often categorized as being at risk because of their high likelihood of living in poverty with parents who have lower levels of educational attainment and English language proficiency. First-generation children who identify as Latino are the most likely to live in poverty (National Center for Children in Poverty, 2002). Children living in poverty face challenges often associated with academic difficulties, including increased family stress and lower levels of cognitive stimulation in the home. Children of immigrants may additionally be forced to confront language barriers in the home and in school that limit their ability to thrive in academic environments.

This chapter explores whether an immigrant advantage is found among the youngest cohort of children in very low-income Latino families. Specifically, I describe the results of a study I conducted that focused on the reading and math achievement of young immigrant and nonimmigrant children living in low-income families prior to formal school entry and as they transition through the elementary grades. The chapter also examines possible differences in parenting and home practices and discusses the role of language factors in understanding the immigrant differences that emerge.

LOW-INCOME CHILDREN AND EARLY ACHIEVEMENT

As of 2007, 21% of children under the age of 5 were living in poverty in the United States (see Kids Count Data Center: http://datacenter.kids count.org/). The alarming nature of this statistic is highlighted by research emphasizing the relationship between living in poverty at a young age and negative academic achievement over the short and long terms (Brooks-Gunn & Duncan, 1997; Duncan, Yeung, Brooks-Gunn, & Smith, 1998). As indicated by Duncan et al. (1998), the effects of economic conditions in early and middle childhood play a more important role in shaping children's achievement than economic conditions later in the academic trajectory. In fact, young children living in poverty are twice as likely to experience grade repetition and dropping out of high school than children not living in poverty (Duncan & Brooks-Gunn, 2000). Votruba-Drzal (2006) found that the negative effects associated with early experiences with poverty set children on achievement tracks that are difficult to change over time.

Several mechanisms through which a family's income or poverty status may affect children's outcomes have been proposed. These include the nature of the home learning environment (Brooks-Gunn, Klebanov, & Liaw, 1995; Chase-Lansdale, Gordon, Brooks-Gunn, & Klebanov, 1997; Smith, Brooks-Gunn, & Klebanov, 1997) and of the parent–child relationship (Davis-Kean, 2005; Pachter, Auinger, Palmer, & Weitzman, 2006), family structure (Brown, 2004; Foster & Kalil, 2007), material hardship (Foster & Kalil, 2005; Gershoff, Aber, Raver, & Lennon, 2007; Heckman & Masterov, 2007; Pachter et al., 2006), and increases in family stress (Formoso, Gonzales, Barrerra, & Dumka, 2007; Parke et al., 2004). These mechanisms may also be understood within a cumulative risk framework: No single risk factor is related to poor child outcomes; rather, an accumulation of factors is associated with parental report of decreased achievement (Friedman & Chase-Lansdale, 2002; Gassman-Pines & Yoshikawa, 2006; Liaw & Brooks-Gunn, 1994).

Among Latino children in the United States as of 2006, 28% lived in low-income families (Fass & Cauthen, 2006). Relative to other racial–ethnic groups, Latino children were more likely to live below the poverty line even after considering family structure and parental employment (Lichter & Landale, 1995). Thirty-three percent of immigrant children lived in low-income working families, relative to only 17% of nonimmigrant families (see Kids Count Data Center: http://datacenter.kidscount.org/). Additionally, increases in immigrant child poverty were associated with declining returns from education, employment, and work experience, with the highest levels of risk experienced by children whose families had the lowest levels of education, worked fewer hours, and had lived in the United States for shorter periods (Portes & Zhou, 1993; Zhou, 1997).

Childhood poverty and associated contextual factors may be related to the substantial gaps in achievement between Latino and non-Hispanic White children, gaps that are particularly evident among children of Mexican and Central American origin (Han, 2006; Jesse, Davis, & Pokorny, 2004; Ryabov & Van Hook, 2007). Moreover, low reading and math achievement appear to be more prevalent among Latino children whose families have lived for longer periods in the United States (Hirschman, 2001; Ryabov & Van Hook, 2007; Valdovinos D'Angelo, 2009), suggesting that length of time in the United States might serve as a useful proxy for acculturative factors that help explain the immigrant paradox.

IMMIGRANT CHILDREN AND SCHOOL SUCCESS

Despite living in disadvantaged circumstances, mixed evidence for an immigrant advantage in the health and educational outcomes of immigrant children has emerged when they are compared with children whose parents were born in the United States (Fuligni, 1997; Hummer, Powers, Pullum, Gossman, & Frisbie, 2007; Kao, 1999; Kao & Tienda, 1995; Palloni & Morenoff, 2001; Portes, 1995; Portes & Rumbaut, 1990). Explanations previously provided for this immigrant advantage include selection bias, social and kinship networks (Palloni & Morenoff, 2001), cultural norms and values transported from the home country, the interplay between immigrants' characteristics and the context of reception within the United States (Portes, 1995), and the process of acculturation over time (Berry, 2007).

Yet, the pattern of results in favor of an immigrant advantage among Latino children is not consistent. Whereas some studies have documented an advantage among first-generation children across a wide range of ages (Glick & Hohmann-Marriott, 2007; Johnson De Feyter, 2008; Palacios, Guttmannova, & Chase-Lansdale, 2008), others found no advantage at all when comparing first-, second-, and third-generation children and adolescents (Crosnoe, 2006; Fuller et al., 2008; Glick & Hohmann-Marriott, 2007; Han, 2006; Padilla, Boardman, Hummer, & Espita, 2002). Given the variability of results for research focusing on Latino immigrant children, particularly when different outcomes are considered, and the lack of research focusing on low-income

Latino preschoolers, it is not clear whether an immigrant advantage is evident among Latino preschoolers from low-income families.

The segmented assimilation hypothesis—attributing the wide variability in child and adult immigrant outcomes once in the United States to the interaction of preimmigration characteristics with postmigration context—may be useful in understanding the immigrant paradox. Within this paradigm, the outcomes of immigrant families and children are a consequence of the interaction between individual-level factors, such as English language ability and age of arrival to the United States, race, family socioeconomic status, and the characteristics of the community into which these families integrate once they have settled in the United States (Portes & Zhou, 1993; Zhou, 1997). Hence, immigrant families with young children who have a wider skill set on arrival in the United States and who immigrate to a location with favorable conditions (i.e., language support programs available for children and adults, schools able to handle a diverse student population) may have children with better long-term academic trajectories than children in families with a smaller skill set in a similarly favorable receiving community or children in families with similar skill sets but an unfavorable environment once in the United States.

A STUDY OF LATINO PRESCHOOLERS FROM LOW-INCOME FAMILIES

In a recent study, I explored the association between immigrant status and reading and math achievement among low-income Latino preschoolers. In particular, the study sought to examine immigrant differences among 2- to 5-year-old Latino children prior to school entry and as they made the transition through early schooling. I used data from Welfare, Children, and Families: A Three-City Study (http://web.jhu.edu/threecitystudy), a multidisciplinary study on the influence of welfare reform on a representative sample of 2,402 low-income children and families in low-income neighborhoods in Boston, Chicago, and San Antonio. Interviews and standardized assessments were collected in three waves (1999, 2000–2001, and 2005).[1] The sample included the youngest cohort of Latino children, ages 2 to 5 ($N = 365$), with an average age of 3 years. Children of immigrants—first- and second-generation

---

[1]In Wave 1 (1999), families living below 200% of the poverty line were randomly selected from more than 40,000 screener households; children ages 0 to 4 and 10 to 14 and the primary female caregiver were interviewed (response rate 74%). More than 90% of caregivers were mothers; "*mothers*" is used to refer to caregivers in the present analyses. Eighty-eight percent of the Wave 1 sample was interviewed at the 16-month follow-up (Wave 2 was interviewed during 2000–2001). Finally, 80% of families from Wave 1 were followed through Wave 3 of data collection (2005).

children—constituted 46% of the sample, and children of nonimmigrant parents—third-generation children—were 54% of the sample.[2] Moreover, English was the first language for 45% of the sample.

Overall, the study lends support for an immigrant advantage in reading achievement that emerges over time in letter–word identification, the measure of reading achievement. Additionally, although it documents an immigrant disadvantage in applied problem-solving skills (the measure of math achievement) at school entry, it documents an immigrant advantage in growth over time. This pattern manifests as parity in math achievement between immigrant and nonimmigrant groups at the end of the 5-year study. For a detailed description of the measures used in the study, see Appendix 8.1; for a description of the analytic plan, see Appendix 8.2.

Letter–Word Identification: Home and School Context

bar children in preschool & likelihood of knowing letter–word

One of the main findings of this study is the evidence in favor of an immigrant paradox in reading achievement. However, this advantage in reading was not evident at the start of the study when children's ages ranged between 2 and 5 years (Figure 8.1). The immigrant advantage emerged in the rate of growth, such that by the end of the study 5 years later, immigrant children experienced a substantial advantage over nonimmigrant children in letter–word recognition. More important, the child and family factors controlled in the study did not reduce the association between immigration and reading achievement.

Why does this pattern of immigrant differences in rate of growth emerge? In general, low-income children experience risk factors that may affect their achievement prior to the start of school (Brooks-Gunn & Duncan, 1997; Duncan et al., 1998; Heckman & Masterov, 2007). Whether low-income families have fewer resources to invest in children's development or because they lack the necessary skills to help their children thrive, low-income children are less likely to experience a cognitively stimulating home environment (Brooks-Gunn et al., 1995; Klebanov, Brooks-Gunn, McCarton, & McCormick, 1998; Smith et al., 1997). For example, children in low-income homes experience lower levels of vocabulary exposure and conversation, are less likely to be read to by their mother or father, and are less likely to have reading materials in the home (Brooks-Gunn & Markman, 2005; Hart & Risley, 2003; Hoff, 2003; Roskos et al., 2008). It is possible that the economic

---

[2]First- and second-generation children are jointly categorized as immigrant children because they are the children of foreign-born parents. Because the children in the sample were very young, the majority were born in the United States; the data set does not include a sufficient number of foreign-born children to allow for comparisons between first- and second-generation children.

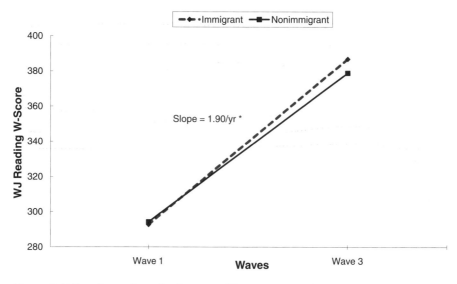

Figure 8.1. Reading trajectories between Waves 1 and 3 of the Woodcock-Johnson letter–word identification, W-scores by immigrant status. No significant differences were found in reading achievement between immigrant and nonimmigrant children at Wave 1 (the intercept). Slope differences result in a significant advantage for immigrant children by Wave 3.
*$p < .05$.

circumstances shared by the Latino immigrant and nonimmigrant children in this sample help explain why few differences emerge at school entry. In other words, immigrant and nonimmigrant families are not differentially providing the type of contexts that nurture early literacy, resulting in no differences in letter–word identification at the start of the study.

However, over the course of 5 years, immigrant children began to outperform nonimmigrant children in early reading. Controlling for the following child and family demographics and family processes did not reduce the association between immigrant status and reading achievement over time: child birth weight, gender, maternal age, education, poverty status, relationship status, number of minors in the home, child behavior problems, family routines, cognitive stimulation in the home, challenges to parenting, parenting style, and use of public services. Two key factors, which were not accounted for in this study, may help clarify these results. First, it is likely that Latino children in immigrant families are more frequently exposed to the use of Spanish in the home. In fact, children from language-minority homes are known to serve as language brokers for their parents, particularly as they get older and are more capable of navigating outside institutions (Morales & Hanson, 2005; Weisskirch & Alva, 2002). This type of continuous exposure may reinforce their early oral-language and literacy skills in Spanish. Moreover, it is possible

190   NATALIA PALACIOS

that the kinds of differences in exposure to language demonstrated by Hart and Risley (2003) between lower and higher income families—especially in the number of words heard per hour and the extent and complexity of the vocabulary experienced by children—may also be evident between Latino immigrant and nonimmigrant groups. As they acquire formal English language skills after school entry, immigrant children may be able to transfer their Spanish language skills toward reading in English (Bialystok, 2006; Lesaux & Siegel, 2003; Quiroga, Lemos-Britton, Mostafapour, Abbott, & Berninger, 2002). The hypothesis is that exposure to dual language use leads to increased metalinguistic abilities in children and thus facilitates their success when reading in English.

The second key factor may be the school context and resources to which children are exposed. If immigrant children take up services for English language learners (ELLs) at higher rates than nonimmigrant children, and ELL services successfully provide initial preliminary reading skills in English, then immigrant children would be able to use their Spanish language skills to improve their English language abilities and, perhaps, eventually outperform their nonimmigrant peers. An alternative explanatory mechanism, although not tested in this study, is that nonimmigrant children receive both lower levels of Spanish language exposure and lower quality English language interactions in the home, whereas immigrant children receive continuous reinforcement of Spanish language skills despite lower quality English language interactions in the home. In this hypothetical scenario, immigrant Latino children would be poised to reap the greatest benefits from English language instruction once they have entered the school environment.

These factors point to the significance of the relationship between home and school during this developmental period. The pattern of results—no initial difference in letter–word identification followed by an immigrant advantage 5 years later—may indicate that the child's exposure to language, in either English or Spanish, will influence their ability to take advantage of the resources that teachers and classroom provide on school entry. Those who have had more or higher quality language exposure in the home may be poised to flourish once exposed to a more formal academic setting.

Moreover, loss of language exposure in the home language over time may be detrimental and may help explain why a reading achievement gap emerges across immigrant and nonimmigrant children. Research suggests that parents often encourage children to become English language monolinguals with the expectation that this will help them do well in school (National Head Start Training and Technical Assistance Resource Center, 2008). Contrary to these expectations, dual language use is beneficial for children's reading comprehension and long-term development (August et al., 2006; Barnett, Yarosz, Thomas, Jung, & Blanco, 2007; Cheung & Slavin, 2005; Espinosa,

2008). The loss of the home language, in turn, results in a less stimulating home environment, along with the potential deterioration of cross-generational cultural ties—ability to communicate effectively with parents and grandparents, understand and maintain rituals and practices, and so on—which have negative consequences for children's achievement outcomes (August et al., 2006). Hence, as language is lost over time and across generations, nonimmigrant children and immigrant children who have been in the United States for longer periods may no longer be able to draw on the strengths within the family and home as additional resources to promote achievement, explaining why recent immigrant children outperform nonimmigrant children on measures of early reading. Future research needs to investigate the cross-generational effect of time in the United States and its potential relationship with loss of the home language and decreased reading achievement in English. It is possible that a well-developed association between home and school could prevent the loss of the home language at school entry. In fact, the Office of Head Start within the U.S. Department of Health and Human Services has recommended that teachers promote maintenance of the home language as a way of improving English language skills (National Head Start Training and Technical Assistance Resource Center, 2008). To accomplish this, the Head Start report highlighted the role that teachers and schools have in informing parents of the value of engaging children in literacy activities in the home language. The central goal of the recommendation is the prevention of home language loss and the promotion of quality literacy practices in the home language so that teachers may use children's skills in their native language for English language promotion on school entry. Many dual language programs share similar goals (Cheung & Slavin, 2005; Tabors & Lopez, 2005).

Applied Problems: Role of Maternal Caregivers

The pattern of findings is different for applied problems solving than for letter–word identification. Latino children of immigrants began the study with a significant disadvantage in math skills relative to nonimmigrant children (Figure 8.2). On the other hand, Latino immigrant children demonstrated an advantage over nonimmigrant children in the growth trajectories associated with math skills. Because of this advantage in growth over time, immigrant children were able to make up the math achievement gap with which they began the study. After a 5-year span, immigrant and nonimmigrant children demonstrated similar skill levels in math achievement. Yet, if the immigrant advantage in slope persists beyond this 5-year period, it is possible that immigrant children would demonstrate an advantage over nonimmigrant children later in their development trajectory despite having started the study with a gap in math skills.

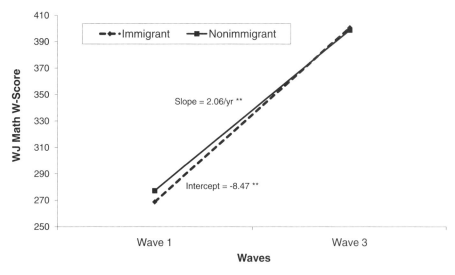

Figure 8.2. Math trajectories between Waves 1 and 3 of Woodcock-Johnson Applied Problems W-scores by immigrant status. Significant differences emerged between immigrant and nonimmigrant children in reading achievement at the intercept, with a nonimmigrant advantage. However, immigrant children's math grew more over time than nonimmigrant children's achievement. By Wave 3, both groups were performing at the same level.
$**p < .01$.

The gap between immigrant and nonimmigrant children in the beginning of the study may be attributable to home environment differences. Within this sample of low-income families, immigrant children experienced lower levels of cognitive stimulation in the home when compared with nonimmigrant children. Perhaps immigrant children have fewer materials (Brooks-Gunn & Markman, 2005) that help them develop and build the basic math skills necessary for problem solving. Yet, controlling for home cognitive stimulation along with other family processes did not account for the initial gap in achievement or advantage in growth over time. This may be expected given that the measure of cognitive stimulation weighed heavily toward assessing home conditions associated with early literacy rather than math skills.

Another factor that may be associated with the initial gap in immigrant achievement is the mother's own math and problem-solving skills. If immigrant mothers have lower skill levels compared with nonimmigrant mothers, then immigrant children may not experience the reinforcement of skills necessary to develop problem-solving skills (Englund, Luckner, Whaley, & Egeland, 2004). Unfortunately, the present study did not contain a measure of maternal skill or ability at Wave 1 that would be a useful first step in understanding the level of math proficiency of those with whom the child most engages.

It is also feasible that immigrant mothers have the necessary math skills but that the true difference between immigrant and nonimmigrant families associated with this initial gap in math skills is cultural. Perhaps immigrant families conceive of education as something that takes place in the school environment and hence do not practice early math skills with their children as an essential component for developing the building blocks necessary prior to school entry (Englund et al., 2004; Starkey & Klein, 2000; Starkey, Klein, & Wakeley, 2004; Willson & Hughes, 2006). Nonimmigrant families, despite having younger mothers, have experienced the educational system in the United States and may be more likely to understand that the practice of rudimentary math principles at home may result in highly valued skills at school entry.

But why does an immigrant advantage in Latino children's math skills develop over time? School may be an important equalizing factor for immigrant children's math achievement. If schools begin teaching basic math concepts in the early grades, despite an initial disadvantage for immigrant children both immigrant and nonimmigrant children would be exposed to the same material. As immigrant children grasp these early concepts, they are experiencing rapid growth that allows them to catch up with their nonimmigrant peers over time. Conversely, because nonimmigrant children may already have been exposed to early math concepts at home or in child care environments, they may demonstrate slower growth trajectories, particularly during the early elementary grades. Although the present study has not followed students beyond the 5-year follow up, it would be interesting to see if the immigrant advantage in growth persists over time, resulting in a level advantage in math skills, or if nonimmigrant children experience an acceleration in math skills once new concepts are introduced that nullifies the present immigrant advantage in the rate of growth.

ACCULTURATION AND ACHIEVEMENT

Acculturation—the bidirectional process by which immigrants are changed by their context and the context is changed by the presence of immigrants (Berry, 2007; García Coll & Magnuson, 1997; García Coll & Szalacha, 2004)—was not directly measured in this study. However, length of time in the United States served as a proxy for the effects of acculturation, with the underlying assumption that the longer one lives in a given context the more likely it is that the influence of that context will manifest in outcomes and behavior. The results for the study support this contention, with an increase

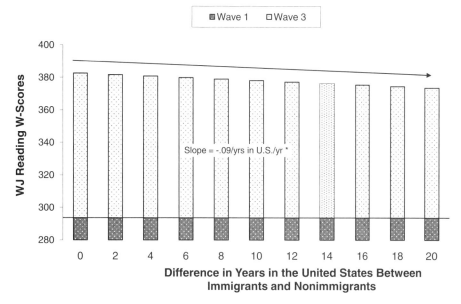

Figure 8.3. Reading Woodcock-Johnson Letter–Word Identification W-scores in Waves 1 and 3 by the difference in years spent in the United States between immigrants and nonimmigrants. No differences in the reading achievement intercept emerged at Wave 1. More time in the United States was associated with lower growth in reading over time.
*$p < .05$.

in the number of years in the United States predicting poorer outcomes in reading and math over time. In fact, it appears that the longer an individual has lived in the United States, the slower they are likely to make gains in reading achievement over time (Figure 8.3) and the higher their initial math score but the slower they make gains in math achievement over time (Figure 8.4).

Overall, these patterns corroborate the immigrant versus nonimmigrant comparisons in reading and math achievement. Yet, the findings may also provide additional insight about the process of acculturation. The results suggest that the longer low-income Latino preschoolers and their families spend in the particular context to which they are acculturating, the more likely they are to have deteriorating outcomes. If Latino immigrant families are more likely to live in poverty, settle in communities with fewer resources, and send children to schools with low-achieving profiles, the negative associations among these detrimental contextual factors may, across time, overwhelm potential protective factors (i.e., family cohesion and extended kin networks, strong work ethic, aspiration for a better life) held by immigrants at the time of migration to the United States. As posited by the segmented assimilation hypothesis—

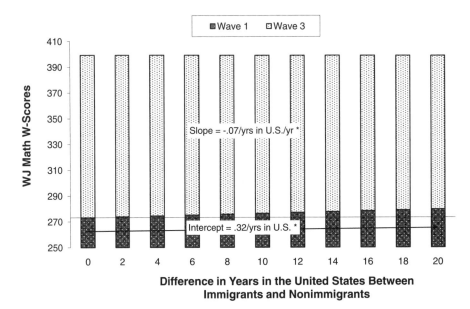

Figure 8.4. Math Woodcock-Johnson Applied Problems W-scores in Waves 1 and 3 by the difference in years spent in the United States between immigrants and nonimmigrants. Additional years in the United States were associated with an advantage in math achievement at Wave 1 but a decrease in the growth over time.
*$p < .05$.

the interaction between premigration characteristics and postmigration context—immigrant families who experience continuous negative environments may experience downward assimilation trajectories, decreasing children's likelihood of achievement across generations.

The importance of context once in the United States does not obviate the possibility that selection forces drive immigration to the United States. Hence, mothers' preimmigration characteristics are important factors, particularly for understanding reading and math achievement at the beginning of the study. To that effect, the analysis controlled for maternal and family characteristics potentially associated with immigration as well as with children's early achievement; controlling for these characteristics did not alter the pattern of results in the present study. Although this study documents a Latino immigrant advantage in reading and an advantage in math skill over time, it does not provide a definitive answer on the question of the immigrant paradox. Variability in the types of outcome measured, the selection of samples included for analysis, and the way that immigrant groups are defined may influence whether positive or negative development outcomes are evident in studies that include immigrant children and families.

CONCLUSIONS

Within the past 5 years, the mean age at entry into the United States has decreased from 9.8 years to approximately 5 years, and 16% of all children under age 10 were born to immigrant parents in the United States (Capps et al., 2005; Chase-Lansdale, Valdovinos D'Angelo, & Palacios, 2007; Tienda & Mitchell, 2006). This figure approaches 50% in major cities such as Chicago, New York, Los Angeles, and Miami. More than 4 million children with limited English proficiency, or approximately 9.3% of total public school enrollment, were estimated to be attending schools in the United States in 2000. This represented a 27% increase relative to the number of English proficient children enrolled just 3 years earlier (Carnoy & Loeb, 2002); the U.S Census Bureau has projected that ELLs will may make up nearly 40% of the school-aged population by 2030.

Integrating increasing numbers of Latino children of immigrants into the academic infrastructure of the United States may be particularly taxing in central cities, which often contend with children's poverty and other disadvantages (Darling-Hammond, 2004; Ingersoll, 2001; Jacob, 2007; Murnane & Steele, 2007; Van Hook, Brown, & Kwenda, 2004). By eliminating economic factors, it is possible to focus on other issues that may be particularly important for immigrant children's academic achievement. Developing a better understanding of children's home language environment may begin to clarify whether immigrant children who excel in reading are experiencing richer, more frequent non-English language environments prior to formal schooling. It is possible that these experiences in the home language translate to skills in English at school entry.

Additionally, understanding the community in which immigrant families settle on their arrival in the United States may be increasingly important, particularly for immigrants to new receiving communities. If longer periods of time in the United States are associated with more negative outcomes overall, then it is possible that the context of arrival may be having a deleterious effect on children's achievement across generational groups. Again, the nexus between home and school is critical for understanding the long-term cross-generational differences in achievement. If school is a community context, and immigrant families live within communities that have generally limited school resources and few or no language services, in particular, to assist in the academic transition, then early differences could be magnified over the long term and across generations. By attending schools with lower quality classrooms or classrooms with lower quality teachers, immigrant children are beginning a trajectory that places them at greater risk over time.

Why is the nexus between home and school important if school services and teacher quality are the factors necessary to understand immigrant differences? School factors alone do not explain the immigrant differences. The nexus between home and school, again, is crucial to understanding why first-generation children excel over third-generation children when both groups have access to similar ELL services or teacher quality at school. In other words, immigrant children may potentially overcome language barriers by taking advantage of school services and by harnessing the potential resources of the language spoken in the home.

Perhaps there is something unique about first- and second-generation children and families that is critical for understanding why they are able to excel academically even in dire circumstances. This key factor may be the *quality* of the language interactions in the native language that take place in the home. Although speaking a foreign language at home may initially manifest in poor outcomes for language-minority children, the quality of the home language is setting up a base of language skills that will allow children to transfer skill from the home language to English at a later time (Bialystok, 2006; Lesaux & Siegel, 2003; Leseman & de Jong, 1998; Quiroga et al., 2002). If the language interactions in the home are of lower quality, then children do not have a foundation of skills in another language that they can transfer during the acquisition of English language skills and achievement. Moreover, if they do not have the foundational skills, children with lower quality language interactions in the home may not be able to obtain the optimal benefits from ELL services offered when they arrive at school. The underlying assumption, however, is that communities and schools will deploy the necessary resources to assist low-income Latino families and their children. Although preparing children for school begins within the home, there is a strong demand for teachers with the necessary training to understand the unique needs of ELLs and of low-income Latino children in particular.

APPENDIX 8.1: MEASURES

Dependent variables. This study focuses on two outcomes: letter–word identification for early reading achievement and applied problem solving for early math achievement.

Letter–word identification. The Letter–Word Identification subscale of the Woodcock Johnson Psycho Educational Battery—Revised (WJ-R) was administered across the three waves of data collection (Woodcock & Johnson, 1990). The items are arranged in order of increasing difficulty with easier items administered first. The subtest required children to identify isolated letters and words represented in large type to assess their reading skills. The letter–word subscale measures reading identification, reflecting children's ability to recognize and decode words ($\alpha = 0.92$).

Applied problems. The Applied Problems subscale of the WJ-R was also administered across the three waves. This subtest measures children's skill in analyzing and solving practical problems in mathematics. Children were required to recognize the necessary mathematical procedures to solve the problem and then perform relatively simple counting, addition or subtraction operations. Because many of the problems include extraneous stimuli or information, the child must also decide which data to include in the count or calculation ($\alpha = 0.91$).

This study uses the w-scores of the Letter–Word and Applied Problems subscales in the longitudinal analyses. W-scores—equal interval, constant-metric scores computed using a transformation of the Rasch-ability scale—do not adjust for age-related improvements and are sensitive to patterns of change over time (Bryk & Raudenbush, 1987; Rasch, 1960/1980; Sanbonmatsu, Kling, Duncan, & Brooks-Gunn, 2006; Wright & Stone, 1979). The scores are centered at 500, the average score at the start of fifth grade (Woodcock & Mather, 1990). The Spanish version of the WJ-R was administered if either the child or parent reported that Spanish was the child's primary language (Woodcock & Muñoz-Sandoval, 1996).

Independent variables. The study seeks to explore differences by generational status and by length of time in the United States. Control variables include child, maternal, and family demographic factors, family processes, and use of public services.

Generational status. The main independent variable is the generational status of the children. Children of foreign-born parents were categorized as immigrant children—the children are first and second generation. Those who were born in the United States to U.S.-born parents were classified as nonimmigrant. Thus, the comparison is between children of immigrants and nonimmigrants.

Time in the United States. Length of time in the United States serves as a proxy for unmeasured acculturation factors. For immigrant children, the variable captures the length of time since the parents arrived in the United States; for nonimmigrant third generation children, the variable is the mother's age.

Additional variables. Child variables include the age of the child, maternal report of child's birth weight measured in pounds, and child gender. Parent variables include mother's age, highest level of education, and whether English is their first language. Family demographic variables provide information regarding the family context, including poverty status, number of minors in the household, and relationship status (single, separated, or married). Home Observation for Measurement of the Environment (HOME) family processes include measures of child internalizing and externalizing behavior problems, family routines ($\alpha = .68$), HOME cognitive stimulation, challenges to parenting ($\alpha = .76$), and authoritative parenting ($\alpha = .54$). Mothers also reported on the family's reliance on public resources, including their take-up of food stamps, Medicaid, WIC, and welfare.

APPENDIX 8.2: ANALYTIC PLAN

The analysis used hierarchical linear models (HLM) with letter–word and applied problems at each assessment—Waves 1 (1999), 2 (2000–2001), and 3 (2005). Multilevel modeling of longitudinal data with repeated outcome measures was used to assess the initial differences by immigrant status in Latino preschooler's level of achievement at the start of the study when children ranged between 2 to 5 years of age. Additionally, the study explored differences among Latino preschoolers in the rate of growth of achievement over time across the three waves of the study, which spanned a 6-year period. Subsequently, a host of potential explanatory factors were included to explore whether the differences in trajectories persisted even after the inclusion of important covariates.

Letter–word trajectories and applied problem trajectories were modeled separately. Level 1, the within-person model, includes a measure of time, describing the individual growth trajectories by capturing the level and the rate of change in letter–word and applied problems achievement over time, such that time at the Wave 1 assessment was coded as 0; time at Waves 2 and 3 were coded as the number of years after the spring of kindergarten assessment. The intercept was centered at Wave 1 because it captures the mean level and variability in both outcomes prior to formal school entry.

To capture between-person differences in the achievement trajectories, child, maternal, and family demographic, along with family processes and use of public services were modeled at Level 2. The first conditional model includes generational status, the second controls for child demographics, and Models 3 and 4 include maternal and family demographic factors, respectively. The remaining variables were entered in separate conceptual blocks, first introducing proximal variables, such as family processes, and then distal variables, such as public service use, to examine how the inclusion of each block of variables would influence the association between immigrant generational status and reading trajectories (Chase-Lansdale et al., 2007). Thus, the final model at Level 2 builds on the preceding models and includes all controls:

$$
\begin{aligned}
\pi_{0i} = \ &\beta_{00} + \beta_{01}\text{Immigrant Status}_i + \beta_{02}\text{Child Demographics}_i \\
&+ \beta_{03}\text{Maternal Demographics}_i + \beta_{04}\text{Family Demographics}_i \\
&+ \beta_{05}\text{Family Processes}_i + \beta_{06}\text{Public Services}_i + \upsilon_{0i}
\end{aligned} \tag{1}
$$

$$\pi_{1i} = \beta_{10} + \beta_{11}\text{Immigrant Status}_i + \beta_{12}\text{Child Demographics}_i$$
$$+ \beta_{13}\text{Maternal Demographics}_i + \beta_{14}\text{Family Demographics}_i$$
$$+ \beta_{15}\text{Family Processes}_i + \beta_{16}\text{Public Services}_i + \upsilon_{1i} \qquad (2)$$

Equation 1 is the Level 2 model of the outcomes at Wave 1; Equation 2 is the Level 2 model for the change in the outcomes between Waves 1 and 3. Note that Equations 1 and 2 are the same for letter–word identification and applied problem solving despite being modeled separately.

An additional model changes the key variable from immigrant status to years of living in the United States:

$$\pi_{0i} = \beta_{00} + \beta_{01}\text{Years in the US}_i + \beta_{02}\text{Child Demographics}_i$$
$$+ \beta_{03}\text{Maternal Demographics}_i + \beta_{04}\text{Family Demographics}_i$$
$$+ \beta_{05}\text{Family Processes}_i + \beta_{06}\text{Public Services}_i + \upsilon_{0i} \qquad (3)$$

$$\pi_{1i} = \beta_{10} + \beta_{11}\text{Years in the US}_i + \beta_{12}\text{Child Demographics}_i$$
$$+ \beta_{13}\text{Maternal Demographics}_i + \beta_{14}\text{Family Demographics}_i$$
$$+ \beta_{15}\text{Family Processes}_i + \beta_{16}\text{Public Services}_i + \upsilon_{1i} \qquad (4)$$

Given that years in the United States for children whose mothers were born in the United States is coded as mother's age, maternal age is removed from the maternal demographics block of variables in this model. The β_{01} coefficient will provide the association between one additional year of living in the United States and letter–word identification in one set of results and with applied problems in the subsequent analysis.

REFERENCES

August, D., Snow, C., Carlo, M., Proctor, C., de San Francisco, A. R., Duursma, E., & Szuber, A. (2006). Literacy development in elementary school second-language learners. *Topics in Language Disorders, 26,* 351–364. doi:10.1097/00011363-200610000-00007

Barnett, W., Yarosz, D. J., Thomas, J., Jung, K., & Blanco, D. (2007). Two-way and monolingual English immersion in preschool education: An experimental comparison. *Early Childhood Research Quarterly, 22,* 277–293. doi:10.1016/j.ecresq.2007.03.003

Berry, J. (2007). Acculturation strategies and adaptation. In J. E. Lansford, K. Deater-Deckard, & M. H. Bornstein (Eds.), *Immigrant families in contemporary society* (pp. 69–82). New York, NY: Guilford Press.

Bialystok, E. (2006). Bilingualism at school: Effect on the acquisition of literacy. In P. McCardle & E. Hoff (Eds.), *Childhood bilingualism: Research on infancy through school age* (pp. 107–124). Clevedon, England: Multilingual Matters.

Brooks-Gunn, J., & Duncan, G.(1997). The effects of poverty on children. *The Future of Children, 7*, 55–71. doi:10.2307/1602387

Brooks-Gunn, J., Klebanov, P. K., & Liaw, F. (1995). The learning, physical, and emotional environment of the home in the context of poverty: The Infant Health and Development Program. *Children and Youth Services Review, 17*, 251–276. doi:10.1016/0190-7409(95)00011-Z

Brooks-Gunn, J., & Markman, L. B. (2005). The contribution of parenting to ethnic and racial gaps in school readiness. *The Future of Children, 15*, 139–168. doi:10.1353/foc.2005.0001

Brown, S. L. (2004). Family structure and child well-being: The significance of parental cohabitation. *Journal of Marriage and Family, 66*, 351–367. doi:10.1111/j.1741-3737.2004.00025.x

Bryk, A. S., & Raudenbush, S. W. (1987). Application of hierarchical linear models to assessing change. *Psychological Bulletin, 101*, 147–158. doi:10.1037/0033-2909.101.1.147

Capps, R., Fix, M., Murray, J., Ost, J., Passel, J., & Herwantoro, S. (2005). *The new demography of America's schools: Immigration and the No Child Left Behind Act.* Washington, DC: The Urban Institute.

Carnoy, M., & Loeb, S. (2002). Does external accountability affect student outcomes? A cross-state analysis. *Educational Evaluation and Policy Analysis, 24*, 305–331. doi:10.3102/01623737024004305

Chase-Lansdale, P. L., Gordon, R. A., Brooks-Gunn, J., & Klebanov, P. K. (1997). Neighborhood and family influences on the intellectual and behavioral competence of preschool and early school age children. In J. Brooks-Gunn, G. J. Duncan, & L. J. Aber (Eds.), *Neighborhood poverty: Context and consequences for children* (pp. 79–118). New York, NY: Russell Sage Foundation.

Chase-Lansdale, P. L., Valdovinos D'Angelo, A., & Palacios, N. (2007). A multidisciplinary perspective on the development of young children in immigrant families. In J. E. Lansford, K. Deater-Deckard, & M. H. Bornstein (Eds.), *Immigrant families in contemporary society* (pp. 137–156). New York, NY: Guilford Press.

Cheung, A., & Slavin, R. E. (2005). Effective reading programs for English language learners and other language-minority students. *Bilingual Research Journal, 29*, 241–267. doi:10.1080/15235882.2005.10162835

Crosnoe, R. (2006). Health and the education of children from racial/ethnic minority and immigrant families. *Journal of Health and Social Behavior, 47*, 77–93. doi:10.1177/002214650604700106

Darling-Hammond, L. (2004). Inequality and the right to learn: Access to qualified teachers in California's public schools. *Teachers College Record, 106*, 1936–1966. doi:10.1111/j.1467-9620.2004.00422.x

Davis-Kean, P. E. (2005). The influence of parent education and family income on child achievement: The indirect role of parental expectations and the home environment. *Journal of Family Psychology, 19,* 294–304. doi:10.1037/0893-3200.19.2.294

Duncan, G. J., & Brooks-Gunn, J. (2000). Family poverty, welfare reform, and child development. *Child Development, 71,* 188–196. doi:10.1111/1467-8624.00133

Duncan, G. J., Yeung, W., Brooks-Gunn, J., & Smith, J. R. (1998). How much does childhood poverty affect the life chances of children? *American Sociological Review, 63,* 406–423. doi:10.2307/2657556

Englund, M. M., Luckner, A. E., Whaley, G. J. L., & Egeland, B. (2004). Children's achievement in early elementary school: Longitudinal effects of parental involvement, expectations, and quality of assistance. *Journal of Educational Psychology, 96,* 723–730. doi:10.1037/0022-0663.96.4.723

Espinosa, L. M. (2008). *Challenging common myths about young English language learners.* New York, NY: Foundation for Child Development.

Fass, S., & Cauthen, N. K. (2006). *Who are America's poor children?* Retrieved from http://www.nccp.org/publications/pub_684.html

Formoso, D., Gonzales, N. A., Barrerra, M., & Dumka, L. E. (2007). Interparental relations, maternal employment and fathering in Mexican American families. *Journal of Marriage and Family, 69,* 26–39. doi:10.1111/j.1741-3737.2006.00341.x

Foster, E. M., & Kalil, A. (2005). Developmental psychology and public policy: Progress and prospects. *Developmental Psychology, 41,* 827–832. doi:10.1037/0012-1649.41.6.827

Foster, E. M., & Kalil, A. (2007). Living arrangements and children's development in low-income White, Black, and Latino families. *Child Development, 78,* 1657–1674. doi:10.1111/j.1467-8624.2007.01091.x

Friedman, R. J., & Chase-Lansdale, P. L. (2002). Chronic adversities. In M. Rutter & E. Taylor (Eds.), *Child and adolescent psychiatry* (4th ed., pp. 261–276). London, England: Blackwell.

Fuligni, A. J. (1997). The academic achievement of adolescents from immigrant families: The roles of family background, attitudes, and behavior. *Child Development, 68,* 351–363.

Fuller, B., Bein, E., Bridges, H., Jung, H., Rabe-Hesketh, S., Halfon, N., & Kuo, A. (2008). *Ethnic differences in infant health and cognition: The roots of the immigrant paradox.* Unpublished manuscript, Policy Analysis for California Education, University of California, Berkeley, and Stanford University, Stanford, CA.

García Coll, C., & Magnuson, K. A. (1997). The psychological experience of immigration: A developmental perspective. In A. Booth (Ed.), *Immigration and the family: Research and policy on U.S. immigrants* (pp. 91–131). Hillsdale, NJ: Erlbaum.

García Coll, C., & Szalacha, L. (2004). The multiple contexts of middle childhood. *The Future of Children, 14,* 81–97.

Gassman-Pines, A., & Yoshikawa, H. (2006). The effects of antipoverty programs on children's cumulative level of poverty-related risk. *Developmental Psychology, 42*, 981–999. doi:10.1037/0012-1649.42.6.981

Gershoff, E. T., Aber, L. J., Raver, C. C., & Lennon, M. C. (2007). Income is not enough: Incorporating material hardship into models of income associations with parenting and child development. *Child Development, 78*, 70–95. doi:10.1111/j.1467-8624.2007.00986.x

Glick, J. E., & Hohmann-Marriott, B. (2007). Academic performance of young children of immigrant families: The significance of race, ethnicity, and national origins. *The International Migration Review, 41*, 371–402. doi:10.1111/j.1747-7379.2007.00072.x

Han, W.-J. (2006). Academic achievements of children in immigrant families. *Educational Research Review, 1*, 286–318.

Hart, B., & Risley, T. R. (2003). The early catastrophe: The 30 million word gap by age 3. *American Educator, 27*, 4–9.

Heckman, J. J., & Masterov, D. (2007). *The productivity argument for investing in young children* (Working Paper 13016). Cambridge, MA: National Bureau of Economic Research.

Hirschman, C. (2001). The educational enrollment of immigrant youth: A test of the segmented-assimilation hypothesis. *Demography, 38*, 317–336. doi:10.1353/dem.2001.0028

Hoff, E. (2003). The specificity of environmental influences: Socioeconomic status affects early vocabulary development via maternal speech. *Child Development, 74*, 1368–1378. doi:10.1111/1467-8624.00612

Hummer, R. A., Powers, D. A., Pullum, S. G., Gossman, G. L., & Frisbie, W. P. (2007). Paradox found (again): Infant mortality among the Mexican-origin population in the United States. *Demography, 44*, 441–457. doi:10.1353/dem.2007.0028

Ingersoll, R. M. (2001). Teacher turnover and teacher shortages: An organizational analysis. *American Educational Research Journal, 38*, 499–534. doi:10.3102/00028312038003499

Jacob, B. A. (2007). The challenges of staffing urban schools with effective teachers. *The Future of Children, 17*, 129–153. doi:10.1353/foc.2007.0005

Jesse, D., Davis, A., & Pokorny, N. (2004). High-achieving middle schools for Latino students in poverty. *Journal of Education for Students Placed at Risk, 9*, 23–45. doi:10.1207/S15327671ESPR0901_2

Johnson De Feyter, J. (2008). *Disentangling the effect of nativity status, race/ethnicity, and country of origin to better predict educational outcomes for young immigrant children.* Unpublished master's thesis, George Mason University, Fairfax, VA.

Kao, G. (1999). Psychological well-being and education achievement among immigrant youth. In D. J. Hernandez (Ed.), *Children of immigrants: Health, adjustment and public assistance* (pp. 410–477). Washington, DC: National Academy Press.

Kao, G., & Tienda, M. (1995). Optimism and achievement: The educational performance of immigrant youth. *Social Science Quarterly, 76,* 1–19.

Klebanov, P. K., Brooks-Gunn, J., McCarton, C., & McCormick, M. C. (1998). The contribution of neighborhood and family income to developmental test scores over the first three years of life. *Child Development, 69,* 1420–1436. doi:10.2307/1132275

Lesaux, N. K., & Siegel, L. S. (2003). The development of reading in children who speak English as a second language. *Developmental Psychology, 39,* 1005–1019. doi:10.1037/0012-1649.39.6.1005

Leseman, P. P., & de Jong, P. F. (1998). Home literacy: Opportunity, instruction, cooperation and socio-emotional quality predicting early reading achievement. *Reading Research Quarterly, 33,* 294–318. doi:10.1598/RRQ.33.3.3

Liaw, F., & Brooks-Gunn, J. (1994). Cumulative familial risks and low-birthweight children's cognitive and behavioral development. *Journal of Clinical Child Psychology, 23,* 360–372. doi:10.1207/s15374424jccp2304_2

Lichter, D. T., & Landale, N. S. (1995). Parental work, family structure, and poverty among Latino children. *Journal of Marriage & the Family, 57,* 346–354. doi:10.2307/353688

Morales, A., & Hanson, W. (2005). Language brokering: An integrative review of the literature. *Hispanic Journal of Behavioral Sciences, 27,* 471–503. doi:10.1177/0739986305281333

Murnane, R. J., & Steele, J. L. (2007). What is the problem? The challenge of providing effective teachers for all children. *The Future of Children, 17,* 15–43. doi:10.1353/foc.2007.0010

National Center for Children in Poverty. (2002). *Children of immigrants: A statistical profile.* New York, NY: Mailman School of Public Health, Columbia University.

National Head Start Training and Technical Assistance Resource Center. (2008). *Dual language learning: What does it take?* Washington, DC: Office of Head Start, Administration for Children and Families, U.S. Department of Health and Human Services.

Pachter, L. M., Auinger, P., Palmer, R., & Weitzman, M. (2006). Do parenting and the home environment, maternal depression, neighborhood, and chronic poverty affect child behavior problems differently in different racial ethnic groups? *Pediatrics, 117,* 1329–1338. doi:10.1542/peds.2005-1784

Padilla, Y. C., Boardman, J. D., Hummer, R. A., & Espita, M. (2002). Is the Mexican American "epidemiological paradox" advantage at birth maintained through early childhood. *Social Forces, 80,* 1101–1123. doi:10.1353/sof.2002.0014

Palacios, N., Guttmannova, K., & Chase-Lansdale, P. L. (2008). Early reading achievement of children in immigrant families: Is there an immigrant paradox? *Developmental Psychology, 44,* 1381–1395. doi:10.1037/a0012863

Palloni, A., & Morenoff, J. D. (2001). Interpreting the paradoxical in the Hispanic paradox: Demographic and epidemiologic approaches. *Annals of the New York Academy of Sciences, 954*, 140–174. doi:10.1111/j.1749-6632.2001.tb02751.x

Parke, R. D., Coltrane, S., Duffy, S., Buriel, R., Dennis, J., Powers, J., . . . Widaman, K. F. (2004). Economic stress, parenting, and child adjustment in Mexican American and European American families. *Child Development, 75*, 1632–1656. doi:10.1111/j.1467-8624.2004.00807.x

Portes, A. (1995). Children of immigrants: Segmented assimilation and its determinants. In A. Portes (Ed.), *The economic sociology of immigrants: Essays on networks, ethnicity, and entrepreneurship* (pp. 248–279). New York, NY: Russell Sage Foundation.

Portes, A., & Rumbaut, R. G. (1990). *Immigrant America: A portrait*. Berkeley: University of California Press.

Portes, A., & Zhou, M. (1993). The new second generation: Segmented assimilation and its variants. *The Annals of the American Academy of Political and Social Science, 530*, 74–96. doi:10.1177/0002716293530001006

Quiroga, T., Lemos-Britton, Z., Mostafapour, E., Abbott, R. D., & Berninger, V. W. (2002). Phonological awareness and beginning reading in Spanish-speaking ESL first graders: Research into practice. *Journal of School Psychology, 40*, 85–111. doi:10.1016/S0022-4405(01)00095-4

Rasch, G. (1980). *Probabilistic models for some intelligence and attainment tests (expanded edition)*. Chicago, IL: The University of Chicago Press. (Original work published 1960)

Roskos, K., Ergul, C., Bryan, T., Burstein, K., Christie, J., & Han, M. (2008). Who's learning what words and how fast? Preschoolers' vocabulary growth in an early literacy program. *Journal of Research in Childhood Education, 22*, 275–290. doi:10.1080/02568540809594627

Ryabov, I., & Van Hook, J. (2007). School segregation and academic achievement among Hispanic children. *Social Science Research, 36*, 767–788. doi:10.1016/j.ssresearch.2006.04.002

Sanbonmatsu, L., Kling, J. R., Duncan, G., & Brooks-Gunn, J. (2006). Neighborhoods and academic achievement: Results from the Moving to Opportunity Experiment. *The Journal of Human Resources, 41*, 649–691.

Smith, J. R., Brooks-Gunn, J., & Klebanov, P. K. (1997). The consequences of living in poverty for young children's cognitive and verbal ability and early school achievement. In G. Duncan & J. Brooks-Gunn (Eds.), *Consequences of growing up poor* (pp. 132–189). New York, NY: Russell Sage Foundation.

Starkey, P., & Klein, A. (2000). Fostering parental support for children's mathematical development: An intervention with Head Start families. *Early Education and Development, 11*, 659–680. doi:10.1207/s15566935eed1105_7

Starkey, P., Klein, A., & Wakeley, A. (2004). Enhancing young children's mathematical knowledge though a pre-kindergarten mathematics intervention. *Early Childhood Research Quarterly, 19*, 99–120. doi:10.1016/j.ecresq.2004.01.002

Tabors, P. O., & Lopez, L. M. (2005). *How can teachers and parents help young children become (and stay) bilingual?* Washington, DC: Administration for Children and Families, U.S. Department of Health and Human Services.

Tienda, M., & Mitchell, F. (Eds.). (2006). *Hispanics and the future of America.* Washington, DC: National Academy Press.

Valdovinos D'Angelo, A. (2009). *Latino immigrant fathers: Implications for the well-being of their preschool-aged children.* Unpublished manuscript, School of Education and Social Policy, Northwestern University, Evanston, IL.

Van Hook, J., Brown, S. L., & Kwenda, M. N. (2004). A decomposition of trends in poverty among children of immigrants. *Demography, 41,* 649–670. doi:10.1353/dem.2004.0038

Votruba-Drzal, E. (2006). Economic disparities in middle childhood development: Does income matter? *Developmental Psychology, 42,* 1154–1167. doi:10.1037/0012-1649.42.6.1154

Weisskirch, R. S., & Alva, S. A. (2002). Language brokering and the acculturation of Latino children. *Hispanic Journal of Behavioral Sciences, 24,* 369–378. doi:10.1177/0739986302024003007

Willson, V. L., & Hughes, J. N. (2006). Retention of Hispanic/Latino students in first grade: Child, parent, teacher, school, and peer predictors. *Journal of School Psychology, 44,* 31–49. doi:10.1016/j.jsp.2005.12.001

Woodcock, R. W., & Johnson, M. B. (1990). *Woodcock-Johnson Psycho Educational Battery—Revised.* Allen, TX: DLM.

Woodcock, R. W., & Mather, N. (1990). *Woodcock-Johnson tests of achievement—Revised examiner's manual.* Allen, TX: DLM Teaching Resources.

Woodcock, R. W., & Muñoz-Sandoval, A. F. (1996). *Bateria Woodcock-Muñoz Pruebas de Aprovechamiento—Revisada* [Woodcock-Muñoz Achievement Test Battery—Revised]. Chicago, IL: Riverside.

Wright, B. D., & Stone, M. H. (1979). *Best test design.* Chicago, IL: MESA Press.

Zhou, M. (1997). Growing up American: The challenge confronting immigrant children and children of immigrants. *Annual Review of Sociology, 23,* 63–95. doi:10.1146/annurev.soc.23.1.63

9

STUDENT ENGAGEMENT, SCHOOL CLIMATE, AND ACADEMIC ACHIEVEMENT OF IMMIGRANTS' CHILDREN

SUET-LING PONG AND KRISTINA L. ZEISER

During the past 3 decades, the U.S. school population has witnessed an unprecedented growth in the number of foreign-born children and children of immigrants (Capps, Fix, Murray, Passel, & Herwantoro, 2005). One concern that policymakers have about this demographic growth is these children's adaptation to the U.S. school system. Their future success as adults hinges on how well they do in school as children. An indicator of students' well-being in school is their *engagement*—the affective component of schooling that includes students' enthusiasm about, interest in, and attachment to school (Newmann, 1992). However, it is also important to consider how children of immigrants perceive their school climate because this shapes both their engagement and their academic achievement. How adolescents view and feel about school is associated with their cognitive achievement (Anderson, 1982), which in turn influences adolescents' access to postsecondary education and labor market success (Farkas & Vicknair, 1996; Jencks & Phillips, 1998). Thus, understanding adolescent students' academic achievement and school engagement would be useful for guiding policies. On the one hand, if immigrants' children fall behind

We thank William Gerhardt for his useful research assistance.

native children, efforts should be made to promote their achievement. If, on the other hand, there is an "immigrant paradox," such that immigrant students outperform native students, then it is important for policies to preserve and maintain the desirable attitudes and perceptions of immigrants' children and to prevent their decline with increasing assimilation.

Immigration research on adolescent children's academic and behavioral achievement in the 1980s and beyond has widely documented an *immigrant paradox*—earlier generations of immigrants' youth showed better academic, behavioral, emotional, and health outcomes than native youth with native parentage (e.g., Harker, 2001; Hernandez & Charney, 1998; Kao, 2004; Kao & Tienda, 1995; Keller & Tillman, 2008; Pong & Hao, 2007; Pong, Hao, & Gardner, 2005). This seems paradoxical because the superior outcomes of the earlier generations counter what would be predicted given their lower socio-economic status and lack of English language skills. However, this phenomenon was not found to be universal in time (Glick & White, 2003) or across different host countries (Levels & Dronkers, 2008; Schnepf, 2007). It is also unclear if this tendency results from a particular migration stream to the United States within a certain period of time. Although more work is needed to discover why the immigrant paradox varies in time and space, it is important to document its existence or absence using more recent data. This chapter uses a recent U.S. database of adolescents collected in the 2000s (the Educational Longitudinal Study of 2002 [ELS]) to help unravel this puzzle.

Immigrant assimilation is a multifaceted process that occurs in diverse contexts and could lead to different adolescent outcomes (Greenman & Xie, 2008). To date, scholars who have examined immigrant assimilation for children have focused largely on their academic achievement and, to a lesser extent, on their psychosocial or affective outcomes. Few have studied generational differences in students' attitudes and their experiences in school. The values immigrants' children place on their schooling, their attachment to school, and their perceptions of school climate would frame their immediate school environments, shaping their emotional and cognitive engagement in school. These intangible school factors are highly associated with students' school performance and persistence (Anderson, 1982; Finn & Rock, 1997; Fredricks, Blumenfeld, & Paris, 2004; Neale, Gill, & Tismer, 1970). Because these social–psychological factors are much needed for students' success, it is important to examine if they too follow a pattern of generational decline that may be responsible for the generational decline in academic achievement.

Generational decline is often used as evidence in support of the immigrant paradox. In this chapter, we detect if the immigrant paradox exists by examining generational differences in students' grade point average, math achievement, student engagement, and school climate. Using data collected in

2002, we ask the following questions: (a) Is there generational decline in academic achievement among adolescents in high school? (b) Is there corresponding generational decline in adolescents' affective engagement in school and their perception of the school climate? (c) Do generational declines in student engagement and perceived school climate explain the observed generational declines in student achievement? (d) Do the generational patterns differ within specific races–ethnicities?

The term *generation* is widely used in the immigration literature to refer to three groups of children. The *first generation* consists of foreign-born children with foreign-born parents. The *second generation* is the group of U.S.-born children with foreign-born parents, and the *third or higher order generation* (*third-plus generation* hereafter) refers to native children with native parents. Past research suggests that race–ethnicity and country of origin are prime predictors of student achievement, which often trump generational status (Glick & White, 2003). Thus, in our investigation of generational differences, we must take into account differences in race–ethnicity and country of origin as well.

GENERATIONS, ASSIMILATION THEORIES, AND THE IMMIGRANT PARADOX

The research on the immigrant paradox is founded on evidence of *generational decline*, that is, earlier generations exhibiting better outcomes than later generations. It is important to note that these generations are neither genealogical nor historical in nature (Smith, 2003). Rather, they are synthetic and cross-sectional. Whereas genealogical or historical generations allow us to test major assimilation theories that span long periods of time, cross-sectional generations enable us to detect contemporary differences in child outcomes due to nativity. A comparison between contemporary first and second generations reveals differences between groups of children who are themselves foreign or native born. A comparison between the first and second generations on the one hand, and the third-plus generation on the other, reveals differences between groups of children with and without parents who are foreign born. These are useful comparisons that facilitate better understanding of the current well-being of immigrants' children.

The differences in outcomes for different cross-sectional generations may not be explained by the framework of major assimilation theories that depict changes of genealogical generations. For example, the classical *straight-line assimilation theory* by Gordon (1964) or others predicts socioeconomic attainment of children that surpass their immigrant parents. A rigorous test of this theory would require more than two genealogical generations. They are difficult to find, and it is impractical to track more than a dozen of the individuals, their children, grandchildren, and great grandchildren in successive genealogical generations.

That said, generational differences have substantive meanings in their own right and need not be used to imply patterns for genealogical generations. Because later generations spend more time in the host country than earlier generations, they tend to be more acculturated and socioeconomically more advantaged. One would expect that their academic, social, behavioral, and health outcomes follow generational improvement. However, this is not consistently found. This negative association between the exposure to the host country and child outcomes—the evidence for the immigrant paradox—may be understood within the framework of the ecological model developed by Bronfenbrenner (1979), which underscores social contexts or ecological systems as explanations for a child's development.

In this chapter, we highlight individual factors as well as the school as a proximal context that plays a key role in the assimilation of adolescents of immigrants. The school is often the first social and cultural institution with which immigrants' children come in contact outside of their homes. This is the place where adolescents of immigrants spend most of their days to learn and develop their cognitive and social skills for future participation in the adult world, and therefore we would expect the school to play a key role in the assimilation of immigrants' children.

STUDENT ENGAGEMENT AND IMMIGRANT ASSIMILATION

Researchers use the term *engagement* to refer to "the extent to which students identify with and value schooling outcomes," a process that "comprises a psychological component pertaining to students' sense of belonging at school and acceptance of school values" (Willms, 2003). Thus, student engagement, broadly conceived, consists of students' attitudes toward schooling or their recognition of the values of schooling.

Previous studies have found that most immigrant children arrive in schools with positive attitudes toward school. A study in the late 1990s conducted by Carola and Marcelo Suárez-Orozco (Suárez-Orozco & Suárez-Orozco, 2001) found that more than 70% of their sample of immigrant students described their schools as their "life," their "second family," or "the path to success." Most immigrant children talked about their school principals as being good and capable, very friendly, and "exciting." They also believed that their teachers were role models or just like parents to them. These positive attitudes are in sharp contrast to the more negative attitudes among their second-generation coethnic counterparts and cannot be predicted by immigrant children's low socioeconomic background. Thus, Suárez-Orozco and Suárez-Orozco (2001) found evidence of the immigrant paradox in school attitudes.

Students are psychologically engaged when they accept the values of schooling, thus developing a sense of purpose at school. Epstein and McPartland (1976) defined two indicators to study the values of schooling. One is the intrinsic value measured by students' satisfaction with their school. The other is the extrinsic value measured by students' perceived benefits of schoolwork. No research to our knowledge has reported whether immigrants' children are more likely to derive intrinsic satisfaction from schooling than their native counterparts. However, immigrant parents tend to hold utilitarian views toward their children's education. Louie (2004) found that Chinese immigrant parents often pressure their children to go into certain fields of study in college that are likely to lead to future financial stability. Because parents' attitudes often influence children's attitudes, children of immigrants are likely to attribute extrinsic or instrumental values to their schooling as well. The values of schooling, be they intrinsic or instrumental, give students a sense of purpose that motivates them to try hard to become better learners. However, past research has reported generational decline in this form of student engagement. Using data from 1992 to 1996, Portes and Rumbaut (2001) found a negative correlation between the number of years since arriving in the United States and students' perceived importance of schooling. These generational patterns in school engagement show evidence of the immigrant paradox: More recently arrived immigrants are more engaged in the school setting despite their lower levels of English proficiency and exposure to the school system. What is unclear, however, is whether these generational differences in school engagement explain the observed immigrant paradox in student achievement.

SCHOOL CLIMATE AND IMMIGRANT ASSIMILATION

Student engagement is shaped by the ecological context of the school. A multifaceted construct, school climate has long been recognized as consequential to child development. The measures of school climate vary but largely fall into two major categories: (a) the formal and informal structures or rules that govern individuals and groups' interactions in school as well as (b) the values and belief systems, such as student peer norms, expectation for success, and discipline in school (Anderson, 1982). These intangible aspects of schooling encompass instructional, interpersonal, and organizational dimensions, and they are indicative of the quality of experiences students have in school. A substantial literature has accumulated to show that school climate shapes adolescents' academic achievement or failure, attitudes, antisocial behaviors, social–emotional adjustment, and other noncognitive development (Anderson, 1982; Fredricks et al., 2004; Loukas & Robinson, 2004; McEvoy & Welker, 2000; Roeser, Eccles, & Sameroff, 1998).

The unequal spatial distribution of immigrants influences the neighborhoods immigrants' children live in and the schools they attend. Immigrant Blacks and Hispanics tend to live with or close to native Blacks in low-income, large metropolitan areas (Iceland, 2009). They also tend to be concentrated in segregated minority schools that contain a disproportionate number of students with limited proficiency in English (Capps et al., 2005; Van Hook & Fix, 2000). The traits that typically characterize the schools that immigrants' children go to, being segregated minority schools and schools with low socioeconomic status, explain a large portion of between-school differences in poor climate expressed in terms of students' perceptions and administrators' reports of school norms, expectations, and beliefs (Brookover et al., 1978).

In the United States, student-reported school climate varies by nativity status and country of origin. Pong and Hao (2007) found that schools attended by Latino children of immigrants, especially Mexican children, have more problem behaviors and perceived negative climate than schools attended by Asian immigrants' children. However, Asian students of Laotian, Cambodian, and Vietnamese origin reported attending the most unsafe schools, including those having a high prevalence of gang activity and violent fights (Portes & Rumbaut, 2001).

Immigrant students' past school experience in their home country, or the stories that immigrants' children have heard about the school system in their parents' native country, could influence their perception of school environments in the host country. Students from developing nations with resource-poor or chaotic school systems can appreciate the resource-rich U.S. schools, and those from authoritarian school systems find U.S. teachers to be personable and approachable. However, classroom norms and expectations differ across national school systems. Immigrant students who are used to an orderly classroom environment are likely to find their American classmates to be disrespectful or the school to be disorderly. Overall, immigrant students' perceptions of the school climate reflect both the objective reality of the school as well as a comparison between the current and past school environments. It is possible that generational patterns in perceived school climate may evidence the immigrant paradox: Because immigrant students have a dual frame of reference, they may have more positive perceptions of their school climate than the objective realities of their schools would suggest. These perceptions are likely to conform to the native students' views as they become more assimilated. Moreover, it is possible that these inflated perceptions of school climate may explain the fact that immigrant children and children of immigrants tend to have higher levels of achievement compared with their native-born coethnics.

DATA AND METHOD

To examine the relationships among student engagement, school climate, and academic achievement of immigrants' students, we used data from the base-year survey of the ELS in 2002 when respondents were in the 10th grade. For details about the survey, see http://nces.ed.gov/surveys/els2002/surveydesign.asp.

There were 15,360 base-year student participants, but we did not include responses from American Indian and Alaska Native students (about 130) and Pacific Islanders (about 60) because they are not immigrant groups. We kept the multiracial individuals (about 740), more than one quarter of whom had immigrant parents. After dropping students (about 1,420) who were missing 10th-grade grade point averages (GPAs), we had in our analytic sample a total of about 13,750 student respondents. About 9% were Asian, 14% Hispanic, 5% multiracial, 13% non-Hispanic Black, and 59% non-Hispanic White.

Our plan for analysis was as follows. First, we detected any evidence of the immigrant paradox from bivariate analysis on the ultimate outcome variable of student achievement as well as the intermediate outcome variables of student attitudes and perceptions of school climates. Then we applied multivariate analysis to examine how the immigrant paradox, if any, could be accounted for by other factors. The multivariate analysis had two main parts. The first was an investigation of generational differences in the intermediate outcomes of student attitudes and perceptions of school climate. We adjusted generational differences by taking into account family socioeconomic status and demographic variables. Because all variables in this first part of the analysis were student-level variables, the ordinary-least-square (OLS) regression model was sufficient for our purpose. The second and final part of our multivariate analysis applied hierarchical linear modeling (HLM; Raudenbush & Bryk, 2002) to student achievement outcomes, that is, GPA and math test scores. The first-level equation included students' background characteristics, their attitudes and perceptions of school climate, whereas the second-level equation included administrators' reports of school climate. The HLM model allowed us to see whether generational differences in student attitudes and perceived school climate could explain the immigrant paradox for achievement.

HLM was appropriate for the second part of our multivariate analysis because we included school-level variables that indicated administrators' reports of school climate. The main advantage of HLM is its treatment of error variance. It corrected for the estimation bias by incorporating a unique random effect for each school. Applying maximum-likelihood procedure, HLM allowed the estimation of individual-level and school-level effects simultaneously by positing a set of relationships at both the individual student level and the aggregate level between schools (Raudenbush & Bryk, 2002).

VARIABLES AND MEASURES

We measured academic achievement with student GPA and math test scores in 10th grade. Students' GPAs were not self-reported; they were collected from high school transcripts. The math test scores were equated to the math test scores in the National Education Longitudinal Study of 1988 (NELS) so that they could be compared with previous NELS results if needed.

The major independent variable was generation status: first, second, and third-plus generations. About 10% of the sampled students were missing information about generational status. We followed Allison's (2002) method for treating missing categorical data by keeping these students in the sample while including a dummy variable to represent them in multivariate analysis. Another important independent variable was student attitudes, which was measured by five variables. The first variable, how much like school, has three values indicating the possible responses of *not at all*, *somewhat*, and *a great deal*. Three other variables indicate the extent to which students accepted the values of schooling. Student respondents were asked to indicate on a scale from 1 to 4 how much they agreed or disagreed with a number of statements about why they went to school. We created a composite of intrinsic value by averaging responses from students' agreement with statements regarding the feeling of satisfaction from what they did in class and their finding school subjects to be interesting and challenging. Another composite was the instrumental value of schooling, created by averaging responses students gave regarding their agreement with statements that education is important for getting a job and teaches them skills useful for a job. The social value of schooling was measured by students' agreement with the statement, "I go to school because it's a place to meet my friends."

The school climate composites were constructed from a number of items on the basis of students' or school administrators' agreement with statements about their current school and teachers. An exploratory factor analysis identified three groups of variables from the students' report, for which we created three constructs by averaging item responses. The constructs are the perceptions of good teacher–student relations ($\alpha = .73$), negative peer behaviors ($\alpha = .68$), and clear rules ($\alpha = .67$). School administrators were also asked, to the best of their knowledge, how often (daily, at least once a week, at least once a month, on occasion, or never) a list of problems occurred at their schools. An exploratory factor analysis helped identify four groups of variables, from which we constructed four composites representing tardiness and absenteeism ($\alpha = .87$), widespread disorder ($\alpha = .76$), and academic press ($\alpha = .87$). See Appendix 9.1 for more details. *Academic press* is defined as the norm of academic excellence shared by teachers, principals, and other school personnel to reinforce the value of intellectual effort and performance. Academic press has been considered to be an important ingredient for identifying effective schools.

It is well known that generational differences vary by students' race–ethnicity and that children in immigrant families tend to have lower socioeconomic status (SES). To control for these potential confounding factors, we controlled for SES and examined differences by students' race–ethnicity—Asian, Black, Hispanic, and multiracial, with White as the reference category. Finally, we controlled for parental expectations for children's schooling, measured by parents' responses from 1 to 7 to the question, "How far in school do you want your 10th grader to go?" If both parents responded to this question, we took the average. Immigrant parents tend to have higher educational expectations for their children relative to native-born parents (Kao & Tienda, 1995), which are likely to influence their children's achievement and therefore partially explain the immigrant paradox. Thus, it is important to control for parental expectations in order to uncover whether generational differences in students' perceptions of school climate and student engagement explain generational differences in academic achievement, independent of their parents' high expectations.

DESCRIPTIVE RESULTS

Our descriptive analyses shown in Table 9.1 suggest that there is some evidence of the immigrant paradox because first-generation students have slightly higher GPAs relative to second-generation students, and the GPAs of first-generation students are just as high as the GPAs of third-plus-generation students. This result differs from Kao and Tienda's (1995) previous study using the NELS data set in which they found both first and second generations to

TABLE 9.1
Unadjusted Means of Student Achievement Outcomes
by Generational Status

| Outcome | Generation | | | |
	First	Second	Third	Full sample
Grade point average[a,b]	2.61 (0.93)	2.53 (0.95)	2.60 (0.91)	2.55 (0.93)
Math test scores[a,b,c]	49.03 (15.23)	51.54 (14.81)	52.20 (13.81)	51.33 (14.19)

Note. Standard deviations are in parentheses. Generational differences significant at the .05 level are indicated by superscript letters: a (first vs. second generation), b (second vs. third generation), and c (first vs. third generation).

have similar grades that were higher than the third-plus generation's. Thus, our finding of the immigrant paradox is much more limited. The result for math test scores is even contrary to the expectation of the immigrant paradox: There is generational improvement for math scores, and each successive generation has significantly higher math scores. This is contrary to the previous NELS results that show generational decline in math scores (Glick & White, 2003). Clearly, earlier results for the NELS cohort are different from our results for the more recent ELS cohort.

Students' attitudes toward school and their perceptions of school climate also varied significantly by generational status, and most of these generational patterns show evidence of the immigrant paradox. Figure 9.1 shows that the less acculturated first generation liked school more, was more accepting of the extrinsic and instrumental values of schooling, and viewed teacher–student relations to be better and school rules to be clearer than the third-plus generation, with the second generation situated in the middle. However, foreign-born students reported more disruptive peers in school compared with third-plus-generation students, which somewhat corresponds to the small variation in administrators' reports about disorder in school. Supporting foreign-born students' claims that teachers in their schools may be preoccupied with students' disruptive behaviors, administrators also reported a slightly lower level of academic press in schools foreign-born students attended compared with schools third-plus-generation students attended. The fact that immigrant children viewed school rules to be stricter may reflect serious problem behaviors at school to such an extent that the school had to adopt strict and clear policies, such as a zero-tolerance policy that leaves no ambiguity for violation of rules and for punishment. In sum, these findings provide evidence of the immigrant paradox because immigrant students and children of immigrants tended to have more positive views of their schools than their native-born peers, even though their schools tended to experience greater levels of disorder and less academic press.

MULTIVARIATE RESULTS

Student Attitudes

Table 9.2 presents the results from our OLS regressions first for a sample that includes all racial–ethnic groups and then separately for each race–ethnicity. Within these results, third-plus generation students serve as the reference group. Supporting the immigrant paradox, we find that generational decline in student attitudes toward school was clear and significant ($\alpha = .01$), even after adjusting for the background variables of SES and parental expectations for children's education in the OLS regression models. Table 9.2 shows

A

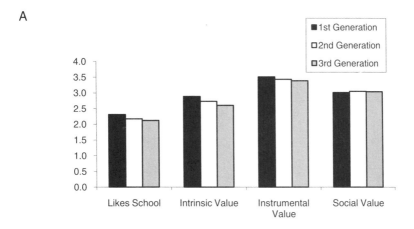

B

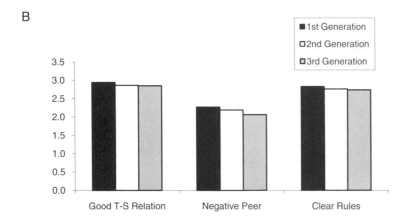

C

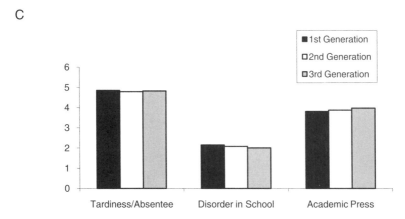

Figure 9.1. A. Student attitudes toward school by generation. B. Student perceptions of school climate by generation. C. Administrator perceptions of negative school climate by generation. 1st generation = foreign-born children with foreign-born parents; 2nd generation = U.S.-born children with foreign-born parents; 3rd generation = native children with native parents; T-S = teacher–student.

TABLE 9.2
Adjusted Attitudes Toward Schooling by Race–Ethnicity
and Generational Status

Variable	Liking school	Intrinsic value	Instrumental value	Social value
All racial–ethnic groups				
First generation	0.169**a	0.259**a	0.109**a	0.014
Second generation	0.044**a	0.114**a	0.038**a	0.027
R^2	.02	.02	.02	.01
White				
First generation	0.165**a	0.127*	0.168**a	−0.107+
Second generation	0.032a	0.038	0.034a	−0.034
R^2	.02	.01	.02	.00
Hispanic				
First generation	0.235**a	0.283**a	0.071+	−0.026
Second generation	0.087**a	0.115**a	0.041	0.034
R^2	.04	.04	.02	.01
Black				
First generation	0.242**a	0.212*	0.007	0.191
Second generation	0.052a	0.148*	0.016	−0.035
R^2	.01	.02	.01	.03
Asian				
First generation	0.253**a	0.146+a	−0.002a	−0.157+
Second generation	0.151*a	0.034a	−0.078a	−0.133
R^2	.02	.03	.02	.01
Multiracial				
First generation	0.060	0.254*	0.134	0.082
Second generation	−0.021	0.059	−0.032	0.004
R^2	.02	.02	.02	.03

Note. Each ordinary-least-squares regression controls for socioeconomic status and parental expectations.
aSignificantly different at 5% between first and second generations.
$+p < .10.$ $*p < .05.$ $**p < .01.$

that the first generation for all racial–ethnic groups exhibited the most positive attitudes toward school, followed by the second generation, and the third-plus generation ranks last. The strongest generational patterns are shown in students' psychological benefits of schooling for almost all racial–ethnic groups. Except for the small number of multiracial adolescents, within every racial–ethnic group, the less assimilated first generation had a stronger liking for school and derived more satisfaction from going to school than the more assimilated second generation, who in turn outscored the third generation in these psychological measures. However, generation decline in the instrumental attitudes toward schooling is only seen among non-Hispanic White students, and Asian first-generation students tended to hold stronger instrumental values than their second-generation counterparts. The only attitudinal variable that does not exhibit any generational pattern is the social value of schooling.

Student-Reported School Climate

Evidence of the immigrant paradox, represented by the generational decline in student-reported school climate, remains after taking into account family background variables in the OLS regression models (see Table 9.3). Although SES and parental expectations explain part of students' perceptions of school climate, supporting the immigrant paradox, foreign-born adolescents perceived significantly better teacher–student relations and clearer school rules than did second or third-plus generation students. However, inconsistent with the immigrant paradox, with each successive generation, students reported fewer peers who put them down, misbehaved, were disruptive, or were engaged in fights or gang activities. There are alternative explanations for the absence of the immigrant paradox in peer evaluation. Because foreign-born students are

TABLE 9.3
Adjusted Student-Reported School Climate by Race–Ethnicity
and Generational Status

Variable	Good T-S relations	Negative peer behaviors	Clear rules
All racial–ethnic groups			
First generation	0.101**[a]	0.165**[a]	0.078**[a]
Second generation	0.018[a]	0.106**[a]	0.018[a]
R^2	.02	.05	.00
White			
First generation	−0.004	0.067	0.069
Second generation	−0.029	0.014	−0.021
R^2	.03	.03	.00
Hispanic			
First generation	0.167**[a]	0.080*[a]	0.121**
Second generation	0.087**[a]	0.018[a]	0.086**
R^2	.02	.04	.01
Black			
First generation	0.246**[a]	0.044	0.202**
Second generation	0.049[a]	0.050	0.050
R^2	.01	.01	.01
Asian			
First generation	0.086[a]	0.158*	0.115[+a]
Second generation	0.005[a]	0.123[+]	0.049[a]
R^2	.02	.03	.01
Multiracial			
First generation	0.097	0.040	0.178*
Second generation	0.072	0.040	0.094[+]
R^2	.03	.03	.02

Note. Each ordinary-least-squares regression controls for socioeconomic status and parental expectations. T-S = teacher–student.
[a]Significantly different at 5% between first and second generations.
+$p < .10$. *$p < .05$. **$p < .01$.

more likely to attend low-quality schools in low-income neighborhoods, they experience more disruptive native peers. Their foreign culture and accents are likely to be targets for discrimination from native students. The second-generation children who were born in the United States are less likely to be teased for cultural and language reasons. It could also be the case that foreign children are less tolerant than the second generation toward disruptive behaviors because they are likely to come from school systems where students are obedient and respectful to teachers and administrators.

Analyses of generational differences of student-reported climate were then performed separately for each racial–ethnic group (see Table 9.3), with the third-plus generation coethnics as the reference group. We found that generational differences were entirely attributed to the Hispanic, Black, and Asian groups. Foreign-born and second-generation Hispanic, Black, and Asian youths were more likely to perceive good teacher–student relations and clear school rules than were the third-plus generation non-Hispanic White youths. This result is consistent with the bivariate findings previously reported in Figure 9.1, supporting the immigrant paradox. Negative peer behaviors decreased over generations among Hispanic and Asian adolescents only. Generational patterns in perceived school climate were not apparent among White or multiracial students, with the exception of first-generation multiracial students reporting higher levels of clear school rules compared with their third-generation counterparts.

Academic Achievement

Results from multilevel analysis predicting ELS students' GPA and math test scores are presented in Tables 9.4 and 9.5, respectively. In all four HLM models estimated, generational patterns appear to go in opposite directions for the two academic outcomes. Foreign-born students significantly outperformed their native-born counterparts in GPA. This is consistent with the evidence of the immigrant paradox found in previous bivariate results. Also consistent with previous bivariate results, foreign-born students lagged significantly behind native-born students in math test scores. These seemingly contradictory generational patterns remain unchanged after student attitudes and school climate variables are considered in Models 2 to 4.

Although student attitudes do not account for generational differences, or for the immigrant paradox in the case of student GPA, it is clear that they are very important for adolescents' academic achievement. When adolescents like school or accept the instrumental value that skills learned in school are useful for future labor market success, they tend to obtain significantly higher GPAs and math scores (Model 2 in Tables 9.4 and 9.5). Students who accept the social value of schooling (i.e., agreeing with the statement that school

TABLE 9.4
Multilevel Analysis of 10th Graders' Grade Point Average

Variable	Model 1	Model 2	Model 3	Model 4
Generation status (ref: third-plus generation)				
First generation	0.138** (0.032)	0.075* (0.031)	0.076* (0.031)	0.078* (0.031)
Second generation	0.034 (0.025)	0.013 (0.024)	0.014 (0.024)	0.015 (0.024)
Race/ethnicity (ref: non-Hispanic White)				
Black	−0.421** (0.024)	−0.468** (0.024)	−0.452** (0.024)	−0.445** (0.024)
Hispanic	−0.316** (0.027)	−0.339** (0.026)	−0.327** (0.026)	−0.323** (0.026)
Asian	0.167** (0.033)	0.149** (0.032)	0.161** (0.032)	0.164** (0.032)
Multiracial	−0.182** (0.034)	−0.178** (0.033)	−0.165** (0.033)	−0.164** (0.033)
Family variables				
SES	0.315** (0.013)	0.314** (0.013)	0.305** (0.012)	0.301** (0.013)
Parents' expectation	0.111** (0.006)	0.095** (0.006)	0.093** (0.006)	0.093** (0.006)
Student attitudes				
Like school	0.198** (0.014)	0.171** (0.014)	0.171** (0.014)	
Intrinsic value	0.115** (0.013)	0.092** (0.013)	0.093** (0.013)	
Instrumental value	0.100** (0.013)	0.088** (0.014)	0.089** (0.013)	
Social value	0.015 (0.010)	0.013 (0.010)	0.013 (0.010)	
School climate (student report)				
Good T-S relation	0.157** (0.017)	0.155** (0.017)		
Negative peer behaviors	−0.095** (0.015)	−0.089** (0.016)		
Clear rules	−0.062** (0.017)	−0.064** (0.017)		
School climate (administrator report)				
Tardiness/absenteeism	0.012 (0.019)			
Disorder	−0.076** (0.026)			
Academic press	0.019 (0.020)			
Constant	2.087** (0.033)	1.074** (0.057)	1.165** (0.082)	1.182** (0.160)

Note. Sample size for each model = 13,750 (rounded to the nearest 10). Mean imputation is used for missing values, and dummy variables representing missing cases are included in the model but not presented here. Standard errors are in parentheses. Academic press = the norm of academic excellence shared by teachers, principals, and other school personnel to reinforce the value of intellectual effort and performance.
[a]Significantly different at 5% between first and second generations.
* *p* < .05. ** *p* < .01.

TABLE 9.5
Multilevel Analysis of 10th Graders' Math Test Scores

Variable	Model			
	1	2	3	4
Generation status (ref: 3rd-plus generation)				
First generation	-1.087**a (0.358)	-1.173**a (0.357)	-1.036**a (0.353)	-1.040**a (0.353)
Second generation	-0.018a (0.279)	-0.041a (0.278)	0.015a (0.274)	0.009a (0.273)
Race/ethnicity (ref: non-Hispanic White)				
Black	-7.342** (0.273)	-7.128** (0.275)	-6.899** (0.272)	-6.801** (0.273)
Hispanic	-4.842** (0.299)	-4.787** (0.297)	-4.540** (0.293)	-4.433** (0.294)
Asian	1.357** (0.373)	1.420** (0.371)	1.660** (0.366)	1.714** (0.365)
Multiracial	-2.047** (0.381)	-1.973** (0.378)	-1.785** (0.374)	-1.735** (0.373)
Family variables				
SES	4.080** (0.145)	4.026** (0.144)	3.843** (0.142)	3.723** (0.143)
Parents' expectation	1.278** (0.065)	1.232** (0.065)	1.185** (0.064)	1.171** (0.064)
Student attitudes				
Like school	1.195** (0.163)	0.805** (0.163)	0.820** (0.163)	
Intrinsic value	-0.597** (0.146)	-0.758** (0.152)	-0.739** (0.152)	
Instrumental value	0.421** (0.155)	0.315* (0.155)	0.323* (0.155)	
Social value	0.668** (0.117)	0.625** (0.115)	0.631** (0.115)	
School climate (student report)				
Good T-S relation	2.279** (0.200)	2.233** (0.200)		
Negative peer behaviors	-2.381** (0.177)	-2.267** (0.178)		
Clear rules	-1.929** (0.190)	-1.962** (0.190)		
School climate (administrator report)				
Tardiness/absenteeism	-0.243 (0.207)			
Disorder	0.096 (0.277)			
Academic press	1.190** (0.209)			
Constant	34.157** (0.365)	29.976** (0.657)	35.632** (0.934)	31.881** (1.745)

Note. N for each model = 13,750 (rounded to the nearest 10). Mean imputation was used for missing values, and dummy variables representing missing cases were included in the model but are not presented here. Standard errors are in parentheses. SES = socioeconomic status; T-S = teacher–student; academic press = the norm of academic excellence shared by teachers, principals, and other school personnel to reinforce the value of intellectual effort and performance.
aSignificantly different at 5% between first and second generations.
*p < .05. ** p < .01.

friends are important) tend to do significantly better in math. However, the result for intrinsic value of schooling is perplexing. Its association with GPA is positive, which we expected, but its association with math scores is negative.

Results of the relationship between school climate and academic outcomes are by and large what we expected. Students' perception of good teacher–student relations is a positive factor in both academic outcomes, but having school peers with undesirable behaviors is a negative factor. Students' perception of clear school rules is also negatively associated with the academic outcomes. It is likely that school rules are clear in schools that experience a lot of discipline problems. Also, administrators' report of disorder in school is a negative factor in both academic outcomes, but academic press is a positive factor.

When each racial–ethnic group is examined separately in Table 9.6, it is apparent that the foreign-born advantage in GPA is evident in all minority groups (Model 1). Among Hispanics, the first-generation advantage in GPA can be explained by the fact that these students have more positive attitudes toward school than their native-born peers (Model 2). However, differences in student engagement and perceptions of school climate do not explain the immigrant paradox in GPA for all other groups, especially Asian and multiracial students. Among Asian and multiracial youths, the second generation also had higher GPAs than their third-plus generation coethnic peers, which cannot be accounted for by student attitudes and perception variables. The immigrant paradox in GPA remains among Black, Asian, and multiracial adolescents after SES, student attitudes, and perceptions of school climate are controlled. Here we caution making comparisons between immigrant and native Black students. Native-born Blacks with native-born parents constitute a historically disadvantaged group who suffered from severe discrimination in the past. Although it is informative to document the educational gap between immigrant and native Blacks, the immigrant paradox is likely to be primarily due to the unique disadvantaged position of the third-generation Blacks than to the material or psychological resources brought by immigrant Blacks.

As for math achievement, Table 9.6 reveals that the foreign-born disadvantage comes primarily from a single ethnic group—Hispanic students. Math achievement improves for each successive generation of Hispanic youths. There is evidence of "second generation super-achievement" (White & Glick, 2009) among Black and multiracial students, and of second-generation underachievement among White students (marginally among Hispanic students). Surprisingly, Asian students show no generational pattern, which contradicts previous findings that Asian students drive the overall math achievement advantage of immigrants' children (Kao & Tienda, 1995).

TABLE 9.6

Multilevel Analysis of 10th Graders' Grade Point Average and Math Test Scores for Each Racial–Ethnic Group

GPA Math Test Scores

Group	Grade point average				Math test scores			
	Model 1	Model 2	Model 3	Model 4	Model 1	Model 2	Model 3	Model 4
White								
1st gen	0.028	−0.029	−0.015	−0.013	−1.516[+]	−1.655*	−1.341[+]	−1.344[+]
2nd gen	−0.142**	−0.158**	−0.151**	−0.152**	−1.077*	−1.120*	−1.014*	−1.031*
Hispanics								
1st gen	0.120*	0.034	0.031	0.030	−1.712*[a]	−1.594*[a]	−1.507*[a]	−1.542*[a]
2nd gen	0.060	0.021	0.014	0.012	−0.179[a]	−0.200[a]	−0.225[a]	−0.290[a]
Black								
1st gen	0.293*	0.238*	0.220[+]	0.213[+]	−0.541[a]	−0.723[a]	−0.674[a]	−0.744[a]
2nd gen	0.126	0.107	0.112	0.103	2.489**[a]	2.838**[a]	2.989**[a]	2.864**[a]
Asian								
1st gen	0.273*	0.240*	0.257*	0.275*	0.855	0.990	1.601	1.573
2nd gen	0.197[+]	0.191[+]	0.206[+]	0.221*	1.537	1.649	2.088	2.097[+]
Multiracial								
1st gen	0.328*	0.261[+]	0.289*	0.293*	0.948	1.041	1.468	1.282
2nd gen	0.377**	0.370**	0.378**	0.397**	3.499**	3.556**	3.647**	3.638**

Note. Reference group is third-plus generation. Models 1–4 have the same variables as those in Table 9.5. 1st gen = first generation; 2nd gen = second generation.
[a]Significantly different at 5% between 1st and 2nd generation.
+$p < .10$. * $p < .05$. ** $p < .01$.

SUMMARY AND DISCUSSION

This research found some significant generational differences that can be interpreted as providing evidence to support the immigrant paradox. Using data from the 10th graders of the ELS survey, we observed foreign-born students having an advantage in GPA over their native-born peers, but we did not find support of a second-generation advantage. Previous findings regarding the second-generation advantage were mixed. Kao and Tienda (1995) found from the NELS data that both the first and second generations outperformed their third-generation peers when SES was controlled. However, using data from the National Longitudinal Study of Adolescent Health (Add Health), Pong et al. (2005) found only the foreign-born advantage in GPA; the second and third generations from similar social backgrounds tended to have similar GPAs. Our ELS results, consistent with the Add Health study, provide evidence of the immigrant paradox in school performance represented by higher GPA among foreign-born students than native students and their more acculturated second-generation peers. This foreign-born advantage in GPA does not translate into foreign-born advantage in math test scores, however. In both bivariate and multivariate analysis, we did not find support for the immigrant paradox in math achievement. Instead we found improvement by each generation for the full sample in bivariate analysis and consistently among Hispanic students in all analyses. The math disadvantage among the second generation, compared with the third-plus generation, is accounted for by students' family background, but the foreign-born disadvantage in math achievement remains even after we controlled for all student and school-level variables. It raises the question of whether generational decline in math skills will continue or whether it was a unique occurrence largely found among adolescents in the 1990s. Glick and White (2003) have shown in their bivariate analysis that generational improvement in math test scores was evident for the cohort of 10th graders in 1980, but generational decline—the immigrant paradox—was observed for the more recent 1990 cohort. Our results based on the 2002 cohort of 10th graders suggests the end of a decade of immigrant advantage in math skills, placing the United States in line with most other countries, where foreign-born children as a group perform lower on math tests than their native-born counterparts (Schnepf, 2007). Future studies need to look into whether the resources immigrant families bring to the United States have changed during the past 3 decades or whether immigrant students' math skills have changed over time, relative to native students. Also, curriculum demands might have changed, making math tests more difficult. More traditional immigrant children's math education back home and the U.S. government's push for math testing are potential explanations for the lack of immigrant paradox in math achievement in the 2000s.

This research also found evidence of the immigrant paradox in that immigrant students were more engaged than U.S.-born students, as indicated by their greater attachment to school and a stronger sense of the purpose of schooling. Foreign-born students held more positive attitudes toward school and were more accepting of the values of schooling than their native peers. In other words, they were emotionally more engaged in school. Immigrant children's greater tendency to perceive good teacher–student relationships is consistent with a recent study reporting that Mexican students who returned to Mexico often praised their former U.S. schools and teachers (Zúñiga & Hamann, 2009). Because students' positive attitudes and perceptions were positively associated with their academic outcomes, it is disconcerting to see that these intangible goods were lost in a generation or two. However, we did not find that generational differences in student attitudes or perceived school climate explained the immigrant paradox evident in student GPA within the complete, ethnically diverse sample. There are two reasons why these attitudes toward school did not mediate the relationship between immigrant status and GPA. First, by including both positive (subjective) and negative (objective) aspects of students' school climate, it is possible that these countervailing forces cancelled each other out. After all, we did find that although foreign-born students reported more positive subjective aspects of their schools compared with their native-born counterparts, they also reported higher levels of negative peer behaviors. Second, our analyses showed racial–ethnic variations in the effect of student attitudes and perceived school climate on student achievement. For example, student attitudes and school climate are useful for accounting for the immigrant paradox in GPA among Hispanic students but not among other students. It is difficult to explain the immigrant paradox within the ethnically diverse full sample. That said, to our knowledge this is the first study on immigrant children's school attitudes and perceptions using nationally representative data. Future research needs to examine why differences in students' attitudes and perceptions account for achievement differences among all students (see Fredricks et al., 2004, for a review) but not for the achievement gap between immigrant generations.

This generational decline in attitudes toward school is especially a concern among Hispanic students, whose attitudes toward school actually explain their higher GPA relative to their native coethnic peers. Foreign-born Hispanic students tend to have more positive attitudes than their native-born counterparts. It is important for schools to find ways to prevent Hispanic children's enthusiasm for U.S. schools from disappearing as they become more acculturated. Teachers can help create positive student attitudes by providing good instructions, forging good relations with students, showing an interest in students, and praising students when they make strong efforts on schoolwork.

All these are measures of student attitudes in our study. Also, school administrators should work hard to eliminate bullying, disruptive behaviors, fighting among students, gangs, and verbal abuse or disrespect toward teachers. Our results suggest that schools without these problems and with positive school climates can promote achievement for all students.

APPENDIX 9.1: SCHOOL CLIMATE COMPOSITES AND THEIR CORRESPONDING SURVEY ITEMS

Composite	Survey items	Cronbach's α
	Student report	
Good teacher– student relations	Students get along well with teachers The teaching is good Teachers are interested in students When I work hard on schoolwork, my teachers praise my efforts	.73
Negative peer behaviors	In class I often feel "put down" by other students I don't feel safe at this school Disruptions by other students get in the way of my learning Misbehaving students often get away with it There are gangs in school Fights often occur between different racial/ethnic groups	.68
Clear Rules	Everyone knows what the school rules are The school rules are fair The punishment for breaking school rules is the same no matter who you are The school rules are strictly enforced If a school rule is broken, students know what kind of punishment will follow	.67
	Administrator report	
Tardiness and absenteeism	Tardiness Absenteeism	.87
Disorder	Physical conflicts among students Student bullying Student verbal abuse of teachers Widespread disorder in classrooms Student acts of disrespect for teachers Gang activities	.76

(*continues*)

APPENDIX 9.1: SCHOOL CLIMATE COMPOSITES AND THEIR CORRESPONDING SURVEY ITEMS (*continued*)

Composite	Survey items	Cronbach's α
Academic press	Student morale is high Teachers at the school press students to achieve academically Teacher morale is high Students place a higher priority on learning Students are expected to do homework	.87

Note. Academic press = the norm of academic excellence shared by teachers, principals, and other school personnel to reinforce the value of intellectual effort and performance.

REFERENCES

Allison, P. D. (2002). *Missing data*. Thousand Oaks, CA: Sage.

Anderson, C. S. (1982). The search for school climate: a review of the research. *Review of Educational Research, 52,* 368–420.

Bronfenbrenner, U. (1979). *The ecology of human development: Experiments by nature and design*. Cambridge, MA: Harvard University Press.

Brookover, W. B., Schweitzer, J. H., Schneider, J. M., Beady, C. H., Flood, P. K., & Wisenbaker, J. M. (1978). Elementary-school social climate and school achievement. *American Educational Research Journal, 15,* 301–318.

Capps, R., Fix, M., Murray, J., Passel, J. S., & Herwantoro, S. (2005). *The new demography of America's schools: Immigration and the No Child Left Behind Act*. Washington, DC: Urban Institute.

Epstein, J. L., & McPartland, J. M. (1976). The concept and measurement of the quality of school life. *American Educational Research Journal, 13,* 15–30.

Farkas, G., & Vicknair, K. (1996). Appropriate test of racial wage discrimination require controls for cognitive skill: Comment on Cancio, Evans, and Maume. *American Sociological Review, 61,* 557–560. doi:10.2307/2096392

Finn, J. D., & Rock, D. A. (1997). Academic success among students at risk for school failure. *Journal of Applied Psychology, 82,* 221–234. doi:10.1037/0021-9010.82.2.221

Fredricks, J. A., Blumenfeld, P. C., & Paris, A. H. (2004). School engagement: Potential of the concept, state of the evidence. *Review of Educational Research, 74,* 59–109. doi:10.3102/00346543074001059

Glick, J. E., & White, M. J. (2003). The academic trajectories of immigrant youths: analysis within and across cohorts. *Demography, 40*(4), 759–783. doi:10.1353/dem.2003.0034

Gordon, M. M. (1964). *Assimilation in American life: The role of race, religion, and national origins*. New York, NY: Oxford University Press.

Greenman, E., & Xie, Y. (2008). Is assimilation theory dead? The effect of assimilation on adolescent well-being. *Social Science Research, 37,* 109–137. doi:10.1016/j.ssresearch.2007.07.003

Harker, K. (2001). Immigrant generation, assimilation, and adolescent psychological well-being. *Social Forces, 79,* 969–1004. doi:10.1353/sof.2001.0010

Hernandez, D. J., & Charney, E. (Eds.). (1998). *From generation to generation: The health and well-being of children in immigrant families*. Washington, DC: National Academy Press.

Iceland, J. (2009). *Where we live now: Immigration and race in the United States*. Los Angeles: University of California Press.

Jencks, C., & Phillips, M. (1998). *The Black–White test score gap: An introduction*. Washington, DC: The Brookings Institute.

Kao, G. (2004). Parental influences on the educational outcomes of immigrant youth. *The International Migration Review, 38,* 427–449. doi:10.1111/j.1747-7379.2004.tb00204.x

Kao, G., & Tienda, M. (1995). Optimism and achievement: The educational performance of immigrant youth. *Social Science Quarterly, 76,* 1–19.

Keller, U., & Tillman, K. H. (2008). Post-secondary educational attainment of immigrant and native youth. *Social Forces, 87,* 121–152. doi:10.1353/sof.0.0104

Levels, M., & Dronkers, J. (2008). Educational performance of native and immigrant children from various countries of origin. *Ethnic and Racial Studies, 31,* 1404–1425. doi:10.1080/01419870701682238

Louie, V. S. (2004). *Compelled to excel: Immigration, education, and opportunity among Chinese Americans*. Stanford, CA: Stanford University Press.

Loukas, A., & Robinson, S. (2004). Examining the moderating role of perceived school climate in early adolescent adjustment. *Journal of Research on Adolescence, 14,* 209–233. doi:10.1111/j.1532-7795.2004.01402004.x

McEvoy, A., & Welker, R. (2000). Antisocial behavior, academic failure, and school climate: A critical review. *Journal of Emotional and Behavioral Disorders, 8,* 130–140. doi:10.1177/106342660000800301

Neale, D. C., Gill, N., & Tismer, W. (1970). Relationship between attitudes toward school subjects and school achievement. *The Journal of Educational Research, 63,* 232–237.

Newmann, F. (Ed.). (1992). *Student engagement and achievement in American secondary schools*. New York, NY: Teachers College Press.

Pong, S., & Hao, L. (2007). Neighborhood and school factors in the school performance of immigrants' children. *The International Migration Review, 41,* 206–241. doi:10.1111/j.1747-7379.2007.00062.x

Pong, S., Hao, L., & Gardner, E. (2005). The roles of parenting styles and social capital in the school performance of immigrant Asian and Hispanic adolescents. *Social Science Quarterly, 86,* 928–950. doi:10.1111/j.0038-4941.2005.00364.x

Portes, A., & Rumbaut, R. G. (2001). *Legacies: The story of the immigrant second generation.* Berkeley: University of California Press.

Raudenbush, S. W., & Bryk, A. S. (2002). *Hierarchical linear models: Applications and data analysis methods.* Thousand Oaks, CA: Sage.

Roeser, R. W., Eccles, J. S., & Sameroff, A. J. (1998, Feb-Mar). *School as a context of early adolescents' academic and social–emotional development: A summary of research findings.* Paper presented at the Seventh Biennial Meeting of the Society for Research on Adolescence, San Diego, CA.

Schnepf, S. V. (2007). Immigrants' educational disadvantage: An examination across ten countries and three surveys. *Journal of Population Economics, 20,* 527–545. doi:10.1007/s00148-006-0102-y

Smith, J. P. (2003). Assimilation across the Latino generations. *The American Economic Review, 93,* 315–319. doi:10.1257/000282803321947263

Suárez-Orozco, C., & Suárez-Orozco, M. (2001). *Children of immigration.* Cambridge, MA: Harvard University Press.

Van Hook, J., & Fix, M. (2000). A profile of immigrant students in U.S. schools. In J. Ruiz-de-Velasco & M. Fix (Eds.), *Overlooked and underserved: immigrant students in U.S. secondary schools* (pp. 9–33). Washington, DC: The Urban Institute.

White, M. J., & Glick, J. E. (2009). *Achieving anew: How new immigrants do in American schools, jobs, and neighborhoods.* New York, NY: Russell Sage Foundation.

Willms, D. (2003). *Student engagement at school: A sense of belonging and participation.* Washington, DC: OECD Publications.

Zúñiga, V., & Hamann, E. T. (2009). Sojourners in Mexico with U.S. school experience: A new taxonomy for transnational students. *Comparative Education Review, 53,* 329–353. doi:10.1086/599356

10

IMMIGRANT GATEWAY COMMUNITIES: DOES IMMIGRANT STUDENT ACHIEVEMENT VARY BY LOCATION?

DYLAN CONGER AND MEGHAN SALAS ATWELL

In addition to facing the stresses of migration and acculturation, foreign-born children in the United States are disproportionately poor and limited in their knowledge of English (Hernandez & Charney, 1998; see also Chapter 1, this volume). Yet many quantitative and ethnographic studies on the schooling of immigrants indicate that they perform as well as or better than their native-born peers who have similar socioeconomic and racial–ethnic profiles (e.g., Fuligni, 1997; Glick & White, 2003; Kao & Tienda, 1995; Perreira, Harris, & Lee, 2006; Portes & Rumbaut, 2001; Schwartz & Stiefel, 2006; Stiefel, Schwartz, & Conger, 2009). Earlier chapters in this volume have offered explanations for this *immigrant paradox*, many of which focus on the potential risks of growing up in the United States (see, e.g., the Introduction). One common concern is that immigrant youth arrive with the values that help them excel in school (e.g., high regard for educational attainment; strong work ethic; respect for elders, teachers, and other authority figures) but that these values are absent in some segments of the native-born U.S. population.

This chapter focuses on how the type of immigrant community in which foreign-born children live affects their academic achievement relative to their native-born peers. Specifically, using administrative records from the state of Florida, we compared the 10th-grade math test scores of immigrant with those of native-born youth across five different Florida communities, each with a different history of immigration. Miami and Fort Lauderdale represent relatively long-standing immigrant gateways with large ethnic enclaves, whereas West Palm Beach, Orlando, and Tampa represent communities that are relatively new immigrant gateways. Our goal was to determine how the direction and magnitude of the nativity gap (the difference between foreign-born and native-born) in test scores varied across these five communities.

We interpreted positive test score gaps (when foreign-born outperformed native-born) and no-difference test score gaps as consistent with an immigrant paradox model and a negative gap (when native-born outperformed foreign-born) as consistent with an *immigrant risk* model, in which immigrant students perform worse than their native-born peers. We further distinguished among the native-born according to whether English was the primary language in the home, treating native-born children in non-English-speaking homes as second-generation immigrant children (with a clear caveat that language at home only approximates immigrant household status). The immigrant paradox theory suggests a consistent decline across generations as they lose their attachment to the immigrant community; first-generation youth are expected to outperform second-generation youth, who in turn are expected to outperform the third generation. We searched for signs of this decline across generations in these additional analyses. This analysis also permitted us to detect evidence of a third model, the *second generation advantage*, in which native-born children with attachments to the immigrant community outperform both immigrant children and native-born children with no such attachments.

By comparing the nativity gap across the five communities, we aimed to shed light on whether certain characteristics of the surrounding community, namely the immigrant share, helps to protect children from the possible risks of being born and growing up in the United States. In the following section, we rely on prior literature to develop expectations about the school performance of immigrant youth across these different communities.

RELEVANT STRANDS OF LITERATURE:
THE EFFECT OF PLACE ON IMMIGRANT YOUTH

Research suggests a number of important influences on the assimilation patterns of immigrant youth in the United States. The characteristics of the children (e.g., gender, race, ability), the human capital of their parents (e.g., education, language ability, employment) as well as the quality of their U.S. schools should all play a large role in how well or how poorly newcomers fare in U.S. schools. Most scholars who study immigrant assimilation also agree that the surrounding community can be expected to further shape the development of immigrant youth. One of the more widely discussed theories is the *segmented assimilation theory*. In their path-breaking study of immigrant youth in two U.S. communities, Portes and Rumbaut (1996, 2001) hypothesized and observed different patterns of acculturation into U.S. society (e.g., on measures of educational performance, English language use). In some national origin groups, a deterioration in academic achievement and other outcomes was found (consistent with the paradox model), whereas in others, a steady improvement in outcomes both across and within generations was found. The authors identified a number of different explanations for these varying pathways and focused much of their explanation on the economic and social characteristics of the communities in which children lived. The authors hypothesized, for instance, that larger numbers of immigrants of a specific national origin group can lead to more densely knit communities, which can provide a supportive social network that helps to prevent family disruption and maintains cultural norms, such as respect for elders (consistent with work by others, such as Massey, 2008). Several ethnographies of Vietnamese and other immigrants in U.S. communities provide examples of the protective influence of ethnic enclaves (e.g., Caplan, Whitmore, & Choy, 1989; Zhou & Bankston, 1998).

It has also been hypothesized, however, that immigrant communities with extensive ethnic labor markets afford opportunities to children outside of the mainstream labor market, which may lower their ambitions to excel in school. For instance, Pérez (2001) observed relatively poor school performance among Cuban immigrants in Miami and suggested that this may be driven by the labor market opportunities that are available to them in Cuban-owned businesses. In other words, living in an ethnic enclave could have both positive and negative influences on the schooling outcomes of immigrant youth.

Although the immigrant community may have direct effects on youth, there are other reasons to expect that a place with a long tradition of immigration might differ from a relatively newer immigrant destination in ways that matter to the educational performance of immigrant youth. For instance, Singer (2004) and Bohon, Macpherson, and Atiles (2005) observed that emerging immigrant gateways, with increasingly diverse populations, are facing resource constraints that differ from established gateways and that new schools, roads, and social services may be needed in these places to accommodate the needs of the growing foreign-born population. Similarly, the schools in these newer destinations may not be geared to deal with the different needs (e.g., English language learning) and cultural norms of the new immigrant groups (Bohon et al., 2005; Wainer, 2004; Wortham, Murillo, & Hamann, 2002). In addition, some have argued that the limited native-born exposure to immigrants in the newer destinations might lead to more prejudice and discrimination against newcomers that reduce the resources available to them. Observations of emerging immigrant destinations with a history of conflict between Black and White residents appear to be facing new strained relations among minority groups as immigrants compete with other minorities for jobs and social services (Waldinger, 1997; Wortham et al., 2002). In addition, at least one study of Hispanic immigrants in newer and older destinations has documented higher levels of residential segregation between Hispanic immigrants and White native-born populations in the newer destinations than in older, more established, immigrant destinations (Lichter, Parisi, Taquino, & Grice, 2010). A recent study of school segregation in North Carolina also found evidence of native-born students sorting away from new immigrant students in emerging immigrant communities, a "native-born flight" of sorts (Santillano, 2009). Schools in established immigrant communities thus might be expected to be better resourced and less segregated than those in emerging immigrant destinations.

On the other hand, some have argued that native-born residents in new destinations may be less hostile to immigrants because they lack preconceived discriminatory or prejudicial attitudes (Atiles & Bohon, 2002). Further, others speculate that the White flight common in many established immigrant destinations may not have yet occurred in emerging destinations, and thus the resources for immigrants may be (temporarily) better in newer destinations (Stamps & Bohon, 2006). In an empirical test of this hypothesis, Stamps and Bohon (2006) compared the educational attainment of adult Latino immigrants in new Latino destinations with those in established destinations and found higher educational attainment among those in the newer destinations. However, the authors attributed much of the observed difference to the self-selection of highly educated Latinos into the newer destinations.

To summarize the previous literature, there are reasons to expect that living in an established immigrant hub versus a newer immigrant settlement community could be both beneficial and harmful to the schooling of immigrant youth. On the one hand, we might expect the immigrant paradox (with foreign-born outperforming native-born) to be more apparent in an established immigrant community because of more densely knit ethnic communities and lower levels of prejudice from native-born residents. At the same time, prior observations of established and emerging immigrant communities have offered a number of reasons to expect that immigrants might fare better in emerging gateways. Whether the positives outweigh the negatives is an open question. To our knowledge, there have been no prior attempts to examine quantitatively how the immigrant gateway type influences the academic achievement of immigrant youth relative to their native-born peers, which is the focus of our analysis in this chapter. We aim to provide a first look at how the relative academic achievement of immigrant youth varies across gateway types and, correspondingly, whether immigrant-rich communities appear to protect foreign-born children from deteriorating academic achievement. Evidence of high foreign-born performance in established gateway communities would be consistent with the theory that living in an immigrant hub is beneficial to immigrant youth.

DATA AND METHOD

Our study used administrative data on 10th graders attending a Florida public high school in school year 2000–2001. In addition to containing information on students' demographic (e.g., birthplace, race–ethnicity, gender) and educational (e.g., test scores, English proficiency) circumstances, the data identify the district and school each student attended in 2000–2001.

Using the school and district identifiers, we subselected high school students attending schools in five Florida districts (the districts that house Miami, Fort Lauderdale, West Palm Beach, Orlando, and Tampa), each of which differ in their history of receiving immigrants and other economic and social indicators (to be described in the following section). For each of the districts, we first computed the raw difference between the foreign-born and native-born students in 10th-grade math scores (note that native-born students include both second- and later generation children). We then estimated regressions of 10th-grade test scores on a foreign-born indicator, holding constant a large set of student-level attributes and indicators for the schools that students attended. Our last model, which we refer to as the *fully specified* model, added students' eighth-grade test scores as an independent variable, which allowed us to control for an additional set of characteristics and experiences, such as early childhood experiences, that likely correlate with foreign-born status and the district in which children live. Finally, we examined the nativity gap for students from different racial–ethnic backgrounds, and we distinguished among the native-born according to whether English was the primary language spoken at home (in an attempt to examine differences between second- and third-generation immigrants). In all of our analyses, we focused on comparisons of these nativity gaps in test scores across communities that differ in the size and history of their immigrant populations.

DESCRIPTION OF FLORIDA COMMUNITIES AND STUDENTS

As the fourth largest state in the United States with the fourth largest immigrant population (Malone, Baluja, Costanzo, & Davis, 2003), Florida is an ideal location for this analysis. In Florida, where approximately 2.7 million public school students reside, an estimated one third of the students are immigrants or children of immigrants (Davis & Bauman, 2008). In addition to housing a large number of immigrants, Florida has both traditional immigrant gateway communities along with several communities that are emerging and reemerging as gateways with rapid increases in their immigrant populations. Miami and Fort Lauderdale are well-known post–World War II immigrant gateways, meaning they have had a large and consistent flow of immigrants since 1950. West Palm Beach and Orlando, in contrast, represent emerging immigrant gateways—communities that had very low immigrant populations up until 1970 and experienced growth from 1980 onward. According to Singer's (2004) typology of immigrant gateway communities, Tampa is also an immigrant gateway, but it is considered "reemerging" because of a large immigrant population in the early 20th century, a lull in immigration, followed by a resurgence after 1980.

Clearly, these five communities differ in other ways that could affect the outcomes of immigrant children. Table 10.1 provides a description of each community on the demographic composition and economic conditions of its population. Miami is by far the largest district with the highest percentage foreign-born. Miami residents also have the worst labor market outcomes; across the five communities, Miami has the lowest median household income, the highest rate of poverty, and the highest unemployment rate. Miami's school system received a grade of "C" from the Florida Department of Education on the basis of the test scores of the students in the schools. It is interesting that although the remaining four districts vary in their immigrant shares (from 25% in Fort Lauderdale to 12% in Tampa), they are surprisingly similar on several other indicators, including the median household income, percentage of people in poverty, percentage of people with college degrees, unemployment rate, and school district accountability grade. West Palm Beach, located just north of Miami and Fort Lauderdale on the eastern coast, has a well-known retirement community and stands out with a disproportionately high percentage of people over age 65. In addition to housing West Palm Beach, the Palm Beach school district also includes many rural communities with a population density of only 573 people per square mile, but it is similar on labor market outcomes to the other three non-Miami gateways.

Table 10.2 provides descriptive statistics on our sample students who attended public high schools in the five communities. As expected, as the longest standing immigrant gateway, Miami had the largest share foreign-born, English language learner, and Hispanic student population. Miami students, on average, also tended to be disproportionately eligible for free and reduced-price lunch, which indicates that they lived in homes that were under 185% of the federal poverty level.

TABLE 10.1
Characteristics of Florida Immigrant Gateways

Characteristic	Miami	Fort Lauderdale	West Palm Beach	Orlando	Tampa
Population	2.25 million	1.62 million	1.13 million	896,344	998,948
Percent foreign born	51	25	17	14	12
Population density [a]	1157.9	1346.5	573	987.8	950.6
Median household income (1999 dollars)	35,966	41,691	45,062	41,311	40,663
Percent of population below poverty line	18	12	10	12	13
Percent of population over 25 with college degree	12	16	18	18	17
Percent of population over 65	13	16	23	10	12
Unemployment rate[b]	5.1	3.6	4.2	3.1	3.3
District grades, 2002–2003 year (A+ Plan)[c]	C	B	B	B	B

Note. Gateway cities are represented by the county school district that houses the central city. Miami is represented by Miami Dade County, Fort Lauderdale by Broward County, West Palm Beach by Palm Beach County, Orlando by Orange County, and Tampa by Hillsborough County. Source is the U.S. Census Bureau (2001) for all statistics except for Unemployment Rate, which is from U.S. Department of Labor, Bureau of Labor Statistics (2000), and the District Grades, which are from the Florida Department of Education (2000).

[a]Measured as the number of people per square mile of land area. [b]Percentage of the civilian labor force that is unemployed. [c]A policy intended to motivate schools to improve their academic performance. Under this plan, each public school in Florida is assigned a grade, A through F, based on the proportion of its students passing the Florida Comprehensive Assessment Test.

TABLE 10.2
Descriptive Statistics on Students in Florida Public High Schools

Variable	Miami	Fort Lauderdale	West Palm Beach	Orlando	Tampa
Foreign born	0.34	0.22	0.19	0.14	0.09
	[0.47]	[0.41]	[0.39]	[0.35]	[0.28]
Free/reduced price lunch eligibility	0.70	0.42	0.42	0.45	0.40
	[0.46]	[0.49]	[0.49]	[0.50]	[0.49]
Limited English proficiency	0.52	0.16	0.22	0.17	0.13
	[0.50]	[0.37]	[0.42]	[0.38]	[0.34]
Hispanic	0.55	0.19	0.16	0.21	0.19
	[0.50]	[0.39]	[0.37]	[0.41]	[0.40]
Asian	0.01	0.03	0.02	0.05	0.03
	[0.11]	[0.17]	[0.15]	[0.21]	[0.17]
Black	0.32	0.37	0.31	0.26	0.21
	[0.47]	[0.48]	[0.46]	[0.44]	[0.41]
White	0.11	0.39	0.48	0.47	0.55
	[0.31]	[0.49]	[0.50]	[0.50]	[0.50]
Male	0.51	0.49	0.51	0.50	0.49
	[0.50]	[0.50]	[0.50]	[0.50]	[0.50]
Exceptional (disability)	0.10	0.09	0.10	0.16	0.12
	[0.30]	[0.29]	[0.31]	[0.37]	[0.32]
Age	16.75	16.58	16.96	16.50	16.61
	[0.87]	[0.92]	[1.03]	[0.74]	[0.84]
Years in school system[a]	1.62	1.63	1.37	1.52	1.57
	[0.64]	[0.72]	[0.78]	[0.83]	[0.59]
Number of students	32,936	20,590	14,179	9,762	13,402

Note. Standard deviations are in brackets. Gateway cities are represented by the county school district that houses the central city. Miami is represented by Miami Dade County, Fort Lauderdale by Broward County, West Palm Beach by Palm Beach County, Orlando by Orange County, and Tampa by Hillsborough County.
[a]Ranges from 0–2, where 2 indicates that a student entered the school system in the eighth grade or earlier and 0 indicates that the student entered in the 10th grade.

Taken together, these results suggest that Miami, in addition to housing many more immigrants than the other communities, had greater economic challenges and more sociodemographically disadvantaged students that may have lowered student performance. The remaining communities largely differed in their immigrant populations but not in other ways; the exception was West Palm Beach, which had a disproportionate share of elderly and whose school district population was more spread out.

RESULTS

Table 10.3 shows the mean 10th-grade math scores for foreign-born and native-born students in each of the communities selected for analysis. The mean scores were lowest in Miami (at 0.28 standard deviations below aver-

TABLE 10.3
10th-Grade Scores by Nativity and District

District	Number of students	Mean math 10th			Foreign born and native born difference
		All	Foreign born	Native born	
Miami	32,936	−0.28	−0.34	−0.25	−0.09
		[0.01]ᶠ	[0.01]	[0.01]	
Fort Lauderdale	20,590	0.04	−0.09	0.08	−0.17
		[0.01]	[0.01]	[0.01]	
West Palm Beach	14,179	−0.01	−0.42	0.09	−0.51
		[0.01]	[0.02]	[0.01]	
Orlando	9,762	0.08	−0.03	0.09	−0.12
		[0.01]	[0.03]	[0.01]	
Tampa	13,402	0.24	0.15	0.25	−0.10
		[0.01]	[0.03]	[0.01]	

Note. Math scores are presented in standard deviation units. Gateway cities are represented by the county school district that houses the central city. The share foreign born at the school level using the student level data is as follows: Miami 34%; Fort Lauderdale 22%; West Palm Beach 17%; Orlando 14%; Tampa 9%. The foreign-born/native-born differences for Fort Lauderdale, West Palm Beach, and Orlando are statistically significant at the 1% level. The difference for Miami is statistically significant at the 5% level. The difference for Tampa is statistically significant at the 10% level. Standard deviations are in brackets.

age for the state) and highest in Tampa (at 0.24 standard deviations above average). In addition, the foreign-born scored below the native-born in all communities, with the largest native-born advantage found in West Palm Beach, one of the emerging gateways: The foreign-born in West Palm Beach scored a full half a standard deviation below the native-born on average. There did not appear to be any relationship between the size of the immigrant community and the nativity gap, however. The gaps were lowest in the communities with the highest (Miami) and lowest (Tampa) foreign-born shares. In addition, the superior performance of native-born students provides no initial evidence of an immigrant paradox across generations in any type of gateway community. In fact, the large negative differences indicate that immigrants are substantially at risk for academic failure.

Of course, the paradox is typically observed when comparing apples to apples—immigrant and native-born youth with similar characteristics and in similar schools. In Table 10.4, we reexamined these nativity gaps, holding constant a large set of inputs to math achievement. The regressions included student-level covariates along with school fixed effects, which hold constant both the conditions in the schools attended and other unobserved differences that drive differential sorting into schools. In addition to providing the results from the regressions, the table reproduces the unadjusted (raw) mean differences between foreign-born and native-born shown in Table 10.3 for comparison. Several of the differences between foreign-born and native-born observed in

TABLE 10.4
Regressions of 10th-Grade Math Score, by District

Variable	Miami	Fort Lauderdale	West Palm Beach	Orlando	Tampa
			Unadjusted		
Foreign born	−0.09**	−0.17***	−0.51***	−0.12***	−0.10*
	[0.05]	[0.04]	[0.05]	[0.04]	[0.05]
			Adjusted		
Foreign born	−0.08***	0.04*	−0.11***	0.08**	0.00
	[0.02]	[0.02]	[0.03]	[0.03]	[0.03]
Free/reduced price lunch eligibility	−0.13***	−0.19***	−0.17***	−0.23***	−0.31***
	[0.02]	[0.02]	[0.02]	[0.03]	[0.03]
Limited English proficiency	−0.16***	−0.24***	−0.33***	−0.33***	−0.17***
	[0.01]	[0.03]	[0.04]	[0.02]	[0.03]
Hispanic	−0.17***	−0.23***	−0.20***	−0.26***	−0.16***
	[0.03]	[0.03]	[0.03]	[0.04]	[0.02]
Asian	0.26***	0.19***	0.18***	0.27***	0.31***
	[0.06]	[0.05]	[0.06]	[0.06]	[0.06]
Black	−0.52***	−0.60***	−0.57***	−0.52***	−0.56***
	[0.04]	[0.03]	[0.03]	[0.03]	[0.03]
Male	0.13***	0.14***	0.20***	0.16***	0.15***
	[0.01]	[0.02]	[0.02]	[0.02]	[0.01]
Exceptional	−1.05***	−0.71***	−0.70***	−0.41***	−0.68***
	[0.04]	[0.04]	[0.04]	[0.04]	[0.03]
Native English-speaking parent	−0.03*	−0.03	−0.09***	−0.03	0.04*
	[0.02]	[0.02]	[0.03]	[0.03]	[0.03]
Age	−0.32***	−0.33***	−0.30***	−0.28***	−0.29***
	[0.01]	[0.01]	[0.01]	[0.01]	[0.01]
Years in school system	−0.13***	−0.08***	−0.10***	−0.11***	−0.11***
	[0.02]	[0.01]	[0.02]	[0.01]	[0.02]
Constant	4.23***	6.29***	5.99***	5.21***	6.03***
	[0.23]	[0.29]	[0.29]	[0.21]	[0.23]
Number of students	32,936	20,590	14,179	9,762	13,402

Note. Coefficients are unstandardized. Gateway cities are represented by the county school district that houses the central city. Standard errors are in brackets. The standard errors in both the unadjusted and adjusted models have been corrected for clustering at the school level. Adjusted models include school fixed effects.
*p < .10. **p < .05 ***p < .01.

Table 10.3 are substantially changed with these model adjustments. In Fort Lauderdale and Orlando, the conditional models led to nativity gaps that favored the foreign-born, and in Tampa, the difference became statistically insignificant and very close to zero. In West Palm Beach, the foreign-born disadvantage of −0.51 was attenuated to a −0.11, and in Miami, the controls changed the results very little: The gap in Miami decreased from −0.09 to −0.08. These adjusted models suggest signs of an immigrant paradox (where foreign-born equal or outperform native-born) in Tampa (where there was no difference), Fort Lauderdale (a marginally statistically significant coefficient), and Orlando but not in Miami and West Palm Beach.

The differences across districts in the nativity gaps presented in Table 10.4 control for many variables but are likely still biased by the endogeneity of district choice. For instance, the foreign-born who chose to live in Fort Lauderdale may have been more positively selected (relative to the native-born) than the foreign-born who chose to live in West Palm Beach on characteristics that the model does not hold constant. In addition, within each district, the estimated gaps shown in Table 10.4 may have been driven by differences between foreign-born and native-born that we did not observe. In an effort to minimize these biases, our next analysis held constant the students' math scores in the eighth grade. We expected that the eighth-grade test scores would hold constant some set of unobserved characteristics that correlated with nativity status and choice of district, such as parental education, attitudes about schooling, and early childhood investments. Table 10.5 provides the results from our "fully specified" model, in which the eighth-grade scores have been added to the equation and multiply imputed for students with missing observations.

The results from models with eighth-grade test scores are very similar to the results without the eighth-grade scores (the adjusted estimates from Table 10.4 are provided on the top row of Table 10.5 to ease comparisons). Even with eighth-grade scores held constant, the foreign-born scored lower than the native-born in Miami and West Palm Beach, higher than native-born in Fort Lauderdale and Orlando, and similar to the native-born in Tampa. Again, no clear pattern emerged in nativity gaps across communities of varying immigrant shares. For instance, though immigrants in Fort Lauderdale (a community with an immigrant share of 25%) earned relatively higher test scores than immigrants in West Palm Beach (a community with an immigrant share of 17%), their relative scores were slightly lower than the relative scores of immigrants in Orlando, a community that is substantially less populated by immigrants. Similarly, immigrant youth in Miami scored relatively higher than immigrant youth in West Palm Beach but not Orlando and Tampa. West Palm Beach may appear to be something of an outlier, where immigrant youth scored disproportionately lower in math (relative to the native-born) than in any other district; however, removing West Palm Beach from the table would not provide a more consistent story about the relationship between the type of gateway community and the relative performance of foreign-born youth.

To examine the heterogeneity in relative foreign-born performance, we reestimated the fully specified model from Table 10.5 separately for each

TABLE 10.5
Regressions of 10th-Grade Math Score Controlling for Eighth-Grade Math Score, by District

Variable	Miami	Fort Lauderdale	West Palm Beach	Orlando	Tampa
		Adjusted			
Foreign born	−0.08***	0.04*	−0.11***	0.08**	0.00
	[0.02]	[0.02]	[0.03]	[0.03]	[0.03]
		Fully specified			
Foreign born	−0.05**	0.04***	−0.11***	0.05*	0.02
	[0.02]	[0.02]	[0.03]	[0.03]	[0.03]
Eighth-grade math score	0.43***	0.58***	0.35***	0.48***	0.55***
	[0.02]	[0.02]	[0.02]	[0.02]	[0.02]
Free/reduced price lunch eligibility	−0.02	−0.04***	−0.07***	−0.09***	−0.14***
	[0.01]	[0.01]	[0.02]	[0.03]	[0.02]
Limited English proficiency	−0.07***	−0.05*	−0.22***	−0.16***	−0.03
	[0.01]	[0.03]	[0.04]	[0.03]	[0.03]
Hispanic	−0.11***	−0.12***	−0.14***	−0.17***	−0.10***
	[0.02]	[0.02]	[0.03]	[0.03]	[0.02]
Asian	0.15***	0.09***	0.09*	0.13***	0.15***
	[0.05]	[0.03]	[0.05]	[0.05]	[0.05]
Black	−0.26***	−0.24***	−0.34***	−0.23***	−0.24***
	[0.03]	[0.02]	[0.03]	[0.03]	[0.02]
Male	0.11***	0.10***	0.16***	0.12***	0.11***
	[0.01]	[0.01]	[0.02]	[0.02]	[0.01]
Exceptional	−0.59***	−0.27***	−0.43***	−0.15***	−0.29***
	[0.04]	[0.03]	[0.04]	[0.04]	[0.03]
Native English-speaking parent	−0.03*	−0.02	−0.07***	−0.03	0.04
	[0.02]	[0.02]	[0.02]	[0.04]	[0.03]
Age	−0.23***	−0.17***	−0.21***	−0.17***	−0.14***
	[0.01]	[0.01]	[0.01]	[0.02]	[0.01]
Years in school system	0.14***	0.08***	0.07***	0.08***	0.05***
	[0.01]	[0.01]	[0.01]	[0.01]	[0.02]
Constant	2.60***	2.93***	3.90***	3.11***	2.07***
	[0.38]	[0.23]	[0.30]	[0.30]	[0.22]
Number of students	32,936	20,590	14,179	9,762	13,402

Note. Coefficients are unstandardized. Gateway cities are represented by the county school district that houses the central city. Standard errors are in brackets, and the standard errors have been corrected for clustering at the school level. All models include school fixed effects.
*$p < .10$. **$p < .05$ ***$p < .01$.

racial–ethnic group.[1] The coefficients and standard errors on the foreign-born variable from these models are provided in Table 10.6 (full results of the models can be obtained from the authors of this chapter). We found large differences in the direction and magnitude of the nativity gap across racial–ethnic

---

[1]We use the racial–ethnic categories that are provided by the school system in which "Hispanic" includes students who originate from Latin or South American countries, irrespective of their skin color.

TABLE 10.6
Foreign Born–Native Born Difference in 10th-Grade Scores
by Race and District: Fully Specified Model

Variable		Miami	Fort Lauderdale	West Palm Beach	Orlando	Tampa
All students		−0.05**	0.04***	−0.11***	0.05*	0.02
		[0.02]	[0.02]	[0.03]	[0.03]	[0.03]
	N	32,936	20,590	14,179	9,762	13,402
Hispanic students		−0.06***	0.09***	−0.07*	0.16***	−0.02
		[0.02]	[0.03]	[0.04]	[0.04]	[0.04]
	N	18,211	3,908	2,307	2,079	2,599
White students		0.13***	0.10***	0.10	0.08*	0.02
		[0.05]	[0.04]	[0.06]	[0.05]	[0.05]
	N	3,468	8,007	6,855	4,582	7,326
Black students		0.00	0.03*	-0.24***	−0.03	0.00
		[0.03]	[0.02]	[0.04]	[0.04]	[0.09]
	N	10,676	7,670	4,394	2,502	2,777
Asian students		−0.02	−0.06	−0.08	0.00	0.05
		[0.08]	[0.05]	[0.08]	[0.07]	[0.07]
	N	388	648	348	440	393

Note. Coefficients are unstandardized. Gateway cities are represented by the county school district that houses the central city. All models include the controls listed in Table 10.5 and school fixed effects. Standard errors are in brackets, and the standard errors have been corrected for clustering at the school level.
*$p < .10$. **$p < .05$ ***$p < .01$.

subgroups. Looking just in Miami, for instance, we saw evidence of an immigrant risk model for all students and for Hispanic students yet evidence of an immigrant paradox for all other racial groups. In West Palm Beach, where the immigrant risk is very large, it appears to be entirely driven by Hispanic and Black immigrants. In Fort Lauderdale and Orlando, foreign-born either equaled or outperformed native-born within every subgroup. In Tampa, there were no nativity gaps. Finally, the direction and magnitude of the nativity gap within racial groups tended to fluctuate dramatically across communities for all groups except White and Asian students. For instance, Hispanic students had relatively low scores in Miami but relatively high scores in Fort Lauderdale. Yet White foreign-born had consistently higher scores across all communities (except Tampa where there was no nativity gap) and Asian foreign-born equaled native-born in all communities. Again, there is no clear pattern in the direction and size of the gap as the immigrant share in the community decreases (moving from Miami to Tampa). The one exception may be among White students, where the paradox appears to grow smaller as the immigrant share decreases; in Miami, White foreign-born outperformed White native-born by 0.13 standard deviations, but their advantage over native-born decreased and reached a low of zero in Tampa.

One explanation for the differences in the within-race nativity gaps across communities may be due to the precise origins of these immigrants. For instance, the Hispanics in Miami were disproportionately Cuban whereas the Hispanics in West Palm disproportionately hailed from Colombia and Mexico. Though our models hold many student characteristics constant, it is still possible that students from different countries have substantially different attributes that matter to their academic achievement even though they share the same race, poverty status, and so on. To better control for these differences, we identified the small set of source countries that had relatively large shares of students. Each of the top four communities was home to a large number of Colombian, Cuban, and Haitian-origin children. In models not shown here to conserve space, we compared these origin groups with similarly situated native-born peers, paying careful attention to how the nativity gap (between, e.g., Colombian children and native-born Hispanic children) differed across the four communities. The models revealed that Colombians equaled or outperformed Hispanic native-born (and Haitian Blacks equaled or outperformed native-born Blacks) in all communities, yet the magnitude of the gap did not consistently increase or decline as the immigrant share in the community increased. Similarly, Cubans equaled or underperformed Hispanic native-born, with no relationship between the magnitude of the gap and the gateway type. Thus, even controlling for the origins of students in these different communities, there was no clear pattern across communities in the direction and size of the gap between foreign-born and native-born.

For our last analysis, we separated the native-born into those who lived in homes where a language other than English was frequently spoken and those who lived in English-speaking homes. Because school systems do not collect information on parental birthplace, we were unable to distinguish among the native-born between those who were second generation and those who were third or later generation. We therefore used home language as a rough proxy for whether the child lived in an immigrant household. By separating the native-born in this way, we could explore whether the native-born children of immigrants looked more similar to their third-generation native-born peers or to their first-generation immigrant peers. Table 10.7 presents the results of these models in which the coefficients of interest are those on the indicator for foreign-born and the indicator for native-born non-English (the reference group is native-born students in English-speaking homes who are presumed to be third generation or later).

Separating the native-born according to their home language alters the findings for Miami and West Palm Beach. In both communities, the native-born students in non-English homes outperformed both foreign-born and native-born English-at-home students. The two groups at greatest risk (with the lowest test scores) were first-generation immigrants and native-born students with possibly little attachment to the immigrant community. This finding suggests a *second-generation advantage*. In Fort Lauderdale and Orlando, the

TABLE 10.7

Foreign Born–Native Born Non-English Difference in 10th-Grade Scores by District: Fully Specified Model

Variable	Miami	Fort Lauderdale	West Palm Beach	Orlando	Tampa
Foreign born	−0.02	0.04**	−0.04	0.04*	−0.01
	[0.02]	[0.02]	[0.03]	[0.02]	[0.03]
Native born non-English-speaking parent	0.04*	−0.01	0.11***	−0.03	−0.04
	[0.02]	[0.02]	[0.03]	[0.02]	[0.03]
Eighth-grade math score	0.43***	0.58***	0.35***	0.48***	0.55***
	[0.02]	[0.02]	[0.02]	[0.02]	[0.02]
Free/reduced price lunch eligibility	−0.02	−0.04***	−0.07***	−0.08***	−0.14***
	[0.01]	[0.01]	[0.02]	[0.03]	[0.02]
Limited English proficiency	−0.07***	-0.03	−0.21***	−0.13***	−0.04
	[0.01]	[0.03]	[0.03]	[0.04]	[0.03]
Hispanic	−0.11***	−0.11***	−0.15***	−0.15***	−0.10***
	[0.02]	[0.02]	[0.03]	[0.03]	[0.02]
Asian	0.15***	0.09***	0.08	0.15***	0.15***
	[0.05]	[0.03]	[0.05]	[0.05]	[0.05]
Black	−0.26***	−0.24***	−0.34***	−0.23***	−0.24***
	[0.03]	[0.02]	[0.03]	[0.03]	[0.02]
Male	0.11***	0.10***	0.16***	0.12***	0.11***
	[0.01]	[0.01]	[0.02]	[0.02]	[0.01]
Exceptional	−0.59***	−0.27***	−0.43***	−0.15***	−0.30***
	[0.04]	[0.03]	[0.04]	[0.04]	[0.03]
Age	−0.23***	−0.17***	−0.21***	−0.17***	−0.14***
	[0.01]	[0.01]	[0.01]	[0.02]	[0.01]
Years in school system	0.14***	0.08***	0.07***	0.08***	0.05***
	[0.01]	[0.01]	[0.01]	[0.01]	[0.02]
Constant	2.57***	2.90***	3.81***	3.10***	2.10***
	[0.38]	[0.23]	[0.29]	[0.29]	[0.21]
Number of students	32,936	20,590	14,179	9,762	13,402

Note. Coefficients are unstandardized. Gateway cities are represented by the county school district that houses the central city. All models include school fixed effects. Standard errors are in brackets, and the standard errors have been corrected for clustering at the school level.
*$p < .10$. **$p < .05$ ***$p < .01$.

first-generation students outperformed both groups of native born, consistent with an immigrant paradox model in which immigrants outperform native-born and there is no benefit to being a native-born child of an immigrant.

Returning again to the focus of this chapter, which is whether there is a pattern in the relative performance of immigrant children across communities with varying immigrant shares, the analysis shown in Table 10.7 points to the same overall conclusion: The gap between immigrant and native-born youth varies across communities, yet there is no clear relationship between whether the community is an established or emerging gateway and whether the gap favors first-, second-, or third-generation youth.

CONCLUSIONS

In this chapter, we have examined whether the type of immigrant gateway in which immigrant children live influences their performance relative to native-born students in the same community. Our examination revealed large differences in relative performance across place, with an immigrant paradox in some communities and a possible second-generation advantage in others. However, the variation observed does not appear to be associated with whether the community was an established or emerging gateway.

Using data from the state of Florida, we compared the nativity gap in high school math achievement across five immigrant gateway communities that differ in their history of immigration and immigrant shares, from Miami, the largest and oldest immigrant destination, to Tampa, a county with a reemerging but small foreign-born population. Our regression models hold constant a large set of student characteristics (including a prior test score) and school fixed effects; thus, our nativity gap estimates compared foreign-born with observationally similar native-born. We also examined these gaps separately for students from different racial backgrounds and among native-born youth from homes where English was and was not the primary language spoken.

The comparisons across the communities revealed that foreign-born students outperformed native-born in some communities, and that native-born students outperformed foreign-born in others. In Fort Lauderdale and Orlando, immigrant performance was relatively high, suggesting a decline from the first generation to later generations (with no difference among the native-born according to whether English was their home language). Yet in Tampa, there was no nativity gap: Foreign-born and native-born (both those in English and non-English homes) had similar test scores. In Miami and West Palm Beach, foreign-born students scored lower than native-born students whose home language was not English, yet they tested equivalent to native-born students in English-speaking homes. The pattern in these two communities suggests that native-born children in immigrant (or at least non-English-speaking) households have an advantage over both first- and third-generation children. The foreign-born scored particularly low, approximately 0.15 standard deviations lower than native-born in non-English-speaking homes, in West Palm Beach. The higher achievement of native-born in non-English-speaking homes is consistent with both the immigrant paradox and immigrant risk models. On the one hand, first-generation immigrant youth are at risk relative to native-born (risk). On the other hand, native-born children with recent immigrants in their household have an advantage over native-born children with no such attachments (paradox). Most of these patterns are driven by the large share of Hispanic immigrant students in each of the communities; among White and Asian students, immigrants outperformed or equaled their native-born peers in all communities (consistent with an immigrant paradox interpretation).

To the extent that native-born children in non-English-speaking homes can be thought of as descendants of immigrants, our findings suggest that in all communities, the highest achievers are either foreign-born children or native-born descendants of immigrants. Thus, we observed either an immigrant paradox or a second generation model, with native-born children in non-English-speaking homes failing to reach the highest levels of achievement. These results call for further policy and research attention to native-born children from underrepresented minority groups who either do not have immigrant parents or live in homes where English is the only language spoken.

The primary goal of our analysis was to explore whether the type of community in which children of immigrants live somehow drives these patterns. Our results suggest large differences in the performance of immigrants across communities, yet there is not a straightforward relationship between the type of gateway community and whether an immigrant paradox or second-generation advantage is observed. For instance, second-generation children fared best in West Palm Beach, a rapidly growing immigrant destination with a current immigrant share of 17%, but they performed no differently from their native-born counterparts in English-speaking homes in Orlando and Tampa, also communities with recent immigrant growth and with similar immigrant shares. Similarly, immigrants in Miami and Fort Lauderdale, both considered established immigrant gateways, had very different outcomes, with immigrants scoring relatively lower in Miami and relatively higher in Fort Lauderdale.

Immigrants in Miami and West Palm Beach appeared to be at a disadvantage in comparison with their native-born counterparts, especially Hispanic immigrant students in these cities. Although Miami and West Palm Beach are very different with respect to their immigrant concentration and history of immigration, they are distinct from the other three communities in several important ways. Miami has the largest immigrant concentration but also has the most poverty, lowest median income, and the highest unemployment rate of any of the other cities observed. West Palm Beach has a large retiree population and a lower population density. The school systems in these two communities may be particularly underresourced and unable to support immigrant students (relative to the schools in the other communities), which could explain the absence of a clear relationship between gateway type and relative immigrant performance.

Our analysis does not call for specific public interventions according to the type of gateway in which immigrant children live. Instead, it shows very clearly that the success of the children of immigrants varies dramatically across communities and that the community context must be considered in future policymaking and research.

With respect to research, there is much more to consider. Our empirical analysis provides an initial examination of the effect of immigrant gateway type on the immigrant paradox, but a more complete model would include this variable (gateway type) along with other characteristics of the communities and schools on the right-hand side of the regression equation. Other variables that would help to understand why such varying patterns are observed across communities could include the quality of the schools and other public resources, the level of nativity and racial segregation across communities, the density and political influence of the surrounding immigrant community, and so on. In addition, we attempted to control for the endogeneity of school district choice by controlling for eighth-grade math scores, but selection biases could be driving the results. Future research could take advantage of natural experiments (e.g., the relocation of children after hurricanes and floods) to explore the true causal effect of place on performance. Finally, future studies should experiment with different measures of academic achievement (e.g., grades) and search for differences between native-born children who are second and third generation.

REFERENCES

Atiles, J. H., & Bohon, S. A. (2002). *The needs of Georgia's new Latinos: A policy agenda for the decade ahead.* Athens, GA: Carl Vinson Institute of Governance.

Bohon, S. A., Macpherson, H., & Atiles, J. H. (2005). Educational barriers for new Latinos in Georgia. *Journal of Latinos and Education, 4,* 43–58. doi:10.1207/s1532771xjle0401_4

Caplan, N., Whitmore, J., & Choy, M. (1989). *The boat people and achievement in America.* Ann Arbor: University of Michigan Press.

Davis, J., & Bauman, K. (2008). *School enrollment in the United States: 2006* (Population Characteristics No. P20-559). Washington, DC: U.S. Census Bureau. Retrieved from http://www.census.gov/prod/2008pubs/p20-559.pdf

Florida Department of Education. (2000). *School accountability report 1999–2000.* Retrieved from http://schoolgrades.fldoe.org/pdf/9900/sg9900allschoolgrades.pdf

Fuligni, A. J. (1997). The academic achievement of adolescents from immigrant families: The roles of family background, attitudes, and behavior. *Child Development, 68,* 351–363.

Glick, J. E., & White, M. (2003). The academic trajectories of immigrant youths: Analysis within and across cohorts. *Demography, 40,* 759–783. doi:10.1353/dem.2003.0034

Hernandez, D., & Charney, E. (1998). *From generation to generation: The health and well-being of children in immigrant families*. Washington, DC: National Academy Press.

Kao, G., & Tienda, M. (1995). Optimism and achievement: The educational performance of immigrant youth. *Social Science Quarterly, 76,* 1–19.

Lichter, D. T., Parisi, D., Taquino, M. C., & Grice, S. M. (2010). Residential segregation in new Hispanic destinations: Cities, suburbs, and rural communities compared. *Social Science Research, 39,* 215–230. doi:10.1016/j.ssresearch.2009.08.006

Malone, N., Baluja, K.F., Costanzo, J. M., & Davis, C. J. (2003). *The foreign born population: 2000* (Census 2000 Brief C2KBR-34). Washington, DC: U.S. Government Printing Office.

Massey, D. S. (2008). *New faces in new places: The changing geography of American immigration*. New York, NY: Russell Sage Foundation.

Pérez, L. (2001). Growing up in Cuban Miami: Immigration, the enclave, and new generations. In R. Rumbaut & A. Portes (Eds.), *Ethnicities: Children of immigrants in America* (pp. 90–126). Los Angeles and New York, NY: University of California Press and Russell Sage Foundation.

Perreira, K. M., Harris, K., & Lee, D. (2006). Making it in America: High school completion by immigrant and native youth. *Demography, 43,* 511–536. doi:10.1353/dem.2006.0026

Portes, A., & Rumbaut, R. G. (1996). *Immigrant America: A portrait*. Los Angeles: University of California Press.

Portes, A., & Rumbaut, R. (2001). *Legacies: The story of the immigrant second generation*. Los Angeles: University of California Press and Russell Sage Foundation.

Santillano, R. (2009). *Avoiding immigrant students in public schools: Evidence from North Carolina*. Retrieved from http://www.ces.census.gov/index.php/ces/seminarslist?down_key=250&down_val=paper

Schwartz, A. E., & Stiefel, L. (2006). Is there a nativity gap? Achievement of New York City elementary and middle school immigrant students. *Education Finance and Policy, 1,* 17–49. doi:10.1162/edfp.2006.1.1.17

Singer, A. (2004). *The rise of new immigrant gateways*. Washington, DC: The Brookings Institution.

Stamps, K., & Bohon, S. A. (2006). Educational attainment in new and established Latino metropolitan destinations. *Social Science Quarterly, 87,* 1225–1240. doi:10.1111/j.1540-6237.2006.00425.x

Stiefel, L., Schwartz, A. E., & Conger, D. (2009). Age of entry and the high school performance of immigrant youth. *Journal of Urban Economics, 67,* 303–314. doi:10.1016/j.jue.2009.10.001

U.S. Census Bureau. (2001). *U.S. Census 2000, Summary Files 1 and 2*. Retrieved from http://quickfacts.census.gov/qfd/download_data.html

U.S. Department of Labor, Bureau of Labor Statistics. (2000). *Local area unemployment statistics*. Retrieved from http://stats.bls.gov/data/#unemployment

Wainer, A. (2004). *The new Latino south and the challenge to public education: Strategies for educators and policymakers in emerging immigrant communities*. Los Angeles, CA: Tomas Rivera Policy Institute.

Waldinger, R. (1997). Black/immigrant competition re-assessed: New evidence from Los Angeles. *Sociological Perspectives, 40*, 365–386.

Wortham, S. E. F., Murillo, E. G., & Hamann, E. T. (2002). *Education in the new Latino diaspora: Policy and the politics of identity*. Westport, CT: Ablex.

Zhou, M., & Bankston, C., III. (1998). *Growing up American: How Vietnamese children adapt to life in the United States*. New York, NY: Russell Sage Foundation.

11

IN SPITE OF THE ODDS:
UNDOCUMENTED IMMIGRANT
YOUTH, SCHOOL NETWORKS,
AND COLLEGE SUCCESS

ROBERTO G. GONZALES

Contemporary immigration scholars have found growing evidence of the immigrant paradox, largely among legal immigrants and their children. However, increases in undocumented settlement over the past 2 or 3 decades prompts us to pay closer attention to the trajectories of undocumented immigrant youth as they grow up, move through school, and are absorbed into the social fabric of the United States. Because of the contexts that receive these young men and women—undocumented status, low parental human capital, and resource-troubled community institutions—they begin behind the starting line and at critical disadvantages vis-à-vis their native-born and legal peers. However, a significant number of these young people are challenging conventional expectations, finding a path to educational success in high school, and making their way to college and university campuses. Given economic and

This project was supported by the National Poverty Center using funds received from the U.S. Department of Health and Human Services, Office of the Assistant Secretary for Planning and Evaluation, Grant 1 U01 AE000002-01. The opinions and conclusions expressed herein are solely those of the author and should not be construed as representing the opinions or policy of any agency of the Federal government. To protect confidentiality, all names of individuals have been replaced with pseudonyms.

legal barriers, how do these students persist? And what sets them apart from their lesser achieving undocumented counterparts?

This chapter focuses on a 4.5-year research project conducted in five-county Greater Los Angeles[1] examining the transition to adulthood of undocumented 1.5-generation young adults[2] of Latin American origin. Hispanics constitute more than 81% of the total undocumented population (Passel & Cohn, 2009). As such, my study focused on the largest segment of undocumented young adults. During my time in the field, I came across scores of community college and university students who, despite great odds, managed to achieve academic success. The circumstances of these young men and women have been championed by the national Development, Relief, and Education for Alien Minors (DREAM) Act (2001) movement that seeks to provide a pathway to legalization for undocumented youngsters who migrated to the United States as children with parents or other family members.[3] The findings of this study provide compelling evidence that undocumented immigrant students are succeeding by using early school success to build networks of support with high-achieving peers and caring adult mentors and accumulating positive experiences in clubs and other youth organizations. These favorable school contexts provide them with opportunities to overcome their initial disadvantages and more freely pursue postsecondary pathways.

These young people are caught in a legal paradox that places special demands over the course of their adolescent and young adult years. Although they are able to receive a primary, secondary, and tertiary public education (as well as gain acceptance to most private postsecondary institutions), they are legally restricted from making use of it in the legal labor market after graduation. Contemporary education and immigration scholarship surmises that many of these young people, in the face of limited and limiting opportunities, might give up and develop oppositional attitudes toward school personnel and other adults in positions of authority (Matute-Bianchi, 1986; Ogbu, 1991; Portes & Zhou, 1993). But key mechanisms within the school system shape different individual pathways with corresponding sets of peer groups and teachers. Although some immigrant students may be acculturating to the norms of low-achieving and delinquent minority peers, others are integrating into environments in which high achievement and active participation in clubs is rewarded by teachers and other school personnel (see especially the-

---

[1]The Los Angeles Metropolitan area consists of Los Angeles, Riverside, Ventura, San Bernardino, and Orange counties.
[2]I define the 1.5 generation as immigrants who come to the country before the age of 12. These young people are born abroad but receive much of their education and socialization in the United States (see Rumbaut, 2004; Smith, 2005).
[3]The DREAM Act was first introduced in Congress in 2001. Although the DREAM Act has not yet been enacted into law, it has a large base of support both in and out of Congress.

ories of segmented assimilation; Portes & Rumbaut, 2001, 2006; Portes & Zhou, 1993)

IMMIGRATION, ASSIMILATION, AND THE PUBLIC SCHOOL SYSTEM

The public school has long been the primary institution of absorption for the children of immigrants. Historically, schools have been some of the most important institutions in the lives of immigrant children, wielding the power to either replicate societal inequalities or to equalize the field. For today's newcomers, this is no exception because they spend more waking hours in school and with peer and friendship groups than with anyone else (Suárez-Orozco, Suárez-Orozco, & Todorova, 2008). Moreover, returns on education have sharply increased in the postindustrial economy, making educational attainment more important today than ever before.

Scholars have long believed in immigrant succession. Although the first generation struggles, the second generation generally does better, and by the third generation the grandchildren of immigrants have outperformed their parents. But scholars studying contemporary incorporation patterns are finding evidence indicating that the reverse might actually be happening. Despite harsh contexts, research shows that the immigrant first generation does moderately well in school (Portes & Rumbaut, 2001). Over subsequent generations, however, academic performance declines. Scholarship on this *immigrant paradox* attributes a certain degree of these negative effects to assimilation and peer influence. Over time, children become increasingly acculturated and regress to the mean of other low-income minority peers. That is, through peer contact and influence they begin to pick up negative American traits as they lose critical sources of resilience and support (Valenzuela, 1999). For youth in urban environments, scholars have argued that negative peer group influence in the schools lead many immigrant children to engage in oppositional behavior, leading to downward trajectories (Matute-Bianchi, 1986; Ogbu, 1991; Portes & Zhou, 1993).

However, recent research on schools has found evidence of within-group differences (Gandara, 1982; Gibson, 1987; Zhou & Bankston, 1998). In particular, scholars have found that a diversity of student outcomes exists even within schools with high poor and minority student concentrations (Gandara, 1995). Indeed, many immigrant students do manage to survive poverty and disadvantage to become successful academic achievers. Relationships with high-achieving peers and school officials, it is argued, can enable poor and minority students to access important sources of social capital and mobilize resources necessary for school success (Gandara, 1982;

Suárez-Orozco, Suárez-Orozco, & Qin-Hillard, 2001). Stanton-Salazar (2001) asserted that students from poor families can overcome economic disadvantage by forging positive relationships with teachers and school staff who can help them to access the necessary information needed to get into college preparatory classes, apply for college, and seek out financial assistance. Croninger and Lee (2001) found that when teachers take time and effort to assist students, they can be an important source of social capital. Indeed, when students are disconnected from the schooling process, they have far fewer opportunities to form relationships with those who can guide their academic progress. But when schools help structure students' peer relationships, they can positively influence their academic achievement (Gibson, Gándara, & Peterson-Koyama, 2004). This is particularly important for students who come from families without a member who has attended a postsecondary institution and, as such, lack knowledge about how schools and the broader society allocate resources and opportunity.

Although the literatures on peer influence and school structure address school success and failure from seemingly different theoretical perspectives, they do not necessarily contradict each other. In fact, their enjoinment enables us to more deeply understand the mechanisms that contribute to school success. Contemporary immigration theory surmises that children from poor immigrant families are likely to be influenced negatively by native-born peer groups. However, as contemporary education scholars have demonstrated, native students from poor and minority populations are not uniformly concentrated in lower tracks and in illicit activity. And immigrant students do not uniformly settle into the lower tracks. In fact, significant numbers of native-born and immigrant students meet each other, develop relationships, and form networks of mutual support in specialized classes and school programs.

When applied to undocumented immigrant students, issues of academic success take on an amplified resonance because these youngsters are arguably more vulnerable and have greater needs than their documented poor and minority peers. Like other members of the working poor, undocumented Latino immigrant youth face notable barriers. Given their parents' job prospects and legal limitations, most undocumented youth live in de facto segregated areas of dense poverty with high rates of crime and attend low-performing schools. Children of immigrants are often doubly unprotected. They are much more likely to be poor, live in crowded housing, lack health care, and belong to families who have trouble paying the rent and affording food (Capps, Fix, Ost, Reardon-Anderson, & Passel, 2005; Hernandez, 1999; Menjívar & Abrego, 2009). Adding undocumented status to the already troubling mix of unfavorable conditions severely undermines efforts to move out of poverty. Like parents in other working poor families, undocumented parents often work in low-paying, unstable jobs for long periods of time, sacrificing job mobility for stability (Chavez, 1998). And like other children who grow up in poverty, children of undocumented immigrants also face high levels of street violence and generally ineffective schools that are at the core of "segregated inner-city residence" (Waters, 1999, p. 243). Furthermore, being undocumented also increases the likelihood that families will lack health insurance (Fortuny, Capps, & Passel, 2007) and lowers their chances of accessing bank accounts and other financial services.

Although family circumstances erect numerous barriers during school, it is perhaps what lies after school that is the cause of most concern. Exclusion from the legal workforce and from the receipt of financial aid narrowly circumscribes postsecondary options for undocumented youngsters. Their inability to legally work forces them into choices that either leave them in a perpetual state of limbo or in jeopardy of being found by immigration officials. For those with resource-poor families, the imperative to provide financial support narrows their choices and heightens their vulnerability. Of equally grave consequences, the denial of financial aid to undocumented immigrant students to support attendance in postsecondary institutions leaves them challenged to come up with the funding necessary to continue their education and keep them engaged in a legally permissible pursuit. Indeed, such structural constraints restrict their ability to participate in many aspects of what is considered a successful adult life. They also have psychological consequences. The fall from protected family and school environments to unprotected environments that correspond with their transitions to late adolescence and early adulthood and the steep barriers to postsecondary schooling can lead to depressed aspirations and negative future outlooks, causing undocumented students to lose motivation in high school or even engage in oppositional behavior.

As the scholarship on other vulnerable populations demonstrates, what happens in high school can exert powerful influence on postsecondary trajectories and aspirations (Conchas, 2001, 2006; Gandara, 1995, 1982; MacLeod, 1995; Portes & Rumbaut, 2001, 2006; Stanton-Salazar, 2001). Indeed, the high school years are important for immigrant and native-born students alike. But for immigrant children and the children of immigrants, it is this experience of schooling in the United States during their formative years that sets them apart from their parents. By participating in the public school system, they are exposed to acculturative forces to which their parents might have no or limited access. They are also exposed to American-born friends and teachers who can influence their decisions and determine access to important information and resources.

Much has been written on their effects when these influences are negative—that is, delayed or downward progress. But what are the possibilities for undocumented youth when these influences are positive?

THE LOS ANGELES ADULT CHILDREN
OF UNDOCUMENTED IMMIGRANTS STUDY

Background and Setting

My research took place in what is arguably the capital of contemporary immigrant America. From 2004 to 2007, and then again in 2009, I carried out fieldwork in the five-county Los Angeles metropolitan area with undocumented 1.5-generation young adults. This period corresponded with the largest periods of inflow of unauthorized migrants into the United States. During the 1990s, 5.1 million undocumented immigrants came to the United States, and during the 1st decade of the new millennium, 5.3 million arrived (Passel & Cohn, 2008). My respondents are representative of this trend toward unauthorized settlement, with many of them making critical transitions from childhood to adolescence and early adulthood during the 1990s.

Over the past 2 decades, dislocations in sending countries, increased labor migration, and accompanying increases in unauthorized settlement dramatically altered the complexity of contemporary migration and the immigrant family. Driving these shifts in settlement patterns in large part were equally dramatic changes in immigration policy (Kanstroom, 2007; Nevins, 2002; Zolberg, 2006). As an unintended result of policy attempts to curb unauthorized migration, specifically a beefing up of the U.S.–Mexico border in the years subsequent to the Immigration Reform and Control Act (IRCA) of 1986, once-circular migratory flows across the United States' southern border were transformed into permanent migrant settlement in the United States, increasing the numbers and changing the composition of the unauthorized population (Cornelius & Lewis, 2006; Massey, Durand, & Malone, 2002). As a result, the number of undocumented immigrants grew substantially and has shifted from predominantly single male migrants working seasonally to larger proportions of women and children (Hondagneu-Sotelo, 1994). By 2008, the number of undocumented immigrants was 11.9 million (Passel & Cohn, 2009). Among these, 1.5 million were under the age of 18.

In California, these demographic changes were the most felt. California is home to more than a fourth of all immigrants in the United States, and more than a fourth of the state's population is foreign born—a significantly greater proportion than any other state (Portes & Rumbaut, 2006). California is also home to 2.7 million, or 22%, of the nation's unauthorized immigrants (Passel & Cohn, 2009). It has an even larger share of the unauthorized student population, about 40% at all grade levels (Passel, 2003). Since 1990, the share of 1.5- and second-generation children in California has steadily increased while the share of the first generation has steadily decreased. This has important implications for the future of California, its workforce, and its schools.

Method

The research for this study involved 3.5 years of ethnographic field work and 150 semistructured interviews with 1.5-generation unauthorized Latino young adults between the ages of 20 and 34. All respondents came to the United States before the age of 12 (some as young as 2 to 3 months), and the median age at arrival was 7.

My field work took place in various settings, including continuation schools, community-based organizations, college campuses, and churches. I accompanied respondents throughout their school or work days, volunteered at local schools and community organizations, and sat in on numerous community- or school-based meetings. Through these efforts, I located the initial group of respondents across various community and educational settings and then used snowball sampling to identify subsequent groupings of respondents.

The entire sample came from the five-county Los Angeles metropolitan area, with respondents from all five counties. The sample was split equally by gender and educational attainment. Half of the sample graduated from high school and went on to college, whereas the other half exited before college, either by dropping out of high school or finishing after the completion of high school. Although this chapter focuses chiefly on college-going undocumented young adults, I incorporated what I learned from the experiences of early-exiters to draw out mechanisms of support. At the time of the last interviews, between 2007 and 2009, the vast majority of respondents' parents were undocumented (92%), and had received less than 6 years of schooling (86%). Parents were employed in low-wage sectors: factory, agriculture, construction, gardening, housekeeping, janitorial work, and the garment industry.

Interviews were conducted only after I had spent lengthy periods of time in the field gaining a rapport with both respondents and community stakeholders. The life history interviews covered aspects of childhood, adolescence, and adulthood, with special attention paid to educational experiences. They ranged from 1 hour and 40 minutes to 3 hours and 20 minutes in length. Transcripts of interviews were analyzed using open coding techniques. Conceptual labels were placed on responses that described discrete events, experiences, and feelings reported in the interviews. Next, each individual interview was analyzed across all questions to identify metathemes. Finally, responses were examined for common metathemes across all interviews.

Growing up, respondents faced notable barriers. Geographically, given their parents' job prospects and legal limitations, most grew up in de facto segregated areas of dense poverty (Chavez, 1998). Their communities were typically beset with low-performing schools, higher than average rates of crime, and few employment opportunities for their residents. Racial–ethnic segregation and limited opportunities have historically concentrated poverty in

Black and Latino communities, subjecting residents to the structural effects of poverty (Waters, 1999). In effect, the low quality of education and low socioeconomic status of urban low-income neighborhoods cumulatively deter the academic progression of the children, shaping their future life chances. Growing up in a poor neighborhood "increases the likelihood of dropping out of high school, reduces the probability of attending college, lowers the likelihood of employment, reduces income earned as an adult, and increases the risk of teenage childbearing and unwed pregnancy" (Waters, 1999, p. 243).

SCHOOL OPPORTUNITY STRUCTURE FOR UNDOCUMENTED YOUTH

Most of my undocumented 1.5-generation respondents attended large school districts in schools with high student-to-teacher ratios, consistent with their poverty profiles. In many Los Angeles area school districts, schools fail to graduate close to half of incoming freshmen. With limited access to teachers and counselors, many students in these schools quickly fall through the cracks. Nevertheless, a significant, albeit much smaller, share of students, navigates its way to the California three-tiered public postsecondary education system.[4]

Among the undocumented young people I interviewed were valedictorians and class presidents in high school (more than 25% finished in the top 5% of their graduating class).[5] Each had been accepted to several colleges and universities. And most of these students exhibited high levels of participation in school and community activities. Of chief importance, nearly all of these college-going respondents indicated that they were connected in important ways to faculty and staff during high school and that their support was an important factor in their school success. They also felt as though they were shielded from other students who were not doing well in school, and that enabled them to focus on doing well in school.

Specialized Classes and Programs

Many of the college-going students with whom I spoke were selected for special classes and programs as early as seventh grade. Schools often select a small number of students who take classes together and advance each year

---

[4]The three-tiered California public higher education system consists of the University of California campuses, the California State Universities, and the California Community Colleges.
[5]Although undocumented females have a slight edge on males in terms of educational attainment (see Batalova & McHugh, 2010), because my sample included equal shares of men and women, I cannot discern educational differences by gender.

together, in many cases sheltered from other students. By the time they reach high school, these students are prepared to compete for slots in the gifted and talented programs, specialized academies, and honors and advanced placement (AP) classes. Esmeralda, who benefited from such selection very early in her schooling explained,

> Before we even moved on to high school, my teachers kind of already recommend[ed] certain classes . . . from middle school to high school they had already chosen for me. "Oh I recommend you for this class or that one."

Particularly in large schools, the smaller environment can be more conducive to learning and can shelter students from many of the problems that plague large, poor, urban schools, such as gangs, large classrooms, and inadequate resources (Hochschild & Scovronick, 2003; Orfield, 2004; Orfield & Lee, 2004). Zulima, another college-goer, described her school and program:

> At the time, [my school] was the second-largest high school in the nation. We had around, I think, 5,400 students. When I started, my class was like 2,200, but by the time I graduated we were I think like 800. Within the school there are little minischools. I was in Odyssey Academy. You have the same classes with the same students, all 4 years. You have to apply to get in and basically you have to take certain classes. I guess it's a division; it was more . . . like a tracking like system. You saw which students were bound for college.

Identified as high achievers and smart kids, the positive labels these students received gave them the affirmation they needed to be confident in their abilities and to assist each other. They modeled positive habits, pushed each other to do more and better, and set up informal mechanisms for information sharing. The experiences of these students provide evidence of the benefits of small, supportive learning environments. Students were shielded from the broader student body; they enjoyed smaller learning environments and gained special access to resources. In addition, they had direct access to teachers and other adults who believed in their potential. These networks provided them with the kinds of advantages Stanton-Salazar (2001) argued are crucial for school success. Smaller learning environments gave them specific advantages over other students—exposure to a pathway designed to get them into college and increased access to teachers and critical information on how to prepare and be competitive for college. These advantages served students well as they moved through high school in the company of other high-achieving peers.

Characteristics of Peer Networks

Indeed, positive tracking through honors, AP, or specialized academies provided undocumented respondents environments that allowed them to feel safe and supported and where they could freely pursue academics. In turn, these environments fostered the development of social capital via peer relationships. These young men and women formed relationships with other high-achieving classmates. They supported, mentored, and competed with each other in ways that enhanced their intellectual development and advanced their academic pursuits.

Many students described to me the benefits of having friends that pushed each other to do well in school. Moreover, among these friendship groups, students tutored each other and studied together. Oscar explained to me how his group of friends helped one other:

> We had study nights or study days and we would help each other and tutor each other. A lot of the students trusted me and knew that I knew the material already, so they would prefer to have me and other friends tutoring them.

Scarlet explained that the transition to high school facilitated her transition of friends. During middle school and the first semester of high school, she was more into boys and hanging out with her friends than her schoolwork. However, the more she accomplished in school, the more excited she became. When teachers started taking notice of her, she slowly began to pull away from her lower achieving friends.

> I was in the popular crowd, and we were into going out and talking to guys and hanging out. We got into an argument, and I stopped talking to all of them and they stopped talking to me. So I made new friends, and the friends that I made were honors students. They were calmer, they were into school. I think in a way that kind of helped me. I think that if I would have stayed with the other crowd, I don't know if I would have done as good as I have. I don't know. I would probably have gone the wrong way or something. Because as far as I know about them, I don't think they go to school or anything.

As Scarlet's experience demonstrates, these peer groups also enhance students' social capital. JD, who grew up aspiring to be a teacher, was the oldest of three sisters. Her parents were very protective of them and insisted that they come directly home after school. Because she did not have free time after school for clubs or friends, she had to maximize her time and resources. She relied on friends for information about academic opportunities. They devised a system and supported each other through the sharing of important information.

> It was more of just a group of people helping. I mean, we were friends. My friend Amanda, she was the one that whenever she would get one piece of information or she heard something I wasn't aware off, she'd let me know, "Hey, did you hear about this that's due?" "No, I didn't." Or we would help each other. There was someone from a different university

coming in to talk. We would sign up and get information and give it [to] each other.

Students in the specialized classes and programs benefited from the relationships they formed within their classes. Undocumented respondents formed friendships and peer networks with other documented and undocumented students in the top strata of their schools. The positive labels they were given as a result of their school placement provided them the affirmation they needed to be confident in their ability to assist each other. They modeled positive habits, pushed each other to do more and better, and set up informal mechanisms for information sharing.

Supportive Adults

Many of the students I interviewed credited individual teachers or counselors who aided them in their academic pursuits. Luis explained to me how he experienced such benefits:

> I had help from counselors, from teachers, from the principal. They were helpful; they were my mentors. Any resources, any help that I needed in terms of questions on writing, you know, your paper, or with school, getting your information, those were the people that I would always go to.

Similarly, Daisy described her positive experiences with her teachers:

> I felt very strongly about their support. I have so many memories about my English teacher and my history teacher who I'm gonna take with me everywhere because they were just so motivating in their teaching style and in the way they showed their support to each student.

Marisol had positive experiences at school that gave her hope during troubled times at home. She enjoyed school and loved the freedom it gave her. While there, she did not have to worry about her problems at home, nor her family's financial woes. "School was an escape," she told me. "There I was happy and calm. . . . I could be myself. I could be recognized at school. I couldn't at home."

Marisol's English teacher helped her through the difficulties at home and encouraged her to pursue college. With her teacher's help, Marisol was able to convince her father of the benefits of going to college versus going straight to work. Although her brothers had little choice because of limited family finances and the families' need for them to contribute, Marisol was able to enroll at a local community college, save money, and transfer to a California State University, where she ultimately earned a bachelor's degree in sociology. Through her relationship with her teacher, she was also able to talk frankly about her legal status and her family's limited financial situation. Ultimately,

Marisol benefited from the trust she gave her teacher because they worked together to find financial solutions and private scholarships.

Similarly, when Aldo was on the verge of dropping out of high school, his AP history teacher intervened. Aldo's earning power was needed by his family as making ends meet each month became increasingly difficult. Feeling the burdens of family needs and not seeing a way to change his immigration status, Aldo decided he would leave school to earn money. However, when she heard the news, Aldo's history teacher pleaded with him to reconsider his decision. Aldo explained his family's circumstances and added that "school probably was not going to be useful anyway" because he could not get a good job even if he went to college. Aldo's teacher mobilized other teachers and started a fund to provide him extra money through the remainder of his senior year.

When it came time for Aldo and other respondents to apply for college, assistance with applications and scholarships was viewed as a natural extension of what they had grown accustomed to in their relationships with teachers over the years. However, it was at this critical turning point when these relationships proved to be pivotal. Whereas many of the early-exiter respondents failed to come up with necessary resources and information for college on their own, those who did go to college were able to do so through assistance from teachers and counselors. Having developed relationships of trust, these students felt comfortable disclosing private details about their immigration status and the related difficulty of paying for postsecondary schooling. As a result, teachers were able to explore options for them, often learning as they went along.

José was on the academic decathlon and debate teams. He did well in school and was well liked by his teachers. Although he did not know how to get past the admissions officer's request that he apply for an international student visa, he was able to rely on his school network to get the assistance he needed.

> When I went to the admissions office they were asking for [my] social [security number] and I was like, "I don't have one." The lady at the administration said that I needed to apply for a student visa which was going to be like, freaking expensive so I went back to my school and [talked to] this guy who works in the office. I went with him and he said, "Okay let me see what I can do." So he called [the admissions office] again and he said, "Well I have this student, this really good student, and he's trying to apply there but he doesn't have a social [security number]." So they told him about AB 540 [Cal. Edc. Code § 68130.5, signed into law in October 2001, which allows eligible immigrant students to pay in-state tuition at public college and universities]. That was the first time I heard about it. The lady in administration didn't tell me anything.

Although Karina, another undocumented student, did exceptionally well in high school, she was quiet and did not garner the attention of her teachers.

264   ROBERTO G. GONZALES

Her high school friends were ethnically mixed but none were undocumented, and Karina did not feel as though she could confide in them, nor did she think they would "understand her situation." When it came time to apply to college, Karina was without any assistance. None of her teachers ushered her through the process, and nobody within her peer network knew any other undocumented students in college. Unaware of her legal options, Karina did not know where to find the necessary information. Instead of going to a 4-year college, she settled for a community college.

> I didn't know anything about AB 540 so the reason I didn't go to university, well first of all was because I was lacking the money so even if I were . . . well maybe if I knew the information I could have gotten a scholarship or something. But I didn't know anything. I didn't even know we had AB 540 so I thought I was going to pay like 20,000 so I was like, "No way I was going to pay that." So that's why I didn't go. Nobody told me anything. I don't know if my counselors knew, but they never told me anything.

José's and Karina's experiences stand in contrast to each other. Each had college aspirations, and each encountered a roadblock during the process. Whereas José was able to reach out to his school network to enlist the assistance of a school counselor, Karina's attempt was stalled because she could not identify anyone within her particular network that had the information or relationships needed to move her over the obstacle. As a result, José moved smoothly into a California State University campus in the fall. On her own initiative, Karina enrolled in a community college. After 3 years of balancing part-time school and work, she is only now beginning the process of applying to 4-year universities.

Because of the inability to receive government-administered financial aid, however, AB 540's reach is limited. Even at in-state tuition rates, the cost of attending institutions of higher learning is prohibitive for most undocumented students. I have met many students like Karina, who end up at the community college after not being able to secure enough money to attend a 4-year university. Some, however, are able to find pots of money through school-based networks.

Margarita, an undocumented student who went on to a prestigious University of California school, explained,

> My counselor was really good. He would tell me more about college and help me out with my essays and everything. He found a lot of scholarships for me. My 1st year of university was entirely paid for. It just seemed so familiar, like this is what I'm supposed to be doing, you know. I didn't know it was gonna be this hard, but this is what I'm supposed to be doing.

Margarita's explanation of the process illustrates the extent to which many of these undocumented successful students saw the college application process to be natural. That is, they grew accustomed to receiving help from teachers and other school personnel.

After Luis was accepted to a university in San Diego, his teacher learned that he was contemplating staying nearby to attend a community college because of the cost differential. Determined to help Luis, she contacted other teachers. Pooling their money to meet her initial $1,000 contribution, their combined donations paid for his 1st-year tuition plus books.

In sum, respondents who were able to find resources were those who had relationships with teachers and who learned supportive institutional and public policies. With very little academic support from their families, such as many middle-class mainstream students possess, peers and school personnel play a critical role in providing opportunities for these students to access the resources available to them so they can attend college.

Extracurricular Involvement

Specialized school programs also led many college-going respondents to extend their networks through participation in school and community extracurricular activities. Respondents viewed their participation in clubs, student government, and community service activities as an extension of school involvement. For many, participation was a direct result of interventions by teachers who recognized talents or abilities and tried to channel them into leadership positions.

Andrea dropped out of school at age 13, but returned 2 years later. Shortly after her return to school, a teacher noticed that she was a leader among her peers in class. During the first weeks of school, he paid close attention to her interactions with other students. He referred her to the vice-principal, who was spearheading a diversity initiative at school. For the next 2 years, Andrea served on an advisory council that gave recommendations to the administration about how to address racial and ethnic tensions at the school. This experience served as a catalyst for later leadership positions for Andrea in college and the community and incited what she referred to as a "sense of ownership of my education and development."

Through participation in extracurricular activities, Andrea and other respondents broadened their horizons and strengthened their networks. These school-sponsored clubs provided students the opportunities to work with teachers and community members. Alexia, for example, attended weekly meetings with the district superintendent. When she applied to college, Alexia felt comfortable about asking the superintendent for a letter of recommendation. Other respondents, who participated in programs such as Upward Bound and the Puente Project and various other clubs and programs, benefited from school-sponsored field trips, university visits, and help with college applications. Participation in extracurricular activities was not the exception but the rule among this group of students. In fact, most of the respondents I spoke with participated in not just one but several activities while in high school.

Undocumented respondents also found that participation in school clubs, social groups, and community organizations provided them with opportunities to gain leadership experience. This gave them confidence to pursue postsecondary education and positions of leadership. These volunteer experiences also helped them to extend their social networks. Many like Alexia, for example, used these networks to gain advantage in the college application process. Similarly, Rosalba, who managed to successfully navigate the educational system and find various private scholarships, has been very active in extracurricular activity since high school and has accumulated an impressive network of support. "I've made it because I've had a support system," she said.

> At every step of my education, I have had a mentor. There's a chain. They are always looking out for you, looking at scholarships for you. It's a thousand times much harder without someone helping you. Being undocumented, it's not about what you know, it's who you know. You might have all of the will in the world, but if you don't know the right people, then no.

WHEN DOORS ARE NO LONGER OPEN

School placement provided select groups of students with opportunities for mentorship, encouragement, exposure, and assistance getting into college. The opportunity to study in small learning environments and to be shielded from the broader student population while receiving resources unavailable to most of that population proved to be critical to their advancement. Moreover, the unique settings that resulted from positive school placement enabled students to forge positive relationships with peers and supportive adults. These relationships proved to be extremely important over time. Seeing the benefits of these relationships, many students expanded their networks by becoming involved in clubs and projects outside of the classroom, where they not only socialized with peers but also worked side by side with school officials and community professionals. This enabled many of these students the opportunities to attend colleges and universities because they learned about institutional and public policies and practices that would support their academic goals.

What do these young men and women do when doors are no longer open? At the time of their interviews, 22 respondents had graduated from 4-year universities (a little more than 28% of all college-going respondents), and nine of them held advanced degrees (more than 13%). These young men and women have been successful despite legal and institutional barriers. None of them, however, is able to legally pursue his or her dream career. The traditional doors to career success are completely shut for these students because they lack legal status. American dream narratives hold a powerful place in the development and schooling of these American youngsters. Through school, in particular, children are taught that if they work hard enough, if they dream boldly, they can reach their goals and be successful in the United States. These narratives are, perhaps, most powerfully internalized among those who actually achieve educational success. As children move through the school system, their success provides proof to them that there is a connection between their hard work and success. The more successful they become, the more meaning gets attached to the belief in meritocracy.

But when achievement and opportunity become delinked, entire meaning systems are thrown into chaos. Among all respondents, those who achieved high levels of school success had a very difficult time reconciling the mismatch between educational attainment and lack of opportunities in adulthood. Instead, many, like Esperanza, found themselves toiling in low-wage jobs.

Esperanza's circumstances diverted long-held aspirations of becoming a journalist to more immediate needs such as making ends meet. In high school, she was in the school band and AP classes. Her high hopes for success were supported by relationships with high-achieving peers and teachers. Until graduation, nothing had prepared her for her circumstances 3 years out of college, when her only available employment options came from restaurant jobs and factory work. These circumstances forced her to eschew the lessons learned from years of schooling. Although she felt out of place in the sphere of undocumented work, she had little choice.

When I interviewed Esperanza, she was having a difficult time reconciling her limited choices and present circumstances. She had graduated from her university with a bachelor's degree in English literature. However, her inability to secure adequate resources for graduate school left her in uncertainty and needing time to make some money. During these years, she had cleaned offices and waited tables at restaurants. When I asked Esperanza to describe her work in restaurants, she recounted the various problems she faced at work, particularly the constant shame and embarrassment.

> I am just ashamed, like I looked [for work] in most restaurants and they would be like, "Why do you want to work for us if you have a BA?" So, I am going to have to lie and I am going to have to tell them that I just dropped out of high school. But eventually it comes out. The people [working] at those places, like the cooks and the cashiers, they are really young people, and I feel really old, like what am I doing there if they are all like 16, 17 years old. The others are like *señoras* who are 35 and have

little kids. They dropped out of school, but because they have little kids they are still working at the restaurant. Thinking about that, it makes me feel so stupid. And like the factories, too, because they ask me, "¿Que estas haciendo aqui? ["What are you doing here?] You can speak English. You graduated from high school. You can work anywhere." They don't stop bugging me.

For years Esperanza assumed different identities—band leader, honors student, college graduate. She believed that by the time she finished school her legal situation would be taken care of and that she would have a job that matched her education. Most of her friends had already started careers. One was a city planner, others were moving ahead in business-related jobs or were teachers. As Esperanza noted, "They have their degrees and they are working at jobs they saw themselves working at. . . . They are following their dreams." But she was hiding her identities that reflected her high achievements. She felt out of place in low-wage work environments and had become wary of the interrogating questions. She chose to assume an identity she felt best matched her coworkers. When I asked her to think of the near future, her outlook was pessimistic, and her expectations were well below those one might hear from recent college graduates.

> I just need a job. It's become about survival. If it used to be a choice, it is not a choice anymore. I am to the point where yes, I will clean somebody's home, I will take care of them, I will clean up somebody's saliva, like, I still can't do that, I don't think I will ever be able to do that, but umm, but more and more it is getting to the point where it is like, I don't care.

DISCUSSION AND CONCLUSION

Why do some undocumented immigrant students do well in school when educational pursuits are met with seemingly insurmountable social, legal, and financial barriers, reinforcing the notion of the immigrant paradox? The school experiences of undocumented immigrant students provide useful data to scholars and policymakers alike. As such, issues affecting their post-secondary matriculation and subsequent academic or career pursuits are important clues to the larger puzzle of what it takes for them to lead healthy adult lives.

The findings discussed in this chapter suggest that important mechanisms exist within the school system to enable high-achieving immigrant students to sustain successful trajectories. As such, this research supports previous studies suggesting that educational advancement is shaped, at least in part, by students' positions within the school hierarchy—that is, their curriculum tracks (Oakes, 1985). In overcrowded urban public schools, students in large, general-track classes have less individualized attention and fewer opportunities to form positive relationships with teachers and school officials. Without access to scarce but critical school resources, many of these students join other delinquent or nonengaged youth, develop a resistance to educational pursuits, lower expectations and aspirations, and fall through the cracks.

However, the young men and women in my study who have done well in school did so because they benefited from environments that fostered learning and the development of school-based social capital and were shielded from the broader problems that plague many of these large urban schools. Smaller learning environments fostered the development of relationships with teachers and adults who could leverage resources needed to advance to institutions of higher learning. School officials actively working to incorporate students into the culture of the school and illuminate the various pathways to postsecondary education provided these young people additional opportunities for achieving educational success. These findings also highlight the importance of supportive policies and practices at the postsecondary educational level and the need to inform these students of their availability.

By taking into account undocumented immigrant status, this chapter extends related inquiries of the immigrant paradox and school structures into a closer examination of the ways they impact vulnerable populations. Besides the already formidable obstacles for low-income students in finishing high school and successfully advancing to postsecondary institutions, undocumented students encounter additional barriers—notably, their unauthorized status and the exclusions attached. Undocumented status arouses the always-present fear of punishment (by immigration authorities or by peer stigmatization) and the discovery of exclusion. Many respondents explained that they did not disclose the details of their unauthorized status to school personnel for fear of negative repercussions. However, by not doing so, they lessened their chances for needed assistance. For those who did have relationships of trust and support with teachers and other school personnel, the ability to confide in these adults proved especially salient when they were attempting to advance through school, move on to college, and secure financial assistance.

Adolescents are at a developmental stage when they are gaining independence but still require a great deal of guidance and help in opening doors (Furstenberg, Cook, Eccles, & Elder, 2000). Most young people, whether documented or undocumented, require adults to shepherd them through important transitions. School provides students with the first opportunities to form important relationships outside the household. The development of these relationships is critical to gaining guidance and support. Through smaller class sizes and ongoing college counseling, respondents in positive tracks were placed in closer proximity to teachers and school personnel. Those with such adult school-based mentors reported that they were more likely to develop trust in adults and to disclose their unauthorized status in order to seek help. These students, then, had distinct advantages in securing resources for themselves. Positioning within the school hierarchy garnered them not only important resources but also relationships from which to draw in order to gain advice about the future, apply to college, and find money for tuition.

This chapter has taken a look at the often-discussed immigrant paradox. After having demonstrated the scholarly implications, I now turn to those for policy. Currently, with the exception of two states (Texas and New Mexico), undocumented students are not eligible to compete for state financial aid and are not eligible for any federally administered financial aid programs. Without financial assistance, it is extremely difficult for most Americans to afford a public or private university. Given the profile of most immigrant families, the cost of college is prohibitive, if not restrictive, for undocumented students.

Indeed, state and federal policies are critical for undocumented immigrant students to access opportunities for postsecondary participation. Current research is just beginning to ascertain these effects (Flores, 2010; Flores & Horn, 2009). However, as this chapter has demonstrated, many of the obstacles to college are also institutional. As many of my respondents found, barriers to postsecondary education can be mediated by K-12 schools. Information about financial resources as well as supportive policies can be accessed through peers or adults.

Undocumented students represent a sizeable, growing, and vulnerable population in our schools. Recent estimates suggest that as many as 2.1 million young people who have been educated in the United States lack legal status (Batalova & McHugh, 2010). Unfortunately, because of educational barriers, of these roughly only 38% would likely benefit from potential legislation. A lack of specialized attention by school personnel to the unique circumstances and experiences of these youngsters is tantamount to allowing them to fall through the cracks. We can, however, look at the experiences of high-achieving undocumented youth to unlock the clues to success. Concerted efforts by schools to promote structures whereby teachers, counselors, and other school personnel work actively to include all students can facilitate the successful transition of undocumented students to college. Indeed, undocumented youth require not targeted but universal access. Further, although proponents of the DREAM Act tout the success of high-achieving undocumented students to make a strong case to Congress, they often fail to point out the mechanisms that promote success. School success is often shaped by students' positions within the school, resilience is shaped by relationships with caring and supportive adults, and civic activity by experience and participation in school-based clubs and leadership positions.

REFERENCES

Batalova, J., & McHugh, M. (2010, July). *DREAM vs. reality: An analysis of potential DREAM Act beneficiaries.* Retrieved from http://www.migrationpolicy.org/pubs/DREAM-Insight-July2010.pdf

Cal. Edc. Code § 68130.5 (October 2001).

Capps, R., Fix, M., Ost, J., Reardon-Anderson, J., & Passel, J. S. (2005). *The health and well-being of young children of immigrants.* Washington, DC: The Urban Institute.

Chavez, L. R. (1998). *Shadowed lives: Undocumented immigrants in American society.* Fort Worth, TX: Harcourt Brace.

Conchas, G. Q. (2001). Structuring failure and success: Understanding the variability in Latino school engagement. *Harvard Educational Review, 71,* 475–504.

Conchas, G. Q. (2006). *The color of success: Race and high achieving urban youth.* New York, NY: Teachers College Press.

Cornelius, W. A., & Lewis, J. M. (Eds.). (2006). *Impacts of border enforcement on Mexican migration: The view from sending communities.* Boulder, CO: Lynne Rienner.

Croninger, R. G., & Lee, V. E. (2001). Social capital and dropping out of high school: Benefits to at-risk students of teachers' support and guidance. *Teachers College Record, 103,* 548–581. doi:10.1111/0161-4681.00127

Development, Relief, and Education for Alien Minors Act, S. 1291, 107th Cong. (2001).

Flores, S. M. (2010). State "Dream Acts": The effect of in-state resident tuition policies on the college enrollment of undocumented Latino students in the United States. *The Review of Higher Education, 33,* 239–283. DOI: 10.1353/rhe.0.0134

Flores, S. M., & Horn, C. L. (2009). College persistence and undocumented students at a selective public university: A quantitative case study analysis. *Journal of College Student Retention, 11,* 57–76. doi:10.2190/CS.11.1.d

Fortuny, K., Capps, R., & Passel, J. S. (2007). *Unauthorized immigrants in California, Los Angeles County and the United States.* Washington, DC: The Urban Institute.

Furstenberg, F., Cook, T. D., Eccles, J., & Elder, G. (2000). *Managing to make it: Urban families and adolescent success.* Chicago, IL: University of Chicago Press.

Gandara, P. (1982). Passing through the eye of the needle: High-achieving Chicanas. *Hispanic Journal of Behavioral Sciences, 4,* 167–179. doi:10.1177/07399863820042003

Gandara, P. (1995). *Over the ivy walls: The educational mobility of low-income Chicanos.* Albany: State University of New York Press.

Gibson, M. A. (1987). The school performance of immigrant minorities: A comparative view. *Anthropology & Education Quarterly, 18,* 262–275. doi:10.1525/aeq.1987.18.4.04x0018r

Gibson, M. A., Gándara, P., & Peterson-Koyama, J. (2004). *School connections: U.S. Mexican youth, peers, and school achievement.* New York, NY: Teachers College Press.

Hernandez, D. J. (1999). *Children of immigrants: Health, adjustment, and public assistance*. Washington, DC: National Academy Press.

Hochschild, J. L., & Scovronick, N. (2003). *The American dream and the public school*. New York, NY: Oxford University Press.

Hondagneu-Sotelo, P. (1994). *Gendered transitions: Mexican experiences of immigration*. Berkeley: University of California Press.

Immigration Reform and Control Act, Pub. L. 99-603, 100 Stat. 3359, enacted November 6, 1986.

Kanstroom, D. (2007). *Deportation nation: Outsiders in American history*. Cambridge, MA: Harvard University Press.

MacLeod, J. (1995). *Ain't no makin' it: Aspirations and attainment in a low-income neighborhood*. Boulder, CO: Westview Press.

Massey, D. S., Durand, J., & Malone, N. J. (2002). *Beyond smoke and mirrors: Mexican immigration in an era of economic integration*. New York, NY: Russell Sage Foundation.

Matute-Bianchi, M. E. (1986). Ethnic Identification and patterns of school success and failure among Mexican-descent and Japanese-American students in a California high school. *American Journal of Education, 95*, 233–255.

Menjívar, C., & Abrego, L. (2009). Parents and children across borders: Legal instability and intergenerational relations in Guatemalan and Salvadoran families. In N. Foner (Ed.), *Across generations: Immigrant families in America* (pp. 160–189). New York, NY: New York University Press.

Nevins, J. (2002). *Operation gatekeeper: The rise of the illegal alien and the remaking of the U.S.-Mexico boundary*. New York, NY: Routledge.

Oakes, J. (1985). *Keeping track: How schools structure inequality*. New Haven, CT: Yale University Press.

Ogbu, J. (1991). Immigrant and involuntary minorities in comparative perspective. In M. A. Gibson & J. Ogbu (Eds.), *Minority status and schooling: A comparative study of immigrant and involuntary minorities* (pp. 3–33). New York, NY: Garland.

Orfield, G. (2004). *Brown* misunderstood. In J. Anderson & D. N. Byrne (Eds.), *The unfinished agenda of* Brown v. Board of Education (pp. 153–164). Hoboken, NJ: Wiley.

Orfield, G., & Lee, C. (2004). Brown *at 50: King's dream or* Plessy's *nightmare?* Cambridge, MA: Civil Rights Project, Harvard University.

Passel, J. S. (2003). *Further demographic information relating to the DREAM Act*. Washington, DC: The Urban Institute.

Passel, J. S., & Cohn, D. (2008, October). *Trends in unauthorized immigration: Undocumented inflow now trails legal inflow*. Washington, DC: Pew Hispanic Center.

Passel, J. S., & Cohn, D. (2009, April). *A portrait of unauthorized immigrants in the United States*. Washington, DC: Pew Hispanic Center.

Portes, A., & Rumbaut, R. G. (2001). *Legacies: The story of the immigrant second generation*. Berkeley: University of California Press.

Portes, A., & Rumbaut, R. G. (2006). *Immigrant America: A portrait* (3rd ed.). Berkeley: University of California Press.

Portes, A., & Zhou, M. (1993). The new second generation: Segmented assimilation and its variants. *ANNALS of the American Academy of Political and Social Science, 530*, 74–96. doi:10.1177/0002716293530001006

Rumbaut, R. G. (1997). Assimilation and its discontents: Between rhetoric and reality. *The International Migration Review, 31*, 923–960. doi:10.2307/2547419

Rumbaut, R. G. (2004). Ages, life stages, and generational cohorts: Decomposing the immigrant first and second generations in the United States. *The International Migration Review, 38*, 1160–1205. doi:10.1111/j.1747-7379.2004.tb00232.x

Smith, R. C. (2005). *Mexican New York: Transnational lives of new immigrants*. Berkeley: University of California Press.

Stanton-Salazar, R. (2001). *Manufacturing hope and despair: The school and kin support networks of U.S.-Mexican Youth*. New York, NY: Teachers College Press.

Suárez-Orozco, M., Suárez-Orozco, C., & Qin-Hillard, D. B. (Eds.). (2001). *Interdisciplinary perspectives on the new immigration: Theoretical perspectives*. New York, NY: Routledge.

Suárez-Orozco, C., Suárez-Orozco, M. M., & Todorova, I. (2008). *Learning in a new land: Immigrant students in American society*. Cambridge, MA: Harvard University Press.

Valenzuela, A. (1999). *Subtractive schooling: U.S.-Mexican youth and the politics of caring*. Albany: State University of New York Press.

Waters, M. C. (1999). *Black identities: West Indian immigrant dreams and American realities*. New York, NY: Russell Sage Foundation.

Zhou, M., & Bankston, C. L., III. (1998). *Growing up American: How Vietnamese children adapt to life in the United States*. New York, NY: Russell Sage Foundation.

Zolberg, A. R. (2006). *A nation by design: Immigration policy in the fashioning of America*. New York, NY: Harvard University Press.

12

IMMIGRANT YOUTH IN POSTSECONDARY EDUCATION

LINGXIN HAO AND YINGYI MA

This volume asks whether there is evidence for the *immigrant paradox*—the phenomenon in which later generations of immigrants perform more poorly on many measures than earlier generations—in a variety of developmental outcomes and, if so, how to explain it. Today, one sixth of the nation's youth ages 18 to 32 are children of immigrants (Kasinitz, Mollenkopf, Waters, & Holdaway, 2008). Relatively little is known about the postsecondary education experience of these adult children of immigrants and whether and why an immigrant paradox exists in postsecondary education. This chapter seeks to fill in this gap. We use the term *immigrant youth* for adult children of immigrants, including those who were born in the United States (the *second generation*) and those who were born abroad but came to the United States before eighth grade (the *1.5 generation*). These immigrant youth are compared with adult children whose parents are both native born, whom we term the *third generation*.

In this chapter we investigate the issue of immigrant paradox by focusing on the population of low socioeconomic status (SES) and non-White immigrant youth because postsecondary education presents a greater challenge than precollege education for this population. Obstacles are financial, social, and cultural because low-SES parents have limited income, little social contact with college-educated people, and a lack of knowledge about navigating higher education. Entering college is a first hurdle to overcome, and completing college is even more demanding. We expect that the immigrant paradox manifests among this population such that low-SES and non-White immigrant children have higher education attainments than their ethnic and racial counterparts and/or native White counterparts. This chapter examines whether patterns of entry into college and bachelor's degree (BA) attainment significantly differ between low-SES immigrant youth and low-SES third-generation youth. If low-SES immigrant youth have a higher rate of college attendance and attainment than low-SES third-generation youth, this would be consistent with the pattern of the immigrant paradox. We drew data from the National Education Longitudinal Survey (NELS; 1988–2000; see http://nces.ed.gov/surveys/nels88/). The base-year survey provides family background information, including children and their parents' immigrant status. Waves 2 and 3 provide the related precollege experience information, and Waves 4 and 5 provide college attendance and attainment information. Evidence from our analysis of the 12-year longitudinal data that followed a nationally representative sample of eighth graders to ages 26 to 27 supports the existence of an immigrant paradox in postsecondary education for some groups and certain outcomes.

Another objective of this chapter is to provide explanations for the paradox, guided by theories on intergenerational education mobility and international migration. At the core of our explanations lies the combination of two related traits of children of immigrants. First, self-selected immigrant parents transmit their ambition, motivation, and drive for upward mobility and instill the home cultural values regarding education to their children, despite the low SES of many immigrant parents. Second, these children actively take advantage of both the home and American cultures in their navigation in the American education system. In this study, we proposed that the combination of these two traits better prepare immigrant youth with disadvantaged backgrounds to face new challenges in the postsecondary education and raise their likelihood of success in comparison with their third-generation counterparts. These ideas were tested using the NELS longitudinal data.

BACKGROUND

A large body of research has addressed the secondary education outcomes of children from immigrant backgrounds, and the evidence is mixed for the immigrant paradox in secondary education contexts. This empirical literature has examined children of the same age or same grade in the same time point or period. The children under study have varied in generational statuses. With adjustment for SES and other family and parental factors, no significant difference has been found between the first and second generations in math and English grades (Fuligni, 1997), grade point average (GPA; Bankston & Zhou, 2002), or math scores (Kao & Tienda, 1995), and both the first and second generations have outperformed the third or higher order generations in virtually all subjects except for reading (Kao, 2004). Combining the first and second generations, Hao and Bonstead-Bruns (1998) reported that first- and second-generation Chinese students did better in GPA and math (but not reading), whereas first- and second-generation Mexican students did worse in the three outcomes than third-generation Whites. In a study that separated all three distinct generations on the basis of census data, Glick and White (2003) found the second-generation advantage in reading scores among Mexican 10th graders compared with first or third generations. Kao (2004) cautioned that this first- and second-generation effect is more robust among Asians than other racial–ethnic groups. Others found first-generation Hispanic students have higher GPAs than do their third-generation peers and similar GPAs as native White students (Kao 2004; Pong, Hao, & Gardner, 2005), which likely results from the high dropout rates among first-generation Hispanic students such that those remaining in school are better students.

Within panethnic categories, there are noticeable variations by country of origin. Both the Hispanic and Asian immigrant populations are heterogeneous, consisting of many national groups. Prior research has reported that Chinese, Korean, and Japanese students had higher GPAs than Hmong, Cambodian, and Lao students (Rumbaut & Cornelius, 1995); Cuban youth outperformed other Hispanic immigrants on academic tests (Portes & Rumbaut, 2001); and Mexicans, who constitute the largest Hispanic immigrant group, have had much less success (Hao & Bonstead-Bruns, 1998; Kao & Tienda, 1995).

To capture the relative pace of intergenerational progress, it is necessary to consider family background and race–ethnicity. The vast difference in educational levels and occupational skills between adult immigrants from Asian and Latin American countries is well documented—for example, high-educated Indian immigrant parents versus low-educated Mexican immigrant parents (Portes & Rumbaut, 2006). Controlling for family factors typically reduces the achievement gap between the immigrant Hispanic students and native White students; in some cases, it reveals the educational advantage of children of Hispanic immigrants over third-generation Hispanic children (Hirschman, 2001; Pong et al., 2005).

Because it is necessary to examine postsecondary education outcomes among high school graduates or GED holders, we should be aware of the well-documented high school dropout rates among Hispanics. Some research has found that the high school completion rate was lower for second-generation than third-plus-generation Hispanics (Rong & Grant, 1992), whereas others have found that foreign-born children who arrived as adolescents were more likely to complete high school than others (White & Glick, 2000). When students' performance and expectations as sophomores are taken out of the analytic model, Hispanic children, among whom three quarters have Mexican origins, are more likely to drop out of high school, which indicates that there are substantial ethnic differences in school performance and expectations that lead to differences in dropping out of high school (White & Kaufman, 1997). Similarly, native-born Blacks exhibit a high dropout rate. We will keep these facts in mind when we interpret postsecondary educational patterns based on the population of high school graduates and GED holders.

THEORETICAL EXPLANATIONS

Parental SES plays a pivotal role in determining children's educational attainment. Explanation for educational disparities across family backgrounds is parents' command of various levels of financial, human, and social capital. *Financial capital*, measured by family income and wealth, largely explains Black–White achievement gaps because both low income and asset poverty is higher among Blacks than Whites (Jencks et al., 1972; Jencks & Phillips, 1998). *Human capital* theory predicts greater investment in children's education by highly educated parents (Becker, 1964). Highly educated parents tend to have higher educational expectations for their children and provide family environments more conducive to stimulate educational attainment (Farkas, 1996; Steinberg ,1996). These theories predict lower educational attainment for children from lower SES families. What might moderate the detrimental effect of low parental SES to yield positive educational outcomes as exhibited in the immigrant paradox? We must turn to other theories.

In explaining the creation of human capital in children, Coleman (1988) advanced the importance of *social capital*. Social capital is a unique type of resource that is generated from social relationships. Concerning the influence of family social capital on children's education, the key social relationship is between the parent and the child. Parents exert influence by sponsoring, supervising, and encouraging children's education. Coleman argued that social capital can compensate for the lack of parental human capital. High levels of social capital, despite low levels of parental human and financial capital, can increase the probability of academic success. This is especially significant for immigrant families, which are often disadvantaged in terms of financial and human capital. Despite SES disadvantages, some immigrants rely on strong family and coethnic social capital, beat the odds, and achieve extraordinary academic success (Caplan, Choy, &Whitmore, 1991; Zhou & Bankston, 1998).

But it is unclear how low-SES immigrant parents create rich social capital that contributes to the immigrant paradox. To search for rationales, we discuss two related themes from the immigration literature: immigrant selectivity and the new second-generation advantage.

The selectivity of immigrants is rooted in the costs of migration and the uncertainty of future adaptation in the host society (Jasso & Rosenzweig, 1990; Massey et al., 1993). The decision of international migration reflects first-generation adults' unobserved traits such as ambition, motivation, and a desire for better life chances for their offspring. The variation in the degree of this self-selection depends on the level of migration costs and whether the migrant is a pioneer or a follower in the family. Thus individuals in the immigrant stock are self-selected, distinguishing themselves from the native-born Americans with unique traits.

Putting immigrant self-selection in the context of their children's education, Kao and Tienda (1995) proposed an *immigrant optimism* hypothesis. It posits that immigrant parents are optimistic about their offspring's socioeconomic prospects, which makes their children behave in ways that promote academic achievement. They found that particularly among Asians, high-achieving students tend to be second generation, although they found a similar but weaker pattern among Hispanic students. It is unclear, though, how immigrant parents' optimism leads to their children's behaviors and attitudes being conducive to academic achievements.

Relatedly, Kasinitz et al. (2008) suggested the idea of "the second generation advantage," where "second generation" is a combination of 1.5 and second generations. The advantage refers to the fact that the "between-ness" of the home and host worlds allows the second generation to draw from the two cultures and develop creative strategies that increase their probability of success. What is yet to be established is why the second generation is oriented to take advantage of the good parts rather than, say, to take the bad parts of the two cultures. In other words, where does the agency conducive to success of the second generation come from? In what follows, we discuss a potential bridge between the self-selection of immigrant parents and the agency of their children.

Theoretical ideas in other studies may help uncover the missing mechanism between immigrant parents' strong motivation for upward mobility and their children's orientation and active role in academic pursuit. Highlighting *mutual expectation*, one of the three major aspects of social capital (Coleman, 1988), Hao and Bonstead-Bruns (1998) developed a conceptual model in which immigrant parents transmit high education expectations to their children through parent–child interaction. Hao and Bonstead-Bruns found that when children hold a level of educational expectation for themselves that is similar to that of their parents as a result of parent–child interaction, they have higher academic achievement, whereas a large parent–child difference in expectations is detrimental for children's academic achievement. This is true for all racial–ethnic and nationality groups. In addition, self-selected immigrant parents provide a unique feature of immigrant family socialization characterized by a collective goal of prosperity and upward mobility. Immigrant parents make a great effort to overcome adversities for their children's future. Witnessing their immigrant parents' sacrifices, children learn to work hard and take responsibility for the whole family, and they grow up to be more upwardly oriented. Previous studies have shown that immigrant youth, Asian youth in particular, appreciated what their parents had done for them and believed that it was their responsibility to the family to do well in school (Fuligni, 1997; Sue & Okazaki, 1990). This stands in striking contrast with the expectations of parental support among many children of native-born parents.

In sum, our theoretical explanations for the immigrant paradox focus on the self-selection effects of immigrant parents and the agency of their children in creating positive educational outcomes for children from low-SES background. Postsecondary education is not free and is embedded in higher education institutions, presenting potentially greater barriers than secondary education to low-SES youth, particularly of racial–ethnic minorities. The attributes associated with the self-selected immigrant parents—high motivations, upward mobile orientation, and huge hopes for their children, coupled with the agency of the children in navigating the higher learning institutions—could potentially help overcome these barriers.

DATA AND ANALYTIC SAMPLES

Our analysis used five waves of data from the NELS. The NELS base-year survey (Wave 1) provided information on eighth graders' and their parents' country of birth and date of arrival so that the students' nationality and generational status could be determined. Family background information includes parental family income, education, and occupation, and in this chapter, we used the SES composite that encompasses the three aspects of income, education, and occupation. Secondary educational outcomes such as high school graduation and GED attainment are crucial for defining the study population of high school graduates. To estimate postsecondary education experiences, we used data from the third and fourth follow-up surveys (Waves 4 and 5) of 12,140 (rounded) respondents in 1994 and 2000. Available information includes enrollment in 1- to 2-year or 4-year colleges and the attainment of various levels of degrees and certificates. Data on college preparation and high school quality depict the precollege conditions, which were taken from Waves 2 and 3. These variables serve as controls in the analytic models.

The NELS is suitable for studying immigrant youth in postsecondary education. It is the only national longitudinal survey that followed a large sample of immigrant youth and their third-generation peers from adolescence to young adulthood during the 1990s. By 2000, most respondents were aged 26 or 27, an age by which most people have graduated from college if they attended college in their 20s. Although the apparent alternative data source during a similar time period, the Children of Immigrants Longitudinal Study (1991–2006; see http://cmd.princeton.edu/cils3shtml) provided a larger sample of immigrant youth, its lack of several key reference groups—for example, third-generation Whites and Blacks—would compromise important comparisons and the estimation of the relative speed of intergenerational progress, which are the two primary objectives of the present study.

The sample size with valid data on generation status, postsecondary education variables, and parental SES for four broad racial–ethnic groups (Asian, Hispanic, Black, and White) was 10,250. Given the sequential nature of postsecondary education, we defined two analytic samples. To analyze college attendance, we used the analytic sample of high school graduates and GED holders (9,810) who were eligible for college entrance. To analyze postsecondary degrees, we used the analytic sample of college attendees (8,240). Results of these analyses provide conditional patterns and are interpreted with necessary cautions.

MEASURES

This study analyzed college attendance and college attainment. Two measures for college attendance are a dichotomous variable for attendance at any college and a three-category variable indicating attendance at a 1- to 2-year college, at a 4-year college, or no college attendance (as the reference). College attainment is a three-category variable: no postsecondary degree (the reference), associate\certificate, and BA or higher.

We have three blocks of explanatory variables, including generation status, race–ethnicity, and family background. As defined in the opening of the chapter, generation status distinguishes between immigrant youth (both 1.5 and second generations) and third-generation youth (third or higher generations). We measured race–ethnicity with four broadly defined groups, including Asian, Hispanic, Black, and White. Although identifying the nationality origin of immigrant youth would be ideal, as with all survey data, including large-scale and national surveys such as the NELS, subsample sizes are a concern. The Mexican group was the only nationality group with a sufficiently large subsample when cross-classified with low and high SES. In addition, African immigrant youth were too few to yield reliable group statistics. Thus we describe the patterns for four racial–ethnic groups of immigrant youth (Mexican, other Hispanic, White, and Asian). Concerning third-generation groups, Asian youths were another small group and excluded from our analysis because most Asian youths were children of post-1965 immigrants. Thus we describe the patterns of four groups of third-generation racial–ethnic students (Mexican, other Hispanic, White, and Black). Taken together, we have eight generation/race–ethnicity groups.

Measures of family background include parental SES, a standardized composite variable created by NELS based on parental education, income and occupation. For group comparisons that address intergenerational progress, we divided each of the eight generation/race–ethnicity groups into a low-SES group (the bottom half of the distribution of parental SES) and a high-SES group (the top half of the parental SES distribution) to yield 16 groups. Because sufficient group sizes in the high school graduate sample and the college attendee sample are important for the statistical power of the analysis, our analysis excludes four relatively small groups (low- or high-SES Black immigrant youth and low- or high-SES third-generation Asians). To identify which component of the three-component family SES may be compensated by parents' self-selection, we also measured separately parental educational levels (lower than high school; high school; some college; and BA, master's, doctorate, or professional degree), family income, and parental occupation (blue collar, middle skilled, and professional).

Students' college access and attainment is conditioned by their academic preparation and expectation during precollege years (Deil-Amen & Turley, 2007; Tinto, 1993). To separate out the immigrant parental influence effect and the immigrant youth agency effect on postsecondary education from effects on secondary education, our analysis controlled for precollege conditions. College preparation was measured by math and reading standardized test scores in 12th grade, and high school quality was captured by a set of dummy variables that distinguished between private and public sector and low to high levels of school lunch program participation. Respondents' educational expectation in 12th grade distinguished between at least BA and below BA. Our analysis also controlled for respondents' gender and age.

ANALYTIC STRATEGIES

The two analytic tasks in this study were to document whether there was an immigrant paradox in postsecondary education using group comparisons of college access and attainment and to estimate the effects of immigrant parent influence and immigrant youth agency. Key to the first task was a proper comparison design. The NELS followed respondents of the same grade from eighth grade. Our analytic sample included immigrant and third-generation youth. Linking respondents' postsecondary education with their parents' socioeconomic background captured the intergenerational progress. The benefit of making the comparison within the same time period was providing a contemporary basis for the comparisons. For instance, if the intergenerational progress of low-SES Mexican immigrant youth had been greater than that of the low-SES third-generation Mexican or White youth, the low-SES immigrant Mexican group must have done a better job in overcoming the same barriers faced by the third generation during the same time period. These advantages might have originated from those unobserved attributes associated with immigrant youth experiences, such as the motivation and drive transmitted from their immigrant parents and immigrant family socialization. The cross-generation comparisons would give us clear signals with regard to how immigrant youth fared.

In addition, our analysis included group comparisons both within and between race–ethnicity groups. Specifically, we compared (a) Mexican immigrant youth with third-generation Mexican youth; (b) other Hispanic immigrant youth with third-generation other Hispanic youth; and (c) White immigrant youth with third-generation White youth. For between race–ethnicity groups, we compared race–ethnicity groups of immigrant youth with third-generation Whites and Blacks, respectively. Specifically, the groups under comparison were (a) Mexican immigrant youth with third-generation White and Black youth, respectively; (b) other Hispanic immigrant youth with third-generation White and Black youth, respectively; and (c) Asian immigrant youth with third-generation White and Black youth, respectively.

We estimated weighted percentage distributions of college attendance and college attainment to provide population patterns. Although one can browse these percentages to make group comparisons, more direct comparisons can be aided with odds ratios of one group to another. For example, the college attendance odds ratio of Mexican immigrant youth to third-generation Mexican is the ratio of the odds (the probability of going to college vs. the probability of not going to college) of the former to the odds of the latter. Odds ratios range from 0 to infinite. A value above 1 indicates the odds are greater for the immigrant youth group than that for the third-generation group, and a value below 1 indicates the odds are lower for the immigrant youth group than that for the third-generation group. A set of logit models (for college attendance) and multinomial logit models (for types of college attended and types of degree received) successively introduce (a) generation/race–ethnicity/SES groups; (b) gender, age, family income, parental education, and parental occupation; (c) college preparation variables such as reading and math standardized test scores and educational expectation in 12th grade; and (d) high school quality captured by sector and lunch program participation level. Three sets of odds ratios and their statistical significance were estimated from these incremental models.

The purpose of our second analytic task was to explain the documented immigrant paradox by focusing on family influence and individual agency. For immigrant youth, *family influence* means the constantly renewed transmission of parents' strong drive for success, and *individual agency* means that immigrant youth turn the transmitted values to action through overcoming obstacles and persevering in college for eventual success. In multivariate analysis, the estimate for the immigrant youth status reveals how the immigrant paradox can be attributed to the immigrant youth agency, controlling for family background, high school academic preparation, and high school quality. To further explain the immigrant paradox, we estimated the differential family effects by generation status using an interaction between a family background variable and the immigrant youth status for each of the four family background variables. Parental SES captures the overall SES, parental family income reflects financial conditions, parental education emphasizes human capital, and parental occupation highlights the current labor market experience and prestige. Human capital theory predicts that children of better family socioeconomic backgrounds have greater educational attainment. This would be represented by a positive coefficient for a family socioeconomic background variable. A negative coefficient for the interaction term would indicate that family socioeconomic background had a weaker positive effect for immigrant youth as compared with third-generation youth. That would indicate that factors other than family socioeconomic backgrounds promote the immigrant youth education success. As we argue in the chapter section Theoretical Explanations, one such key factor could be the intergenerational transmission of values and orientations, though we do not have direct measures for it.

RESULTS

We present the results in three parts. The first part shows the population pattern of postsecondary education access and attainment. The second part presents pairwise comparisons highlighting differences in intergenerational progress between an immigrant youth group and a third-generation group, within and/or between race–ethnicity. The last part presents the estimates of differential family background effects between the second and third generations.

Population Patterns of Postsecondary Education Access and Attainment

How does high school graduates' access to postsecondary education differ by generation status and family SES? Do low-SES immigrant youths gain

TABLE 12.1
Weighted Percentage Distribution of College Attendance Among High
School Graduates and Postsecondary Education Attainment Among
College Attendees by SES, Generation, and Race–Ethnicity,
National Education Longitudinal Survey, 1988–2000

Group (immigrant youth)	Among high school graduates			Among college attendees	
	Any college	1- or 2-year college	4-year college	AA/ Certificate	BA+
Low SES					
Mexican	78.3	61.1	17.2	29.3	14.5
Other Hispanic	88.6	61.4	27.2	23.1	20.3
White	87.7	57.2	30.5	29.5	33.5
Asian	93.8	53.7	40.0	15.6	42.3
Low SES, third generation					
Mexican	75.9	60.1	15.8	31.2	12.8
Other Hispanic	69.8	59.7	10.1	19.7	4.7
White	69.6	45.4	24.1	29.3	23.7
Black	72.9	51.1	21.8	29.0	16.1
High SES					
Mexican	98.3	48.3	50.0	8.8	43.3
Other Hispanic	95.9	33.5	62.4	12.5	60.0
White	95.6	33.1	62.5	10.6	69.6
Asian	97.7	24.7	73.0	11.4	69.7
High SES, third generation					
Mexican	97.7	56.9	40.8	7.9	28.9
Other Hispanic	96.0	57.3	38.7	9.9	39.8
White	93.5	36.2	57.4	13.0	54.5
Black	92.4	31.9	60.5	13.2	45.3

Note. Second-generation Blacks and third-generation Asians have small cell sizes and thus are excluded from group comparisons. Low- and high-SES statuses are defined as the lower and upper half of the SES distribution, respectively. SES = socioeconomic status; AA = associate degree; BA+ = bachelor's degree or above.

greater access than their third-generation counterparts? We seek answers to these questions from columns 2 to 4 in Table 12.1 that show the weighted percentage distribution of attending any colleges, attending 1- to 2-year colleges, and attending 4-year colleges. The results clearly show that high-SES youths have greater access to any colleges in general and to 4-year colleges in particular. This high-SES advantage is largely consistent across racial–ethnic generation groups.

For instance, the percentage difference in any college attendance between low- and high-SES Mexican immigrant youth is 78.3 and 98.3 respectively, similar to the corresponding gap for the third-generation counterparts (75.9

and 97.7). However, the percentage gap between low- and high-SES Mexican youth in 4-year college attendance is 17.2 to 50.0 for immigrant youth, greater than 15.8 to 40.8 for the third-generation counterparts. In contrast, a higher percentage of low-SES Mexican immigrant youth attended 1- to 2-year colleges than their high-SES counterparts (61.1 vs. 48.3), which is similar to the third-generation pattern (60.1 vs. 56.9). The 1- to 2-year college education appears to be a low-SES family strategy; that is, low SES may constrain youths' college options even after they manage to continue with postsecondary education.

Focusing on low SES helps answer the second question about intergenerational progress, so we examine the columns headed by "Low SES." Within-racial–ethnic comparisons can be made for Mexican, other Hispanic, and White groups, and the results show that immigrant youth have higher college attendance rates than third-generation youth, suggesting an immigrant paradox. For Mexican-origin youth, the percentages of immigrant youth and third-generation youth are 78.3 versus 75.9 for any colleges, 61.1 versus 60.1 for 1- to 2-year colleges, and 17.2 versus 15.8 for 4-year colleges. The immigrant-youth lead in college attendance is more salient for other Hispanics: The corresponding percentages are 88.6 versus 69.8, 61.4 versus 59.7, and 27.2 versus 10.1, respectively. Similar generational differences are found for White youth. Between-racial–ethnic comparisons revealed that Asian, Mexican, and other Hispanic immigrant youth fared better than third-generation Blacks and Whites in access to college in general and 1- to 2-year colleges in particular. Concerning 4-year colleges, the immigrant youth advantage still held, except for Mexican immigrant youth, who lagged behind third-generation Black and White youth, but they were still ahead of third-generation Mexicans. The patterns of the lead of racial minorities over Whites in college attendance should be understood in connection with the patterns among low-SES high school graduates. Specifically, third-generation White youth had a greater high school graduation rate than third-generation racial–ethnic minority groups. This means that third-generation racial–ethnic minority students were already more selected than their White counterparts among high school graduates. This selection may have contributed to the higher rate of college attendance of racial minorities than Whites.

Moving from access, our next two questions focused on postsecondary attainment. In particular, we examined how postsecondary education attainment differed by generation status and family SES and whether immigrant youth fared better in terms of degree attainment than their third-generation counterparts. Columns 5 and 6 in Table 12.1 show the weighted percentage distribution of associate/certificate (AA/certificate) and BA or higher (BA+) degrees among college attendees. The results reveal a contrast between

AA/certificate and BA+ attainments by family SES: Low-SES youths exhibited a higher rate of AA/certificate attainment than their high-SES counterparts whereas the opposite was true for BA+ attainment. This pattern is consistent with the pattern we see in Table 12.1, which shows higher 1- to 2-year college attendance rates among low-SES youth. Little generational and race–ethnic difference is observed for the attainment of AA/certificate, except that the rate of Asian immigrant youth was much lower than the rates of the third-generation Blacks and Whites The immigrant youth advantages are more salient for the outcome of BA+ attainment for both low-SES and high-SES students. The Mexican, other Hispanic, and White immigrant youth all exhibited a higher rate of BA attainment than their third-generation counterparts, again in support of the immigrant paradox. On the other hand, the between-racial–ethnic comparisons show a lower rate for Mexican immigrant youth than third-generation Black and White youth, which stands in sharp contrast with the Asian immigrant youth, who have an advantage over third-generation Black and White youth.

In sum, the top panel of Table 12.1 suggests an immigrant paradox in access to 4-year college and BA+ attainment. Mexican, other Hispanic, and White immigrant youth groups had greater 4-year college access and BA+ attainment than their racial–ethnic third-generation counterparts. Except for Mexican immigrant youth, all other immigrant youth groups appear to have had greater access to 4-year college than third-generation Whites. With regard to the BA degree, only Asian and White immigrant youth were more likely to complete their degree than third-generation Whites.

Pairwise Group Comparison of Postsecondary Education Access and Attainment

Two further questions regarding group comparisons are whether the group differences shown in Table 12.1 are statistically significant and how these differences hold up after controlling for individual, family, and pre-college variables. To provide evidence for the immigrant paradox, we are especially interested in whether the immigrant youth advantage holds up for the low-SES students. We used odds ratios that explicitly measure group differences in event occurrences. Because statistical power depends on the sample size and subgroup sizes, we did not use sampling weights in generating odds ratios.

We obtained odds ratios from multinomial logit models for three category outcomes: attending 1- to 2-year colleges, attending 4-year colleges, and no college attendance as the reference category. Model 1 specifies the 16 generation/race–ethnicity/SES groups without controlling for other variables. Model 2 adds individual characteristics including age; gender; and

TABLE 12.2
Odds Ratios for College Attendance Among Low-SES High School Graduates, National Education Longitudinal Survey, 1988–2000

Pairwise group comparison	Model 1	Model 2	Model 3
1- to 2-year college			
Within race–ethnicity			
Immigrant Mexican with 3rd-gen Mexican	0.89	1.03	0.91
Immigrant oth-Hisp with 3rd-gen oth-Hisp	2.73 **	3.26 **	2.96 **
Immigrant White with 3rd-gen White	2.35 **	2.31 **	2.38 **
Between race–ethnicity			
Immigrant Mexican with 3rd-gen Black	1.37 †	1.50 *	1.41 †
Immigrant Mexican with 3rd-gen White	1.56 **	2.05 **	1.90 **
Immigrant oth-Hisp with 3rd-gen Black	2.72 **	2.75 **	2.66 **
Immigrant oth-Hisp with 3rd-gen White	3.10 **	3.76 **	3.61 **
Immigrant Asian with 3rd-gen Black	4.34 **	4.57 **	3.60 **
Immigrant Asian with 3rd-gen White	4.95 **	6.26 **	4.87 **
4-year college			
Within race–ethnicity			
Immigrant Mexican with 3rd-gen Mexican	0.94	1.46	1.05
Immigrant oth-Hisp with 3rd-gen oth-Hisp	5.73 **	7.78 **	5.82 **
Immigrant White with 3rd-gen White	2.56 **	2.48 **	2.48 **
Between race–ethnicity			
Immigrant Mexican with 3rd-gen Black	0.75	1.00	0.69
Immigrant Mexican with 3rd-gen White	0.87	1.75 **	1.60 *
Immigrant oth-Hisp with 3rd-gen Black	2.64 **	2.61 **	2.04 *
Immigrant oth-Hisp with 3rd-gen White	3.06 **	4.56 **	4.75 **
Immigrant Asian with 3rd-gen Black	7.61 **	7.98 **	3.00 **
Immigrant Asian with 3rd-gen White	8.82 **	13.96 **	7.00 **

Note. Presented are odds ratios and their significance derived from estimates of logit or multinomial logit models. Model 1 includes a set of dummy variables to indicate the 16 generation/race–ethnicity/SES groups. Model 2 controls for gender, age, family income, parental education, and parental occupation; Model 3 adds reading test score, math test score, educational expectation in 12th grade, and high school quality variables. SES = socioeconomic status; 3rd-gen = third generation; oth-Hisp = other Hispanic.
†$p < .10$. * $p < .05$. ** $p < .01$.

family background, including parental family income, parental education, and parental occupation. Model 3 further controls for precollege conditions, including reading and math test scores and educational expectation in 12th grade and high school sector and lunch program participation level. Results for low-SES youths' college attendance are shown in Table 12.2.

The top panel for 1- to 2-year college attendance shows that except for low-SES Mexican immigrant youth, all other low-SES immigrant youth are more likely to attend 1- to 2-year colleges than their low-SES third-generation counterparts. The bottom panel shows odds ratios of 4-year college attendance. The within-race–ethnicity patterns remain similar to those from the first two panels. The between-race–ethnicity patterns, however,

TABLE 12.3
Odds Ratios for Postsecondary Attainment Among Low–Socioeconomic Status College Attendees, National Education Longitudinal Survey, 1988–2000

Pairwise comparison	Model 1	Model 2	Model 3
AA/certificate versus no degree			
Within race/ethnicity			
Immigrant Mexican with 3rd-gen Mexican	0.94	0.88	0.91
Immigrant oth-Hisp with 3rd-gen oth-Hisp	1.58	1.56	1.68
Immigrant White with 3rd-gen White	1.10	1.11	1.10
Between race/ethnicity			
Immigrant Mexican with 3rd-gen Black	1.11	1.08	1.16
Immigrant Mexican with 3rd-gen White	0.85	0.78	0.79
Immigrant oth-Hisp with 3rd-gen Black	1.26	1.27	1.37
Immigrant oth-Hisp with 3rd-gen White	0.96	0.92	0.93
Immigrant Asian with 3rd-gen Black	0.86	0.87	1.01
Immigrant Asian with 3rd-gen White	0.65 *	0.63 *	0.69†
BA versus no degree			
Within race/ethnicity			
Immigrant Mexican with 3rd-gen Mexican	1.27	1.66 †	1.47
Immigrant oth-Hisp with 3rd-gen oth-Hisp	3.70 *	4.35 **	3.57 *
Immigrant White with 3rd-gen White	1.67 *	1.69 *	1.81 *
Between race/ethnicity			
Immigrant Mexican with 3rd-gen Black	0.95	1.19	1.01
Immigrant Mexican with 3rd-gen White	0.62 **	0.94	1.03
Immigrant oth-Hisp with 3rd-gen Black	1.40	1.40	1.14
Immigrant oth-Hisp with 3rd-gen White	0.91	1.10	1.17
Immigrant Asian with 3rd-gen Black	3.58 **	3.79 **	2.24**
Immigrant Asian with 3rd-gen White	2.34 **	2.98 **	2.30**

Note. Presented are odds ratios and their significance derived from estimates of multinomial logit models. Model 1 includes a set of dummy variables to indicate the 16 generation-race/ethnicity-SES groups. Model 2 controls for gender, age, family income, parental education, and parental occupation; Model 3 adds reading test score, math test score, educational expectation in 12th grade, and high school quality variables. AA = associate degree; 3rd-gen = third generation; oth-Hisp = other Hispanic; BA = bachelor's degree.
†$p < .10$. *$p < .05$. **$p < .01$.

depart from those for any college or 1- to 2-year colleges. In contrast to the unfavorable access among low-SES Mexican and other Hispanic immigrant youth, low-SES Asian immigrant youth exhibited superior odds of attending 4-year colleges compared with low-SES third-generation Black and White youth.

Turning to postsecondary attainment, we examine the odds ratios in Table 12.3. The top panel shows the odds ratio for AA/certificate versus no postsecondary degree. The only significant result is for low-SES Asian immigrant youth: Their odds of earning an AA/certificate were about 30% to 40% lower than among third-generation Whites (see the last row of the top panel).

This can be explained by the lower probability of Asian youth attending 1- to 2-year college. With this exception, there is no significant difference in AA/certificate attainment between immigrant youth and third-generation youth. Odds ratios in the bottom panel show a number of interesting findings for attaining a BA degree. Other Hispanic immigrant youth had significantly higher odds ratios of BA attainment than their third-generation counterparts (3.70, 4.35, and 3.57), and odds ratio for Whites were smaller but still significant (1.67, 1.69, 1.81). Compared with third-generation Whites, Mexican immigrant youth had lower odds to gain BAs when no variables were being controlled (0.62). This difference, however, disappeared (0.94) after controlling for individual and family background variables. This suggests that among the lower half of the SES, Mexican immigrant youths' parents were in a much lower socioeconomic position than their third-generation White counterparts, which accounts for the lower odds of BA attainment for the Mexican immigrant youth. Asian immigrant youth had greater success when compared with third-generation Black and White youth. For example, compared with low-SES third-generation White youth, the odds of low-SES Asian immigrant youth completing a BA are 2.34 without controlling for any variables. After controlling for family background, the odds ratio increases to 2.98. This suggests that low-SES Asian immigrant parents occupied a lower socioeconomic position than their low-SES native White counterparts, and after controlling for SES, the lead of Asian immigrant youth in completing BA is even more salient. This odds ratio, however, declined somewhat after controlling for precollege variables. It suggests that precollege conditions not only matter for college entry but also for BA degree attainment.

Taken together, Tables 12.2 and 12.3 provide strong evidence in support of the immigrant paradox in the access and attainment of postsecondary education for all racial–ethnic immigrant youth except for Mexican immigrant youth. Despite low-SES background, the advantage of being an immigrant youth significantly enhances the probability of degree attainment. The magnitude of the immigrant youth advantage is large when compared with Blacks and Whites of native-born parents. The patterns for Mexican immigrant youth also do not show any disadvantage of this group compared with third-generation Mexican, Black, and White youth.

Immigrant Family Effect and Immigrant Youth Agency Effect

Our second analytic task was to estimate the relative importance of immigrant family effects and immigrant youth agency effect on college attendance and degree attainment, controlling for precollege variables and individual and family characteristics (all continuous covariates were centered at their

TABLE 12.4
Differential Family Background Effects on College Attendance Among High School Graduates, National Education Longitudinal Survey, 1988–2000

Variable	Model 1	Model 2	Model 3	Model 4
1- to 2-year college				
Immigrant youth status	0.270 †	0.307 *	0.562 **	0.565 **
Family SES	0.790 **			
Family SES × Immigrant Youth	−0.491 **			
Family income		0.011 **		
Family Income × Immigrant Youth		−0.013 **		
Parent BA			0.867 **	
Parent BA × Immigrant Youth			−0.649 *	
Parent professional				0.518 **
Parent Professional × Immigrant Youth				−0.418
4-year college				
Immigrant youth status	0.439 **	0.431 **	0.816 **	0.743 **
Family SES	1.410 **			
Family SES × Immigrant Youth	−0.726 **			
Family income		0.018 **		
Family Income × Immigrant Youth		−0.015 **		
Parent BA			1.583 **	
Parent BA × Immigrant Youth			−1.056 **	
Parent professional				0.865 **
Parent Professional × Immigrant Youth				−0.567 †

Note. Coefficients (log odds) of logit and multinomial logit models are presented. All models control for race, gender, age, reading test score, math test score, educational expectation in 12th grade, high school sector, and lunch programs. Continuous covariates are centered at their grand mean so that the interpretation of coefficients for dummy covariates is for the typical situation of these covariates. SES = socioeconomic status; BA = bachelor's degree.
†$p < .10$. *$p < .05$. **$p < .01$.

grand mean). Table 12.4 shows results for college attendance from four models, each including an interaction term between the immigrant youth status and a different measure of family SES: (a) family SES, (b) family income (controlling for parental education and occupation), (c) parental education (controlling for family income and parental occupation), and (d) parental occupation (controlling for family income and parental education). Presented are coefficients (log odds) for the immigrant youth status, a measure of family SES, and their interaction. In the bottom panel for 4-year college attendance, the Model 1 coefficient for the immigrant youth status is 0.439, and the significance level is less than 1%. This is interpreted as a significantly higher likelihood of attending a 4-year college than third-generation youth at the mean level of family SES, implying a stronger agency effect for immigrant youth than for third generation, all else being equal. When measured with the composite family SES variable (Model 1), the family SES coefficient

(1.410) was positive and significant for the third generation, whereas the coefficient for the interaction between family SES and immigrant youth status was −0.726, significant at the 1% level. Thus the SES effect for immigrant youth remained positive, but the magnitude was reduced by about one half. Model 2 examined a component of family SES—family income—while controlling for parental education and occupation. The immigrant youth effect was stable at 0.431, and significant. The income effect, which was positive for the third generation (0.018), almost disappeared for immigrant youth (0.018–0.015). Model 3 examined parental education at BA or above. The immigrant youth effect was 0.816 and significant. The effect of parental BA, which was positive for the third generation (1.583), was weakened by two thirds for immigrant youth (−1.056). The positive effect of parental professional occupation in Model 4, however, differentiated by generation status only at the 10% significance level. Parents' professional occupation mattered equally across generations, and a lack of it could not be compensated by the immigrant youth status.

The second and third panels estimate 1- to 2-year college attendance and 4-year college attendance with no college attendance as the reference category. The significance of each coefficient in the second and third panels is similar to that in the first panel. The magnitude, however, is somewhat smaller for 1- to 2-year college attendance and considerably greater for 4-year college attendance.

Table 12.5 presents the corresponding results for postsecondary education attainment among college attendees. The top panel shows that immigrant youth status significantly increased the likelihood of obtaining an AA/certificate in two out of the four models. Family socioeconomic background, however, did not play a positive role at all, and when measured with the composite family SES, the role was negative. This is not surprising because 1- to 2-year colleges target lower SES youth. The bottom panel presents results for BA attainment. The immigrant youth effect was much stronger on BA attainment than on AA/certificate attainment, suggesting the importance of agency among immigrant youth in pursuing, navigating and succeeding in 4-year colleges. Family socioeconomic background continued to strongly influence BA attainment. A small negative interaction effect was significant for the composite SES, marginally significant for parental education, and insignificant for family income and parental professional occupation. The declining concurrent transmission of parents' values and orientations and the rising importance of immigrant youth's agency during college years are understandable given that immigrant youth in college were involved in the very different environment of a higher education institution, which in most cases was quite foreign to immigrant parents.

TABLE 12.5
Differential Family Background Effects on Postsecondary Degrees Among
College Attendees, National Education Longitudinal Survey, 1988–2000

Variable	Model 1	Model 2	Model 3	Model 4
Associate degree/certificate				
Immigrant youth status	0.281 *	0.249 *	0.173	0.239 †
Family SES	−0.197 **			
Family SES × Immigrant Youth	0.172			
Family income		−0.003		
Family Income × Immigrant Youth		0.002		
Parent BA			−0.078	
Parent BA × Immigrant Youth			0.247	
Parent professional				−0.071
Parent Professional × Immigrant Youth				−0.107
BA				
Immigrant youth status	0.558 **	0.489 **	0.605 **	0.549 **
Family SES	0.833 **			
Family SES × Immigrant Youth	−0.315 **			
Family income		0.008 **		
Family Income × Immigrant Youth		−0.001		
Parent BA			0.830 **	
Parent BA × Immigrant Youth			−0.302 †	
Parent professional				0.369 **
Parent Professional × Immigrant Youth				−0.169

Note. Coefficients (log odds) of AA/certificate vs. some college without a degree from multinomial logit models are presented. All models control for race, gender, age, reading test score, math test score, educational expectation in 12th grade, high school sector, and lunch programs. Continuous covariates are centered at their grand mean so that the interpretation of coefficients for dummy covariates is for the typical situation of these covariates.
**$p < .01$. *$p < .05$. †$p < .10$.

CONCLUSIONS

To document and understand the immigrant paradox in developmental outcomes, this chapter provides national patterns of and potential explanations for the immigrant paradox in postsecondary education. Overall, we found some evidence to support the immigrant paradox. Our descriptive analysis of observed patterns shows that among low-SES youth, non-Mexican Hispanic immigrant youth fared better than their third-generation counterparts in both college access and BA attainment. In addition, low-SES Asian immigrant youth had a higher college attendance rate and BA attainment rate than low-SES third-generation Whites and Blacks. Both patterns are significant before and after taking into account individual, family, and precollege variables.

Our investigation into explanations of the immigrant paradox found weaker effects of family SES on postsecondary educational outcomes for immigrant youth than for the third generation. Then what might immigrant parents use to compensate for the low SES during their children's college years? A plausible answer is cumulative intergenerational transmission in immigrant families, where immigrant parents continuously instill their ambition and drive for success in their children. In addition, controlling for precollege conditions and family background, immigrant youth status plays an increasingly positive role in college access and success whereas low-SES parents become less able to guide their children. That is, during college years, immigrant youth must rely more on their own initiative and creativity, which is in part derived from the cumulative transmission of their parents' values. This study focused on factors at family and individual levels to explain the immigrant paradox. Future research should also look into the role of institutions and communities.

Our foremost finding is that racial–ethnic groups of immigrant youth, except for Mexicans, follow the immigrant paradox in postsecondary education. However, Mexican immigrant youth would not have been disadvantaged in postsecondary education provided the same family background. Our multivariate results for Mexican immigrant youth did not show any disadvantage compared with third-generation Mexican, Black, and White youth controlling for other covariates. In particular, the observed disadvantage of Mexican immigrant youth in 4-year college access and BA attainment disappeared after parental education, income, and occupation were controlled.

Nonetheless, why Mexican immigrant youth are exceptional to the immigrant paradox in postsecondary education remains a puzzle. A core of this puzzle is whether Mexican immigrant parents at the same level of parental education, income, and occupation transmit greater motivation and drive for upward mobility than their third-generation counterparts. Future research can start to tackle this question by conducting in-depth studies on Mexican immigrant families. Our conceptual focus on the selectivity of immigrant adults could be a useful starting point. Researchers may examine from the perspective of international migration the relatively low cost of migration from Mexico, the circular and temporary migration of some Mexican immigrants, and the mounting illegality facing many Mexican immigrant families in recent decades.

REFERENCES

Bankston, C. L., & Zhou, M. (2002). Being well vs. doing well: Self-esteem and school performance among immigrant and non-immigrant racial and ethnic groups. *The International Migration Review, 36,* 389–415. doi:10.1111/j.1747-7379.2002.tb00086.x

Becker, G. (1964). *Human capital: A theoretical and empirical analysis, with special reference to education*. Chicago, IL: University of Chicago Press.

Caplan, N., Choy, M. H., & Whitmore, J. K. (1991). *Children of the boat people: A study of educational success*. Ann Arbor: University of Michigan Press.

Coleman, J. S. (1988). Social capital in the creation of human capital. *American Journal of Sociology, 94*, S95–S120. doi:10.1086/228943

Deil-Amen, R., & Turley, R. (2007). A review of the transition to college literature in sociology. *Teachers College Record, 109*, 2324–2366.

Farkas, G. (1996). *Human capital or cultural capital? Ethnicity and poverty groups in an urban school district*. New York, NY: Aldine de Gruyter.

Fuligni, A. J. (1997). The academic achievement of adolescents from immigrant families: The roles of family background, attitudes, and behavior. *Child Development, 68*, 351–363.

Glick, J. E., & White, M. J. (2003). The academic trajectories of immigrant youth: Analysis within and across cohorts. *Demography, 40*, 759–783. doi:10.1353/dem.2003.0034

Hao, L., & Bonstead-Bruns, M. (1998). Parent–child difference in educational expectations and academic achievement of immigrant and native students. *Sociology of Education, 71*, 175–198. doi:10.2307/2673201

Hirschman, C. (2001). The educational enrollment of immigrant youth: A test of the segmented assimilation hypothesis. *Demography, 38*, 317–336. doi:10.1353/dem.2001.0028

Jasso, G., & Rosenzweig, M. R. (1990). Self-selection and the earning of immigrants [Comment]. *The American Economic Review, 80*, 298–304.

Jencks, C., & Phillips, M. (1998). *The Black–White test score gap*. Washington, DC: Brookings Institution Press.

Jencks, C., Smith, M., Acland, H., Bane, M. J., Cohen, D., Gintis, H., . . . Michelson, S. (1972). *Inequality: A reassessment of the effect of family and schooling in America*. New York, NY: Basic Books.

Kao, G. (2004). Parental influences on the educational outcomes of immigrant youth. *The International Migration Review, 38*, 427–449. doi:10.1111/j.1747-7379.2004.tb00204.x

Kao, G., & Tienda, M. (1995). Optimism and achievement: The educational performance of immigrant youth. *Social Science Quarterly, 76*, 1–19.

Kasinitz, P., Mollenkopf, J. H., Waters, M. C., & Holdaway, J. (2008). *Inheriting the city: The children of immigrants come of age*. Cambridge, MA: Harvard University Press.

Massey, D. S., Arango, J., Hugo, G., Kouaouci, A., Pellegrino, A., & Taylor, J. E. (1993). Theories of international migration: Review and appraisal. *Population and Development Review, 19*, 431–466. doi:10.2307/2938462

Pong, S. L., Hao, L. X., & Gardner, E. (2005). The roles of parenting styles and social capital in the school performance of immigrant Asian and Hispanic adolescents. *Social Science Quarterly, 86*, 928–950. doi:10.1111/j.0038-4941.2005.00364.x

Portes, A., & Rumbaut, R. G. (2001). *Legacies: The story of the immigrant second generation*. Berkeley and New York, NY: University of California Press and Russell Sage Foundation.

Portes, A., & Rumbaut, R. G. (2006). *Immigrant America: A portrait*. Berkeley: University of California Press.

Rong, X. L., & Grant, L. (1992). Ethnicity, generation, and school attainment of Asians, Hispanics and non-Hispanic Whites. *The Sociological Quarterly, 33*, 625–636. doi:10.1111/j.1533-8525.1992.tb00147.x

Rumbaut, R. G., & Cornelius, W. (Eds.). (1995). *California's immigrant children: Theory, research, and implications for educational policy*. San Diego: University of California.

Steinberg, L. (1996). *Beyond the classroom: Why school reform has failed and what parents need to do*. New York, NY: Simon & Schuster.

Sue, S., & Okazaki, S. (1990). Asian-American educational achievements: A phenomenon in search of an explanation. *American Psychologist, 45*, 913–920. doi:10.1037/0003-066X.45.8.913

Tinto, V. (1993). *Leaving college*. Chicago, IL: University of Chicago Press.

White, M. J., & Kaufman, G. (1997). Language usage, social capital, and school completion among immigrants and native born ethnic groups. *Social Science Quarterly, 78*, 385–398.

White, M. J., & Glick, J. E. (2000). Generation, social capital and the routes out of high school. *Sociological Forum, 15*, 671–691. doi:10.1023/A:1007515100190

Zhou, M., & Bankston, C. L., III. (1998). *Growing up American: How Vietnamese children adapt to life in the United States*. New York, NY: Russell Sage Foundation.

IV
CONCLUDING REMARKS

13

THE INTERSECTION OF ASPIRATIONS AND RESOURCES IN THE DEVELOPMENT OF CHILDREN FROM IMMIGRANT FAMILIES

ANDREW J. FULIGNI

The story of the immigrant paradox is a tale of unexpected success in the face of adversity. What intrigues observers is the possibility that children from immigrant families may show better developmental outcomes than predicted by their socioeconomic resources, ethnic minority status, and position as new-comers in a new and sometimes unwelcoming society. The authors of this volume highlight the initial research that first gave rise to the idea of the paradox, such as the surprising birth outcomes and health status of children from poorer, foreign-born mothers. The authors thoroughly address the logical and analytical issues involved in empirically testing the existence of the paradox, including the all-important question of the proper comparison group: Should it be all American-born members of the same ethnic group, only those of the same socioeconomic status, or American-born members of the European American majority group? Finally, the chapters include a comprehensive collection of tests of the paradox across a variety of ages, outcomes, and ethnic groups from impressive and varied data sets.

Perhaps not surprisingly, the answer provided by these chapters to the question driving this volume is, "It depends." What is clear is that the immigrant paradox is not universal across all children and all aspects of development. Nevertheless, some immigrant children do show similar or better developmental outcomes than their American-born counterparts than would be expected from their socioeconomic background and status as newcomers in American society. There is variability in the existence of an immigrant paradox across a number of factors, including children's age, immigrant and ethnic group, and the specific developmental outcome being addressed. Yet there appears to be a pattern in this variability that allows us to offer a story of the development of children from immigrant families that is more complex than that offered by the immigrant paradox and more revealing than simply saying, "It depends."

The story about the development of immigrant children offered by the authors in this volume has four primary points: (a) Immigration is a highly selective process in complex ways; (b) partially as a result of this selection, immigrant families come to the United States with high aspirations for their children, high levels of family stability, and a strong work ethic; (c) despite facing numerous social and economic challenges, families keep their children out of trouble and maintain good health; and (d) when immigrant families have access to information, resources, and opportunities, they succeed in education, but significant numbers of immigrant families do not have access to such resources, and their children are unable to achieve their goals.

IMMIGRATION IS A HIGHLY SELECTIVE PROCESS

Immigration is by nature a selective process. Members of sending nations are not randomly chosen to emigrate, and those who do leave their home societies are not randomly placed in receiving nations around the world. The settlement of immigrants in specific locations in the United States, whether they are specific regions in the country or large cities versus suburban or rural areas, is highly selective. Complicating things even further, the forces of selection operate differentially for immigrants from different sending nations, such as those from Asia compared with those from Latin America (Portes & Rumbaut, 2006). The selection of immigrants from the same country even changes across time and history, resulting in qualitatively different pools and samples of immigrants that feed into the different generations that are often compared in research on immigrant adjustment.

Any attempt to address the sources of the developmental patterns of children from immigrant families must at least acknowledge the selection forces at play. The difficulty is that it is usually unfeasible to control for all these forces. Most notably, researchers often cannot control for the exact dimensions on which immigrants are selective members of their native countries. None of the authors in the present volume have been able to do this with the current data resources that are available to them. As a result, the authors could not empirically determine whether the children from immigrant families in the United States are healthier, better behaved, or show better academic achievement than their counterparts whose families did not emigrate. Similarly, the authors could not estimate whether immigrant parents are more or less educated, wealthy, or healthy than parents who remained in their native societies.

Getting a better handle on the role of selection is critical in order to answer the provocative question of whether "becoming American" is a developmental risk for children. Without being able to properly estimate whether immigrant families are selected from their native societies on the basis of the eventual developmental outcomes of their children and whether that selection process differs from the previous immigrant families who contributed to what are now the third and later generations in American society, we cannot determine whether being in American society by itself contributes negatively to children's development. Given the inherent and sometimes indefinable complexity in immigrant selection across history and nations of origin, it is unlikely that we ever could convincingly conclude that becoming American is a developmental risk.

Nevertheless, we do have knowledge about two key selection effects involved in contemporary immigration to the United States that allows us to at least better understand their potential role. First, the system by which the government determines who can enter the country from specific sending nations gives first preference to reunifying applicants who have close family members already in the United States, followed by those who possess occupational skills deemed lacking and needed in the country. On average, those admitted under family reunification provisions tend to have lower levels of education and occupational skills than immigrants who enter under employment preferences (Fuligni & Yoshikawa, 2003). As a result, newer immigrant flows from countries with historically low numbers of immigrants in the United States have greater socioeconomic resources than flows from countries with large numbers of immigrants already in the country. At the introduction of the family reunification and employment preference system in 1965, there were many more individuals from Latin America (particularly Mexico) than Asia who were already living in the United States. This fact, combined with the cost and difficulty of coming from more distant nations, is one reason why all of the analyses described in this volume show that immigrant parents from many Asian countries have higher socioeconomic standing than those from many Latin American countries. This is a critical point to consider when making comparisons involving children from immigrant families from Asia and suggests that children in Asian families start out with a socioeconomic advantage over both those from Latin American and even their counterparts in American-born families. Over time, however, immigrants from Asia have increasingly entered under family reunification preferences, suggesting that the socioeconomic advantage of the foreign born from these countries may attenuate over time (Portes & Rumbaut, 2006).

A second and perhaps equally important selection factor to consider is that immigration to the United States is largely voluntary. Except in some cases of asylum seekers or refugee resettlement, most immigrants come willingly. In fact, given the arduous nature of entering and staying in the country both legally and illegally, current immigrants are likely selected for a high level of motivation, diligence, effort, and desire to succeed in American society. As described in more detail later in this chapter, it should not be surprising that immigrant parents should have very high aspirations for their and their children's success, betraying a belief in the value of hard work and the opportunity structure in American society.

IMMIGRANT FAMILIES HAVE HIGH ASPIRATIONS AND VALUE WORK AND FAMILY TOGETHERNESS

Numerous studies have shown that foreign-born parents come to the United States with a high level of optimism and a strong desire to succeed in American society (Fuligni, 1997; Gibson & Bhachu, 1991; Kao & Tienda, 1995; Suárez-Orozco & Suárez-Orozco, 1995). It appears that regardless of their country of origin or socioeconomic standing, immigrant parents have educational aspirations for their children that consistently tend to be higher than those of American-born parents. These aspirations, in turn, seem to be quickly and easily internalized by their children. Pong and Zeiser (Chapter 9, this volume) observed higher levels of motivation on the part of students from immigrant families. These students liked school and found it more interesting and satisfying than their peers from American-born families. It is interesting that Pong and Zeiser also report that students from immigrant families believed school to be more useful for getting a job later in life, consistent with a tendency for immigrants to emphasize the importance of obtaining stable and gainful employment (Fuligni & Yoshikawa, 2004).

The focus on hard work is evident in the employment patterns of immigrant parents. As Hernandez, Denton, Macartney, and Blanchard describe in Chapter 1 of this volume, immigrant parents work at rates that are equal to or even higher than those from American-born parents. There is great variability in the level of this employment and the financial returns for the family, as described in more detail later, but high rates of employment are generally linked to better educational, mental, and physical development in children.

Hernandez and colleagues (Chapter 1, this volume) also report that immigrant families have higher rates of dual-parent households and show lower rates of divorce. Likely because of both selection effects from the country of origin and more traditional views about the stability of marriage, the family structure of immigrant families also likely confers an advantage to their children. These findings on family structure are consistent with a large number of other studies that highlight the value immigrant families place on family togetherness, stability, and support. Immigrant parents tend to emphasize the importance of all family members chipping in to help the family make it in a new society, with children playing an important role. In addition to providing instrumental support to the family at times, children's obligation to the family is to stay out of trouble and try hard in school (Fuligni, Rivera, & Leininger, 2007). Most children from immigrant families share this sense of obligation to the family, which is an important source of good behavior and academic motivation. As described in the next section, however, it is easier for most children from immigrant families to stay out of trouble than it is for them to succeed in school, the latter of which requires resources and opportunities that are not shared equally across all immigrant groups.

IMMIGRANT FAMILIES KEEP THEIR CHILDREN OUT OF TROUBLE AND IN GOOD HEALTH

Perhaps the most consistent immigrant paradox or advantage appears in the area of problem behavior, particularly during the adolescent years. Hernandez and colleagues (Chapter 1, this volume) summarize analyses conducted by Harris (1999) that showed consistent generational increases in risky and problem behavior by youth. First-generation, foreign-born adolescents were significantly less likely to engage in a variety of delinquent behaviors such as painting graffiti, vandalism, shoplifting, and burglary than second- and third-generation youth. Similarly, first-generation teenagers were less likely to engage in violent behavior such as fighting and using weapons. Drug and alcohol use was lower in the first and second generations compared with the third generation. These findings were observed after controlling for socioeconomic factors and were generally the same across different ethnic and national groups, with less consistency in the differences between the second and third generations. Bui (Chapter 6, this volume) reports similar trends from the same data set as that used by Harris (1999) but goes further to suggest that the generational differences are attributable to better academic performance and behavior among Asian immigrants and better family relationships and lower neighborhood violence among immigrants from Latin America. Finally, Raffaelli, Kang, and Guarini (Chapter 5, this volume) report similar trends in sexual behavior. First- and second-generation adolescents reported less sexual involvement, earlier age at first intercourse, and increased use of birth control at first intercourse compared with third-generation adolescents.

The consistency of these patterns led Crosnoe (Chapter 3, this volume) to offer the intriguing suggestion that socioemotional and behavioral developmental outcomes may be particularly likely to show an immigrant paradox or advantage. This trend does appear to show up in other developmental outcomes reported by other authors in this volume. For example, Turney and Kao (Chapter 4) found that teacher reports of both internalizing and externalizing behavior among young children were lower among immigrant children than American-born children. These findings were evident despite the fact that immigrant parents suggested that their children may be more lonely and less socially connected, which may not be surprising if they are newcomers to the United States who are having difficulty being integrated into American peer groups. The potential social isolation of these children is a cause of concern, but it makes their apparently better socioemotional development compared with American-born children even more surprising.

Hernandez and colleagues (Chapter 1, this volume) also summarize analyses regarding the self-reported health status of adolescents by Harris (1999) that suggest that at least in some aspects of health, those from immigrant families reported better outcomes than those from American-born families. Generally speaking, first- and second-generation teenagers reported fewer health problems and lower rates of asthma, obesity, and being in fair or poor health than those from the third generation. These results are perhaps more surprising than those regarding problem behavior and are largely unexplained by the chapters presented in this volume. It is possible, however, that to the extent that these particular health problems are related to behavior and diet, teenagers from immigrant families may be benefitting from family behaviors, diet, and routines that are more typical of their families' native cultures compared with those typical of American society. It remains to be seen, however, what these behaviors, diet, and routines may be.

TRANSLATING ASPIRATIONS TO SUCCESS IN SCHOOL REQUIRES RESOURCES AND OPPORTUNITIES

The ability of immigrant parents and children to turn their aspirations and optimism into lower levels of risky and problem behavior provides an interesting contrast to the educational arena. As suggested by Crosnoe (Chapter 3, this volume), developmental outcomes such as education that are more related to the social and economic stratification system in the United States are less likely to show a consistent immigrant advantage or paradox. More so than perhaps staying out of trouble, doing well in American schools requires access to information, resources, and opportunities that are highly variable among the immigrant population. Hernandez and colleagues (Chapter 1, this volume) describe the remarkable variability in resources available to immigrant families, with many possessing extremely low levels of income, education, and school quality. Therefore, immigrant families are highly variable in their ability to translate their aspirations into success in the American educational system. Those with higher levels of parental education, more financial resources, and greater information and access regarding educational opportunities show levels of academic success that are sometimes greater than that of their American-born peers.

The inconsistency of the immigrant paradox or advantage in education is evident across several chapters in this volume, with some even reporting evidence of an immigrant risk in student achievement. It is difficult to derive overall conclusions from these results, but there do seem to be patterns that are contingent on age, ethnic group, and specific aspects of the achievement being examined. In terms of age, Crosnoe (Chapter 3, this volume) and Palacios (Chapter 8, this volume) present results that together suggest an initial immigrant disadvantage or risk in some academic skills at kindergarten that goes away and even becomes an immigrant advantage over the early years of elementary. Han (Chapter 7, this volume), in turn, shows analyses that suggest that any immigrant advantage or at least equity with American-born students only develops during this period for children who appear to be bilingual in English and their family's native language. Suggesting the potential merits of bilingualism, whether they are conferred cognitively or through an ability to better connect with the different worlds of home and school, Han's findings highlight a potentially important source of diversity in immigrant advantage in the educational arena.

The results from early childhood that suggest a reversal from a story of immigrant risk to one of immigrant advantage seem to be consistent with previous work during the teenage years that suggests an immigrant advantage in achievement (Fuligni, 1997; Kao & Tienda, 1995). Pong and Zeiser (Chapter 9, this volume) report a similar immigrant advantage during adolescence in academic grades, although the advantage is less evident when standardized test scores are examined. Hao and Ma (Chapter 12, this volume), in turn, suggest an immigrant advantage in terms of 4-year college enrollment and bachelor's degree attainment.

Yet these attempts to draw general conclusions must be tempered with significant caveats that suggest that there is no overall immigrant paradox or advantage in terms of achievement. First, as highlighted by Crosnoe (Chapter 3, this volume), a paradox in achievement is often only revealed when controlling for socioeconomic background. Given the dramatically low levels of parental education of many immigrants, such as some from Mexico or

Southeast Asia, the real-world meaningfulness of these statistical comparisons can be brought into question. Second, the paradox is often only revealed when generational comparisons are made within ethnic groups. Therefore, an apparent immigrant advantage for some groups, such as those from Mexican immigrant families, does not mean that they are achieving at levels equal to those of their peers from the American-born, European American majority. The only students from immigrant families who sometimes show this advantage are those from Asian immigrant families. As discussed earlier, this is partially due to the fact many immigrant parents from Asian countries have higher levels of education, occupational status, and income than American-born parents. Many immigrant Asian parents also have access to social capital and information in their communities that help them to navigate the often complex American educational system (Zhou, 2008). Third and finally, there can be substantial diversity in immigrant advantage or risk across schools and communities, as shown by analyses reported by Conger and Atwell (Chapter 10) in this volume. It is unclear why different communities show different patterns or advantage or risk, but Conger and Atwell's findings highlight the important role that educational systems and practices may play in the educational adjustment of children from immigrant families.

CONCLUSION

Collectively, the chapters in this volume nicely unpack and complicate overly simplistic conclusions about an immigrant paradox or advantage in child development. They demonstrate how immigrant parents come to the United States with high aspirations for their children and a strong belief in the value of hard work and the economic returns of education. Most immigrant parents succeed in socializing these same values in their children despite the distractions and pressures involved with being a child growing up in American society. Most immigrant families succeed in cultivating good behavior and keeping their children out of trouble during adolescence, a time when many American children begin experimenting with risky behavior and substance use. The ability of immigrant families to translate their aspirations into academic achievement in their children is much more variable and less well understood. There are success stories, but the educational success of children from immigrant families, like that of all American children, depends a great deal on the availability of information, resources, and opportunities. Immigrant families often do quite well with the often few opportunities that they have available to them, but the educational fortunes of many of their children can be thwarted by their inability to access needed resources. Given the remarkably high level of motivation, effort, and desire of this population, meeting these needs would seem to be an investment with a high probability of payoff for American society.

REFERENCES

Fuligni, A. J. (1997). The academic achievement of adolescents from immigrant families: The roles of family background, attitudes, and behavior. *Child Development, 68*, 351–363.

Fuligni, A. J., Rivera, G. J., & Leininger, A. (2007). Family identity and the educational progress of adolescents from Asian and Latin American backgrounds. In A. J. Fuligni (Ed.), *Contesting stereotypes and creating identities: Social categories, social identities, and educational participation* (pp. 239–264). New York, NY: Russell Sage Foundation.

Fuligni, A. J., & Yoshikawa, H. (2003). Socioeconomic resources, parenting, and child development among immigrant families. In M. H. Bornstein & R. H. Bradley (Eds.), *Socioeconomic status, parenting, and child development* (pp. 107–124). Mahwah, NJ: Erlbaum.

Fuligni, A. J., & Yoshikawa, H. (2004). Investments in children among immigrant families. In A. Kalil (Ed.), *Family investments in children's potential: Resources and parenting behaviors that promote success.* (pp. 139–162). Mahwah, NJ: Erlbaum.

Gibson, M. A., & Bhachu, P. K. (1991). The dynamics of educational decision making: A comparative study of Sikhs in Britain and the United States. In M. A. Gibson & J. U. Ogbu (Eds.), *Minority status and schooling: A comparative study of immigrant and involuntary minorities* (pp. 63–96). New York, NY: Garland.

Harris, K. M. (1999). The health status and risk behavior of adolescents in immigrant families. In D. J. Hernandez (Ed.), *Children of immigrants: Health, adjustment, and public assistance* (pp. 286–347). Washington, DC: National Academy Press.

Kao, G., & Tienda, M. (1995). Optimism and achievement: The educational performance of immigrant youth. *Social Science Quarterly, 76*, 1–19.

Portes, A., & Rumbaut, R. G. (2006). *Immigrant America: A portrait* (3rd ed.). Berkeley: University of California Press.

Suárez-Orozco, C., & Suárez-Orozco, M. (1995). *Transformations: Immigration, family life, and achievement motivation among Latino adolescents.* Stanford, CA: Stanford University Press.

Zhou, M. (2008). The ethnic system of supplementary education: Nonprofit and for-profit institutions in Los Angeles' Chinese immigrant community. In M. Shinn & H. Yoshikawa (Eds.), *Toward positive youth development: Transforming schools and community programs* (pp. 229–253). New York, NY: Oxford University Press. doi:10.1093/acprof:oso/9780195327892.003.0013

INDEX

Externalizing behaviors
  in early childhood, 80
  in school context, 67–68
  teacher-reported, 97, 304
Extracurricular activities, 266–267

"Failure feedback," 163
Families, immigrant. *See* Immigrant
  families
Family context
  behavior in, 10, 82, 96, 102–103
  characteristics of, 86, 167
  effects of, 150, 284
  English language learners in, 18–19
  and health status, 304
  literacy programs for, 29
  in Mexican-origin immigrants, 53–54
  and school experience, 152
  and socioeconomic stratification, 71
  values in, 303
Family reunification, 301–302
Family structure, 302–303
Farm work, 48, 150
Fathers, 53
Favorable self-concepts, 52–53
Feliciano, C., 50
Females, 118–119, 260n5
Fernandez, R. M., 45
Financial aid, 257, 265–266
Financial capital, 278
First-generation immigrants
  academic performance of, 179–182
  acculturation of, 7
  assimilation of, 140
  behavioral outcomes for, 86, 303–304
  biculturalism in, 38
  bilingualism in, 181–182
  categorization as, 189n2
  defined, 166, 211
  delinquency among, 138, 142
  educational expectations among, 170
  externalizing behaviors in, 67
  family context effect on, 150
  grade point average for, 225, 227
  health status of, 24–25, 304
  high school graduation of, 31–32,
    43–44
  Latino, 180
  math achievement of, 64–65, 173,
    174

and native-born peers, 17
reading achievement of, 173, 174
school climate reported by, 221–222
selection factors for, 12
sexual behaviors of, 25–27, 111–114,
  125
support and assistance for, 153
uniqueness of, 198
upward/downward mobility of, 42–43
Florida, 237–238
Florida gateway communities, 237–247
Fort Lauderdale, Florida, 238–240,
  242–249
14th Amendment, 6
Fromm, E., 51–52
Functioning, 67–70

Gamio, M., 42, 52
Gandara, P., 43
Gang involvement, 46–47, 151
García, H. D. C., 46
García, Matt, xiii–xiv
García Coll, C., 163
Gateway communities, 233–250
  data and methods in study on, 237
  discussion from study on, 248–250
  effect of place on youth in, 234–237
  in Florida, 237–240
  results from study on, 240–247
Gender, 260n4
  and romantic relationships, 118–119
  and sexual behaviors, 111–114, 116
Genealogical generations, 211, 212
Generational decline, 211, 234
Generational status. *See also specific*
    headings, e.g. Third-generation
    immigrants
  in academic performance, 165–166,
    217–218, 222–226
  and assimilation, 138
  and attitude about school, 210–211,
    218–220
  and bilingualism, 165–166, 179–180
  differential patterns with, 10
  and educational outcomes, 44
  within ethnic groups, 306
  and health status, 24–25
  and high school graduation, 31–32
  in immigrant paradox, 7–8
  in language status, 168–169

and math test scores, 27–28, 162–163, 170–178, 224–227
measurement of, 7–8
and parent–child relationship, 122
and peer group relationships, 123
and reading test scores, 28, 162–163, 170–178, 277
and school environment, 211–212
and sexual behavior, 25–27, 110, 115–116, 124–127
and student-reported school climate, 221–222
Generational status and delinquency study, 135–155
conceptual framework for, 136–138
data analysis in, 142–149
discussion section from, 149–153
methods used in, 138–141
results from, 142–149
Generations, 211–212
Glick, J. E., 227, 277
Gonzales, R. G., 50
Gordon, M. M., 39, 211
Grade point average (GPA), 217–218, 222–227
Grades, 27
Gratification, deferred, 51
Grebler, L., 43, 44
Guarini, T., 303–304

Haitian immigrants, 246
Han, W.-J., 305
Hao, L., 214, 277, 279–280, 305
Harmon, T., 116
Harris, K. M., 28, 303, 304
Hart, B., 191
Head Start program, 41, 192
Health care system, 17, 32, 123
Health insurance, 32, 257
Health status
and generational status, 24–25, 304
immigrant advantage in, 187–188
in immigrant families, 4, 303–304
immigrant risk in, 69
parent-reported, 68–69
teacher-reported, 68–69
Henderson, R. W., 44–45
Heritage, racial/ethnic, 39, 82, 93
Heritage language, 29–30
Hernandez, D. J., 302–305

Hierarchical linear modeling (HLM), 215
Higher-order generation, 211
High School and Beyond study, 45
High school context, 62, 257
High school graduation, 31–32, 43–44
Hispanic immigrants
attitudes toward school in, 228–229
behavioral outcomes for, 101
delinquency among, 46–47, 150
early childhood behavioral outcomes for, 96
educational outcomes for, 225, 277–278
in gateway communities, 245, 246
neighborhood context of, 214
as racial–ethnic category, 244n1
HLM (hierarchical linear modeling), 215
HOME (Home Observation for Measurement of the Environment), 199–200
Home context
cognitive stimulation in, 189–190, 193
language in, 191–192, 197, 198, 246–247
letter–word identification in, 189–192
and math test scores, 193
and school context, 197–198
Home Observation for Measurement of the Environment (HOME), 199–200
Homeownership, 21–22, 51
Host society, xii
Human capital, 278

ICE (Immigration and Customs Enforcement), 33
IDEAS, xiv
Identity, 54–55
Ideological movements
Americanization, 39–40
anti-immigrant, 5–6
Immigrant children
adaptations of, xi–xii
agency effects on, 290–293
characteristics of, 167, 179
citizenship of, 20
demographics of, 17

Immigrant children, *continued*
  with parents who lack English
    fluency, 19
Immigrant communities, 11–12, 197.
    See also Gateway communities
Immigrant families, 17–34, 299–307
  aspirations of, 302–303
  citizenship in, 19–21
  constraints for, 22–24
  educational outcomes for, 304–306
  effects of immigration on, xi–xii
  in Florida, 237–238
  health status in, 4, 69, 303–304
  homeownership by, 21–22
  in immigrant paradox, 24–29
  language environments in, 18–19
  opportunities for, 304–306
  and postsecondary education, 290–293
  problem behavior in, 303–304
  public policy recommendations for,
    29–33
  resources available to, 304–306
  resources in, 21–22
  selection factors in, 300–302
  as two-parent families, 21, 82
  values of, 302–303
  work ethic in, 21
Immigrant generation, 7
Immigrant paradox, xiii, 3–13
  and academic achievement, 248–249
  acculturation in, 7–8
  adolescent sexual behavior in,
    110–114
  in behavioral outcomes, 9–11, 82
  complexities in, 180
  concepts in, 4–6
  and crime, 136
  definitions of, 17, 62, 80, 109–110,
    161–162, 275
  in delinquency, 153
  in educational outcomes, 11–13, 210
  in gateway communities, 248–249
  generational status in, 7–8
  for immigrant families, 24–29
  inconsistency in, 61–62
  and language background, 181
  for Mexican-origin families, 62–63
  perspectives on, 9
  research on, 255

and school environment, 209–211
  socioeconomic status in, 305–306
  theoretical frameworks for, 8–9
  variability in, 61–63, 72–74,
    299–300, 305
Immigrant parents
  and adolescent sexuality, 120–122
  Asian, 120–121
  aspirations of, 302–303
  attitudes about school in, 213
  behavioral outcomes reported by, 10,
    89, 93–96, 101, 103
  caught in worksite raids, 33
  and delinquency, 149–150, 152, 278
  divorced, 82, 302–303
  education level of, 22–23, 73,
    149–150, 152, 278
  employment rates for, 23, 83
  English fluency of, 17, 19–21
  expectations of, 121, 279–280
  Latino, 120, 192–194
  optimism in, 52, 279, 300, 304
  socioeconomic status of, 23–24, 61,
    70–73, 185–187
  U.S.-born or U.S. citizen, 19–20
  work ethic of, 302
Immigrant risk
  in academic achievement, 66
  defined, 63
  as double stratification, 73
  in gateway communities, 248
  in health status, 69
  test score evidence for, 234
Immigrant status, 85–86
Immigrant student paradox, 37
Immigration and Customs Enforcement
    (ICE), 33
Immigration Reform and Control Act
    (IRCA), 258
Impulsive behavior, 102
Imputation, multiple, 141n1
Income. *See* Socioeconomic status
Individual factors
  in adolescent sexual behavior,
    116–118
  child characteristics, 167, 179
  in segmented assimilation
    hypothesis, 188
Institutional systems, xii, 70

316   INDEX

Low-income families, *continued*
    achievement in, 186–187, 194–198, 256
    constraints on children in, 23–24
    Latino preschoolers from, 185–201
    and postsecondary education, 275–276, 284–290

Ma, Y., 305
Macartney, S., 302
Maccoby, M., 51–52
Macias, T., 54
Macpherson, H., 235
Males, 260n4
Manual laborers, 150
Marriage rates, 82
Martinez, J. L., 37–38
Maternal employment, 83
Math achievement
    and acculturation, 195–196
    for adolescents, 27–28
    for Asian immigrants, 174
    and bilingualism, 170–178
    for first-generation immigrants, 64–65, 173, 174, 227
    in gateway communities, 240–247
    and generational status, 27–28, 162–163, 170–178, 224–227
    for Hispanic immigrants, 225
    immigrant advantage in, 188–189
    immigrant paradox in, 218
    for Latino children, 173–178, 192–196
    as measure for academic performance, 165
    national patterns of, 64–66
    for second-generation immigrants, 64–65, 173, 174, 225
    for third-generation immigrants, 64–66, 173, 174
McPartland, J. M., 213
Measurement
    of acculturation, 7, 153
    of assimilation, 153
    of bilingualism, 182
    of language status, 166–167
    of prejudice against racial–ethnic groups, 153
    of socioeconomic status, 282

Measures
    for academic performance, 165
    in Latino families early achievement study, 198–200
    for letter–word identification, 198–199
    of neighborhood context, 141
    in postsecondary education study, 281–282
    of school context, 167
    in school environment study, 216–217
Media, 124
Melville, M. B., 43
Mendoza, R. H., 37–38
Mentors, 270–271
Merrit, C. G., 44–45
Methodological approaches
    anthropological, 9
    in culture deprivation research, 41–42
    for immigrant paradox, 7–8
Mexican American War, 46
Mexican-origin families, 37–56, 61–74
    biculturalism in, 52–56
    bilingualism in, 44–46
    in cultural integration hypothesis, 37–42
    delinquency and crime in, 46–47
    developmental stage for children of, 63–67
    early education enrollment in, 31
    early education studies on, 43–46
    economic and occupational mobility in, 42–43
    health insurance coverage of, 32
    health outcomes for, 25
    immigrant paradox for, 62–63
    and immigrant paradox variabilities, 72–74
    parenting practices of, 120
    and postsecondary education, 294
    school stage for children of, 63–67
    selection factors for, 38–39, 47–52
    in socioeconomic stratification, 70–72
    socioemotional functioning in, 67–70
Miami, Florida, 238–240, 242–249

Minority children, 96
Mobility, 42–43, 52–54
Moore, J. W., 47
Mothers
    age of, 83
    caregiver role of, 192–194
    employment of, 21, 83
    immigrant status of, 85–86
    race background of, 85
Mother tongue, 179
Multiple environments, 8
Multiple imputation, 141n1
Mutual expectations, 279–280

National Academies/Institute of
    Medicine, 24, 27
National Center of Education Statistics
    (NCES), 83, 85n3
National Education Longitudinal Study
    (NELS), 64, 66, 73, 216, 218,
    276, 280, 281, 283
National Longitudinal Study of
    Adolescent Health (Add Health),
    110, 124, 138, 142, 227
National Opinion Research Center, 45
National origin, 125, 246, 300
Native Americans, xi
Native-born families
    compared to immigrant peers, 17
    grade point average for, 225
    in immigrant communities, 236
    poverty rates for, 23
"Native-born flight," 236
Native English speakers (NES), 162
Naturalized citizens, 20
NCES (National Center of Education
    Statistics), 83, 85n3
Negative stereotypes, 52–53
Neighborhood context. *See also*
    Gateway communities
    for Black immigrants, 151–152, 214
    of first destination, 3
    of Hispanic immigrants, 214
    measures of, 141
    negative conditions in, 150–151
    and parental education level, 152
    racial–ethnic groups in, 137
    and school context, 150–152
    for undocumented youth, 259–260

NELS. *See* National Education
    Longitudinal Study
NES (native English speakers), 162
Nielsen, F., 45
Noncoital sexual development, 115
Non-White immigrants, 275–276
Norms, 214

Occupational background, 48–49
Occupational mobility, 42–43
Odds ratios, 283
OLDS (Oral Language Development
    Scale), 165, 167
OLS (ordinary least square) regression,
    215
1.5 generation
    behavioral paradox for, 10
    defined, 254n2, 275
    designation as, 7
    education level of, 44
    and second-generation immigrants,
    279
    sexual behavior of, 125
Optimism
    in cultural integration hypothesis, 52
    and second generation advantage,
    279
    as selection factor, 300, 304
Oral Language Development Scale
    (OLDS), 165, 167
Ordinary least square (OLS) regression,
    215
Orlando, Florida, 238–240, 242–249
Ortiz, V., 44, 54, 55

Palacios, N., 305
Parent–child relationship
    and acculturation, 121
    generational changes in, 122
    as protective factor, 126–127
Parenting, authoritarian, 120
Parents, immigrant. *See* Immigrant
    parents
Peer groups
    characteristics of, 261–263
    influence of, 136–137
    and sexual behaviors, 122–123
Perez, Cinthya Nathalie Felix, xiii, xiv
Pérez, L., 235

Perez, W., 47
Piehl, A. M., 47
Place, 234–237
Pong, S., 214, 227, 302, 305
Portes, A., 48, 55, 137, 213, 235
Positive stereotypes, 52–53
Post-educational opportunities, 267–269
Postsecondary education, 275–294
  access to and attainment in, 284–292
  analytic strategies in study on,
    282–284
  data and analytic samples from study
    on, 280–281
  immigrant family effects on, 290–293
  immigrant youth agency effects on,
    290–293
  measures from study on, 281–282
  research on, 276–278
  results from study on, 284–293
  theoretical explanations in study of,
    278–280
  undocumented youth in, 253, 254
Poverty
  and Earned Income Tax Credit,
    32–33
  of Latino immigrants, 185
  public policy on, 23–24
  rates of, 23, 186
  of undocumented immigrants,
    256–257, 259–260
Prejudice, 137
Preschool. See Early education
Preventive health services, 123
Problem-solving skills, 193
Productive-exploitive character, 52
Productive-hoarding character, 51
Property delinquency, 147–149, 151–152
Proposition 187, 47
Protective factors, 126–127
Psychological factors, 51–52
Puberty onset, 125
Public education system. See School
    system
Public policy
  on access to services, 47
  for adolescent sexual behaviors,
    126–127
  Americanization ideology in, 39–40

employment preference system,
    301–302
  for English language learners, 161
  for gateway communities, 249–250
  for immigrant families, 29–33
  of immigrant family reunification,
    301–302
  immigrant paradox in, 73–74
  on poverty, 23–24
  research-informed, 6, 12–13
  and statistical controls for SES, 72
  for undocumented youth, xiv, 271
  unintended consequences of, 258
Puerto Rican-origin families, 25n1,
    166n1
Push–pull model, 48

Qualitative sociology, 9

Race
  behavioral outcomes comparisons
    within, 97–101
  de facto segregation by, 259–260
  in early childhood behavioral
    outcomes, 85–86
  and problem behavior, 81
  segregation by, 137–138, 259–260
  as term, 80n1
Racial–ethnic groups, 9. See also specific
    headings
  academic performance in, 165–166,
    225
  attitudes about school in, 219–220
  behavioral outcomes in, 103
  bilingualism of, 165–166
  comparisons across, 136
  dating within, 119
  demographic transformation of, 18
  differential patterns of, 10
  education levels among, 152,
    277–278
  generational differences in
    delinquency in, 142–149
  generational status comparisons
    within, 306
  in immigrant paradox, 12, 138
  inner-city neighborhood concentra-
    tion of, 137
  peer group friends within, 123

postsecondary degree attainment for, 286–287, 289–290

poverty rates for, 23, 186–187

prejudice and discrimination against, 137

socioeconomic status effects on, 28–29

test score differences within-group for, 245–246

Racial heritage, 39, 82, 93

Racialization, 54–55

Raffaeli, M., 303–304

Ramirez, M., 45–46

Ratios, odds, 283

Reading achievement

and acculturation, 195–196

and bilingualism, 170–178

and generational status, 28, 162–163, 277

immigrant advantage in, 188–189

for Latino children, 173–178, 189–190, 195–196

as measure for academic performance, 165

Receptive-passive character, 51

Relationships

in adolescent sexual behavior, 120–123

in immigrant success, 255–256

peer group, 122–123, 261–263

undocumented students and teachers, 264–265

Religious traditions, 93

Remittances, 51

Research

on culture deprivation, 41–42

on early achievement, 10

on gateway communities, 250

on immigrant paradox, 255

on postsecondary education, 276–278

public policy informed by, 6, 12–13

on sexual behavior, 125–126

on sexuality, 114–116

on within-group differences, 41–42, 255–256

Resilience, 52

Resources. *See also* Socioeconomic status

access to, 11

available to immigrant families, 304–306

of immigrant families, 21–22

and math achievement, 227

for native mainstream families, xii

Reunification, family, 301–302

Risk, cumulative, 186

Risk taking, 51

Risky behaviors

of adolescents, 25–27

immigrant paradox in, xiii

long-term consequences of, 10–11

and socioeconomic status, 25–27

Risley, T. R., 191

Rivadeneyra, R., 124

Romantic relationships, 118–120

Rumbaut, R. G., 11, 55, 213, 235

Salgado de Snyder, V. N., 50

Sampling issues, 66–67

"Save Our State" initiative, 47

SCHIP (State Children's Health Insurance Program), 32

School climate

and academic achievement, 228

and assimilation, 213–214

composites of, 216–217, 229–230

student perceptions of, 218

student-reported, 221–222

School context, 209–230

and academic achievement, 222–226

and assimilation, 5, 211–214

attitude toward, 212–213, 218–220, 302

bilingual education in, 162

engagement in, 212–213

English language learners in, 161

enrollment in early education programs, 31

generational status in, 211–212

hierarchy of, 269–270

and home context, 197–198

and immigrant paradox, 209–211

letter–word identification in, 189–192

measures of, 167

mediation effects of, 10

for Mexican-origin families, 63–67

negative conditions in, 50, 149–150

and neighborhood context, 150–152

School context, *continued*
  quality of education in, 153
  safety conditions in, 153
  and school climate, 213–214,
    221–222
  of secondary school, 66
  segregation in, 236
  specialized classes/programs in,
    260–262
School effort, 55
School environment, school climate
  composites for, 229–230
School environment study, 215–230
  data from, 215
  descriptive results from, 217–218
  discussion from, 227–229
  measures for, 216–217
  methods for, 215
  multivariate results in, 218–226
  variables in, 216–217
School system
  in areas of de facto segregation,
    259–260
  as assimilation vehicle, 255–257
  California three-tiered, 260n4
  immigrant children as challenging
    to, 17
  immigrant success in, 187–188,
    304–306
  opportunity structure of, 260–267
  past experiences with, 214–215
  and undocumented youth, 255–257
Secondary school, 66
Second generation advantage, 234,
  246–249, 279
Second-generation immigrants, 7
  academic performance of, 179–182
  advantage for, 234, 246–249, 279
  Asian, 180
  attitudes about school in, 11
  behavioral problems in, 10,
    303–304
  biculturalism in, 38
  bilingualism in, 181–182
  categorization as, 189n2
  defined, 166, 211
  delinquency among, 142
  externalizing behaviors in, 67–68
  health status of, 24–25, 304

high school graduation of, 31–32,
  43–44
Latino, 180
math achievement for, 64–65, 173,
  174, 225
native-born peer comparisons with,
  17
and 1.5 generation, 279
racial–ethnic group differences in, 12
reading achievement for, 173, 174
in research on behavioral outcomes,
  86
school climate reports of, 221–222
sexual behaviors of, 25–27, 112–114,
  125
socioeconomic status of, 150
success rates for, 24
uniqueness of, 198
upward/downward mobility of, 42–43
Segmented assimilation
  community in, 235
  and delinquency, 137, 138, 152–153
  and generational status, 152–153
  in immigrant paradox, 62–63
Segmented assimilation hypothesis, 188
Segregation, 137–138, 236
Selection factors
  in academic achievement, 196,
    279–280
  in child development, 300–302
  in cultural integration hypothesis,
    47–52
  education level as, 49–50
  in first-generation advantage, 12
  in immigration, 300–302
  for Mexican-origin families, 38–39,
    47–52
  optimism as, 300, 304
  in postsecondary education, 276
Sensitivity, cultural, 29
SES. *See* Socioeconomic status
Settlement patterns, 258
Sexual behavior, 25–27, 303–304. *See
  also* Adolescent sexual behavior
Sexual development, 115
Siblings, 122
Singer, A., 235, 238
Single-parent families, 82, 102

Welfare programs, 32–33
Welfare reform, 20–21
West Palm Beach, Florida, 238–249
White, M. J., 227, 277
White flight, 236
White immigrants
  academic achievement of, 245
  behavior differences in, 86n7
  immigrant paradox for, 152
Within-group differences
  in behavior outcomes, 97–101
  and country of origin, 153
  in cultural deprivation research,
    41–42

in gateway community test scores,
    245–246
generational status in, 306
research on, 41–42, 255–256
Woodcock Johnson Psycho Educational
    Battery–Revised (WJ-R),
    198–199
Work ethic, 21, 46, 302
Worksite raids, 33

Zeiser, K. L., 302, 305
Zhou, M., 137

ABOUT THE EDITORS

Cynthia García Coll, PhD, is the Charles Pitts Robinson and John Palmer Barstow Professor of Education, Psychology and Pediatrics at Brown University in Providence, Rhode Island. She has published on the sociocultural and biological influences on child development with particular emphasis on at-risk and minority populations. She has been on the editorial boards of many academic journals, including *Child Development, Development and Psychopathology, Infant Behavior and Development*, and *Infancy and Human Development* and is the current editor of *Developmental Psychology*. She was a member of the MacArthur Foundation Network's "Successful Pathways Through Middle Childhood" from 1994 to 2002. Dr. García Coll has coedited several books: *The Psychosocial Development of Puerto Rican Women; Puerto Rican Women and Children: Issues in Health, Growth and Development; Mothering Against the Odds: Diverse Voices of Contemporary Mothers*; and *Nature and Nurture: The Complex Interplay of Genetic and Environmental Influences on Human Behavior and Development*. She is a fellow of the American Psychological Association. Presently, her scholarship is largely focused on the role of race and ethnicity in children's development, specifically, the role of culture, acculturation, and different sources of oppression (i.e., poverty, racism, and discrimination) in shaping human development.

Amy Kerivan Marks, PhD, is an assistant professor and the director of graduate and undergraduate studies in psychology at Suffolk University in Boston, Massachusetts. She is coauthor with Cynthia García Coll of the book *Immigrant Stories: Ethnicity and Academics in Middle Childhood,* and has published numerous other edited and peer-reviewed works on the acculturation, ethnic identities, and development of immigrant youth. Her doctoral work on the measurement of ethnic identities was supported by a graduate fellowship from the National Science Foundation, and her current work is supported by the W. T. Grant and Jacobs Foundations. Dr. Marks was recently awarded a Jacobs Foundation Young Scholar Award for her research with immigrant youth. Her present research is focused on understanding person–context interactions in the development of ethnically and racially diverse children and adolescents.